E

Honey from the Rock
--A Daily Devotional--

"He nourished him with honey from the rock, and with oil from the flinty crag." Deut. 32:13

Dr. Tim Paulsen

Printed by Createspace.com, an affiliate of Amazon.com. Additional copies may be ordered through Amazon or any other book distributor.

ISBN-13: 978-1505810981
ISBN-10: 1505810981

Dedication

To my beloved wife, Ann.   You have been my inspiration and encouragement from the beginning. Without your graciousness and patience, this book would never have happened. You are my "honey from the rock", and it has been your daily devotion to the Lord that has been my light on the journey. Together we'll make it.

Honey from the Rock

"He nourished him with honey from the rock, and with oil from the flinty crag."
Deut. 32:13

The image of God being like a rock is a dominant one throughout scripture (Deut. 32:4, Psa. 18:2, I Cor. 10:4). It is a symbol for his strength, stability, safety, and surety. We can depend on him and trust in him, even when everything and everyone else fails us. When Moses is told to strike the rock, then, in order to provide water for the Israelites in the desert, there is a definite correlation with Christ being crucified, and the living water, eternal life, pouring out from him to all who believe (I Cor. 10:4, John 7:38).

Yet, water from the rock is only the beginning of our spiritual journey. As God drew the Israelites closer to himself in the wilderness, he also gave them "honey from the rock" (Deut. 32:13). The Promised Land was said to be a "land of milk and honey" (Ex. 3:8). The problem, though, is that in Israel the honey wasn't always easily accessible. Besides the trees, the bees often sought shelter for their hives in the clefts of the rocks. In order to get the honey from the rocks, then, the Israelites had to get a reed and suck the honey right from the honeycombs through the reed like a straw. The phrase "honey from the rock", in fact, means literally, "sucked from the rock". The honey comes from the pollen of flowers, but must be transformed by the bee before it becomes sweet enough to eat. The honey, therefore, is a symbol for those spiritual truths that are transformed by the Spirit so that they are more digestible for our own personal maturity level. Some spiritual truths are easier to come by, like the bee hives in the trunk of a tree. Yet, others are ones that we really have to seek the depths of, like sucking honey from the crevices of a rock. These truths aren't meant to be easy to come by. They are meant to be savored as rewards for our faithfully seeking Him.

As we continue to seek Him, He also nourishes us with "oil from the flinty crag" (Deut. 32:13). The olive trees are well-known in the holy land, for they don't grow in fertile valleys. They grow on mountain cliffs and rocky plains. From these trees comes the bitter fruit of the olives, but these olives are made into oil which is very useful for cooking, light, and worship. The oil, in fact, is a symbol for consecration, and is used in the ordination or consecration of the priests and kings of Israel. God doesn't want us to just be saved. He wants us to continually grow closer to Him, and to be completely consecrated to serving Him.

He not only gives us water from the rock, then, but honey and oil too. He gives us spiritual life through his water of salvation, spiritual growth through the honey of his Word, and spiritual maturity through the oil of consecration, squeezed by the pressure of the bitter fruit of affliction, persecution, and discipline. If we just keep coming back to the Rock, He'll always give us what we need.

When God is a Tortoise

"God will go before me."
Psalm 59:9

Most people are followers. Even the so-called leaders of our society are often merely imitators of other people whom they admire. They have an ideal in their mind of the kind of person they want to be, based upon someone they have known, a pop star, or leader in their community, school or workplace. Perhaps they are a composite person, where they have chosen different qualities from different people to imitate, sort of like choosing foods in a cafeteria. Sometimes we follow people because we like them or something about them. Other times we follow them because they can help us get something we want or achieve a goal that we have, even though we don't like them personally.

Even the non-conformists of our society choose to non-conform in similar ways as other non-conformists so that they can be easily identified as non-conformists. The clothes they wear, the cars they drive, the foods they eat, the pleasures they seek, all fall into a pattern of what other non-conformists might choose. They want to be individualists, but they also want to belong and be accepted by other individualists. So they follow the trends.

Yet, even though most of us are followers by nature, we all seem to have a problem following in one area—that of following God. Of course, people who do not know God personally are not going to want to follow him. They are taught even as children never to go with strangers, and God is a stranger to them. Yet, we as Christians also tend to have trouble really following the Lord. We have problems, first of all, in following His example, for after all, He is God, and we are only human.

Another problem, though, in following God is that we are often in too big of a hurry to plow ahead with what we want to do, and we expect God to come behind to help us. We want to lead and for God to follow. We have it in our brains that our plans, our goals, our decisions and our ministries are the best ones, and we just need to convince God to help us a little bit. We do the planning, and God does the providing. It's teamwork, our style. What God wants us to do, however, is to wait upon Him and to follow His lead. That is really hard. Sometimes it seems like the Lord is a tortoise, and we are the hare. We can't wait to rush into things with great enthusiasm and effort, and we can't understand why God is taking so long. So we push forward ourselves, and hope that He catches up.

Don't you hate it when you are excited about going somewhere, and you are sitting outside in the car, impatiently waiting for the rest of the family to hurry up, especially when you have a little brother, sister, or child who just loves taking their time? Sometimes we feel the same way about God. God wants us to slow down, wait upon Him, and only go forward when we are following Him. If we don't learn to follow, we will never learn to lead.

May You Rest In Peace

"My soul finds rest in God alone." Psalm 62:1

When someone dies, we often hear the saying, "May he rest in peace". This is a nice gesture, but it doesn't really mean anything. Somehow, psychologically, it makes us feel better if we think of a dead person as resting, and that is why we have them lying down in soft, cushioned caskets, as if they are just taking a long, winter's nap. Some Indian tribes in early America used to bury their dead standing up because they believed in immortality, and that the person was just on a long journey into the spirit world. In some ways this is actually more consistent with our own views of immortality as Christians, for we too believe that the after-life is not just a time of sleeping, but of actively serving and worshipping God for eternity.

Part of our problem is our misconceptions about what "rest" and "peace" are. Society seeks and offers all kinds of solutions for how to escape the stress and anxiety of life. We live for the weekend, long for the vacation, dream about island paradises, seek saunas and hot tubs, practice Yoga, go jogging, do jazzercise, go to movies or meditate for hours--anything and everything just to relax and escape our problems, even if it is just for a few moments here and there. Even the restroom stall seems like a shrine of solitude at times, for just being alone seems like heaven.

Yet, all of these escapes are only Band-Aids for the real problem. We are really searching for peace for our souls, but we are trying to sooth our minds and bodies instead. Don't get me wrong. There is nothing wrong with trying to relax, either mentally or physically. Yet, these should never be substitutes for the solace of the spirit. We wouldn't try to cure cancer by getting a massage. Why try to cure a troubled heart by going to aerobics?

The scriptures tell us, "My soul finds rest in God alone". Only God can give us true peace. The main question is, are we right with God? Do we have any area of our lives that we have not turned over to Him? Is our life ruled by faith, love and truth, or are we driven by fear, worry, anger and deceit? Are we trying to run from our problems, or are we willing to let God bare our heart so we can become more like Him? Are we trying to hold on to the safety zone of who we are, or are we willing to submit to the molding hands of the Lord upon our character?

You see, much of the stress in our lives is not caused by the pressures of the outside world. It is caused by the internal struggle between God and us about one issue—who is going to rule our life? We would like it to be us, but that is not one of the choices. It is either the Devil or God. When we are in bondage to the Devil, there is never any rest or peace, for he always leaves us feeling empty, futile, and frustrated. The only true rest and peace is in submission to the will of God. May we rest in peace in Him alone.

The Right Response to Rebuke

*"If you had responded to my rebuke, I would have poured out my heart to you
and made my thoughts known to you." Prov 1:23*

One of the hardest things to do in life is to know how to respond to rebuke. Everything seems to be going okay until one day our boss, our pastor, our spouse, a police officer, a teacher, or a friend comes to us and criticizes something that we have done. Our first response is usually to become defensive, justifying what we have done or trying to downplay it, as if it is no big thing. We also might come back with our own criticisms, such as, "Who do you think you are criticizing me? You are just as bad or worse than I am!"

Part of our response is based on who is giving the rebuke. There is a big difference in receiving criticism from a friend, and getting it from someone that we don't like or respect. Yet, even when it comes from someone we love, sometimes it hurts so bad that it creates a huge wall between us, and reconciliation may take years. Criticism from a parent, even after you are an adult, especially hurts because hurts are accumulative, and they build upon each other through the years. Our feelings get hurt, and healing takes time. It doesn't matter to us whether what they have said is true or not. It just hurts to be criticized, true or not. We feel they are looking down on us, judging us, thinking they are better than we are.

Part of our response, of course, is based on how the rebuke is given. If it is given in a harsh, insensitive tone, our reaction can range anywhere from open anger to simmering, quiet rage; deep depression or despair to open rebellion and obstinate refusal to change. The more we resent the rebuke, the stronger our response tends to be. In the extreme, we may feel like slugging the person in the mouth, or quitting and running away. If, on the other hand, someone comes to us as a trusting friend, and they gently, patiently, and tactfully talk to us about a fault that we have, we may be hurt, but we are more likely to get over the pain much quicker, and our friendship may grow even stronger in the end.

This is where accountability groups or partners can really play an important part in our lives, if we are really serious about our spiritual growth. If we are willing to change, to be more Christ-like, and that is our priority in life, then loving rebuke can be a transforming tool in the hands of friends. The Lord may use our friends to rebuke us, or He may deal with us more directly, through His Word or the Holy Spirit, but much is dependent upon our response. If we respond with a stubborn heart, He cannot teach us or use us. If, on the other hand, we yield to His gentle nudges, He longs to open His heart to us and share the fire of His glory, but He has to test us, through rebuke, to see if we can take the heat.

Will the Real God Please Stand Up?

"I appeared to Abraham, to Isaac and to Jacob as God Almighty,
but by my name the Lord I did not make myself known to them." Ex. 6:3

All of us have probably seen different pictures of what artists through the ages have imagined Christ to look like. Yet, what if an artist tried to paint a composite of God in all of the different ways that He is described in scripture? He would have to be part lion, part lamb, part eagle, part mother hen, part jasper and sardius, part rainbow, part transparent spirit, part white-haired grandpa, etc. etc. Of course, He probably doesn't look like any of the above. They are probably only metaphors to help us understand His complex character, but who knows for sure?

Even God's character is so varied, puzzling, and apparently contradictory that it is hard to get a firm grasp on who He really is. As one reads the Bible, one often feels that he is reading about a Chameleon, who is constantly changing based on the setting that He is in. At one time, God appears to be a ferocious giant on his holy mountain throwing down huge lightning bolts of wrath upon sinful man. At other times He is the compassionate, self-sacrificial, merciful one, who loves mankind so much that He is willing to die for even His enemies.

Part of the problem is God's complexity, and part of the problem is that He has chosen to reveal Himself to different people at different times based upon His eternal purpose, and his changing relationships with different people. With the Jews, for example, God first reveals himself just as "Almighty God", which emphasizes his power and divine right to rule the world. Later, however, when Moses comes along, He reveals himself as "Yahweh", which is translated "LORD", but refers to God as redeemer, and the personal relationship that He has with His chosen people. He still is Almighty God, who gives them the rules to live by, but He wants them to know Him as more than just a dictator. He wants them to know "Him", not just his position.

This new relationship with God is hard for even Christians today to understand experientially. It is hard for many of us to get past our fears of "the Judge", so we never really know him as Father or friend. We understand the concepts intellectually, but in our hearts we have never felt the freedom of forgiveness, or known the intense delight of walking with God in the coolness of the morning in the garden of his light and love. We are still trapped in the slavery of guilt within our own spiritual Egypt, and we haven't allowed God to give us the liberty to walk with Him to the Promised Land.

God's revealing different aspects of himself through time, then, is partly due to his timing and purpose, and partly due to our readiness to see Him in a new light. Most of us are still seeing God in black and white, when He can't wait to show us the latest 3-D, multimedia, Technicolor, fully-interactive "Divinivision". We have the capability. All we have to do is to let Him turn on the power.

Why Do the Wicked Prosper?

"Why does the way of the wicked prosper? Why do all the faithless live at ease?"
Jer. 12:1

We understand that God is both just and merciful. Yet, we want to put stipulations on His judgments. We want Him to be just with the wicked, and merciful with the righteous. We want Him to punish others, but forgive us. So, when we see the wicked prospering, we are jealous of their success, and we want God to throw down lightning bolts upon their heads. It doesn't seem fair somehow that they should be doing so well, and we are struggling every day to make ends meet.

There are a couple of things that we need to understand about how and when God chooses to bring judgment on the wicked. First, His main priority is to lead them to repentance, not to destroy them. As the gentle Father of all mankind, He has decided in His wisdom to win them over through His goodness first, and only to use judgment as a last resort. He points the finger back upon us when He asks, "Do you show contempt for the riches of his kindness, tolerance, and patience, not realizing that God's kindness leads you toward repentance?" (Rom. 2:4). God wants people to be drawn to Him because of His loving kindnesses, not because they fear Him.

Secondly, if God does choose to finally condemn the sinners and to make them pay for their wickedness, it isn't so much that He has lost patience with them as much as that He has lost patience with us. That's right. The blame is put back upon us. When Jeremiah asks the Lord, "Why does the way of the wicked prosper?" he wants the Lord to take action. He tells the Lord to "Drag them off like sheep to be butchered!" (Jer. 12:3). The Lord's response is a powerful rebuke to Jeremiah. He says, "The whole land will be laid waste because there is no one who cares" (Jer. 12:11).

In other words, the wicked will be judged not just because of their own evil, but because of our lack of love. Since we do not love the world, as God loves the world, we are not trying to reach out to them with gentle patience. We just want them judged, not forgiven. We are like Jonah who didn't really want Nineveh saved. He didn't want them to repent, because he wanted them to be judged. It is the same today, for Christians do not care enough about the lost to share the gospel. We are actually glad when a sinner is condemned, for they have finally gotten their due.

Solomon tells us, "Do not gloat when your enemy falls" (Prov. 24:17). Instead, we should be loving our enemies so much from the heart, that when they fall, we would grieve as much as if it were our own child. The Lord is very blunt about His judgments. He says that when He does finally judge the wicked, we are partly to blame. He says, "The sword of the Lord will devour…so bear the shame of your harvest" (Jer. 12:12-13).

When God Doesn't Make Sense

"Lean not on your own understanding." Prov. 3:5

We can understand why life would be confusing at times, for people do crazy things for crazy reasons. Yet, if any one is "sane", it is God, so why is He so confusing at times? Sometimes it is just because we are finite and He is infinite, and His thoughts are higher and deeper than our thoughts (Isa. 55:9). What do we do, though, when God's ways don't seem higher or deeper, just dumber or plain "wrong"?

For example, when the children of Israel went into the Promised Land, they were commanded to kill all of the men, women and children. We can understand why they might kill the men who are fighting against them, but why the innocent women and children? Doesn't this seem unjust? Also, why wasn't Moses allowed to enter the Promised Land? He unselfishly led the Israelites through the wilderness for forty years, and only made one error in judgment. Somehow it doesn't seem fair that he should be excluded for one moment of anger and frustration. Where is God's mercy and love?

One of the biggest mistakes that we can make is second-guessing God. When we start thinking that we know better than God, we are trusting our own understanding more than God. Do we know what would have happened if the people of Israel just killed the men, but not the women and children? The Bible tells us what would happen, for they sometimes are not killed, and the results are disastrous. The Israelites follow the pagan gods of the women, and the pagan children seek revenge for their fathers' deaths (Judges 2:3).

As far as Moses goes, who knows what would have happened to Moses if he had gone into the Promised Land? Maybe he would have fallen into great sin, and been much worse off than he was. Maybe his death was actually an act of mercy, instead of punishment. Maybe God wanted to develop the leadership qualities of Joshua, and He needed Moses gone to help Joshua mature. Maybe He needed to provide a way for Joshua to prove himself, so that the people would trust his authority and position. When they crossed the Jordan River on dry ground, just as they had with Moses across the Red Sea, God was making a statement: Joshua is my man. The people needed to know that fact before they started conquering the land. Joshua had gone into the Promised Land forty years before, and they hadn't believed his glowing report. Why should they believe him now?

We do not know all of God's thoughts or reasons for doing things, but we do know that He is always wise and always just and always working out His eternal plan, even when we can't understand a minute part of it. He sees the whole picture, and we do not, so we need to let God be God, even when He doesn't make sense to our miniscule brains. We may need His help when we have our own Jordan to cross.

When Darkness Reigns

"This is your hour—when darkness reigns." Luke 22:53

When Jesus was teaching his disciples and preparing them for his persecution and death, he told them, "If you don't have a sword, sell your cloak and buy one" (Luke 22:36).   They told him they already had two swords, and he said that would be enough. The disciples were ready to rumble, and it sounded like the Lord wanted them to. Yet, when it came time to confront the enemy in the garden of Gethsemane, and one of the disciples cut off the ear of one of the servants of the high priest, Jesus put a stop to it. He healed the servant's ear, and went without a struggle to be crucified.

What went wrong? He could have called ten-thousand angels if needed (Matt. 26:53), but He chose to let himself be captured, tortured and killed. What kind of spiritual battle is this, when the good guy just lets the bad guys win? Or so they think. From all appearances, even to his closest followers, Satan just won.

Yet, Jesus had a plan from the very beginning. It was like the Israelites when they fought against the king of Ai. Joshua lured the king and his men out of the fortified city by appearing to be weak and losing, but when the enemy was outside their walls, they were ambushed from behind and completely surrounded by the children of Israel (Joshua 8:1-29). God did the same thing at the cross. He made it look like Jesus was losing so that everyone would feel bold enough to show their true selves, and then he "ambushed" them through the resurrection. He let the darkness reign for a short time, for it was their hour, but the ultimate victory was always in the master's hands. He was like a grand champion in chess, who lets his opponent think that he is winning by letting him capture his queen, only to get him in checkmate the very next move. It may have been the Devil's hour, but it damned him to hell for eternity.

When we are fighting our spiritual battles, then, we need to remember the example of our captain. When it seems like we are losing, and we turn the other cheek instead of seeking revenge, the whole world might call us fools and cowards, but we are really seeking to "ambush" them with love or "kill them with kindness". Spiritual warfare is never a matter of getting back at people who deserve it. It is always a matter of fulfilling God's purpose for our lives at that moment.

God's purpose for Christ was to suffer at the hands of the enemy, to be like a lamb led to slaughter, so that his ultimate sacrifice would provide a way of salvation for all mankind. He had to die so that we might live. When we suffer for righteousness sake, we too are fulfilling a higher purpose. We are examples of God's patience and love. The greatest victory is not won by protecting ourselves so we are never crucified. It is rising again in the power of Almighty God, after the Devil has knocked us down and counted us out.

What is God Bringing to You?

"He brought them to the man to see what he would name them." Gen. 2:19

One of the most astounding stories in the Bible happens right after creation. God has just finished creating man, and God starts to bring each animal to him, one by one, and asks Adam what he wants to name it. Can you imagine God bringing the elephant, the giraffe, the anteater, etc. one by one to Adam, and saying "What do you think about this one, Adam? Use your imagination. Whatever you decide, that's what it will be called." First of all, Adam had never seen these things before, he had no idea what animals were or what they were good for, and he had never used his mind, imagination, or even language before, let alone trying to name all these things.

God does the same thing to Noah before the flood. He tells Noah that it is going to start raining, that he needs to build this huge boat, and take all the animals on board to take care of until the flood is over. First of all, he has never seen rain before, he is a farmer, not a boat builder, he doesn't live anywhere near the water, and he doesn't know how to take care of all these animals. God brings the rain, teaches him how to build the boat, and he brings all the animals to him. All he has to do is obey.

God also tests Moses in the same way. He tells him that he is going to use Moses to lead the children of Israel out of Egypt. It doesn't matter that there are more than two million Jews, that they don't know or trust Moses, or that Pharaoh will do everything he can to keep them there. In fact, God tells him that he is going to purposely make it more difficult by hardening Pharaoh's heart, so that he will refuse to let them go. God wants to use this experience not only to set the Israelites free, but to judge and punish the Egyptians and their pagan gods. So he sends several plagues, which attack the specific gods of the people, to show that his power is greater than theirs. This, of course, makes the Egyptians even angrier, and less likely to let them go, but God wants it that way. He wants everyone to know that he is God, and that there is no other.

Do we see a pattern here? God often brings us things—tasks, people, responsibilities—and He asks us to do things that we have never done before, aren't qualified to do, and may not even want to do. Yet, He brings them anyway, and asks, "What are you going to call this one?" or "How are you going to take of this one?", and we are tested way beyond our capabilities. That is exactly where He wants us. He wants us to grow by trusting and obeying Him, whether or not we feel up to the task.

With God, all things are possible. Yet, instead of just doing everything himself, He keeps bringing things to us, and allowing us to participate in His masterful plan. What a wonderful God. Has He brought us anything lately? If so, what have we done with it?

We Preach Christ Crucified

"Jews demand miraculous signs and Greeks look for wisdom, but we preach Christ crucified."
I Cor. 1:22

What are we looking for in our religion? What makes us think that our church is the right one? What are we seeking, really? It is so hard to be a Christian in our society. We are so used to the media blasting us with the idol worship of entertainers, politicians or geniuses of one variety or another, that we carry those thoughts and priorities into our churches. We want bigger and better church buildings, elaborate surround-sound and entertainment systems, programs, and professional personnel at every level. We have to dress, sing, and talk according to whatever is popular in our area. We feel that we must compete with the world and every other church in order to get more people to come to our services. There is jealousy and resentment between pastors of different denominations, and comparisons are always being made on who has the most people, how many conversions, baptisms, and new members.

Somehow it seems that we have missed the point. There is only one church, the universal body of Christ, and we are all parts of that same body. The apostle Paul speaks against the kind of divisions that we see today when he says, "One of you says, 'I follow Paul'; another, 'I follow Apollos'; another, 'I follow Cephas'; still another, 'I follow Christ.' Is Christ divided?" (I Cor. 1:12-13). Popularity contests have no place in the body of Christ, and church services were never meant to be entertainment hours for the exclusive social club of people who call themselves Christians.

The validity and effectiveness of a church is also not based on how many spiritual gifts the people have, or how many miracles they have seen. These are wonderful, but if they only serve to glorify the people who perform them, even miracles are vanity. Paul says that different people are looking for different things. The Jews are looking for miracles, and the Greeks for wisdom. Yet, he says that the emphasis of Christianity is not to be on either one of these things.

The focus should be on Jesus Christ, and Him crucified. The emphasis is on the self-sacrificial, unconditional love of God, and the need for us to be like Him, regardless of how foolish that looks to the world. Instead of watering down the truth to get more people to attend our churches, we need to tell it like it is. Discipleship means taking up our cross and following the Lord—being crucified with Christ and being completely submissive to Him. We are meant to be slaves to Christ, pure and simple.

The gospel was never meant to be popular. Narrow is the gate to heaven, and only few will find it because only a few will really want what God has to offer. We need to stop confusing them by trying to make the gospel to appear to be something it is not.

Was Jesus Crazy?

"When his family heard about this, they went to take charge of him, for they said,
'He is out of his mind'" Mark 3:21

Jesus had been healing people and casting out demons. Then he gave his disciples the ability to heal and cast out demons also. This was spiritual warfare, and Jesus had just equipped his disciples with the spiritual weapons to take on the enemy. So, what was the response to this increased spiritual tension? First, the religious leaders of the day committed the unpardonable sin by saying that Jesus was demon possessed, and that he cast out demons through the power of Satan himself. Then his own family attacked him by claiming, "He is out of his mind."

Secular authorities, like the family or the government, tend to respond to the antisocial person as mentally ill. Why else would anyone dare to go against them unless they are crazy? Although both of these explanations, religious or secular, could be right at times, oftentimes it is just the opposite. Those in authority can also be of the Devil or insane, and the people who are challenging them may be the sane ones.

In the case of Jesus, the Lord says that the religious leaders of his day were "a brood of vipers," and "belonging to your father, the Devil." Since we believe that Jesus is Almighty God incarnate, proven through his miracles and his resurrection, his appraisal of the religious leaders must be correct. They are the ones being empowered by Satan, not Jesus, and they view his miracles and teachings as threats to their own power, as well as their father's power, the Devil himself.

As far as the claim that Jesus is crazy, though, it is a matter of interpretation. It is based upon the definition of words. The word "crazy" means broken or deranged. In some senses, Jesus was both of these. He was physically broken at the crucifixion, emotionally broken at Gethsemane, and spiritually broken-hearted as he approached Jerusalem at the triumphal entry. He was broken, a "man of sorrows" (Isa. 53:3), yet there was nothing broken about his reasoning ability or the truth of his words. He was never "out of his mind", like his family claimed, for He had the mind of God.

Yet, in one way, he was "deranged". The word deranged means "out of order", or "disturbing the regular order of something." If the regular order of things was Satanic hypocrisy, pride, idolatry, and power mongering, then everything that Jesus stood for would have been "disturbing the regular order of things." Jesus was truth, life and light, and men of darkness abhor all three of these things. So in this limited perspective, we could say that Jesus was "crazy", but never insane. He may have been "deranged", but never delirious. He was crazy about the truth, but never crazy because of it. After all, He was the creator of the mind. We can assume, then, that he would understand how it works.

Using God's Name in Vain

"These are the words of the Amen, the faithful and true witness." Rev. 3:14

Why do we pray in the manner that we do? Most of us do things because we are followers by nature. We see or hear others do something, and we follow their example, usually without even thinking about why things are done that way. For example, why do we say "Amen" at the end of our prayers? Well, we think, it is sort of the reverent way of saying "the end", to let everyone else know we are done. If so, then why do we say it even when we are alone with God? Does God need to have a cue card to let him know that we are done praying? What we don't realize is that the word "Amen" doesn't mean "the end". Like it says in the verse above, the word Amen is actually a name for God. It means "the one who in his very essence is true and faithful."

Even when we pray in the name of Jesus Christ, do we know what we are saying? The name Jesus is the Greek derivative of the Hebrew "Joshua", which means Jehovah or Yahweh, our savior. The word "Christ" is the Greek derivative of the Hebrew "Messiah", which means the one who is anointed for a special purpose. Jesus was anointed to be not only the king of the Jews, but the savior of the world, because he was the only one who could die for others, being true and without sin himself.

When we end our prayers, then, what we are really saying is, "In the name of Jesus, who is Jehovah our savior, who was the anointed one to die for the sins of the world, for he is the only one who in essence is completely true and faithful." In our mindless world, though, we have abridged it to just, "in Jesus name, Amen".

Okay, let's shorten it. But let's do it with understanding what we really mean--"In Jesus name, which is the Amen." The name of Jesus at the end of our prayers is not just the way to politely bow out. It is the access card that we have to the throne of God in prayer. It really should be stated at the beginning of our prayers instead of at the end, for it is like going to the throne of the Father with our petition, and we are stopped at the door by St. Peter, who asks us "who goes there?" We have no right to even enter the presence of God unless we say, "I come in the name of Jesus." The name of Jesus gives us the right to pray.

It is not just something we tack onto the end, as some magical phrase to get us what we want. Neither should the word "Amen" just be tacked on, for it is not just saying "Goodbye God", but glorifying the very nature of who God is—the only true and faithful one, who will answer our prayers, not because of anything we deserve, but because it is his very nature to do so. If we just say the words, then couldn't it be said that we are in danger of breaking one of the Ten Commandments, "Do not use the name of the Lord our God in vain?"

They Missed the Point

"He prophesied that Jesus would die for the Jewish nation." John 11:51

It usually doesn't matter how close you are to attaining something of value. You either have it, or you don't. We don't like this principle. We would rather that things not be so black and white, either/or. Being close should count for something, right? Sometimes teachers will do away with the absolute standard of right or wrong. They will say, "I'll give you an 'A' for effort." In other words, it doesn't really matter that we got the answer wrong, as long as we did our best. Well, this may work if our main goal is helping someone to feel good about themselves, but it still doesn't help them to get the answer right.

In the Bible, it gives a similar situation. The Pharisees were feeling threatened by the miracles and teachings of Christ. He was criticizing their hypocrisy and challenging their legalistic interpretations of scripture. There were some, in fact, who became so angry that they started plotting how to kill Jesus. Murder, though, didn't quite fit most of their ethical justifications, so they kept looking for a "good reason" to have him killed. That reason came in the form of a prophecy to the high priest. God had told him that it would be better for the nation of Israel if one man died, so that the nation as a whole would not be destroyed.

The Pharisees did not see the spiritual implications of this prophecy. They only interpreted it from a political standpoint. They thought that God was telling them to kill Jesus in order to save them from their political enemies, as if his death would be a sacrifice that would get God's favor upon them. Yes, they actually felt that they were doing God's will by killing Jesus. The high priest told the Sanhedrin, "You do not realize that it is better for you that one man die for the people than that the whole nation perish" (John 11:50). That's all the excuse that many of them needed. From that day on, they plotted to kill him with a clear conscience, thinking that it was best for God's chosen people to get rid of this heretic.

How close, and yet so far away? In one sense, they were actually doing the will of God, at the same time that they were rebelling against it. They were fulfilling the prophecy of God by killing Christ, but his death had nothing to do with politics. His death and resurrection would bring spiritual salvation to the nation of Israel, as well as the rest of the world, even though their political and religious powers would be stripped from them. Christ's kingdom was an internal one, and his death would only further his reign in people's hearts, not end it. What the Pharisees thought would bring the end of something, was actually just the beginning, and they really served God in establishing the very thing that they tried to destroy.

The Wise will Stumble

"Some of the wise will stumble, so that they may be refined, purified, and made spotless."
Dan. 11:35

It is easy for us to understand when those who are foolish fall by the wayside. They seem to deserve the consequences of their folly, and we have little sympathy for their "learning the hard way." What is harder for us to comprehend is when those who are usually very wise stumble along the way. What happened? Were they really not wise at all, but merely hypocrites acting a good role? Was God punishing them for their "pretend wisdom", or were they just attacked by Satan, and they got caught off guard?

The fact is, Christians continue to sin after they are saved. It doesn't matter if they are wise or foolish, they still sin. We don't become robots when we become Christians. We still have a will, and sometimes even the wise choose wrongly.

Why doesn't God protect the wise and keep them from falling? It can be explained by a very important principle: God's pressure to conform us to Christ's measure is more important than our pleasure. In Daniel, it says that even the wise stumble so they may be "refined, purified, and made spotless". Things are often purified and refined by either heat or pressure. This is also how certain things, like glass and metals, are molded into what the maker has designed. God, then, allows the wise to stumble so He can apply the heat or pressure that is necessary to refine and mold us into the image of Christ. Even the saintly Paul said that he had not reached the point of perfection yet, but tried to stay focused on the mark, or the model of perfection, which is Christ.

This is also why God allows problems in the lives of wise Christians. He is testing, polishing and molding us into a finished product that will be more than just enough—it will be a supernatural masterpiece. God is an artist, and we are His art. Some of us may think that God is a Picasso, and all of his art is too abstract for our taste. We would rather that he just keeps it simple and less stressful, plain and less ambiguous. Yet, God cannot "dumb-down" his art for our sake, and limit his art to childish finger-painting. The complex intricacies of God's nature are being recreated in us, and that can't happen without getting rid of a lot of scrap metal or useless clay in our lives.

We may stumble over the pieces that God is chipping away, and we may even try to glue them back on. Yet, if we just yield to his design, his master blueprint, the Bible, we don't have to keep tripping over the same things all the time. We can walk boldly forward in the light, and shouldn't be so surprised by the things that we see. When we see the broken pieces at our feet, we can be assured that they are there because God has been doing his workmanship, and we are being crafted into his image. When God takes something away, he is trying to make room for something better.

The Whisper of God

"After the fire came a gentle whisper." I Kings 19:12

God speaks to us in different ways. Sometimes He speaks through acts of Nature, such as thunder, lightning, earthquakes, floods and rainbows. Sometimes He talks to us through other people, such as ministers, families and friends. Other times He speaks to our hearts through His Word, convicting us of our sins or our need to be more like Him. The method that He uses to talk to us depends on our need at the moment, our willingness to listen and obey, and God's immediate purpose or plan for our lives. It also depends on His attitude toward us at the time, whether it be anger, compassion, or frustration. God has moods just as we do, and His patience can run a little thin at times.

One of the ways that I believe He talks to us most of the time, though, is through a still small voice. This is hard for us to imagine, for we picture Him as only majestic, and His voice like that of thunder. Yet, when He spoke to Elijah, one of the two men who have ever lived who never died, He spoke to him in a "whisper"(I Kings. 19:12). First, though, God had to get Elijah's attention. He used earthquakes, wind and fire, and then finally the still small voice. I believe that God was trying to whisper to Elijah all along, but Elijah wasn't listening. He was feeling sorry for himself, for he felt that he was the only one left in Israel who still worshipped the true God.

Self-pity may be quiet, but it is never silent. It shouts in our ears, like fanatical fans at an athletic event. It stirs our minds and hearts to a fever pitch, and we become delirious and frantic, shutting out anything and anyone who may try to comfort us. It doesn't matter if it is self-pity, anger, lust, envy or any strong emotion, if we become drunk with being controlled by it, we can no longer be controlled by the Holy Spirit. Our emotions become idols, for they are more important to us than our relationship with God, and they make us deaf and dumb to anything that He tries to say to us.

God is like the tender bridegroom whispering into our ears the sweetest words of devotion and encouragement, but we often don't hear a word, for the trauma of our inner struggles is deafening. So He nudges us gently to get our attention, always whispering, never forsaking His attempt to draw us nearer to Himself. If we continue to drown Him out, He will allow things to come into our lives to draw our focus on Him, so that we will finally hear His precious words of love, and respond with intimate affection. We begin to hear the secrets of God's heart, which He had been trying to tell us all along. God will never tell us something in His thunder that He didn't already try to tell us in His whisper, but we just weren't ready to hear.

The Value of Affliction

"Before I was afflicted I went astray, but now I obey your word." Psa. 119:67

My mother always used to tell me, "You're as stubborn as a Kansas mule." It was a gentle rebuke for my willfulness—my wanting "my way or nothing". I was throwing a teenage temper tantrum, and she knew that I needed an attitude adjustment. She knew that I needed to be disciplined to help me to understand that there were negative consequences to my behavior, but as a teenager, I resented any kind of limitation put upon my freedom to just be me. So I did everything that I could to fight back against any added restrictions or controls, making the discipline even worse than it would have been if I had just submitted to the correction.

God, as our heavenly Father, also tries to discipline us when we rebel against His will. He tells us, "Do not be like the horse or mule, which have no understanding, but must be controlled by bit and bridle, or they will not come to you" (Psa. 32:9). The horse and mule love their freedom, but their owner has the right to show them who their master is. He has the right to induce pain, through the bit and bridle, to keep the animal going in the right direction, based upon his desires and purposes, not the animal's. The animal may not like it, but the more he fights against the bit and bridle, the more pain that he brings upon himself. If he is smart, he will quickly learn who the boss is, and he will yield to the controls of the master's hand. In time, he may even learn to obey verbal commands and to respect the gentle mastery of the one in control.

David talks about this attitude adjustment. He says, "Before I was afflicted, I went astray, but now I obey your word" (Psa. 119:67). He recognizes that the pain or affliction that he had to go through was from God, and that it, like the bit and bridle, was meant to keep him in line. He says, "I know, O Lord, that your laws are righteous, and in faithfulness you have afflicted me. May your unfailing love be my comfort" (Psa. 119:75-76). David comes to realize that God is not just trying to "control" him. God loves him, and every kind of discipline or affliction that God allows is because of that faithful love. It isn't something to fight against, for there is comfort in the master's hand.

When we learn to trust the master's wisdom and love, even his afflictions can seem like embraces, for they keep us from going astray and from hurting ourselves and others. If we fight against the Lord's bit and bridle, we will become either sore and irritated, or "callous and unfeeling", like the wicked of the world (Psa. 119:70). On the other hand, if we yield to His will, we, like David, can truly say, "It was good for me to be afflicted so that I might learn your ways" (Psa. 119:71). The ultimate goal is to learn, not just to stay like some "dumb animal" or "brute beast". God wants us to become more like him, more elevated and divine, not to become less than human by acting like mules. We need to get smart, and let God do his part.

The Temple and the Jar

"Don't you know that you yourselves are God's temple,
and that God's spirit lives in you?" I Cor. 3:16

I love the passage where we are called the "temple of the Living God" (2 Cor. 6:16). What a majestic honor! What a spiritual responsibility! It is a beautiful picture, but not one that is meant to make us feel comfortable. We sense the joy of privilege, but also feel the weight of the burden that it places upon us to be holy. It doesn't feel natural. In fact, it isn't. Our natural self is sinful, lost, and rebellious against God, so being the temple of God is exactly the opposite of what our sinful nature wants to be. We, as Christians, may be God's temple, but it is like being given our father's suit when we are boys. We are thankful, but we won't really appreciate it until we grow into it.

On the other hand, the apostle Paul also compares us to a "jar of clay". He says, "We have this treasure in jars of clay to show that this all-surpassing power is from God, and not from us" (2 Cor. 4:7). This image isn't as glamorous as a temple, and maybe even a little demeaning. I mean, couldn't we have been compared to a silver chalice? Why a clay jar? On the one hand, we are called the temple of God to emphasize the sacred importance of our spiritual communion and submissive service to Christ. On the other hand, we are only jars of clay, in that, our bodies are frail and temporary. We must be shown our powerlessness apart from Him so that we can appreciate that His power is only made perfect in our weakness. If we are weak, then he is the only one who gets the glory.

So, we are a temple in our relationship with the Father, but a jar of clay in our relationship with others. The temple is made for worship; the jar of clay for service. We are at once both God's dwelling place and his chosen instrument to share his "treasures" with others. In both cases we are "containers" of God, but God doesn't like being "contained", so our job is to share Him with other "jars of clay" until they too overflow.

The ironic thing is that when the jars of clay were used in the temple to cook the burnt offerings so that the priests could eat the meat, the jars then had to be broken, for they had touched a most holy thing. They could not be used for anything else. We, too, as jars of clay must be broken when we are touched by the Holy Spirit. We are broken because we need to be humbled in the presence of a holy God, but we are also broken because, like the clay jar, once we have been touched by the holy, we aren't meant to be used for anything else. We are his and his alone. We have become consecrated clay, and our jars are broken so God can take each piece and make a beautiful mosaic for his temple. The mosaic, though, is not just made up of clay from our jars, but all the broken jars that have come before us.

The Sun Stood Still

"The sun stood still, and the moon stayed,
until the people had avenged themselves upon their enemies." Joshua 10:13

One of the most amazing events in history occurred because of the tremendous faith of a single man. When he was much younger, Joshua went into the Promised Land, to spy out the land with a group of men. When he returned, only Caleb and Joshua had the faith that God would give them the land. Everyone else feared the giants in the land, and the impossible odds of fighting against walled cities and trained armies. God punished the Israelites by making them wander around the wilderness for forty years until they all died, but he rewarded Joshua and Caleb by allowing them to enter the land of Canaan. Joshua received an additional blessing by being appointed as the successor to Moses, to lead the Israelites in their battle to conquer their new land.

God knew that Joshua was a man of faith, and that He could trust him to obey Him, no matter what. When the Israelites had to fight against five kings and their armies all at once, then, God not only blessed Joshua for his faith, but he used his faith to show to the world that God was fighting for them, and that their end was near. So, God put it into Joshua's heart to command the sun and the moon to stand still until the victory was complete, giving the enemy no means of escape into the darkness, and giving the Israelites the strength that they needed to fight non-stop without sleep, food or water. It wasn't just any act of faith. "There was no day like that before it or after it, that the Lord hearkened unto the voice of a man" (Joshua 10:14).

Wow! How did Joshua get so much faith? Well, for one thing, Joshua had been the personal assistant to Moses for forty years. In many ways he had been closer to Moses than even his own brother, Aaron. Before the tabernacle was built, Moses set up a tent of meeting outside the camp for people to come to seek wisdom and decisions from God. Moses would meet the people there, and then he would go do other things. Yet, Joshua always stayed at the tent of meeting. He saw first hand how God dealt with Moses, and he sensed the presence of God when he came upon them. No wonder he had faith when it counted. He had been the apprentice to God's anointed, and he was being prepared from the beginning to be the next in line. He never had it in his mind that they would ever fail, for God was on their side, and he was always there.

Yet, we often doubt God and think we can only do so much because we are only one person. If God used Joshua to stop the sun, think what He can do with us if we only believe. God specializes in the impossible, so if you're impossible, watch out. He may be headed your way.

The Servant Heart

"Drink, and I'll water your camels too." Gen. 24:14

When Abraham sends his servant to another land to find a wife for his son, Isaac, the servant is looking for a certain kind of girl. He knows that Isaac is going to want a beautiful woman, of course, but the servant is looking for something else. He looks for a girl with a servant heart. How is he going to find one? He sets forth a test. When he goes to a well to get water, he prays that God will send him a woman who will not only offer to give him water, but to give water to all of his camels as well, even without his asking for this special favor. Amazingly, God answers his prayer in exactly this way, and Rebecca is recognized as the girl of choice. What a special gift this servant has found for his master's son—a woman who is beautiful inside and out.

Unfortunately, this isn't the end of the story. Rebecca becomes the wife of Isaac and the mother of two boys, Jacob and Esau. When Abraham dies, Isaac becomes the leader of the Hebrew clan, and Rebecca becomes "mother superior". Her attitude changes from servant-hearted to manipulator. Instead of seeking to please her husband, she works behind the scenes to trick him and to get her own way, by helping Jacob, her favorite, to be blessed instead of Esau, Isaac's favorite. She lies and teaches her son to lie also. When she was a poor shepherd girl, she had no problem giving the utmost to even strangers. Yet, now that she is rich and powerful, she becomes greedy for even more.

The seed of greed is an ugly thing, but it is within each one of us, as part of our sinful nature. We may think that we don't have a problem with it because we don't have a lot of money to spend on the things that we covet. Greed, though, is not just limited to money. It also can involve wanting power over people. The desire for power is what tempts many people into the occult, for they are willing to do anything in order to get the power that they crave.

I doubt that Rebecca went that far, but the way that she used her own son to manipulate her husband makes us wonder if she ever really had a servant heart at all. Maybe she only offered to water the camels to impress Abraham's servant, to maybe get something in return. It is one of the tricks of the Devil that one of his servants can pretend to be a servant of God, but really be a slave to the dark side. It is called "false humility", where a person puts on an air of servanthood in order to gain our trust and admiration, and then they twist us around their little finger to get what they want. Some children learn how to do this with their parents at an early age. Some never outgrow it.

What kind of servants are we? Ones that really would be willing to go the extra mile, no matter what the cost, to serve others and the Lord, or ones who only water their camels so we can hide our true selves behind their humps?

The Rainbow of God

"I have set my rainbow in the clouds,
and it will be the sign of the covenant between me and the earth." Gen. 9:13

The story of Noah and the ark is an awe-inspiring story, for God's power and sovereignty is without limit. The magnitude of the destruction and the impact that it must have had on Noah and his family when they came out of the ark onto dry land must have been overwhelming. Whatever their thoughts, God tried to comfort them and assure them that such a destruction of the earth by water would never happen again. As a symbol of this promise, he said that he would send the rainbow to relieve their fears.

Why did he choose the rainbow as a symbol of hope? One clue, I think, is found in the wording of his promise itself. God says, "I have set <u>my</u> rainbow in the clouds". He doesn't say "a rainbow". Why would He use this possessive pronoun to describe this celestial phenomenon? In the book of Revelation, when John is describing his vision of God in heaven, he says that, "The one who sat there had the appearance of jasper and sardius. A rainbow, resembling an emerald, encircled the throne" (4:3). God appears like transparent gems, and His light shines through these gems to create a magnificent rainbow all around the throne. It is <u>His</u> rainbow, and after a huge storm, when we are afraid and worried about the possible devastation of God's Nature, He reveals a little of His beauty and creativity in the sky, and possibly a glimpse of His throne itself, to set our hearts at ease.

He does the same thing when we endure other kinds of storms, as well. He may not reveal a physical rainbow, but he reveals different facets of his nature and light, and they open our eyes to all different colors of his love. When a light shines through a prism, it separates the light into its many colors. A prism has three sides, just like the Trinity. There is only one God, but when his light shines through the prism of the Trinity, we can see more of his beautiful complexity than we ever could if it had just stayed one light. When we go through our storms of life, then, the light of God diversifies through the Father, Son, and Holy Spirit. We can feel the strong, warm embrace of the Almighty God, the compassionate understanding of the Son, and the indwelling, enabling power of the Holy Spirit to see us through.

It is like going into a clothing store and looking at ourselves in a three-sided mirror. We are only looking at one person, but we see ourselves from three different perspectives, as the light reflects off of us and the glass. God's light does the same thing when it reflects off of us in the midst of our afflictions. We are able to see different colorful sides of God as he helps us. He wants us to know that he will not leave us in the clouds. There is a light at the end of the tunnel—the kaleidoscope of the King.

The Nazarite Vow

"...a vow of separation to the Lord as a Nazarite, he must abstain...".
Num. 6:2-3

There is great confusion about the Nazarite vow, partly because of the similarity of its name to the town where Jesus grew up, Nazareth. Many assume that Jesus was a Nazarite because of where he was from, but this is not true. There is no evidence that Jesus ever took this vow, and the word Nazarite is not derived from Nazareth. The word Nazarite means "vow of holiness or consecration", and has nothing to do with where a person lives. In fact, the town of Nazareth did not even exist at the time that the vow was instituted.

The second point of confusion is that many feel that this vow only applies to men. The Bible clarifies this, though, by saying, "If a man or woman wants to make a special vow" (Num. 6:2). Yet, the vow affected them differently. For the man, it required him to let his hair grow long. This would be a sign of humiliation, because he was usually not supposed to have long hair (I Cor. 11:14). On the other hand, the woman was supposed to have long hair, so the vow required her to shave it all off (Num. 6:18). This too would be a sign of humility before the Lord.

Besides the hair issue was the command to abstain from drinking wine or to eat or drink anything made from the vine. There is usually nothing wrong with drinking wine, as many Christians would like us to believe, for the Bible only speaks against drunkenness, not drinking itself (Eph. 5:18; I Tim. 5:23). Yet, the Nazarite vow requires complete abstinence, for during this time of consecration, God wants us to be completely focused on Him and not the pleasures of this world.

This kind of abstinence is the same reason why someone might fast today. Fasting, like the Nazarite vow, though, is not meant to be a permanent situation. The Nazarites only took vows for 30 to 60 days. The only exceptions to this were when the parents dedicated their child to God at birth, and they became Nazarites not by their choice, but their parents'. Samson and Samuel would be examples of this. For the most part, though, it was meant as a temporary time of purification and dedication, not a lifestyle.

There is no example in scripture of anyone joining a communal group, such as a monastery, for the purpose of abstinence. The Nazarite vow was a very personal thing, between a person and God, for a specific, temporal purpose. We are told in scripture to be the salt of the earth (Matt. 5:13) and the light of the world (Matt. 5:14). We can't do that if we are hiding in seclusion some place, trying to become holy through abstinence. The Nazarite vow may be good for a time, but then it is time to move on in your renewed dedication to God, and reach the world for Christ, instead of just hiding from the Devil.

God's Bodyguards

"I bear on my body the marks of Jesus." Gal. 6:17

When I was young, I used to get pushed around a lot by the other kids because I was the preacher's kid. They felt that I couldn't fight back because it wouldn't be right for a preacher's kid to fight, so they took advantage of every opportunity to use me as a punching bag. I hadn't done anything wrong. I felt isolated, abused and worthless as a human being. Everyone treated me like a reject, so that means I must be one, I thought.

Then I grew up, and I learned that all the persecution had nothing to do with me. I was being abused because they were angry at my father for taking a stand against the immorality in our community. It was just easier for them to strike out against me instead of him, for his status in the community made him more unapproachable. I really resented all this persecution, and I blamed my dad for making my life miserable.

Then as I became an adult, and I started making moral choices of my own, I found that I was being persecuted for my own beliefs, instead of my father's. I couldn't get away from it, and I blamed God for my problems, just as I blamed my father when I was young. "Why can't I just be left alone? I didn't hurt anyone. I know I am in a spiritual warfare, but I don't want to fight anymore. Please leave me alone."

Then I remembered President Reagan being shot, and how one of his assistants also took a bullet that was intended for the president. The assistant was crippled for life, but he probably saved the president from being assassinated. Being a bodyguard for the president must be a glorious job, I thought. It would take a real hero to want to put your life on the line for someone else.

Being a disciple of Christ is the same way. We need to think of ourselves as bodyguards for the Lord. Satan and his followers hate the Lord. They will do everything they can to get to him. Look at what they did to him when they had the chance at the crucifixion. Yet, now they can't reach him in the same way. Now they can only get to him through us. They throw their punches or arrows to attack the Lord, but we are his bodyguards, and we quickly stand in the way, receiving the blows upon ourselves instead.

When Paul says that he has "the marks of Jesus" on his body, then, he is talking about the afflictions that he has received for Jesus' sake. People who hated Jesus, struck out in anger, and Paul stepped in between to spare the Lord any more pain. The Lord had been through enough already for our sake. Now it was time for Paul to take some of the heat.

When we are persecuted, then, we shouldn't start feeling sorry for ourselves, for we have the greatest job in the world—bodyguards for the Master. We are heroes of the faith every time we take a blow for the Lord, and the "marks of Jesus" are medals of honor.

The Lord of the Flies and the Moths

"I am like a moth to Ephraim, like rot to the people of Judah." Hosea 5:12

Can you imagine anyone thinking of God as a "moth" or "like rot"?   Yet, some people, like the people of Ephraim thought of God in those terms. Oh, they did not imagine him as a literal moth, but as having the characteristics of a moth. A moth lacks the romantic beauty of the butterfly which innocently flitters away, enjoying the warm spring time or summer breeze. A moth is the butterfly's homely cousin, and he enjoys the night rather than the day. He spends his time as a scavenger of the dead or decaying things. He is also known for destroying perfectly good clothing by eating holes right through them. In fact, the moth is probably named after the Canaanite god of death, Mot, and is related to worms and flies in scripture as creatures that devour "dead meat".

Why, then, would anyone imagine God as a moth? The problem is that many people only see God as a grouchy, old man whose main goal is to make life miserable. They picture God as enjoying bringing trials into our lives, taking away the things that bring us pleasure, and zapping us if we do wrong. They see him as the angel of death and judgment, and cannot comprehend how He can possibly love them. Without knowing it, their image of God is really an image of the Devil. For even though the Devil tries to counterfeit the light of God, and lures many into his web of deceitful pleasures, his real name is "Beelzebub", which means "the lord of the flies" (Luke 11:15). He is really the spiritual "moth", "worm", "locust", "lion", or "fly" that only seeks to devour (I Peter 5:8), yet he tries to make everyone think that God is the one who is out to get you.

God is more like the butterfly, who went into the cocoon of the grave and came out transformed for us, so that we too can be transformed into the beauty of the celestial monarch. Which one are we most attracted to—the creature of the night or the one who stretches his wings by the warmth of the "Son"? It is our responsibility to show the beautiful side of God to the world, instead of the many distortions that they may have. The world, though, is not going to believe in the beauty of God if all they see is the ugliness in our lives and attitudes. They are not going to believe that God is like the butterfly that has been transformed if we are no different than they are. They are not going to be able to picture God as one who can fly with wings of freedom, joy, and love if all they see is us weighted down with heavy burdens of guilt or soberness. Instead of being lights to the world, we are more like eclipses, shielding the light from ever getting to the world.

It's no wonder that the world pictures God as a moth, for his believers spend all of their time "bugging" them. We are the moths, ever attracted to the light, but only flying in endless circles, and burning out in the end.

The Lord is my Banner

"Moses built an altar and called it 'The Lord is my Banner'". Ex. 17:15

We have many different kinds of banners today. We have banners in support of athletic teams, schools, clubs, social causes, and political parties. Banners are great for drawing attention to something or someone that you support with great enthusiasm, or they can be used to take a stand against something as well. In the time of Moses, though, banners were usually used to identify a king or kingdom that an army was willing to fight or even die for. The banner helped to identify which side you were on in the battle.

When Moses builds an altar to honor God for helping them win an important battle, then, he names the altar, "The Lord is my banner". He recognizes that it was only through God's help that they were able to have victory over their enemies. Yet, more than that—he wanted the Lord to be the king that they were fighting for. He wanted everyone to know that God was not only their deliverer—He was their whole purpose for living.

This is an important distinction because it is one that is often overlooked in today's world. People often have no problem accepting Christ as savior or deliverer from their problems. What they have difficulty with is allowing Him to be the king or Lord of their lives. They are "secret agents for the Lord", who are known by other secret agents, but they wouldn't dare let the world know what they believe. They don't want the stigma that they feel is associated with being a Christian, so they seek the blessings of being saved, but try to avoid the responsibility of the battle. They may be willing to carry a banner of love, but it is a self-seeking kind of love, and "me" is still the king.

What God asks of each one of us is that we, like Moses, build an altar of self-sacrifice and devotion to the King of Kings, and Lord of Lords, and that we carry His banner unashamedly, as His loyal followers and warriors in the spiritual battle that is all around us. Nothing short of being willing to die for what we are living for is acceptable. Sometimes, though, Christians are known more for what they are against than what they are for. They carry around banners of anti-this, or anti-that, but in the process become anti-Christ's. In other words, we end up doing more harm than good because all that the world sees is that we are a bunch of negative, uptight bigots. They don't see our good motives. They don't see us as standing up for the truth. All they see is a dark pessimism, instead of the light of the world.

Is it wrong to stand up against things that we believe are wrong? Absolutely not! Even Jesus threw the money changers out of the temple. Yet, Christ is not remembered in human history for his fancy use of the whip in the market place. His banner around the world is love and humility, and this should be ours, as well. God wants us to be banners, not pickets.

The Lion and the Bear

"It will be as though a man fled from a lion only to meet a bear." Amos 5:19

God is compared in many places in scripture to both a lion and a bear (Rev. 5:5, Hosea 11:10, Hosea 13:7, 8). They are both big, fearful creatures, who can rule their territory like kings. The difference, though, is in how they respond to their children. Both are loving parents, to be sure, but the bear is much more protective about its young if they are threatened by danger. The bear becomes far more upset, and takes it personally if someone endangers its cubs. Hosea refers to this protective spirit when he says that God is "like a bear robbed of her cubs," who will "attack" the predators if they even get near (Hosea13:7.8).

We can understand why God would feel this way. After all, He is the creator, He is the one who chose Israel as His special people, and He bought us back with the price of His own blood. He has a right to be defensive and protective about what rightly belongs to Him. So, when He sees His children being lured away by the enemy and kidnapped, He has the right to act like an angry bear that has had her cubs stolen. When it says in Amos, then, that a man is trying to flee a lion "only to meet a bear," it is the same as the old saying, "out of the frying pan and into the fire." Though a man might feel that he is able to flee God and His commands or judgment just by running away, he has actually made things worse, and God's anger is the kind that only a parent who has lost a child or a child's love can understand.

Of course, if we are walking with God, and not trying to run away from Him, we have no reason to fear Him as either the Lion or the Bear, for they both love their children. Yet, if we choose to be God's enemy instead, the Lion has probably already been nipping at our heels and breathing down our neck. We don't want to know what will happen if the Bear catches up with us.

The same thing is true if we are seeking to hurt one of God's children, either physically, emotionally, or spiritually. God will hold us accountable. The Bible says, "Woe to the world because of the things that cause people to sin. Such things must come, but woe to the man through whom they come" (Matt. 18:7). Everyone sins, for we are all human. Yet, if we are the cause of someone else sinning, then our punishment is even more severe. From a parent's perspective, if someone is trying to hurt my child physically, I am going to be very upset.

When a child is led away from God, though, the consequences can be eternal, so the parent can be even more enraged. God feels the same way when someone tries to lead one of his children away from him. I would be "lion" if I told you that his fury will be easy to "bear". I would rather have all my skin peeled off inch by inch with a razor blade for eternity than to face for an instant the motherly/fatherly wrath of God. He is no teddy bear.

The Knowledge of Good and Evil

*"God knows that when you eat of it your eyes will be opened,
and you will be like God, knowing good and evil." Gen. 3:5*

The world calls it the "fortunate fall". Whether man even believes in the literal truth of the original fall of man, there seems to be the predominate opinion, that even if it did happen, it was a good thing rather than a bad one. In other words, they have bought into Satan's lie that God is just some "meany" in the sky who is just trying to keep us from having fun and from becoming gods ourselves. Sin is really a good thing because it helps us to grow wise, and it establishes that we are not going to let God bully us around or hold us down. Innocence, in contrast, is looked at as a bad thing because it keeps us ignorant and dependent upon God instead of being able to decide for ourselves.

These arguments are hard for Christians to debate, for we all have "learned things the hard way", and probably feel that we are wiser for our mistakes. It almost seems like we should sin on purpose just so we can grow closer to God. Paul deals with the same questions in the church at Rome. He says, "Shall we go on sinning so that grace may increase?"(Rom. 6:1). His answer is, "By no means." The problem is that we think of sin as a form of freedom, whereas, it is really a form of slavery (Rom. 6:7). Instead of giving us wisdom, it blinds us to the truth, and we become trapped in a prison of self-delusion (2 Cor. 4:4). It is not sin which teaches us wisdom, but only the grace of God, who out of His love for us, picks up the pieces that are left from our fall, and draws us to Himself, who is Wisdom and light. True wisdom is never just knowing more. It is knowing Him more (Psa. 111:10; Isa. 33:6).

People have the impression that being innocent means being a naïve simpleton, who is just too ignorant to know any better. This is one reason that even Christians speak out against parents who want to home school their children. They feel that we are actually hurting our children by keeping them from experiencing life in the "real world". The right to know the whole truth is our constitutional right, isn't it? We can learn from whatever we see, can't we? We are told, "Don't put blinders on the eyes of your children. The imagination is more important than knowledge, so the more things they are exposed to, the more their creativity will be developed."

The Bible says that, "I want you to be wise about what is good and innocent about what is evil" (Rom. 16:19). God will shed light on the darkness, so that we will not be too naïve. But, that doesn't mean that we need to live in a pitch black cave in order to learn about the bats that live there. We don't need to dive into quicksand in order to learn that it doesn't make a good swimming hole. Slaves throughout history have never been the best educated. Slaves to sin are no exception.

The Happiness of God

"Come and share your master's happiness." Matt. 25:21

Everyone has different ideas about what will bring them happiness. Wealth, fame, material possessions, power and pleasure are only a few of the many choices. As we mature, though, we discover that our own happiness is often connected to making others happy. When we see the joy in a child's face when he is given a special gift, or making someone laugh to lift their spirits, somehow our own spirits are lifted too. When we share our wealth, material possessions or pleasures with others, our joy is increased. It is not what we have that brings us happiness, but what we do with it. If we hoard it like Scrooge, all of the possessions in the world will not bring us happiness. If we use it to bring others happiness, though, our happiness is based on personal fulfillment, not just personal gain.

Jesus deals with this principle when he tells the parable of the talents. The master gives his servants different amounts of money, based upon their abilities, to see what they will do with them. Some use their money wisely, and they make twice the money as they were given. One just hides his money, and he gains nothing in return. The master praises the good servants, for they have been "faithful with a few things," therefore, they will be put "in charge of many things" (Matt. 25:21).

The key is not just that they made more money. The important thing is that they took what the master had given them, and then did with it what they knew would please their master. They were not motivated by just adding to their own selfish gain. The result was that when the head of the household came back, he tells them, "Come and share your master's happiness" (Matt. 25:21). Since they were not focused on their own happiness, they were able to share in the happiness of someone else, and that, in turn, increased their own.

The same thing happens with our relationship with the Lord. If we only seek our own happiness, apart from him, we will never experience the joy of the Lord. If, on the other hand, we seek to please and glorify the Lord in whatever we do, he will say to us as well, "Come and share your master's happiness." Which would be better to have, the temporal high of a moment of pleasure, or the eternal exuberance of a God in ecstasy?

If we are in love, we are constantly asking ourselves, "What would make the other person happy?" Sometimes this means giving up some pleasure that we would enjoy, like skipping Monday Night Football to go see a romantic movie with our wife, or going camping in a tent with our family instead of sleeping in our nice, warm bed. The same thing is true in our relationship with Christ. Sometimes he asks us to give up things that stand in the way of fellowship with him, but because we love him, his happiness, not ours, is our ultimate goal.

The Green Tree and the Stagnant Stump

"If men do these things when the tree is green,
what will happen when it is dry?" Luke 23:31

Jesus was being led to the place called "The Skull" to be crucified. On the way, he noticed some women mourning and wailing for him. He turns to them and says, "Daughters of Jerusalem, do not weep for me; weep for yourselves and for your children" (Luke 23:28). Instead of feeling sorry for himself, he felt compassion for these people because he could foresee their future and the terrible persecution of the Jews. He tells them that things are going to get so bad, they are going to wish they were dead, and cry out to the mountains to fall on them. Things aren't that bad yet, for God is still patiently blessing Israel, but even the religious leaders are so evil, that things are going to get much worse.

Jesus' comment about this growing degradation is, "If men do these things when the tree is green, what will happen when it is dry?" If men are evil in spite of the fact that they have seen the miracles and compassion of Christ, as well as being blessed by God as a nation, what will they be like when the Messiah and the blessing are gone? They will become so hard-hearted and wicked that God will just give them over to their enemies and to Satan himself to bring them into bondage.

We look at the Jews at the time of Christ, and we say, "What fools", yet we often do the same thing ourselves. God blesses us so much and shows us His love and power in a variety of ways, yet we take the "green trees" of God's goodness and mercy for granted, until we become strangled by the poison ivy of sin that climbs its way up the trunks of our lives. Before we know it, our hearts and souls are dry, and our spiritual lives are barren.

The only tree that is an evergreen is the cross, for out of it comes eternal life. For though the green trees of the world are drying up fast, and God's final judgment is drawing ever nearer, the "branch of Jesse" was planted in the hillside outside Jerusalem long ago, and it has been growing up to heaven ever since. The water of the Word is keeping it alive, and the tree of Life will be with us forever. We just need to make sure that we don't become so comfortable in its shade that we fall asleep spiritually speaking. We need to keep cultivating it in our hearts until even the birds of Paradise sing in its branches.

We also need to realize that every tree goes through different seasons of change, even the evergreens. Sometimes they grow cones or seeds. Sometimes they shed dry leaves or needles. Sometimes they even lose a branch in the heavy winds, rains or snow. Being a green tree doesn't mean a stagnant tree. It is vital and growing, ever changing and reaching out. It stretches toward the sun at one end, and deep into the earth at the other. It is blessed by God, and, in turn, spreads out to bless others.

The First Lord's Supper

"They saw God, and they ate and drank." Ex. 24:11

When Jesus celebrated the Passover feast with his disciples, his breaking the bread and drinking the cup was nothing new. They were part of the normal Passover rituals. However, he gave them a new meaning—they were meant as symbols of the body and blood of Christ, and as a memorial to the new covenant that he was making with his bride, the church.

It was customary in Old Testament times for people to have a meal to commemorate a new covenant (Gen. 26:30; 31:54). One of the best examples, though, is often overlooked completely. It was when Moses, Aaron, Aaron's sons, and the seventy elders of Israel all went up to Mount Sinai, and they all "saw the God of Israel" (Ex. 24:10). Moses had just finished reading to the people the Book of the Covenant which God had given to them. He had then sacrificed young bulls and taken blood from the bulls to sprinkle on all the people, saying, "This is the blood of the covenant" (Ex. 24:8). Then he goes with the leaders up the mountain, and they see God, and "they ate and drank."

Can we imagine for a moment Moses and the rest eating and drinking with God on Mount Sinai, as a memorial feast to the new covenant that was being made between God and His chosen people? The implication is huge. First, we have God appearing to the Israelite leaders and having a covenant meal with them, establishing the covenant of the law, and then, we have God incarnate, Jesus, sitting down with the leaders of the church and having a covenant meal with them, establishing the New Covenant of Grace. Then, at the end of the age, He sits down with all those who have believed at the marriage feast of the Lamb, and He eats once again, establishing the Covenant of Eternity. That means that the Lord's Supper before his crucifixion was really neither the first Lord's supper, nor the last supper. It was merely a reaffirmation of His sacrificial love for us, that always has been, and always will be.

All three suppers of the Lord involve the shedding of blood. Moses sheds the blood of bulls and sprinkles their blood on all of the people as the "blood of the covenant" before they eat with the Lord. This is not the blood of atonement for salvation, but one of commitment and dedication by the people to the Lord, and the Lord to the people. The blood of the New Covenant, of course, is the blood that is shed on the cross for our sins, which is symbolized by the Passover Feast that Jesus has with his disciples. At the final supper of the Lamb, which is often called the Marriage Feast of the Lamb, the blood that is shed is the blood of all the people at the Battle of Armageddon who have bowed down to worship the Beast (Rev. 19). Their flesh is feasted upon by all of the birds of prey that the Lamb brings with him to the battle. It is blood of vindication and revenge against the Devil for all of his torment of God's chosen people. What a meal.

The Finger of God

"The magicians said to Pharaoh, 'This is the finger of God'". Ex. 8:19

Children love to compare themselves to their friends. There is such competition, in fact, that sometimes their parents get involved, and things really turn ugly. Usually, though, it is just harmless bantering, such as "I can do anything you can do better." Such one-upmanship is common amongst adults too, and competition can turn to rivalry, where those who were once friends become enemies.

We live in a competitive world, where we compete with other countries at the Olympics, but also in the marketplace. Sometimes the competition is fair, with judges to make sure that no one cheats. Yet, often times there are countries that use the competition to sabotage or spy on another country. They use the openness of the American economic system to take advantage of our freedoms, then they stab us in the back by stealing or counterfeiting products without giving credit to the original owners or inventors. The Chinese, particularly, have a repetition for bootlegging our products in order to take advantage of their cheap labor to create bigger profits. It is almost impossible to stop such pirating techniques when the Chinese government is behind it.

Competition is nothing new. In the time of Moses, God had given Moses the ability to perform miracles in order to convince the Egyptians and Israelites alike that he was God's spokesman. He is able to turn a rod into a snake, is able to cause plagues, and he is able to make leprosy appear on his arm and then disappear. The trouble was that Pharaoh had some magicians who were not just illusionists, but actual practitioners of the secret occult arts. Every time that Moses performed a miracle, the magicians were able to duplicate the supernatural act. The only difference was that Moses acted with the power of God, and the magicians used powers from the dark side.

There came a time, though, when the magicians reached the limit of their abilities, and even they acknowledged the legitimacy of the power of Moses' God. They not only admitted that the miracle was an act of God, but they glorified His power by saying that God was able to do it by only using His one finger. It wasn't some great exertion that took all of God's effort. It was an easy miracle for Him, even though it was too difficult for them to perform.

If their power was from the Devil, this is a huge victory for the Lord and His people. It isn't very often that the Devil's disciples give praise to their enemy. Someday, though, every knee will bow and praise God as Lord (Phil. 2:10), and all the magical powers in the world will not be able to prevent it. If we think the finger of God is impressive, wait till we see Christ in his entirety ruling the world. "Amen. Come, Lord Jesus" (Rev. 22:20).

The Divine Vacancy

"He did not know that the Lord had left him." Judges 16:20

One of the most terrifying things that a parent can experience is going shopping with a child, and turning around to discover that the child is missing. We know that they were there a minute before, but while we were focusing on something else, they disappeared. Our emotions range from anger at the child to fear for the worst, or even blame for ourselves. How could we have lost someone so precious to us, without even knowing that they were gone, until it was too late?

Samson experienced something very similar, but he lost God without knowing it. He was so over-confident in his own ability, that he took God for granted. Maybe he didn't really need God after all. Even when he sinned before, God had always come through for him, so what difference did it make what he did? When he told Delilah the secret of his strength, then, and she has his hair cut off, he awakes to the attack of the enemy thinking that it would be just business as usual. He would rise up and have victory over the attackers without problem. Yet, it didn't work out that way. His strength was gone, he was taken captive, and he had his eyes cut out.

What happened? Well, when he sinned before, such as marrying a Philistine woman instead of a Hebrew, God overlooked the sin so that He could bring judgment upon the Lord's enemies. Now, however, Samson had broken his Nazarite vow, and God had left him, without his even knowing it. What an empty feeling that must have been, to be filled with the Spirit of God one moment, and then, to have nothing the next. Yet, Samson was so filled with himself and his stubborn pride, that he didn't even notice the vacancy.

Sometimes we are the same way. Oh sure, we may not lose the Holy Spirit in the same way that he did, for we have been baptized with the Spirit for eternity. However, we can still experience being filled with the Holy Spirit, and then lose that filling without even realizing that His power is missing. We can become so filled with ourselves, and even pride in what the Holy Spirit has done through us, that our focus is turned to ourselves, instead of the Spirit who empowers us. We are pumped up with adrenaline and with the praise of others, and we are feeling so good about ourselves, that we don't even realize that we have pushed God aside. We become like a beautiful car with no battery. We still may look glorious to the crowd, but we no longer have the power to move forward. We are stuck in park, with the emergency brake on, and don't even realize that we are not moving because of all the activity that is still going on around us. We have a "vacancy" sign on our window, that only the Lord can see, but sooner or later, the vacancy becomes a vacuum, and we're left wondering where everyone went.

The Divine Nature of God

"For since the creation of the world God's invisible qualities—
his eternal power and divine nature—have been clearly seen." Rom. 1:20

There are many in our pagan world that would consider the divine nature of God as meaning that Nature itself is divine. We just need to get closer to Nature so we can tap into the power and beauty of this majestic force. When the scriptures talk about the divine nature of God, though, they are speaking of the spiritual qualities of the Creator and ruler of all things.

We, as Christians, understand and trust in the power of the Almighty, and have learned to love his divine character. Yet, our impression of God is based upon the Bible and upon God incarnate, Jesus Christ, and his demonstration of the intimate nature of our Maker. We love him because he first loved us. However, Paul seems to imply in Romans that we can know the divine nature of God through his creation, not just the Bible and Jesus.

Beyond the obvious—God is all-powerful—what can we learn about God's inner being from the external world? First, he is an artist. His imaginative powers, creativity, love of the unique, appreciation of beauty and majesty, as well as the minutest complex design, all point to a God who produces nothing but masterpieces and originals. Second, His intelligent design of the universe and how even the smallest part fits together and contributes to the whole demonstrates not only his intelligence, but the depth and breadth of his concern for holding it all together in perfect harmony. Third, He can be seen as a God of mercy and justice, for he provides rain for the just and the unjust, gives the rainbow for all to share, and blesses even the pagans with the ability to produce new life.

Yet, He can destroy whole countries with floods, fire, famine or plague. His acts of Nature demand both our faith and our fear. Fourth, the creation of the world isn't just about trees, waters, and animals. It also includes the creation of man. Mankind was created in the image of God, so that we could see even in our own reflection, a little of the divine. We are not gods, only mirrors to reflect the light of the one and only true God. For many, the only God they'll ever see is the God they see in me. This places a huge responsibility upon each one of us, for the world has suppressed the image of God in Nature by promoting the godless theory of evolution. That makes it doubly important for them to be able to see Jesus in us. We are part of God's creation. Do we truly reflect the divine qualities of this invisible deity, or is our Christianity also invisible?

The Dandelions of Defeat

"The more they were oppressed, the more they multiplied." Ex. 1:12

There is something about weeds that really bothers some people. It doesn't matter how beautiful a weed may be, they try everything they can to get rid of them because the weeds are "the enemy". I remember as a young boy trying to get rid of the dandelions in our front yard because my daddy said they were bad. So I would pick off their "wish balls", and blow them all apart, thinking that was the best way to destroy them. I didn't realize that I was actually spreading their seeds, and creating a worse problem than we had before.

The same thing happens when we try to deal with people we can't stand. The more that we try to fight against them, the stronger that they become. Since they sense our resistance, they become even more determined to resist us, and the problem only becomes worse. When the Egyptians, for example, tried to persecute the children of Israel because they felt threatened by the strength of their numbers, "the more they were oppressed, the more they multiplied." Instead of defeating the Jews, the oppression made them even more determined to survive.

It's funny because I picture Satan as the little kid trying to blow "wish balls" in order to destroy them. He tries to destroy the Israelites, but it only makes them stronger. He tries to destroy Christ, but Christ's death and resurrection make salvation available to the world. Even today, he tries to destroy the church, but it is up to us whether Satan is just blowing wish balls, or if he is truly able to crush us in defeat. Will we stand up and fight against the wiles of the Devil with the full armor of the Lord, and become stronger the more he attacks us, or will we break under his oppression, and weaken the cause of Christ?

Whether we are "dandelions", who spread the Word even more the more that we are "blown" by the winds of adversity, or whether we are "real lions", who stand up against the Devil, toe to toe, to fight his every scheme, we can only have victory if we trust in the power of Christ instead of our own strength. It is only in Christ that we are actually made stronger when we are attacked, and the enemy is made weaker the harder he tries.

The Courage to Obey

"Be strong and very courageous, that you may observe to do according to all the law." Joshua 1:7

Moses had just died, and Joshua was appointed to be the new leader. His job was to lead the children of Israel into the Promised Land and to conquer the enemy. There were walled cities, like Jericho, and there would be giants fighting against them. They would be outnumbered and out-trained in fighting men, and they would have to fight against one city after another, until the whole country was conquered. Yet, when God tells Joshua to "be strong and very courageous," it isn't because of the enemy that he would have to face at all. He was told to be courageous so he could "observe to do according to all the law."

This is a new slant to the old hymn, "Trust and Obey," but now it is "Be courageous so you can obey." We can understand how trust fits with obedience, for we have to be able to trust the Lord to want to follow Him. Yet, what does courage have to do with obedience? I'm sure that anyone who has first hand experience in spiritual warfare could tell you. Unfortunately, it is possible to both trust in God, and at the very same time not to trust yourself. You know that God is able, but Satan has shaken your own self-confidence, and your fear keeps you from doing what you know you should because you are afraid of your own failure, not God's. So, God patiently tells Joshua to be courageous, so that he can obey, for He knows that even though God has the power to bring victory over the physical enemies, Joshua's fear may cause him to lose the spiritual warfare. It takes both faith and courage to be a leader, for there is a lot more riding on your outcome, and a multitude depending on your success.

It also takes courage to obey the Law because many of the commandments of the Lord require us to be different from the rest of the world. We would rather just blend in so we can be accepted by the crowd, but God's standard is holiness, and there is no room for compromise. The world says that it is alright for people to commit adultery or fornication, and celebrities often flaunt their infidelities and their "baby bumps". Yet, the bible says that we need to stay virgins until marriage, and to stay faithful to our spouses till death separates us. It does not matter how much teasing we get for staying pure, or how turned off we get when our spouse becomes obese, diseased, or just plain grumpy. Marriage is a life-long commitment which symbolizes our marriage with the Lord. Would we want Jesus to be unfaithful to us when we become old or useless? We need to be faithful to our spouses, then, as if they are the Lord himself. Will this take courage? Absolutely. Yet, the world is watching us to see if we really mean what we say when we call ourselves Christians. Are we really one with him, or just when it is convenient?

The Best of Both Worlds

"May God give you of heaven's dew and of earth's richness." Gen. 27:28

People often speak of wanting the best of both worlds. When they use this phrase, though, they are usually referring to different contrasting conditions here on earth, such as being married, but living the lifestyle of the single crowd, having a steady job, but having the freedom to roam, or having kids, but having someone else take care of them. They can enjoy the benefits of the one condition without having to deal with the responsibilities or negative aspects of the condition. Of course, this philosophy is idealistic and escapist, and sooner or later everything hits the fan of reality.

When Isaac blesses his son, however, he is not contrasting romanticism versus realism. He blesses him with the refreshing goodness of heaven, as well as the richness of earth. This really is the best of both worlds—heavenly and earthly. It is asking God to bless his son both spiritually and materially. It is speaking of God's healing power to revive and renew each day, as a fresh spring dew brings rejuvenation to the earth each new morning. What a special gift that Isaac wishes for his son.

Ironically, though, he thinks that he is blessing his favorite son, Esau, but he is really blessing the deceitful Jacob, who has pretended to be Esau. It is frustrating as a parent sometimes, for we do everything we can to bless our children through our words and actions, and yet their characters are molded by so many other factors around them, that our blessings often fall on deaf ears. So, we satisfy ourselves by blessing them through our prayers instead.

Unfortunately, we often stop at praying for them to experience the richness of the earth, without praying for the dew from heaven. The greatest blessing we can give our children is the legacy of God's love, for what has a man gained if he gains the whole world, but loses his soul? Pray for peace in their souls first, and then it won't matter if they ever experience worldly wealth, for the best of both worlds can only be truly enjoyed while abiding in the heart of God.

Sweet and Sour

"The Lord showed him a piece of wood.
He threw it into the water, and the water became sweet." Ex. 15:25

One of the greatest difficulties that faced the Israelites as they journeyed through the desert was the lack of good water for their families, as well as their livestock. Where do you go to find enough fresh water to meet the needs of millions of people, and millions of animals? This is an impossible task, and people can become very angry and desperate if this simple, basic need is not met. After wandering around for some time, Moses finally found enough water, but it was bitter. Can you imagine the great happiness that must have been felt when the water was first sighted, and then the even greater disappointment when it turned out to be sour? The people grumbled and blamed Moses for bringing them out to the desert to die.

Moses, out of desperation and maybe even fear for his own life, cried out to the Lord for help. The Lord could have answered his prayers in several different ways. He could have caused a great rain storm, or opened up fresh springs from the earth, or, even just wiped everyone off the face of the earth because of all their complaining. What He did do, though, was to tell Moses to go over and pick up this stick and throw it in the bitter water. Moses obeyed, and immediately the water was made sweet.

We can learn a couple of lessons from this. First of all, when we are faced with the bitter circumstances and people of this world, the answer is not to become sour ourselves, but to turn to God for help. When we do this, we may be surprised by God's solution to the problem. Instead of some mighty miracle, with all the thunder and lightning that God can muster, He may just ask us to take the simple tools or gifts that we have, and to use them, with his guidance and blessing, to turn the bitter into sweet. He told Moses to use an old stick. He may ask us to pick a flower to give to our foe, or to make a cake, or to buy a cup of coffee. It may mean just getting the old grouch to laugh, or to offer to help them with a project that they are overwhelmed with. It doesn't have to be something big. It just means using the little that we do have, instead of complaining about what we don't.

Second, if we ask God for guidance, we have to be willing to follow His advice. God doesn't always make sense from our human perspective. He tells us what we should do, and we think we know better. After all, didn't He tell Moses to change bitter water to sweet by just throwing an old stick into it?   Yet, Moses obeyed, without question, and the water was purified instantaneously.

It doesn't take much to see God move in wondrous ways. It just takes a willingness to use whatever we have, and a submissive spirit to follow God's directions.

Suppressing the Truth

*"The wrath of God is being revealed from heaven against all godlessness
and wickedness of men who suppress the truth by their wickedness." Rom. 1:18*

So often the world tries to give the impression that the greatest hindrance to growth and progress is ignorance. If we just educate people properly, they will know the truth, and the truth will set them free. According to scripture, though, the problem with people is not ignorance, it is sin. First, we are born into sin, with an inherited sin nature, and then we willfully choose to rebel against God's claim to rule our lives.

We become "godless" in the sense that we choose to leave God out of our decisions, our values, and our souls. We become so self-centered, that God just doesn't matter any more. In other words, we become "wicked". Wickedness is egotism that is so caught up with self, that it totally disregards justice, righteousness, truth, virtue and honor. It not only disregards these things, it seeks to suppress them as much as possible so that others will disregard them also. The problem here is not ignorance. It is a willful choice not to know the truth, because the truth will convict them of their sinfulness, and they do not want to be accountable for their hard-hearted focus on self.

Unfortunately, this is not just a problem with non-Christians or pagans. There are many people who say they have accepted Christ as their saviors, but who still reject Him as their Lord. They go to church on Sundays, but during the week they leave Him out of their decisions, and their values are based on personal pleasures and immediate gain, rather than trusting in God's leading, or submitting to His priorities. I'm not talking about back-sliding Christians, who have walked away from Christ to live in sin. I'm talking about Christians who by all appearances are God-fearing, Bible believing proclaimers of the gospel. They talk the talk, and walk the walk, in public, that is. Yet, it's all a show. They are masqueraders in a pageant, but their true selves are not revealed until the parade is over. The Bible calls them hypocrites. Immediately, when people see that word, "hypocrite", they shut down their psyches, saying to themselves, that's not talking about me. Yet, remember, the wicked person is not someone who is ignorant of the truth. It is someone who knows better, but sins anyway. It is someone who suppresses the truth.

So, when the Holy Spirit tries to convict us of our sin, how do we respond? Do we face it square on, turn it over to the Lord, and move on to the next test of our faith, or do we hem and ha, squirm away, and completely avoid thinking about anything that might imply that we are guilty or that we need to change? God is speaking to each one of us. Are we really listening, or just playing the game?

Stand Firm and Be Still

"Do not be afraid. Stand firm and you will see the deliverance the LORD
will bring you today." Ex. 14:13

Fear is something we all face from time to time. It is a natural response to danger, and is helpful as a self-defense mechanism. Sometimes it motivates us to move out of harm's way. Other times it moves us to fight back against the threatening foe, or irrationally, even against the people who are trying to help us. The drowning man can sometimes be his own worst enemy, as well as a danger to the lifeguard trying to save him.

Though our natural tendency is to struggle when we are afraid, sometimes the best thing to do is just "stand firm", and let God do the fighting for us. We understand this principle when we are children, for we often have to just stand and watch as our older brother or father protects us from the bullies of the neighborhood. We know that we cannot fight the battle ourselves. We have to trust in others who are more powerful than we are. When we become adults, though, we find this harder to do. Our pride makes us believe that we can fight our own battles, and our David/Goliath mentality often backfires.

The Israelites didn't have a chance against the mighty Egyptian army. If they tried to protect themselves, they would have been wiped out. God told them instead to not be afraid, and just "stand firm" and watch God do the fighting. It wouldn't do any good to fight, or to run away, or to just run around in circles. The only thing that would work was to stand firm, and to "be still".

This second part is almost always more difficult than the first, for even when we know we can't fight the battle, we love to hurl hurtful words at our foes, and to provoke them to even greater anger. God's command to stand still and be quiet is like a matador trying to tell a raging bull to calm down and stand still, while he stands over his head with a raised sword in hand.

If we are relying only on our own strength, such a command only makes us more afraid and more angry. If, however, we have learned to trust in the Almighty God to fight our battles for us, we can be like the little child again who has complete faith in his father to take care of the big guy next door. Let God take care of the bullies, and you won't end up with any spiritual black eyes.

Spiritual Deafness

"Moses reported this to the Israelites, but they did not listen to him." Ex. 6:9

There are many reasons for spiritual deafness, or the inability to hear what God is saying to us. It is easy to conclude that it is just because of spiritual rebellion, or refusing to listen because the person doesn't want to obey. However, there are many other causes for being "hard of hearing" the still small voice of God. One is that there are too many other distracting signals being sent toward our spirit sensors. Satan and the world love to drown out the divine messages being sent our way, so that compared to the quiet, calm, love whispers of our bridegroom, Christ, the adrenaline rushes of sinful temptations force us to only hear the fast, furious, frenzied frequencies of egomania.

The reason for the Israelites being spiritually deaf, though, has nothing to do with the distractions of pleasure. It is something that Christians don't often like to talk about, for it seems to fall outside of the normal "biblical" reasons. In fact, it is from the unpopular realm of the psychological that sneaks its way into the Bible while the Christians aren't watching. Many Christians feel that psychology has nothing to do with spiritual things, but Moses gives us an interesting insight into some of the problems of the chosen people. He says that "they did not listen to him because of their discouragement and cruel bondage" (Ex. 6:9). They were spiritually deaf, not due to rebellion, but due to being pushed down, beaten, abused, oppressed and despised for so long, that they were too discouraged to even hope for a savior.

The psychological term for this is "despair", or "manic depressive", where someone is so overwhelmed with sadness and being victimized, that they can hardly lift their hands to feed their faces, let alone look past the misery of the moment. It wasn't the world's temptations that were drowning out the voice of God for the Israelites. It was the spiritual vacuum of hopelessness. In such cases, God has to heal the brokenness of their hearts enough for them to hear His voice before they can learn to accept His love. Usually this comes only through Christians patiently reaching out to them in unconditional love, not judging them for their inability to hear or respond, but encouraging them through open-ended listening, instead of just trying to "preach at them". This takes time.

In the case of the Israelites, though, God encouraged their hearts through His awe-inspiring miracles and their supernatural deliverance from their enemies. Sometimes God steps in and jump-starts hope, so people will listen "now", because he has a plan that requires immediacy. Most of the time, however, He relies upon us to encourage people through love until they can finally listen to Him-- As long as we don't become discouraged ourselves first(2 Chron. 32:8, Gal. 6:9).

Sons of the Living God

"They will be called sons of the living God." Hosea 1:10

Have you noticed how Christians often talk in a language all our own? We use King James English when we pray, or we use terminology that a non-Christian would not understand. Phrases such as "born again" are just plain confusing and make unbelievers uncomfortable when they come to our churches. We sing hymns that are even more old-fashioned, and though they are powerful and meaningful to us, the unbelieving visitor just shakes his head at such phrases as "the balm of Gilead" or "I raise my Ebenezer."

In one sense, this is very similar to Paul's point about the use of spiritual gifts in the church. He says that it is better to use gifts in the church that everyone can benefit from. What good does it do if we use a gift that no one understands? Those personal gifts can still be used alone with God, but should not be used in church without an interpreter (I Cor. 14:1-5). Maybe the same thing holds true for the songs we sing and the terminology that we use in church. The purpose should be clear communication, not just spiritual symbolism.

On the other hand, there are some phrases that Christians don't use, even though the Bible does. We have no problem with calling Christians the "children of our Heavenly Father". However, we save the term "son of God" for Jesus alone. How can we be children, but not "sons" or "daughters"? It is true that Jesus was the "only begotten son" of God, but we are His adopted children, and we are promised that we are going to inherit the kingdom with Christ (Rev. 21:7), and that we will be God's "sons". If God himself calls us His sons, then why are we afraid to use this term? We are both trapped in a spiritual language that doesn't communicate, and in fear of saying the wrong thing. Jesus is the Word. Let Him free us in our words.

Sifted as Wheat

"Satan has asked to sift you as wheat. But I have prayed for you."
Luke 22:31-32

When we read the story of Job, we tend to think of it as an isolated case, like some extreme example to scare us into obedience. Or maybe, we think, it was just something that happened in Old Testament times, and we don't have to deal with that anymore because Satan was thrown out of heaven, right? Wrong. At the Last Supper, when Jesus was preparing his disciples for his death, he turned to Peter and said, "Satan has asked to sift you as wheat". Satan asked God if he could sift Peter, just like he sifted Job, by causing him to be persecuted and tested to his absolute limit.

Jesus' response to Satan's request of God is that he prays for Peter. He is Peter's advocate with the Father, and he pleads for mercy. Yet, he doesn't pray that God will keep Satan from sifting Peter. He just prays that Peter's "faith may not fail". He knows that Peter will fall, just like he fell when he tried walking on water, because his enthusiasm is great, but his faith is weak. He wants God to strengthen his faith, so "after he falls", he will turn back to strengthen his brothers (Luke 22:32).

We don't like this. We would much rather that God keep Satan away from us, so that we would never fall. Yet, God, in his infinite wisdom, knows that we need to be tested to grow in our faith. The problems that we go through are not as punishment for our past sins, but preparation and training for our future victories. God has a wonderful plan for our lives. Jesus said, "I have come that you might have life, and that you might have it more abundantly" (John 10:10). Yet, that plan takes discipline and training of the good parts and purging of the bad.

Satan and his angels are like the practice squad of a football team. They never get to play a real game, but are merely there to help the starters get in shape for the real competition. Our real competition is not the Devil or his demons, but our sinful natures, which we battle with every day of our lives. Even Paul, who seemed to have victory over Satan from the very beginning of his ministry, still struggled with his "old self". He says, "I do not understand what I do. For what I want to do I do not do, but what I hate I do…It is no longer I myself who do it, but it is sin living in me" (Rom. 7:15-17). He doesn't blame the Devil or something outside of himself for his problems. He recognizes that the battle is within. He says, "I see another law at work in the members of my body, waging war against the law of my mind and making me a prisoner of the law of sin" (Rom. 7:23).

Yes, the Devil is out there, and God may allow him to test us to help our faith to grow, but we can't cop out and say, "The Devil made me do it" every time we sin. Our greatest enemy is our inner man.

Servant, Sent and Set Apart

*"Paul, a servant of Christ Jesus, called to be an apostle
and set apart for the gospel of God." Rom. 1:1*

Paul is identifying himself as the writer of this letter to the Romans. Yet, he is doing far more than that. He is also identifying his position, his purpose and his priority in Christ. His position is that of a servant in relation to Christ, who is the King of Kings and Lord of Lords. This position is based upon humility and a realization that he is nothing apart from God. He believes that he is the worst of all sinners, and that he is only saved by grace (I Tim. 1:15).

This position, though lowly, is not meant to imply that he is given little to do. His purpose is the high calling of being an apostle. He is to be a servant of Christ, but a leader of men. An apostle is a "sent one", a messenger or torchbearer, who is meant to lead the way and show others the right path by his example, as well as his teachings. His purpose is that of a pastor or shepherd, who leads his flock beside the still waters, as well as through the valley of the shadow of death.

His priority, though, is never to glorify himself, but to lift up the name and saving power of his Lord. He knows that he has been set apart for that very purpose, and that his life only has meaning as it relates to that priority. So, verse one is more than just a name tag—it is a calling card, a passport, and itinerary. It tells us who he is, where he is going, and what he is going to do when he gets there. He keeps it clear and simple so he can stay focused on the who's, what's and why's of his mission, instead of the "whines". If we are to be followers of Christ, and Paul's example, we too should have a clear focus on the fact that we are servants, sent ones, and set apart for the gospel and glory of our Lord.

Scribes and Prophets

"I wish that all the Lord's people were prophets
and that the Lord would put his Spirit on them." Num. 11:29

Two of the most respected roles in Jewish history were the scribes and the prophets. The prophets were the ones who received messages directly from God, and then told those messages to others. The scribes were the ones who wrote down the messages, and then made copies so that many others could read them. Both positions were important and necessary, for without them both, we would not have the Holy Scriptures that we have today.

Yet, Moses says that he wishes that "all the Lord's people were prophets". He doesn't say that he wishes that they all could be scribes. Why does he make this distinction? The scribe didn't have to think about what he was writing, or even understand the truth behind the words. He was just a copy or duplicating machine. Anyone could be a scribe, as long as they could read and write with a legible handwriting. Although it was a position of great honor and respect because of the sacred content of what they were writing, they could be replaced today by anyone in the local secretarial typing pool.

The prophet, on the other hand, had direct contact with God. He heard God's voice and knew God's heart. He was a channel of God's mercy, as well as His wrath. He was a conduit of God's power and a mediator of God's will. What an exciting privilege and awesome responsibility. No wonder Moses wished that all God's people could be prophets. Just think of the possibilities—having every believer be filled with the Spirit so that they could hear the Lord speaking directly to them, instead of having to go through some human advocate. What a wonderful dream! Yet, then the Lord came in human form to die for the sins of the world, and he changed that dream into a reality. He broke down the barriers between God and man, and now every man and woman can be a prophet who hears directly from God.

The problem is, though, that people don't want to deal with God one on one. They are too afraid of His holiness and judgment, so they hold Him off at a distance. They would rather have God speak to someone else, and then have that person filter out all the harsh stuff, to make God's will easier to swallow. In other words, they want pastors to be like mother birds who chew up the spiritual worms before they give them to the babies to eat. What a shame. Instead of the church being a vibrant powerhouse of prophets proclaiming the Word of God, we have become a secondhand store of borrowed blessings. God wants all of us to be Elijah's, and yet we are satisfied with being Xerox machines. Don't just hide by being a scribe. Profit more by being a prophet.

Ruins or Rainbows

*"Throughout the night the cloud brought darkness to the one side
and light to the other side." Ex. 14:20*

The children of Israel had escaped Egypt, and the Egyptian army was rapidly advancing to take them back. The Israelites were trapped in a valley, with the Red Sea in front of them and the enemy right behind them, and there was no way to escape. So the Lord, who appeared as a cloud by day and fire by night, moved from before His people, and came between the Jews and the army. Then mysteriously, the same cloud brought darkness upon the enemy, but light to the Israelites.

How can this be? First of all, a cloud does not have any light of its own. It is like the moon, which only gives light by reflection. Clouds, then, can either block the light of the sun, or they can reflect its light, and cause beautiful sunsets or even rainbows. The clouds of life (discouragements, heartaches, failures and fears) can either come between God and us, or they can help to reflect His light by revealing His love, forgiveness, patience and power.

The difference is in our perspective. We can either choose to see the clouds as barriers, keeping us from our pursuit of happiness, or we can choose to see them as opportunities for God's miraculous, awesome power to shine through. The clouds of life are prisons to some and prisms to others—prisons of confusion, anger and self-pity or prisms that reflect God's glory, truth and love. The clouds are there to test us. They can either be a blessing or a curse. If we love, serve and obey God with all our hearts, minds and souls, the greatest problems always point to His loving, wise providence, and we end up growing stronger and closer to Him. If we rebel against God and His leading in our lives, though, the clouds bring only darkness, depression, and despair to our souls, and we are completely blind to the light of God. We are so completely self-focused, that even though the greatest light in all the world is all around us, we can only see the darkness within. Which would you rather see—the ruin of self or the rainbow of God?

Rescue Me

*"The Lord Jesus Christ, who gave himself for our sins
to rescue us from the present evil age."* Gal. 1:3 - 4

Sometimes we get the impression that Jesus died on the cross only to save us from eternal damnation, but this is not true. Salvation is not just being saved from something in the future. The Bible says that Christ's death for us was also to save us from the "present evil age". What does this mean? It certainly doesn't mean that we are immediately removed from the earth, or that we can never sin again.

I believe that the key to this question can be found in Col. 1:13-14. It says, "For he has rescued us from the dominion of darkness and brought us into the kingdom of the Son he loves, in whom we have redemption, the forgiveness of sins." It doesn't say that he "will" rescue us. It says he "has rescued us" from the dominion of darkness. Yes, Satan is still the ruler of this earth, but we are no longer his subjects. We have a different lord and master, and his kingdom is not of this world. We may be in the world, but we are no longer of the world. Christ's kingdom is within us now. We have been redeemed or bought back from the slave-driver through the blood of Christ, and Satan no longer has any claim on us.

Yes, we are still sinners, but we are saved by grace, and all of our sins have been forgiven. Satan cannot hold them against us anymore. Salvation and eternal life do not begin after we die. They begin the moment we are born again. Old things have passed away. Behold, all things have become new. Now, just claim it, and live it. Stop trying to hold on to the past. Someone who has been rescued from a burning building doesn't go rushing back in. Someone rescued from sin shouldn't either.

Remember Your Roots

*"Remember that you were slaves in Egypt
and the Lord your God redeemed you."*
Deut. 15:15

A number of years ago, there was a book and movie called *Roots*, which explored the history of slavery and racial prejudice in our country. It showed how many people were destroyed by this terrible moral plague which poisoned the minds and hearts of many Americans, who may have been completely "Christian" in every other way, but totally depraved in their hatred of other human beings.

Why do "good people" act so badly toward others? One of the reasons that is given in scripture is that we forget our roots. When the children of Israel came to the Promised Land, and they started becoming more prosperous, God warned them about the way they treated their slaves and servants. He said, "Remember that you were slaves." Remember how bad it was, and how cruelly you were treated. Remember how you prayed and begged to God for deliverance, and how "the Lord your God redeemed you." Remember the way that you wished to be treated, and treat them in that way. It is the golden rule with a twist, based on your memories of the past, not just your desires for the present.

This same principle not only applies to how we treat those under our authority, but people in general. There is an old saying that says, "If not but for the grace of God, there go I." When we look at others who have fallen into sin, and who are slaves to their sin natures, we are told not to judge them too quickly or harshly, but remember our own sinfulness. We too have been slaves to sin at different times, and it is important that we all remember our roots. If we remember our "roots", maybe we will have an easier time removing the "trees" from our own eyes before we try to remove the "splinters" in the eyes of others.

Remember Lot's Wife

"Remember Lot's wife! Whoever tries to keep his life will lose it."
Luke 17:32-33

Lot and his wife and daughters were told by two angels to leave Sodom and Gomorrah and to flee to the mountains. They were told not to look back or to stop anywhere on the way. Lot's wife did look back, though, and she was immediately turned into a pillar of salt. Why did she look back? Only God knows what was in her heart. Yet, Jesus uses her as an example of those who don't want to leave their lives of wickedness to follow him. Lot had chosen to settle in Sodom because the land was fertile and rich. The people there were used to having whatever they wanted, and getting it easily. It was no wonder that Lot's wife didn't want to give up her home and life of luxury and ease. It didn't matter that the town was depraved, and that homosexuals were openly raping whomever they wished. She had it good. She didn't care about the angel's warnings. All that she thought of was what she was having to give up.

The Israelites reacted the same way when they faced their first trials in the wilderness. "Why can't we go back to Egypt where we at least had good food to eat?" It didn't matter that they were slaves, as long as their stomachs were filled. It is amazing how pleasure can be so strong in our imaginations, that it completely obliterates any memory of the misery that the pleasure may have brought us. We may get as sick as a dog after partying all night, but all we remember is the good time that we had when we felt so high. Jesus says, "Remember Lot's wife."

We can't be true disciples of Christ if we are always looking over our shoulder, wishing that we could be back enjoying the pleasures of our past. Nostalgia is a good thing when it comes to remembering the pastimes of innocence. It is deadly if we can't let go of our longings of the sinful self. What good would it do us if we threw the anchor overboard, yet continued to hold on to the chain? The same thing happens when we hold on to the memories of our self-indulgences. We will end up drowning in our dreams, and any attempt to go back will be a nightmare. Longing after past sins is like lusting after a corpse. No one in their right mind would do such a thing. Why, then, lust after our old sinful self, which is dead spiritually? We shouldn't try to revive it. If we try to use CPR on sin, it will suck the life out of us much faster than we will ever breathe life into it, and our pillar of salt may be a dung heap.

Rejoicing in the Morning

"Weeping may remain for a night, but rejoicing comes in the morning." Psa. 30:5

I have often heard this verse at various occasions, such as funerals, where the preacher is trying to encourage people to not be in despair. Sorrow may last for a while, but it doesn't need to be permanent. Each day is a new day, and the sunrise helps us to put our sorrows behind us. This verse, however, is not dealing with how to cope with grief. It is talking about how we deal with the chastisement of the Lord. If we have fallen away into sin, for example, and the Lord punishes us or disciplines us, then our response is weeping, for not only are we hurting from the discipline, we feel the weight of the grief that we have caused the Lord. We may weep for a while, but then there is a sense or realization that God chastens those He loves, and we are thankful for His gracious correction and forgiveness. We, then, can walk on in a refreshing newness that comes from being purged, and our heart is filled with joy.

Some, however, may have a hard time accepting this interpretation of this verse because it is so foreign to what we have always heard. In fact, we may even like it better the other way. Yet, let's look at the context. It says, "Sing to the Lord, you saints of his; praise his holy name. For his anger lasts only a moment, but his favor lasts a lifetime; weeping may remain for a night, but rejoicing comes in the morning…When you hid your face, I was dismayed…to the Lord I called for mercy: what gain is there in my destruction? You turned my wailing into dancing; you removed my sackcloth and clothed me with joy" (Psa. 30:5-11).

The weeping and wailing, then, are results of God's anger and His hiding His face from him. David is so dismayed, in fact, that he feels that God may actually destroy him because of his sin. He wears sackcloth and mourns his loss of fellowship and favor with God. God doesn't leave him in his sorrow, though. That is the difference between the guilt trip that Satan puts on us and the conviction of the Holy Spirit. The Devil keeps trying to rub our noses in our sins, and he won't let us forget our failures. He not only defeats us through our sins, he defeats us again through our memories. God, on the other hand, convicts us of sin, forgives us of guilt, and then forgets that it ever happened.

This is why we are able to start the new day with renewed hope and joy. We know that God has given us another chance, a fresh start. That doesn't mean that we can just take advantage of God's forgiveness and just keep sinning. God will chasten us even more if we take Him for granted, and if we are not sincere with our repentance, there will be no joy the next day. We will have a spiritual hangover from our sin in the morning instead of the dance of forgiveness, and wonder where all the fun went. Joy only comes in the morning if peace with God leads the way. A rebellious heart doesn't find either one.

Rebuke your Neighbor

"Rebuke your neighbor frankly so you will not share in his guilt." Lev. 19:17

It seems that this verse is an obvious contradiction to Christ's teaching to "Judge not, lest ye be judged" (Matt. 7:1). However, the reason for the misunderstanding is that Christ's teaching is taken out of context. The problem that Christ is dealing with is not judging other people. It is hypocrisy. He is saying that it is wrong for us to judge others if we are doing the same thing or even worse things ourselves. Yet, then he says, "First take the plank out of your own eye, and <u>then </u>you will see clearly to remove the speck from your brother's eye."

In other words, if we are right with the Lord, and not a hypocrite, then it is alright for us to judge others. In fact, it is not only alright, it is our responsibility to do so. First, we have the command in Leviticus to rebuke our neighbors frankly. We cannot rebuke someone unless we have first judged them. Second, if we don't rebuke them, but just look the other way, we actually share in their guilt. Those who are mature in the Lord have a responsibility to oversee those who are less mature, and if they see that they are falling into sin, they must rebuke them, or they will be held accountable.

Yet, some may say that this only applies to the Old Testament times, for they were under the law. What about Christ's teaching to his disciples, "If your brother sins, rebuke him, and if he repents forgive him" (Luke 17:3)? Again, how can they rebuke someone for their sins unless they first judge them? Paul gives advice to Timothy on how to be a good pastor. He tells him, "Preach the Word…correct, rebuke, and encourage—with great patience and careful instruction" (2 Tim. 4:2).

Is it right, then, for us to judge someone? If we are living in sin, no. If we are not, yes—as long as we do it to build someone up in the Lord, and not to tear them down, and if we do it with great patience, humility, and careful instruction. In other words, if we do it the way the Lord would.

One Man's Junk is another Man's Treasure

"She named her son Ben-Oni, but his father named him Benjamin." Gen. 35:18

Garage sales and flea markets are based on the principle that there are people out there who highly value the things I just want to throw away. It doesn't matter how broken or worn out or out-dated something is, someone still probably wants it. It's amazing how we can look at the exact same thing, and come to completely opposite opinions about it. Sometimes we value things because we know they are worth a lot of money. Sometimes we just feel attached to things because they have sentimental value—they remind us of special people or memories. If someone else doesn't have those same memories, they may just miss the point.

In Jacob and Rachel's case, it is a matter of perspective. Rachel has just given birth to a son, which is normally a very joyful occasion, but this birth is traumatically difficult. It is so hard, in fact, that Rachel is going to die because of it. From her perspective, then, it is the worst possible thing that could happen, so she calls her son, Ben-Oni, which means "son of my trouble". When Rachel dies, though, the baby becomes even more precious to Jacob, for he knows that his wife loved him so much that she was willing to even die to give him another son. He cherished the boy as a token of his wife's love. So, he renamed the boy, Benjamin, which means "son of my right hand". To the wife, the boy was a curse. To the husband, he was a blessing.

This is very similar to the way that people view the cross. From the world's perspective, the crucifixion was just a tragedy, for it rid the world of a great teacher, healer, and possible Messiah. To those who love him, though, the cross is precious, and the means by which all may be saved. What the world views as Christ's great defeat, we view as His greatest victory, and its value grows greater and greater through the ages as many thousands more become a part of God's family because of what Jesus did. The world casts Jesus aside as junk, a reject and failure, but we see him as priceless treasure to our souls. Sacrificial love is what makes the difference between trash and treasure, but only those who are willing to die to themselves can truly appreciate someone who has died in their place.

On the Wings of an Eagle

"I carried you on eagle's wings and brought you to myself." Ex. 19:4

Imagine for a moment a mother eagle pushing its baby out of a nest which is perched high on a mountain cliff. The baby flaps its wings frantically, while falling at a tremendous speed toward the rugged canyon below. At the last minute, the mother eagle swoops beneath it to keep it from dashing itself on the jagged rocks. She catches her eaglet on the back of her wings, and carries it back to the safety of the nest. Why does the mother treat its child in what seems like such a harsh way? It is because she wants her baby to learn how to fly. What appears to be an act of cruelty is really an act of love.

Most of the time, when a mother eagle takes this drastic step, the eaglet is able to fly on the very first try. For some, though, it takes more patient training. The mother has to catch the baby on its wings, and return it safely to the nest. Then, when the baby's wings are a little stronger, the mother flies near the baby while it falls, and merely uses its wings to create an updraft for the baby to fly easier. Finally, the baby is able to fly on its own, but always with its mother's watchful eye.

When the Lord, then, says to the Israelites that He carried them on eagle's wings, it is a beautiful picture, but it really is talking about the immature level of the chosen people. They have just been taken out of Egypt, and they have yet to understand what following God really means. They are still holding on to the stability of their memories of the "nest" back home. Sure it was slavery, but in their minds, it was still better than being "pushed out of the nest" into a desert to die. They didn't yet know that they could trust God to swoop down like an eagle to catch them whenever they fell. They may have even felt like the baby eagle probably feels—"Doesn't my "mommy" really love me?" What is God trying to do, punish me? If God really loved me, he wouldn't let me suffer like this—falling aimlessly, terrified, fighting for my life. Yet, God, like the eagle, is not trying to hurt us by letting us struggle. He wants to teach us how to "fly" spiritually.

Isaiah 40:31 says, "Those who hope in the Lord will renew their strength. They will soar on wings like eagles." Before we can "soar" we first have to have our wings strengthened, and that only comes through hoping in the Lord. What is our hope? As God said to the Jews, He carried them on eagle's wings to bring them to Himself. Our hope, even when we are "falling", is that God is always there to lift us up, and His goal is always to bring us to Himself. He wants us to be with Him and to be like Him, even if it means pushing us out of our nest or comfort zone in order to get us to trust Him more. We can always count on Him to be the wind beneath our wings.

Old Grouches Can't Be Saved

"We played the flute for you, and you did not dance." Luke 7:32

Have you ever known anyone who was an old grouch? No matter what you did to cheer them up, nothing would make them happy. In fact, often your attempts to bring light into their world only made them more grouchy, and more determined to fight off your Pollyanna smile. Jesus talks about this kind of person and how difficult it is to try to reach them for God. He says that the Pharisees fit into this category because they fought off every attempt by God to soften their hearts. First, God tried to reach them through John the baptizer, whose ascetic lifestyle was meant to appeal to the legalistic Jews. Then came Jesus, who ate and drank with tax collectors and sinners, showing God's love to everyone. Yet, neither extreme met the approval of the religious leaders, for they judged anyone and everyone who wasn't exactly like themselves, for they set themselves up as the standard. They were old grouches, and religious ones are the worst.

Jesus says, "To what, then, can I compare the people of this generation?...We played the flute for you, and you did not dance; we sang a dirge, and you did not cry" (Luke 7:32). No matter what way that God used to reach them, they were stiff-necked and rebellious, refusing to be happy or at peace with the God that they claimed to profess. It was as though they believed that it was their religious duty to be either miserable themselves or make everyone else around them miserable. What a contrast to when King David saw the Ark of the Covenant returning to the Holy City, and he greeted it with singing and dancing. The presence of God in our lives should be music to our ears and a reason for celebration, not a funeral march.

Yet, even if our churches were filled with joy and laughter, there would still be the majority of people who would not dare to enter its doors. They are just like the Pharisees in many ways, and no matter what God does to soften their hearts and draw them to himself, they will still rebel and turn the other way. Most people would rather be their own gods, even if it means misery and woe, than to bow down to a God who demands self-denial and submission. It doesn't matter how appealing of a show the church makes, true disciples are never drawn by entertainment alone. Old Grouches can't be saved, no matter what method is used, unless they first become like children, and that is impossible. Thank God, He specializes in the impossible.

You Will Not Reap What You Sow

*"You will sow much seed in the field
but you will harvest little." Deut. 28:38*

We have all heard the verse, "You will reap what you sow" (Gal. 6:7). This applies to the area of morality, where if we sow the "wild oats" of our sinful nature, we will reap destruction. Yet, there is another area where we do not reap what we sow. That is the area of good works. We think that it should work the same way—that if we put in a lot of effort doing good things, that it should reap great rewards. However, God makes an important distinction in this area. The Israelites were hard workers, and they planted much seed, but God said that they would "harvest little."

The reason for this discrepancy was that even though they worked hard, they were doing it for selfish gain, and God would not bless them. They were following the idols of the heathen nations around them, and they were not being obedient to the law of the Lord. Their priorities were all messed up, and they were not thankful for the times when God had blessed them in the past. Moses tells them, "because you did not serve the Lord your God joyfully and gladly in the time of prosperity, therefore in hunger and thirst…you will serve your enemies" (Deut. 28:47).

This sounds like a lot of Christians today, who are running around doing a multitude of good things, but for the wrong reasons. They think that it is the quantity of "sowing good works" that matters, but they are doing it for the idols of self-glorification, fame or wanting rewards in heaven, instead of humble obedience to the leading of the Holy Spirit. Their ministries may still grow for a while, just out of hard work and natural abilities, but God will not bless them the way that He would if they were obeying Him and follow His leading, instead of just following after their own selfish ambitions. They will end up spinning their wheels much of the time on wasted efforts, and burning themselves out because they are doing everything with their own strength. They will reap what they sow morally, but they will be greatly disappointed in how little they are able to harvest in rewards based upon the tremendous amount of effort that they exert in the sowing. If all we sow is self, then all the digging just makes our grave bigger.

You Reap What You Sow

"They sow the wind and reap the whirlwind." Hosea 8:7

The wind is a fascinating thing. It is powerful, unpredictable, and almost magical at times. It helps to move ships, give flight to the birds and planes, and even helps a little boy fly his kite. Yet, it can also be very destructive. It can knock down trees and houses, destroy crops, and even kill innocent people. Since it is so powerful, in both good and bad ways, it is often compared to God, as well as demons. Yet, in Hosea it speaks of the wind not as just a mighty force, or even a heavenly being, but a way of life. There are those in life who are addicted to adrenaline. They go from one rush to another, as if searching for the ultimate thrill ride of their lives. Each one needs to be a little bit better, a little bit scarier, or a little bit more awesome than the last one. Some have a death wish, I'm sure, but most are just seeking to live as close to the edge as they possibly can without falling off into oblivion. They want to dare death to a challenge, or live for the ultimate pleasure, and they are never satisfied in their search except for their occasional climactic high, which is only a temporary, fleeting moment of excellence. After that, there is a great let down and depression, a spiritual hangover of sorts, which leaves them eager to pursue the next wild ride to escape their spiritual vacuum.

What they don't realize is that when "they sow the wind", they "reap the whirlwind." The whirlwind is the wild ride out of control. It is fascinating to watch, but destructive to everything in its path. It tosses you all around, upside down and backwards, and then it throws you down to the ground as a mangled, wretched blob. It is the drug trip gone bad, the sexual escapade that ends in unwanted pregnancy or AIDS, or the exciting, otherworldly adventure into the occult that is turned from bizarre fun into demonic terror. There is never a right way to ride the wind, unless the wind is the Holy Spirit, for only then is there calm at the eye of the storm, and that calm is Jesus.

Magnify the Lord with Me

"On that day the Lord magnified Joshua in the sight of all Israel." Joshua 4:14

We are often told to magnify the Lord, for He above all is worthy of praise and glory (Psalm 34:3). Yet, what does it mean to magnify the Lord? To magnify means to enlarge, clarify, or lift up in honor. When we use a magnifying glass it enlarges the words that we are trying to read or object that we are trying to see. It seems to lift the words right off the page, bringing them closer to us for better observation. When we magnify the Lord we are doing the same thing. We are bringing God into greater focus, lifting Him closer to ourselves, and allowing Him to enlarge Himself within us, filling us with His power and love.

Yet, magnifying people, in contrast, seems totally inappropriate, for who is man that he should be lifted up? We are finite, fallible creatures, at best, who are taught to humble ourselves, and to have servant hearts. When God led the children of Israel into the Promised Land, though, it says that He "magnified Joshua in the sight of all Israel; and they feared him, as they feared Moses, all the days of his life" (Joshua 4:14). Why would God magnify a person? Aren't we supposed to give God all the glory and honor? In spite of all of our weaknesses and insufficiencies, it is a fact of history that God uses the foolish things of this world to confound the wise (I Cor. 1:27). He purposely chooses the weak, the stubborn, or the misfits, who in spite of the failures still believe in God, and He magnifies them before the world as examples of His grace. In other words, He magnifies them so He can be magnified through them.

So when others try to glorify us, and lift us up to positions of honor, don't fall away in humble shyness, as if it is our Christian duty to be a wallflower. God wants His disciples to be magnified, so they can be a light upon a hill, where others may see the power of God's grace working in our lives. It is all right to be held up in the lime light, as long as you see yourself as a prism, which when held in the light, magnifies the light into a beautiful rainbow, glorifying the light, not the prism. When we are glorified, it is a greater opportunity to glorify the Lord, who has given us whatever ability that we have which is being honored. We need to acknowledge the source of our power, and we will receive more. If we claim it all for ourselves, we will lose the little that we have.

Like a Dumb Ox

"He followed her like an ox going to the slaughter." Prov. 7:22

It is amazing to watch someone gently leading a huge ox to the slaughter-house, and this powerful animal not having a care in the world, as if he is just being taken for a stroll in the park. He doesn't realize that it will be his last walk, or that the gentleness of the person is just a ploy to bring him to his death. Solomon uses this description to talk about those who are seduced by the wiles of the wild woman, who sweet talks a man into his own destruction. He is blinded by her beauty and the promise of great pleasure, and he is completely oblivious to the negative consequences of his actions. He is living in a fantasy world and feels invincible. In reality, though, he is just a dumb ox being led to slaughter.

      This illustration by Solomon is especially interesting because his own mother committed adultery with his father, and Solomon himself was enticed by the physical charms of thousands of women. Was he speaking from experience, after learning a lesson the hard way? Not according to scripture. He was seduced more and more through his life, to the point that he not only fell for their sexuality, but also was lured by their idolatry. Instead of being the wisest man on earth, he too became as dumb as an ox, and became a victim of his own folly. He couldn't use ignorance as an excuse, for God had given him wisdom, but he consciously chose to go his own way. He had experienced all that life had to offer, and concluded that all was "vanity", so why even try to be better? His search for wisdom became just a search for the ultimate experience, and his wise proverbs were turned into the emptiness and futility of Ecclesiastes. How dumb can you get?

Like a Doe Set Free

"Naphtali is a doe set free that bears beautiful fawns." Gen. 49:21

There is something truly beautiful about seeing a deer out in its natural environment, enjoying the freedom of its wild yet gentle nature, bounding away in smooth, fluid grace. In the cramped, often suffocating world that we live, we are envious of its freedom. The image in the scriptures, though, is not just of a "Bambi" born free in the forest. The deer is one that was in captivity, but is now "set free". People are the same way. We are born into the captivity of sin, and we are only set free with the liberty that we have in Christ. Only then can we be compared to a "doe set free", bounding victoriously in fluid grace.

The important principle that I would like to focus on in this passage, though, is not just the freedom that God's grace gives to us. It is the effect that that freedom has on others. When we are in bondage to sin, or the overwhelming burden that even the memories of sin can often leave, it has a tremendous impact on the people around us. We are so wrapped up inside of ourselves and our own needs, wants, and cares, that we cannot be sensitive to the concerns of our loved ones. We are a slave to our lusts, anger, bitterness, pride, or envies, and we take out our frustrations and dark spiritual anguish on our family and friends. What wee are doing, without even knowing it, is extending the bars that have been around us so that they begin to imprison everyone else within our reach. Our captivity is like a malignant cancer that affects all the healthy cells around it, like a hungry monster seeking others to devour.

When we are truly set free by the empowering, saving grace of our Lord, we, then, are not the only ones who are set free. We also make it possible for the others in our sphere of influence to escape the poison of our perverted persona. It may take a while, for the arsenic of our attitude may have done a lot of damage over the years. Yet, when they see the transformation that has happened in us, and that it is not just a temporary reformation, it will give them hope for their own captivity, that they too can be "does set free".

That is why there is a promise in this blessing, that not only will freedom come to us as individuals, but we will have "beautiful fawns" as well. It doesn't say perfect fawns, for there still may be negative consequences to our sinful, rebellious past. Yet, there is real beauty in the forgiveness and healing of the Spirit in our lives, and the spiritual energy from our regeneration can empower and flow through the others that we embrace. They still must make choices of their own, to remain captives or be set free, but our own freedom will give them another good reason to believe.

February 27

Light and Darkness

"He separated the light from the darkness." Gen. 1:4

Have you ever thought about what actually happened at the creation of the world? I'm not talking about whether everything happened the way that it is recorded. I believe in the literal interpretation of scripture, and that every word in the creation story is inerrant truth. I'm talking about the truth which lies beneath the surface. Have you ever considered the significance behind God separating the light from the darkness? At first glance, we assume this is just talking about God creating day and night, and it must involve the creation of the sun, moon and stars. However, the celestial spheres are not created until the fourth day. God separates light from darkness on the first day. There must be some mistake, we think. There can't be day and night without the sun. How were the first three days measured if the sun wasn't created until the fourth day? Is it possible that day and night have nothing to do with the earth's relationship to the sun? Is it possible that what is going on with the separation of light and darkness involves more than just the physical world? Think about it. God is light. It doesn't say God became light. He is light and always has been. The Bible also says that God is everywhere. The logical question, then, is how is darkness possible if God is everywhere?

I believe that the answer can be found in the incarnate Christ. Is Christ God? Absolutely! And yet, he was also completely man. How can this be? Through God's divine wisdom, He chose to subdue or hide his glory within a human form so that He could pay the price for man's sin, and fulfill His divine plan for eternity. He was never not God, yet He chose to confine His deity for a period of time into a form that would be easier for man to comprehend, so that man would better understand God's love, forgiveness and divine power. In other words, He subdued His divinity to better reveal His divinity in a way that our finite minds could accept.

Is it possible, then, that God could have been doing this very thing all a long? That even at the beginning of the world, God subdued His divinity by separating light from darkness? That even in this limitation of His light, it actually increased our appreciation and understanding of His light in contrast to the darkness? That this is true not only in the physical world, but the spiritual world as well? That God allowed darkness and evil into our world for the same reason—that we would see what it means to be separated from the Light and how futile living in darkness can be, so that we would choose to be close to God instead of separated from Him for eternity? God chose to separate the light from the darkness. We choose which side we want to be on.

Labor Pains

"When the time comes, he does not come to the opening of the womb." Hosea 13:13

As a man, I cannot imagine the intense suffering that is involved in giving birth to a child. There is nothing in my experience that even comes close, so it's difficult to even pick a metaphor or draw a word picture that captures even a tenth of the agony or the ecstasy of that powerful moment. Yet, the scripture passage here paints a picture of labor pains from a different perspective than the mothers'. It is the baby who is fighting being born. He is safe and comfortable in the warm sac that he has called home for nine months, and now his world is being turned upside down, and he is being forced out of his shelter. Rather than being eager to see and experience his new life, he is afraid of the unknown, and he struggles to hold on to the familiar darkness. This makes it more difficult for the mother, of course, for the baby just doesn't ever seem ready to come. He wants to hold on to the past, while she is anxiously working toward his wonderful future.

The same thing happens spiritually. There are some, of course, who enter their new life with Jesus as smoothly as if they are lubricated with the oil of the Holy Spirit, and they just squirt out into their exciting adventure. Many of us, though, fight being born again. We struggle and rebel and kick the hands of the divine physician who is tenderly trying to pull us into life. We feel too comfortable and safe where we are, and we don't want to let go of our worldly umbilical cord. We would rather stay in our familiar darkness than to enter a world of scary light that exposes all our sins, and demands conformity to the image of Christ. In other words, we are going to be expected to grow up. Those who make this choice still are pushed out, but they are a spiritual miscarriage, and they end up experiencing another darkness—the darkness of death.

Just Call Me Ishmael

"You shall name him Ishmael, for the Lord has heard of your misery."   Gen. 16:11

In the great American novel, *Moby Dick*, by Herman Melville, the narrator says, "Just call me Ishmael." He says this because he is a homeless outcast who goes out on a whaling boat, even though it is dangerous, because it doesn't really matter to anyone whether he lives or dies. He is named after the biblical Ishmael who was cast out of Abraham's household, along with his mother, for no other reason than the jealousy of Abraham's wife, Sarah. So, he and his mother almost starve out in the desert, and the name of Ishmael becomes the symbol for outcasts of the world.

Anyone who feels victimized by the unfairness of life and the arbitrary judgments of the so-called "in-crowd" are able to identify with Ishmael's dilemma. The name Ishmael, though, doesn't mean "outcast", as many suppose. It means, "God hears". God has heard the cries of Ishmael and his mother, and He promises to save them from their misery. It is a promise of grace and blessing, for it says that even though Ishmael will be "a wild donkey of a man," God "will make him into a great nation" (Gen. 21:18). His descendants, in fact, are the entire Arab world.

The world, then, may treat people like outcasts, and reject anyone who appears to be a threat to their egos, but God hears their cries of misery, and promises His gift of grace and love. It is up to us, though, to accept this gift. Sometimes people are so convinced that they are dysfunctional rejects, that they cannot accept the fact that anyone could love them, especially not someone as holy as God. They feel like saying, "Just call me Ishmael, the outcast", but God responds, "I will call you Ishmael, for God hears." It is not enough, then, for us to hear the call of God. We must also be willing to accept that He hears us.

The Sacrifices of God

"The sacrifices of God are a broken spirit; a broken and contrite heart." Psa. 51:17

I am very thankful that I was not a Jewish priest in the time of Moses, where I would be required to sacrifice animals and be around blood almost every day. I know that it was a much honored, respected position, but I cannot imagine a worse job in the world. Due to the grace of God and the sacrificial death of Christ on the cross, no one will have to ever sacrifice another animal for eternity. Thank God.

Yet, there is a sacrifice that every believer must make, for we are all called to be priests in Christ. It is the sacrifice of a broken spirit and contrite heart. From our human perspective, it seems that anything that is broken just needs to be fixed. There is something wrong with it, a defect, and it should be repaired or discarded. With the Lord, however, a broken spirit is exactly what he wants. He, in fact, won't use us unless we are broken, and unless we stay that way. He doesn't want to fix our brokenness.   If we are not broken when he gets us, in fact, He will try to break us.

The spirit of a man is his immortal will, where he chooses whether he wants to serve God or Satan. It is naturally self-centered and stubborn. It is like a wild stallion, which may be very beautiful in its passionate freedom, but still needs to be tamed if it is going to be useful to the owner. A man with a broken spirit is one who has been tamed. The Holy Spirit is like a cowboy whose job it is to be the bronco buster. It is his job to bring us under his control enough so he can put our master's brand on us, and to tame us enough to be used effectively for his service. The more we fight against his spiritual spurs, the more we hurt ourselves. It is better if we just yield to his training and discipline.

The contrite heart is different than the broken spirit. The spirit deals with the will. The heart deals with the emotions. When the Holy Spirit deals with our will, we need to submit. When he deals with our heart, we are able to feel the pain internally that Jesus felt on the cross for our sins. Our conscience is like a whip that the Holy Spirit uses to train our hearts to feel about things the way that God feels about them. I'm not talking about a little wince of regret here. The word contrite means "beat up, bruised, and crushed to a powder". The spirit may be broken, but the heart is pulverized.

We have a choice. We can either offer a sacrifice of our heart and spirit to the Lord willingly, and be rewarded generously, or wait to be broken and tamed by the Lord, and end up looking like spiritual "Spam", crammed and canned and put on the shelf. Being broken and contrite, though, doesn't mean being resentful for being tamed. The heart and spirit are also the means by which we are able to love the Lord, and the more He conforms us to His image, the more we love Him.

A Famine of Hearing the Word

"I will send a famine…of hearing the words of the Lord." Amos 8:11

There are many starving people around the world. Some are starving out of laziness or rebellion, for they just refuse to work. So they go around begging or stealing in order to get what they want, without having to work for it. Some, though, are starving through no fault of their own. There is a famine in their land, and they cannot make food grow where there is no water. Sometimes God is the one who sends famine upon a land as punishment for their wickedness or idolatry. Other times, famine has more natural causes, and thousands may die as innocent victims of Nature.

A more tragic kind of famine, though, is not the one that causes physical starvation. It is the famine of the Word. This kind of famine has similar reasons to the physical realm. People starve physically because they are lazy or rebellious. People starve spiritually for the same reasons. They are too lazy to pick up the Word to read and meditate upon it every day, or they are too rebellious to apply the Word that they have read or heard. Instead of reading the Word themselves, they depend on others to spoon feed them. They are like beggars at the church, and they give out nothing in return. So, God stops trying to teach them until they learn what they have already been given. It is spiritual stagnation, which is the same thing as starvation.

Sometimes, though, they can be innocent victims living in a barren land. If you live in a country that doesn't allow you to have a Bible, and there is no one there who knows it or who can teach it, you can literally be spiritually starved just because the resources are not there.

The worst kind of famine of the Word, however, is when God sends it to you because a nation as a whole has refused to hear the Word. Then, even the prophets are shut out from hearing from God. They plead for God to speak to them, but He is silent (Amos 8:12). When God stops talking even to those who are close to Him, in order to keep them from guiding everyone else, you know that the end is near for that people. Those of us in western cultures have taken the Word for granted, for it has come too easily to us. What would you do if it was taken away, and all you had to rely on was your memory?

What about the Misfits?

*"All those who were in distress or in debt or discontented gathered around him,
and he became their leader." 1 Sam. 22:2*

When the Jewish leaders were looking for a messiah, they were looking for someone like themselves. They were hoping that he would be one of their friends, so that when he came into power, they could be swept into the kingdom on his coattails, like politicians often do today. When Jesus, a simple carpenter, came, then, they were not impressed. He didn't meet their expectations or their desires for their kind of leader. When Jesus chose common fishermen and tax collectors as his disciples, this further increased their disgust and denunciation of this common man's hero.

In one sense, Jesus, who was of the lineage of King David, was following his famous ancestor's example. Before David became king, he was a wanted man. King Saul was trying to kill him, for he was jealous of David's popularity, and fearful that David would take his throne from him. David refused to kill Saul, even when he had the chance, for he respected Saul as God's anointed. So he ran instead, always keeping one step ahead of Saul's army. In the process of running, he met a lot of others who were running also. They were the misfits of society. They were the failures and discontents, so they were constantly running, searching for meaning and purpose in their lives, and someone who would appreciate and value their strengths instead of focusing on their weaknesses. David was that person, and he became their leader. It was through these new found friends, disciples of sorts, that he won some of his greatest victories.

What about us? Are we reaching out to the misfits of our community, or are we, like the Pharisees, only interested in reaching out to people like ourselves? Some church leaders sooth their consciences by having ministries to the homeless, the addicted, or the orphans, but they have other people do the ministering. They are too busy doing more important things themselves. Yet, the people in the congregation aren't any better. They have paid ministers, paid missionaries, and paid outreach people, so they can justify to themselves that they are doing the right thing, even though they would never think of even speaking to the undesirables of their town.

If we want to be more like Christ, and David, we aren't going to do it by being a cheerleader of the church, while others play the game. We have to be willing to be a quarterback, if God asks us to, and to go out into the world so we can understand the meaning of loneliness, desperation, and rejection, and in the process become a more effective, sensitive minister to those in need. Sometimes it takes a misfit to understand or reach a misfit. After all, Jesus is the King of Misfits, for we are all sinners and failures without him.

Concerning the Wicked

"Concerning the wicked: there is no fear of God before his eyes." Psa. 36:1

All of us are in contact with non-Christians around us. They are our neighbors, our community leaders, and our fellow-workers. Yet, how many of us know a truly "wicked" person? Somehow wickedness seems to carry a deeper sense of evil than just sin. We all sin, but we are not all wicked. What makes the difference? The scriptures tell us that "the fear of the Lord is the beginning of wisdom" (Psa.111:10). The verse above, though, says that with the wicked, "there is no fear of God". The wicked, then, is going to be characterized by both a lack of fear of God and a lack of wisdom. He is going to be, in fact, a fool.

There is, then, in one sense, no difference between an atheist who says there is no God, and the wicked man who believes in God, but doesn't fear him. They are both fools. How could it be possible to actually believe in God, but not fear him? The same passage above tells us the reason. It says, "For in his own eyes he flatters himself too much to detect or hate his sin" (Psa. 36:2). In other words, he has an ego problem. He is so proud that he is either blind to his own sinfulness, or he loves his sin so much that he sees nothing wrong with it. His wickedness serves to build his ego, and since he doesn't fear God, he thinks that no one can stop him. There is a sense of invincibility, that he can do whatever he wants and get away with it.

Yet, the Holy Spirit can give us the gift of discernment, to discern the spirits, whether they are of God or the Devil (I John 4:1). We can tell if a person is genuine, or if they are a wolf in sheep's clothing, and it really bothers the wicked person that we can see through them. They know we know, and it irritates them to no end. We become their enemies and their victims because we are not deceived by their slyness, and we are not afraid of their schemes. They have no fear of God, and this makes them fools. We have no fear of them, but fear God instead, and this makes us wise.

Unfortunately, it is not just out in the world that we face the wicked. It is also in our churches and Christian ministries. There are some people who are even ministers who are so egotistical, that they spend all their time in self-promotion, and in trying to build bigger and bigger buildings, so they can out-do the churches down the street. Then, when they are tempted by the Devil to fall into sin, they fall easy prey because they flatter themselves that they are so powerful that they can do whatever they want and get away with it. They are invincible in their gilded pulpits, and no one can touch them, so they think. The true believer, though, sees through this masquerade, and the Bible says that "pride comes before a fall" (Prov. 16:18). It is our responsibility to make sure that the wicked do not prosper in our churches or Christian ministries. We need to weed them out, if we have the power to do so, or pray that they be removed if it is out of our control.

The Sin of Neglect

"Far be it from me that I should sin against the Lord by failing to pray for you."
I Sam. 12:23

It is easy for us to identify actions that are sins—murder, rape, lying, stealing, adultery, etc. The "Thou shalt Nots" in scripture are very clear. It is much more difficult, however, to identify the sins of neglect. It isn't that the Bible is not clear about what we should do, it is just that it doesn't seem as important to us. Somehow the focus of the church has been on the negatives of the Law of Moses, so much so, that we have forgotten or pushed to the side the positives of what we are supposed to be doing. Christianity is not supposed to be Judaism revived. It is suppose to be Judaism fulfilled. We need to stop focusing on the don'ts, and start doing the do's.

For example, the scriptures tell us to pray for one another (James 5:16), but do we do it? I'm not just talking about general prayers in church for the congregation, or the nation, or the world. I am talking about specific prayers about the spiritual needs of specific people. It is as if we are afraid to embarrass people or infringe upon their privacy if we pray for their personal lives. We limit our prayer requests to physical needs, like someone's second cousin who has a mole on her left gluteus maximus, but we fail to mention that she is also suffering from deep depression, anger, and bitterness. James tells us to "confess your sins to one another and pray for one another that you might be healed." That's the kind of praying we should be doing for one another, not the shallow fluff that often takes place in our churches today.

God isn't interested in our angelic eloquence, our rehearsed, written-down religiosity, or our over-simplified, charitable, child-like prayers, that speak of the bumped-up bodies but never the shattered souls. God wants our honesty, our genuine love, and our humility in our prayers, not just when we are alone in our prayer closets, but in the openness of our churches.

This is the kind of prayer that Samuel was talking about in reference to his prayers for the Israelites. He prayed about their idolatry, their wanting to be like all the other nations by having a king instead of a prophet lead them, their need to remember all the great things that God had done in the past, and their need to love and serve God with their whole hearts. Then he told them that if he didn't pray about these things, he would be sinning against God.

Do we understand the importance of praying this way for those we love? It is our responsibility to intercede on their behalf. God has asked us to be mediators between God and man, not for salvation purposes, for only Christ can be that, but for the sake of their spiritual growth. If we don't pray for them in this way, we have committed a sin of neglect, and we have robbed them of some of the spiritual power that is necessary for their progress.

The Shadow of Death

"Even though I walk through the valley of the shadow of death,
I will fear no evil, for you are with me." Psa. 23:4

Humanism would like us to believe that man is evolving into a superman, who is a god unto himself, and the potential for his future is limitless. He just needs the right education, environment and time, and all of his problems will be solved. Yet, the evidence all around us points to just the opposite. There are wars and rumors of wars, senseless crimes, abuses of all kinds, and battles of rage and discrimination all around us. When even the most successful adults and a growing number of children are taking drugs to calm them down and control their anxiety, there is a real problem that is growing more explosive every day. The world seems like a runaway train headed for a steep cliff, with no hope for stopping the inevitable devastation, and all we hear are the echoing cries of desperate people shouting, "Stop the world! I want to get off."

There are so many people who face panic attacks on a daily basis, who are so lonely, desperate, angry, and fearful that they can hardly function, that sometimes it is hard to distinguish between the good people and the bad, for everyone seems like they are falling apart at the seams. Who can we trust when even our so-called role models are so messed up and twisted in their values and priorities that they make us want to become hermits and hide from the world? Where can we turn when even the churches seem dead or consumed with materialism, and the pastors lack the spiritual maturity or vision to lead the way out of the chaos?

Everything that I have just described is part of what is meant by the "valley of the shadow of death". This verse is not just talking about facing the possibility of physical death. Our whole world is under a deep shadow of spiritual death that can become such a heavy weight, even to Christians, that it burdens our souls with fear and depression and robs us of our joy and peace in Christ. It is part of Satan's strategy to enslave mankind by constantly keeping us off balance, fearful, angry and confused so that we seek the mindless and soulless escapes of our society just to be able to survive.

Yet, God offers an alternative. He tells us that we do not need to fear any evil, for even though we have to walk through this spiritual shadow of death, He is always there with us to comfort us, guide us, and strengthen us. He will never allow us to be tested above what we are able to bear if we trust in Him. We shouldn't be surprised by all the evil around us. The closer we are drawn to the light of God, the more everything else will appear to be darkness in contrast. If we just keep our eyes on Him, we will never need to be discouraged or distracted by the shadows.

The Secrets of God

"The secrets things belong to the Lord our God, but the things revealed belong to us." Deut. 29:29

People seem to love secrets. They have secret gardens, secret hide-a-ways, secret relationships, secret clubs and secret sins. Some people can keep a secret; others can't wait to tell them. So, some people we can trust with our secrets, and others we wouldn't dare tell. God also loves secrets. He knows everything, but he also knows that most people cannot be trusted with His secrets. So He picks and chooses who he will trust his secrets with according to our faithfulness in living according to what he has already revealed.

The disciples were puzzled by Christ's secretive nature. They asked him why he taught in parables instead of just coming right out and saying things clearly. His response was, "The knowledge of the secrets of the kingdom of heaven has been given to you, but not to them. Whoever has will be given more, and he will have an abundance. Whoever does not have, even what he has will be taken from him" (Matt. 13:11-12). He talks about secrets as if they are possessions or inheritance that a father might pass on to his children. Not everyone receives the same inheritance. Not every human receives the same knowledge from God about Himself. Not even every Christian receives the same knowledge of God.

God gives out His secrets just as He gives out His other blessings—as tokens of His love and grace, and they aren't meant for just everyone. I believe that the ancients knew more about our physical and spiritual worlds than we do today, in some areas, in spite of all our learning and technology. How was Adam able to name all of the animals even though he had never used language before, and had no background of knowing anything about the animals before, unless God revealed his secrets to him?

God wants to reveal his secrets to us too, but we have to be willing to listen and act according to his revelation. It is very easy for Christians who have been saved for a long time to feel that they know it all already. Church is boring to them because they feel that the pastor can't teach them anything new. They go to church more to show off their spirituality than to learn or grow. Or, if they want to grow, they church hop, going from one speaker to another, one program to another, thirsting for something new in the same way as a shopper might look for a new outfit.

God is not going to reveal his secrets to people who are just curiosity seekers or thrill ride surfers on the waves of what's popular in Christian realms. God tells His secrets to those who love Him with their whole hearts, minds and souls, not to those who have read the most books, have the most college degrees, or been Christians the longest. God's secrets are never given to the know-it-alls, just to those who really know Him.

March 9

The Rod of God

"Your rod and your staff they comfort me." Psa. 23:4

When we think of the rod of God, our first impression is that of punishment, in contrast to the shepherd's staff, which would be used more to guide and rescue. A rod, however, was used for various purposes in Bible times, and each one gives added meaning to how God uses His rod with us.

First, there is the idea of chastisement, which sometimes is presented as pure punishment for open rebellion and wickedness. However, it is also used as a means of discipline or correction for someone who just needs the fine tuning of growing more mature. In this case, even a gentle word from the Father about our need to change course can be presented as the "rod of His mouth" (Isa. 11:4), for that is all that it takes sometimes to convict us of our need to change.

Second, the Bible refers to the "weaver's rod" (I Sam. 17:7), which was used in weaving blankets or rugs. We are not talking about a knitting needle here. Goliath's spear is compared to a weaver's rod, so it must have been big. Yet, even this powerful beam was used for something creative when it was used to weave things for the home or the market. God's rod is also like a weaver's rod, in that, it too is large and powerful, yet used to create beautiful rainbows of texture and design into our lives.

Another use of the rod in scripture was as a measuring rod (Ez. 40:5), similar to how we would use a yard stick today. The word of God is God's measuring stick for our lives, whereby we are not compared to other people, but to the "whole measure of the fullness of Christ" (Eph. 4:13).

Christ, then, is the Rod of God, whereby the whole world will be judged. He is the root of Jesse (Isa. 11:10) and the branch of David (Jer. 23:5), and out of this rod God has made a scepter of righteousness who will rule the world for eternity (Num.24:14). God gave his rod to Moses to stretch out over the Red Sea before it parted to set the Israelites free (Ex.14:16), and He has given us his rod also to set us free. Christ, as the rod of God, chastens us in his love, weaves into us the very nature of God himself, compares us to himself, as the only standard for true holiness, and empowers us to become just like him.

The rod of God is more than just a shepherd's staff, then. It is the shepherd himself. So, when we read the twenty-third Psalm, we can read it a little differently. We can read, "Jesus, my rod and my staff, you comfort me." When the Lord is our shepherd, we have no wants. When he is our rod and staff too, we are more than comforted. We are able to rest and be nourished in his green pastures, and be refreshed by his still waters. What more could we want than to be "led and fed" by the "rod of God"?

The Prayer of Jabez

"Oh that you would bless me and enlarge my territory. Let your hand be with me, and keep me from harm so that I will be free from pain." I Chron. 4:10

There are a lot of people today who have glorified this prayer into almost a mantra, where they have to repeat it word for word every day in order to be blessed by God. Why? Is there something special about this prayer? Are we commanded in scripture to pray this prayer? What is all the fuss about?

First, we are not commanded in scripture to say this prayer. Second, there really isn't anything special or unique about this prayer at all. Jabez's mother went through a lot of pain when she gave birth to Jabez, so she gave him his name, which means, "much pain". She probably also told him as he was growing up why he was named that, laying a guilt trip upon her son for something he had no control over. He grew up to be an "honorable man", but according to his prayer, I would say he was also a self-centered man. The entire prayer is just "me, me, me". He wants more things, and he wants to be free from pain.

This prayer fits right in with today's prosperity theology and "meism idolatry". Some people believe that it is God's will for all Christians to be prosperous and healthy, and if they are not, then they are living in sin. This philosophy is not biblical. It is a vain attempt at using a single prayer in the Bible to justify their own materialistic egotism. Jabez was feeling sorry for himself, and God, in his grace, listened to his cries of self-pity and answered his prayers, just like he listened to the whining of the Israelites in Egypt. It had nothing to do with their worthiness or the exceptional value of their prayers. God just had compassion on their suffering.

Poverty and pain are not just results of sin. Job experienced great suffering and had all of his possessions taken from him, with God's permission, even though he was a righteous man. God was just testing his faith. Yet, how does Job respond to his trial? He prays a prayer that is far more worthy than the prayer of Jabez. The words of his prayer are not recorded, but the essence is. He didn't pray for God to relieve his pain or to give him more things. He prayed for his friends, that God would forgive them for their unbelief and be merciful to them.

What was the result of his prayer? God not only forgave his friends, but blessed Job by taking away his suffering and doubling everything that he had had before. He didn't whine about himself, or ask for more. He was like Solomon, who just asked for wisdom, but God gave him prosperity also because his priorities were right. Job prayed for his friends, not himself, and God blessed him because his priorities were right.

We need to forget about Jabez and imitate Job. It is more important that we learn from our pain than it is to pray that we don't have any.

The Monument of the Testament

"In the presence of the Israelites, Joshua copied on stones the law of Moses." Josh. 8:32

The Israelites had crossed the Jordan into the Promised Land and had conquered Jericho. Then the Lord told Joshua to stop for a short time at Mount Ebal, where he was told to build an altar for sacrifices, and to write a copy of the Law of Moses. The place where he was to build this altar was the same place where Abram had built an altar when he first came to the Promised Land, and God had promised this land to his descendents. Joshua's building his altar, then, was a renewal of this covenant as they came to claim their inheritance. His writing a copy of the law was in fulfillment of a command by Moses before his death (Deut. 27:2-4). Moses had told them to write the copy of the law on huge stones, not to take with them, but as monuments for all to see as they came to worship the Lord on this mountain. Joshua didn't engrave the letters into the stones with chisels. He smeared plaster on the stones first, as Moses had commanded, and then he wrote into the plaster. All of the Israelites stood around Joshua as he wrote not only the Ten Commandments, but the entire Law of Moses, including all of the blessings and curses, rituals and requirements. Then Joshua stood and read the law out loud to everyone there, and sacrificed animals to their God. They were now ready to go on to possess the land.

It doesn't say how long this whole process took, but it shows the tremendous importance and prominence of the Law, and the accountability of each person to its dictates. The people had learned after wandering through the desert for forty years that it didn't do any good to try to win this battle alone. Every step must be guided and blessed by the wisdom and power of God, and without His law, they were lost. When they left that mountain, they left the monuments behind, but they carried God's word in their hearts wherever they went.

What kind of prominence does the Word of God have in our lives? Is it a monument of God's light, hope and grace every step that we take, or is it shoved under the bed, and only taken out before we go to church? How do we treat the Word? Do we throw it into the trunk of our car, put it on a dusty shelf, or hit our friends with it when they give us a hard time? Do we only read it when we have to, or do we search it diligently for nuggets of spiritual truth every moment that we can? Is it a monument on a mountain top for all to see, or is it the Last Will and Testament of our faith that died? We will never gain possession of the promised land of God's blessings unless we put God's Word first in our lives, and unless we live it out in the open for all to see, not as pillars of pride, but monuments of mercy.

The Lord is with You

"The Lord is with you, mighty warrior." Judges 6:12

Have you ever had someone compliment you, applaud you, or ask you to be their leader, and then you responded, "Who me? You've got to be kidding"? That's exactly how Gideon felt when the angel of the Lord came to him and said, "The Lord is with you, mighty warrior." Gideon had never fought in a war. He was just a farmer's son, and he was busy threshing wheat in his father's winepress. "Mighty Warrior?" You've got to be kidding. Gideon responds, "But sir, if the Lord is with us, why has all this happened to us? Where are all the wonders that our fathers told us about?...The Lord has abandoned us."

Maybe you have felt the same way when God has asked you to do something. "I can't do that." "I don't have the power or ability to pull that off." "If we only lived in the time of the Heroes of our Faith", like Elijah, David, or Paul, we could do great miracles." " But, this is today, and I'm just me." "Mighty Warrior? Yeah, right! Maybe you're in a time-warp, God, and you're thinking of the good old days. Maybe you're having a senior moment, Lord. Remember, this is just me."

Notice how the Lord responds to Gideon's doubts. He says, "Go in the strength you have...Am I not sending you" (6:14). In other words, it doesn't matter what Elijah and David could do in the past. It doesn't matter how many miracles Paul could perform. You, yes you, just go in the strength that you have, whatever that is, no matter how little it is, and do what God has asked you to do. If God has asked you to do something, He will give you the strength to do it. If God sends you, He has promised to go with you and to be your strength.

Sure, it would be nice if you had the ability to perform all kinds of miracles and do powerful stuff. But, maybe if you could do all those things, you would feel that you didn't need God. You would end up getting all the credit instead of giving the praise to God. Have you ever thought that God may have chosen you to do something precisely because you can't do it with your own strength? He wants to be needed. So, just take whatever you have, do whatever you are asked, and expect whatever results God intends. You may not be a silver chalice, but even a clay pot can be used to quench the master's thirst. It's not your ability that matters. It is your availability.

Never hesitate to follow the Lord into battle. He can make even the farmer's son, or the farmer's daughter, into a mighty warrior. Just take what you have, and give it to Him. Who knows? You might just be another Gideon, and people in future generations may wish they could be like you.

The Justice of the Peace

"How can there be peace…as long as all the idolatry and witchcraft…abound?"
2 Kings 9:22

The world longs for peace, or so it says. What they really want is more power. Those who are evil want the power to do their evil. Those who consider themselves to be good, want their power to bring about justice. They want to stop all the oppression, violence and abuse that is happening in the world, no matter what the cost. The problem is that everyone has a different idea about who the oppressors are, what is right or wrong, who has the right to enforce justice, and even what justice is. So we have people arguing and fighting over who has the best plan on bringing peace to the world.

People are ironically fighting for peace, with no end in sight. How can we solve this dilemma? We can't. It is humanly impossible. The reason that we can't is clearly stated in the scriptures—"How can there be peace…as long as all the idolatry and witchcraft…abound?" We are living in a world, not just of physical violence, but spiritual warfare. That spiritual warfare is not going to stop until God destroys this world and creates a new heaven and a new earth (Dan. 9:26). It doesn't matter how much we pray, or even if there is a great revival on earth. If Christians are praying and growing, it just makes the enemy fight that much harder. If there is revival, there will be persecution to try to thwart it.

Will idolatry and witchcraft ever stop this side of eternity? No. Anyone who puts himself on a pedestal as lord of his own life, even though Satan is his real master, is an idolater. Anyone who yields themselves to any being in the spirit world other than God is looking for power outside of God's will, and their power is witchcraft. Will people stop seeking power apart from God before the last judgment? Absolutely not. So, accept the fact that there will never be peace on earth as we know it, and seek for spiritual peace instead. War is a result of man's sinfulness and God's condemnation. God can be called the Justice of the Peace because there will be no peace apart from His final justice. We might even say that it is God's will that there is war on earth as part of His justice. He is hoping that this part of his condemnation will bring people to repentance before He comes in the end. So, instead of praying for world peace and the brotherhood of man, pray for the salvation of individual men, that they might have peace with God in spite of all the war.

The Intercessor

"My advocate is on high. My intercessor is my friend."
Job 16:19-20

I remember seeing a movie once of a stranger being pulled over by the police for speeding in a small town. He was arrested and taken to court immediately where he stood trial. He was in big trouble because the sheriff's father was the judge, the district attorney was his brother, and court appointed attorney pleading his case was the sheriff's second cousin. He didn't have a chance.

The Bible talks about a similar situation, where the Father is the judge, the son is the court appointed attorney, and the Holy Spirit is the district attorney. The Holy Spirit's job is to convict people of their sins (John 16:7-8). Jesus, on the other hand, is our advocate with the Father, who admits that we are guilty, yet says the crime is already paid for. The penalty was already paid by him on the cross. The ransom has already been paid, so the case needs to be dismissed.

On the one hand, family justice in the small town was doomed for judgment from the very start. On the other hand, family justice in heaven is tempered by grace and mercy, and even the convicting of the Holy Spirit is for our own good. What makes this heavenly court case so different? It is the relationship that we have with the Justice of the Peace, the public defender and the D.A. First, the judge is not just the Father of the lawyer, he is our Father as well, if we know Him. Second, the Holy Spirit's job is not just to convict us of sin, but to help us to have victory over sin. He has the dual role of district attorney and public defender. If we accept his advice, he is all for us. If we reject his counsel, there is no hope for us. Third, Jesus is not just our lawyer; he is our brother, our husband, and our friend. So, it's not us versus the "Family". If we are saved, we are part of the family, and our lawyer has arranged for a plea bargain agreement before we even get there. Praise God! We have a "Get out of jail free" card, the blood of Christ, and the judge has already been paid off. We are home free.

One of the amazing things about this story, though, is that it didn't just start after Christ's death and resurrection. Two-thousand years before Christ even lived on the earth, Job wrote about his relationship with the heavenly intercessor. He said, "Even now my witness is in heaven; my advocate is on high. My intercessor is my friend as my eyes pour out tears to God; on behalf of a man he pleads with God as a man pleads for his friend" (16:19-21). That means that Jesus has been the intercessor for man from the very beginning, not just after he paid the price for their sins. He was the prophet-public defender, pointing forward toward the payment for sin, and the judge accepted his word for it. He didn't have to swear on a stack of Bibles, for he is the Word of God.

The Informer

"Even now my witness is in heaven." Job 16:19

Criminal investigators often rely on informers to get their evidence. An informer is someone on the inside who is a first hand witness of a crime being planned or committed. Without the use of informers, many cases would never be solved, for there is no other way to prove what happened behind the scenes. The same thing is true about what we know about God, and how He has worked in people's lives throughout the ages. There is absolutely no way for us to know what happened unless God revealed it through the prophets, and there is no way for them to know it unless there is an informer in heaven. He, you might say, is our inside man. He knows what he is talking about because he is there. He is our witness, and he is ready to testify on our behalf.

The Bible puts it this way: "Even now my witness is in heaven; my advocate is on high. My intercessor is my friend as my eyes pour out tears to God; on behalf of a man he pleads with God as a man pleads for his friend" (Job 16:19-21). Doesn't this sound familiar? Try 1 John 2:1, "If anyone does sin, we have one who speaks to the Father in our defense—Jesus Christ, the Righteous One."

We all have heard about Jesus being our advocate with the Father, but how on earth did Job know about that? Job lived approximately 2000 B.C., not only before Christ, but before any of the scriptures were written. Job, in fact, is considered the oldest book in the Bible, not Genesis. How, then, did Job know about Christ and what his role was in heaven?

Well, I believe that he must have had an informer, for there is no other way for him to know the things that he did. Job, as the father, before the law was given, was the priest of his own family. He sacrificed animals for his children's sins. How did he know about the need for sacrifice? How did he know all the doctrine that he talks about with his friends before the law? How could he say, "I know that my Redeemer lives, and that in the end he will stand upon the earth?". And after my skin has been destroyed, yet in my flesh I will see God" (Job 19:25-26). Was he a prophet as well as a priest? Did he know the Redeemer and Advocate with the Father, Jesus Christ, even before Jesus was born or prophesied about by any other prophet? If so, it must have been an inside job. Jesus must have chosen to reveal himself to this holy and upright man, whom even God called "blameless". What a privilege that would have been to learn about God first hand, face to face, and not have to learn second hand through what God told someone else.

When you think about it, that's what the Holy Spirit does for us today.

The Idolatry of Arrogance

"Rebellion is like the sin of divination, and arrogance like the evil of idolatry."
I Sam. 15:23

Pride is a terrible sin, even listed in scripture as one of the things the Lord hates (Prov. 6:16). Yet, there is one kind of pride that the Lord hates more than any other, yet is often overlooked completely in our churches today. It is spiritual pride. Spiritual pride can be seen in the pastor who thinks he's the greatest because he has a bigger church than any of the other pastors in his community or denomination. It is seen in the choir director or worship team leader who thinks of himself as a paid entertainer who needs to have grandiose programs or special effects to make the worship time more powerful. It is seen in the people who feel that they have to compete with the other parishioners on how well they are dressed at church,, who gives the most money for special projects, who is on the most committees, etc. etc. It is seen in all the busyness in our churches today, where people are running themselves ragged in their religious ringside circuses, thinking that all their activity for God makes them somehow more worthy of special honor or blessings.

King Saul was the same way. He was going into battle, fighting one of the enemies of God, doing God's service—putting his life on the line for the Lord. Then he comes back victorious with plans to sacrifice the animals that were taken as plunder, to glorify and thank God for the victory. What's wrong with that? He is serving God, and he is giving God the glory. Are we missing something here? Yes. Samuel comes to Saul and criticizes him severely, saying that God has rejected Saul as king because of his actions. The problem is that God told Saul to fight the battle, but not to bring any plunder home. He was to kill all the animals and people at the battlefield. King Saul tries to excuse himself by saying that he only brought them home to sacrifice to God, but that wasn't good enough. He missed the point. Samuel tells him, "Does the Lord delight in burnt offerings and sacrifices as much as in obeying the voice of the Lord?" (I Sam. 15:22).

In other words, God doesn't care about how big our church is, how many hours we spend serving him, or how much money we give for good causes. These are all like Saul's burnt offerings. They may be nice for us, but they are nothing to God. What God wants more than anything is a humble heart and obedience. If we cannot serve God without getting any credit or honor for it, then we are doing it for the wrong reason. We are like the Pharisees, who stood in the market places saying fancy prayers out loud to draw attention to themselves. He says that this kind of arrogance is "like the evil of idolatry". We don't need a stone statue to be an idolater. Our arrogance is idolatry, and the stone statue of our pride is deaf to the voice of God.

The Heart of a Fool

"The fool says in his heart, 'There is no God'." Psa. 14:1

We can understand how a person who is mentally ill or incapacitated could come to the conclusion that there is no God, for they are unable to be rational. However, how do we explain the fact that there are so many people who are intellectually sound who have come to the same conclusion? How can something which seems so obvious to us, seem so irrational to others? It is because they are using their minds to interpret and judge their hearts, and we are using our hearts to guide our minds. If they feel something in their hearts, but their minds tell them it is irrational, they will discount it as being foolish. If we, on the other hand, have a conviction in our hearts that something is right or wrong, it doesn't matter if our brains tell us it is irrational.

"Faith is being sure of what we hope for and certain of what we do not see." (Heb. 11:1). Faith is not meant to be scientific. "God chose the foolish things of the world to shame the wise; God chose the weak things of the world to shame the strong. He chose the lowly things of this world and the despised things-and the things that are not-to nullify the things that are" (1 Cor. 1:27-28). God's plan of salvation isn't suppose to make sense to the human mind. He purposely chose an irrational, "foolish" plan so that no man could come to God through using his mind alone.

That doesn't mean that belief in God itself is illogical. When scientists have studied the intelligent design of the universe, which points to the absolute need for a divine designer, the greatest irrationality comes from those who claim that it all just happened by chance. In spite of the obvious evidence of God's creation, their minds refuse to acknowledge the truth because their "foolish hearts are darkened" (Rom. 1:21). The problem is not with their mental capabilities. Their hearts are like the speed regulators that many places put on school buses. The bus engine has the capability to go much faster, but the regulator controls and limits that capability. The hearts of unbelievers regulate and limit how much their brains can assimilate. It doesn't matter how plain and obvious the evidence is of God's existence, their hearts put blinders on their brains.

They refuse to even think about any possibility that their theories might be wrong. That is, until the Holy Spirit comes in through the back door of their conscience and convicts them of their sin. Once they recognize and admit their need for a savior, and accept Christ as Lord, their minds and hearts begin to blend together like a beautiful duet. The heart plays the melody and the brain plays the harmony, and the music can do nothing else but glorify God. It's only when people try to make the brain sing the melody and force the heart to be silent that there is discord.

The Gift of Wisdom

"Give your servant a discerning heart to govern your people." I Kings 3:9

The story of Solomon asking for the gift of wisdom is well-known, but it is greatly misunderstood. It is true that God gave him wisdom, but he still acted like a total idiot in some ways. Think of all the thousands of wives and concubines that he had, and how he let them build idols to their pagan gods on the mountain tops. Think of his Ecclesiastes and how he tried every kind of pleasure to see if it would bring him happiness, only to decide in the end that all is vanity. Does a truly wise person have to go through all of that in order to get more wisdom? Wouldn't he know better already without having to learn the hard way?

The problem is that we think of wisdom as all-inclusive, applying to every area of our lives. Although this is the ideal, this is not usually the way that it happens. We may be wise in one area of our lives, but be completely dysfunctional in another. Maybe we are a wise leader at work, where we are able to give advice to others, and handle millions of dollars without a blink. Yet, when we get home, we don't have a clue how to raise our kids, how to treat our spouse, or even how to get our daily tasks organized. Our office is immaculate, but our garage at home is chaos.

Part of the problem is just lack of energy. We have exerted so much creative energy at work, that we just don't have any left when we get home. Our family ends up getting only the leftovers. Part of the problem, though, has to do with our giftedness. Giftedness is compartmentalized. We can be really smart when it comes to accounting, but completely helpless when it comes to changing the oil in our car. We can be very effective in leading adults, but fall apart when it comes to nurturing children. We can be a great boss, but we have trouble when we start bossing people around at home. Somehow the principles that we use in one place just don't work someplace else.

Wisdom is the same way. It is compartmentalized. We can be really wise in some ways, but foolish in others at the same time. For example, we can be very wise as a pastor, sharing nuggets of truth from the scriptures that help others to grow and flourish, and yet be foolish in how we handle the church finances or in our inter-personal relationships. We have wisdom to help people when we preach, but don't have a clue how to counsel them one on one.

Solomon didn't ask God for an all-inclusive wisdom. He asked him for discernment on how to run his government. He was given the ability to be a wise ruler, but it didn't carry over to his personal life. God promised to give wisdom liberally to anyone who asks (James 1:5), but we need to be very specific in each area that we need the wisdom.

The Conclusion of the Matter

*"Let us hear the conclusion of the whole matter: Fear God, and keep his commandments:
for this is the whole duty of man." Eccl. 112:13*

This statement is made by Solomon, the wisest man who has ever lived. Yet, somehow, my spirit wants to rebel against this conclusion. Is this all there is—the chief end of man—to fear God and to obey? Somehow I want more than this. I want an intimate relationship with my maker. What about love, faith and hope? What about sharing the love of God with others? What about glorifying and worshiping the Father? If all I have to do is fear and obey, I might as well be a robot following the commands of a divine, digitized commander.

The reason that my spirit rebels against this concept, though, is because it makes the mistake of taking this verse out of its context, and not understanding the purpose of this conclusion. First of all, Solomon, in all of his wisdom, still did not know the Lord in the intimate way that we know Him. The main focus of his time was on the Law of Moses, for Christ had not yet come to fulfill the law. God's emphasis was on the Israelite people more than individuals, and the Holy Spirit was only given for short times for specific needs, not as the indwelling comforter/counselor that he is today.

Second of all, Solomon doesn't say that fear and obedience are the only purposes of man. He uses the word "duty", which implies indebtedness. What did the Israelites owe God because of all that He had done for them? He had saved them out of bondage and chosen them as His special people. He provided for their needs through the wilderness, and had given them an inheritance in the Promised Land. He had demonstrated His power and His right to rule them. He had earned their reverence and respect, and now He was holding them to their promise of fear and obedience (Josh. 24:14-22).   Sure, there were a few during this time who achieved more than this, for some, like Abraham and David, were even called the friends of God. Yet, most of the Israelites only knew God as their master, and fear and obedience were their only duties.

Today, however, we are under a new law—the law of Christ—where our obedience is motivated more by our love for our savior than any fear of judgment. We are indebted to Christ for what he did on the cross, and in response, need to be crucified with Christ each day to our sinful nature and desires. Yet, we follow Christ not in fear but in excited anticipation for all that we know he is going to do for us and through us as we walk in His steps. We respect and reverence our Maker, but not as robots or slaves who have no choice. We are the children of the King of Kings, and our focus is not so much on "what is my duty?" as "what is my honor and privilege to do for my precious Lord?"   Fear and obedience are still our duties, but they are definitely <u>not</u> the "conclusion of the matter".

Test Me, O Lord

"Test me, O Lord, and try me, examine my heart and my mind." Psa. 26:2

At first glance, this seems like a foolish prayer. "Go ahead, God. Put me to the test. Cause trials to come in my life. I dare you. Go ahead; give it your best shot." It's like praying for patience, and then having God zap you with problems so you can learn your lesson. Yet, this isn't really what this prayer is asking for. The words "test" and "try" do not necessarily mean "give me problems". They go along with the second part of this verse—"examine my heart and mind". Think of God as a scientist, who is putting our heart and mind under the spiritual microscope to test them for our faith, love and obedience. He is the Great Physician, and David is asking Him for a "complete physical" of his soul. There are different reasons why David asks for such an examination. They are clearly stated in Psa. 139:23—"Search me, O God, and know my heart; test me and know my anxious thoughts. See if there is any offensive way in me, and lead me in the way everlasting."

There are three reasons stated here for wanting God to search our hearts. First, we want God to know us. Don't get me wrong. God knows us whether we want him to or not. He knows everything. The point is, do we want Him to really know us? We tend to put walls around ourselves, defensively keeping people, and even God, at a distance. We don't really want him to examine us closely because we are ashamed of what we are doing, and we don't really want to change. For David, then, to come to the place where he genuinely wants God to know his heart and anxious thoughts, with all of their flaws and nothing held back, is a tremendous sign of spiritual maturity, and shows a sincere desire for continued growth and communion with the Father.

Second, he wants to better know himself. So often, we are blind to our own sinfulness. We feel comfortable with who we are, and we have come to accept our own flaws as being "normal". For someone to come to the place where they actually want God to reveal their sinfulness by exposing their impurities in the light of God's holiness is a huge step in the complete submission to the will of the Lord. It's hard enough to confess the sins that we know about already. It's impossible, humanly speaking, to really want God to expose even more sin, so we can be closer to God. We would rather keep God at a distance where we don't feel so vulnerable. The Holy Spirit, though, can bring someone to this point of wanting more intense communion with God, no matter what the cost.

Besides wanting God to know us more intimately, and wanting to know ourselves better, there is also the conscious choice and commitment to change. We have to want to be led "in the way everlasting", to move toward eternal goals, values and priorities. In other words, we have to want our earthly life to line up with our heavenly destiny.

Simple Integrity

"He is blameless and upright, a man who fears God and shuns evil.
And he still maintains his integrity." Job 2:3

God is describing Job, and He gives a very glowing account. To be praised by God in this fashion seems to be the highest honor that He could ever pay a human. Can you imagine, with all that God knows, for Him to declare that a human is blameless? Wow! I wish I had known Job. Yet, in my mind, the last characteristic that God mentions is far more valuable than the first—"He still maintains his integrity."

Why is this more important than being blameless? The word integrity means "complete". When Jesus was teaching the multitude, a young man came up to him and asked what he needed to do to have eternal life. Christ told him to obey the commandments. The man said that he already did, but wanted to know what he still lacked. Christ then said, "Sell your possessions and give to the poor, and you will have treasures in heaven" (Matt. 19:21). The man was blameless, just like Job, but he still lacked one thing. He feared God enough. He just didn't love Him enough. He loved things more than he loved God. There are a lot of good people in this world, who by their goodness are trying to earn their way into heaven. They want eternal life, like the rich young man, but they don't really want God there when they get there. Heaven is just one more thing or possession for them to acquire.

Job, on the other hand, was a man of integrity. He didn't lack in any way. He was complete because he loved God more than possessions. God was his priority, not the things that God had given him. He was completely satisfied, content, and whole, just in knowing God. He didn't need anything or anyone else to make him complete. Everything else was just a fringe benefit.

Another meaning for the word integrity is "simplicity". Have you ever heard the saying, "Keep it simple, stupid"? Why do we try to make things so complex? Christianity is really quite simple. Notice that I didn't say "easy". There is a big difference between "simple" and "easy". Jesus tried to emphasize the simplicity of the gospel by summarizing all the law and the prophets in just two commandments—"Love the Lord your God with your whole heart, mind and soul, and love your neighbor as yourself." It can't be any simpler than that. It is the nitty-gritty of truth. Job had discovered this truth. He knew the simplicity and completeness of only needing God, and showing his love for God by loving others. It didn't matter if everything and everyone else was taken away from him. God was his all-in-all.

What about us? Are we blameless? I hope so. Yet, more importantly, are we men or women of simple integrity—complete in Jesus and wanting nothing more?

Returning to the Lord

"Surely goodness and mercy shall follow me all the days of my life, and I will dwell in the house of the Lord forever." Psa. 23:6

This is a beautiful promise, with hope for each day, through eternity. It is a peaceful picture of the Lord being our shepherd, and how he leads his sheep. He makes sure that we are nourished, protected, disciplined and directed. Yet, there is a subtle inference in this verse which is often overlooked. For example, the word "follow" does not just mean to continue with us. It means "to pursue aggressively", and is used other places in scripture to describe the Israelite army chasing after their vanquished foe. This chapter, though, is not dealing with warfare, is it? It is talking about green pastures, still waters, and quiet rest.

The reality behind this beautiful pastoral setting is that it is very much involved with spiritual warfare. Why does the shepherd have to "make" us lie down in green pastures? The shepherd is trying to protect his sheep from the hungry wolves that are out there. It will be much easier to detect any wolves trying to attack if all the sheep are lying down. If they have been following the shepherd all day, feeding at his feet, and doing what he wanted them to do, they also may need to lie down to rest. Some people are workaholics. God has to stop us sometimes and make us rest, because we are wearing ourselves out, and the Devil loves to take advantage of weary sheep. He knows we are vulnerable, and he doesn't hesitate to tempt us in areas where we are normally strong enough to fight.

The shepherd not only makes us lie down when we need to, he uses his rod and staff to correct us when we go astray. The Devil loves to get us one on one, so he purposely leads us away from the fellowship of others who might help to strengthen us. Sometimes, though, we refuse to listen to the voice of the shepherd or heed the leading of his rod and staff, and we wander off, doing our own thing. It is then that the shepherd's assistants, mercy and goodness, pursue us until they bring us back into the fold. They are determined that the Devil is not going to get one of the master's little lambs, so they chase after them as if their lives depended on it.

When it says that "I will dwell in the house of the Lord forever", the word "dwell" actually means "return to dwell", implying a temporary absence and a reconciliation. It is talking about someone who has been persuaded by the enemy to be a traitor for a time, but now is brought back into full communion and fellowship with the Lord. Even the word "forever" fits into this metaphor, for it isn't just talking about eternity. It means "from day to day continually". In other words, for the rest of my life I can depend on the fact that God will never give up on me in the battle, but will from now to eternity, pursue me with His love, patience, and mercy. That means right now. Isn't that better than just a promise for peace and mercy in the next life?

Pure Prayer

"My prayer is pure." Job 16:17

In English we have two words which are very similar in meaning—pure and virgin. It is possible, though, to be pure without being a virgin, and it is possible to be a virgin without being pure. If someone is a virgin, which means they have not had sex, they could still be impure in their thoughts and actions. Also, if someone has lived an immoral life, but they have been forgiven and cleansed by the Lord, they could be said to be pure even though they are no longer a virgin.

The same distinction can be made when talking about prayer. There is no such thing as a virgin prayer, for we are all tainted by sin, even the most innocent child. However, we can have a pure prayer. The word "pure" means "clean, refined, and unmixed with anything else." It means without sin. That doesn't mean that if we sin, we can't pray. We need to pray to confess our sins. However, it's possible to sin even while we are praying. Jesus said that the Pharisees were sinning when they prayed loudly in the marketplace, seeking to draw attention to themselves in their pride. We may not do that now, but do we ever try to impress others in the church by our public prayers in the congregation? Have we ever even lied in our prayers by promising God that we will never do something again, even though we have no intention of really keeping that promise? A pure prayer cannot have any sin in it.

Second, it must be refined. Something is refined by experiencing extreme heat or pressure in order to get all of the impurities out of it. It isn't perfect or virgin to begin with, it must be transformed. Since we are all sinners, no one is perfect, but we can be refined. We can be purged of our sinful hearts, so that we truly love God more than our selves. It is in that state of total submission and love to God that pure prayer can be made.

Third, a pure prayer cannot be mixed with anything else. As stated before, pure prayer cannot be mixed with any kind of sinful intention or prideful act. This isn't the only kind of mixing that goes on in prayer, however. Prayer is open and honest communication with God, which involves both sharing and receiving, speaking and listening. Have we ever tried talking to someone, but sensed that they weren't really paying attention? Well, we do the same thing when we pray. We are going through a routine or ritual, but our hearts are not there. We are there in the flesh, but not in the spirit.

We cannot pray a pure prayer unless we are one-hundred percent filled with God's spirit in heart, mind and soul, and one-hundred percent attentive and receptive to His speaking to us, as well as our speaking to Him. We are Christ-minded because we are one with Him, and not mixed with anything else. We may not be a virgin, but we are pure, and our prayers reflect who we really are.

O Lord, Open my Eyes

"O Lord, open his eyes so he may see." 2 Kings 6:17

It never ceases to amaze me how I can be so familiar with someone or something, and yet completely miss an important aspect of their character or appearance. How could I be so blind? Sometimes our blindness to things has to do with our personal giftedness. Some of us are able to see the whole picture, like a huge panorama of life, and yet completely miss the details. Others are very detail oriented, but totally miss the big picture. The same thing is true on a spiritual plane. Some of us live almost completely in the physical world, with almost no sensitivity to spiritual things whatsoever. Others are so spiritually minded, they are of no earthly good. They see God's hand in everything, but they can't keep a job or have lasting relationships in the real world. These are two extremes. Most of us fit somewhere in-between. We have spiritual perception, but we are also able to focus on our daily physical responsibilities.

Sometimes, though, the Lord opens our eyes, and we are able to see life from His perspective. Our spiritual awareness is quickened, and suddenly we can see clearly in areas that were just clouds before. It isn't a matter of our opening our eyes to see better. God has opened our eyes and healed us from our self-centered perspective. When that happens, it's almost as if we have left our bodies and entered into a spiritual dimension. We are no longer bound just to the physical realm. We see with God's eyes.

For example, Elisha was being sought by his enemies, and a huge army was completely surrounding his house. His servant was very nervous and afraid for his life. Elisha, on the other hand, was very calm and controlled. It was because he looked at things from God's perspective. He asked God to open his servant's eyes so that his servant could see what Elisha could see. When God opened his eyes, he could see an army of angels who were also surrounding the house, protecting Elisha from any harm.

There is a lot more going on around us than we could ever imagine. The spiritual warfare that is present would blow our minds if we were able to see all that is going on behind the scenes. It isn't necessary for us to see all of this, but it is important to understand that it is going on. We need to be conscious that everything that happens has eternal consequences and significance, and that we are wrestling against spiritual powers of darkness in high places. We need to be aware that there are angels that are there to protect us and help us, and that the Holy Spirit is always present. We need to think beyond the here and now, and allow God to open our eyes to the constant eternal moment of the I AM. He won't show us everything right now, but as the hymn goes, "Open my eyes that I might see, glimpses of truth thou hast for me." Thank God for the glimpses.

My Soul Pants for God

"As the deer pants for streams of water, so my soul pants for you, O God.
My soul thirsts for God, for the living God." Psa. 42:1-2

This is a beautiful picture of the gentle deer by a rippling brook calmly quenching its thirst in the stillness of a forest. There is something powerfully peaceful and idyllic about this setting that appeals to our hearts. Yet, at second glance, this is not a peaceful picture at all. The deer doesn't pant for water unless it has been running in fear from an enemy or the danger of fire. The deer pictured here is probably not only thirsty but exhausted from running in desperation. It is panting to get its breath as it gulps for air in between gulps of water. Its heart is pounding with fear still as it drinks, not knowing if the enemy or danger is catching up as it takes a few moments to rest and be refreshed.

King David felt the same way. He had enemies all around him, and he wasn't even sure he could trust his friends. His only solace was when he was alone with God, for it was then that he could be refreshed by the living water of the Lord's love, hope, and grace. He was like that deer panting by the streams of water, never quite sure when the next attack by the enemy would occur.

Unfortunately, we often find ourselves in the same situation. We are in spiritual warfare all of the time, never knowing who we can trust, and being let down by even our closest friends. We long for and desperately cling to every quiet moment of meditation that we have alone with God, where we can quench our thirst for spiritual intimacy, strength, and renewal.

Yet, why is it that we tend to only seek this refreshment when we are panting from exhaustion, fear and desperation? Isn't this same spiritual nourishment available at all times? Do we need to have crises in our lives before we seek the living waters? It seems so. Of course the Lord wants us to come to Him in our time of need, for He wants us to realize how inadequate we are without Him. However, the Lord is much more pleased when we come to Him because we thirst for Him, not just for his help. He wants us to drink from His spirit—to internalize His presence and power—and to want Him, not just what He can give to us.

So often, we drink water only when our mouths and throats are dry. We don't realize that our whole body thirsts and needs water to survive and function in a healthy manner. We take care of the surface thirst, but often neglect the deep drinking and quenching of thirst that the whole body pants for. The same thing is true spiritually. We take a sip here and there of spiritual refreshment, or gulp it down in a hurry when we are desperate, but we neglect the daily, continual communion with the living water himself, Jesus Christ. He wants us to pant for Him with intense desire for fellowship with Him, not just because we are afraid of the enemy. He doesn't want to be just the rescue squad that saves our life. He wants to be our life.

It's Your Choice

"I have set before you life and death, blessings and curses. Now choose life."
Deut. 30:19

As a child, I often played with invisible ink. I would write a secret message to my friend, and then he would hold it up to a flame, and the heat would turn the letters brown so he could read it. Jesus did the same thing, in a sense, when he taught using parables. He was sending messages to His friends in a way that only His friends could understand, if they held them up to examine them in His light. When the crowds were not around, though, such secrecy was not necessary. He taught them plainly and to the point.

In the Old Testament, God did the same thing. When He was speaking to His own chosen people, He made His truth very clear. He tells them, "I have set before you life and death, blessings and curses. Now choose life." He had made it very clear what was expected of them, and what the consequences would be. Everything was black and white. No invisible ink was necessary. What does it mean to choose life? He tells us—"The Lord is your life" (30:20). What does it mean to have the Lord be your life? "That you may love the Lord your God, listen to his voice, and hold fast to him" (30:20).

Wow! Can we understand the significance of what was just promised? If we choose the Lord as our life, we will be given the ability to love Him as Lord, to hear Him speaking to us, and to cling to Him without any barrier between us and Him. Each one of these three things is a personal gift of God—a gift of himself to us. First is the gift of love. God is love. We cannot love God unless He first gives of himself to us. "We love him because he first loved us" (I John 4:19). We cannot hear His voice speaking to our heart unless He has first given His Spirit to us, and our spiritual sensors are rejuvenated and sensitized to hear His voice (John 10:27). We are His sheep, and He is our shepherd, and when He speaks, we are able to hear his voice, and we follow Him. We do not follow Him from a distance, though, for we hold fast to Him, as if we are glued or bonded together. The Holy Spirit is the "Super Glue" that holds us together, and nothing can separate us ever from the love of God (Rom. 8:39).

When we choose the Lord as our life, then, it is an eternal choice. It is not, though, just choosing eternity. If we just want to live longer, we have missed the point. When we are choosing life, we are choosing the Lord—His life, His eternal love, His intimate voice, and His abiding oneness. When the only other choice is spiritual death, why would anyone choose anything but the Lord? Have we made our choice yet? Choose life.

It Ain't Much, but It's Paid For

"Silver and gold I do not have, but what I have I give to you." Acts 3:6

I remember a friend who just bought a used car. It was old and beat up, and he could tell I was snickering under my breath as I looked at it. He read my mind, and he said, "It ain't much, but it's paid for." In our world of easy credit, and maxed-out indebtedness, he had a real treasure—freedom from monthly payments. What a unique idea—an ideal that few Americans ever realize. We are blinded by the lie of getting something for nothing, and we end up spending the rest of our lives trying to free ourselves from the prison that we have allowed others to build around us.

Unfortunately, this philosophy is often held to be true by even those who are physically or emotionally handicapped in our world. They often believe that the world should feel sorry for them and just give them things to help compensate them for their suffering. Why should I have to work? It's hard enough just to survive. It's "something for nothing" all over again.

Perhaps this is what is going through the mind of the beggar who sits at the temple gate as Peter and John approach. He knows that people who are coming to the temple often bring money to give as offerings, or to buy animals for sacrifices. Why not take advantage of their religious piety to plead for their generosity? There is no indication that he was there for any other reason than money. Peter's response to the beggar is, "Silver and gold I do not have, but what I do have, I give unto you." Peter reaches down and lifts him up, healing him instantly. It wasn't what he was asking for, but it was exactly what he needed. He started "walking, and leaping, and praising God." Peter and John didn't have any money, and even if they did, they probably wouldn't have given it to him. They had a higher purpose than just feeding this man's appetite. They knew that they could help him far more by making God's power real in his life than just giving him a handout.

A lot of Americans today, if given the choice between money and a closer relationship with God would choose the money. It's a lot like the ungrateful children today who get a nice sweater carefully knit by a loving mother or grandmother, but respond, "next time just give me money." Just a closer walk with Jesus "ain't much", from the world's perspective, but at least it's paid for.

In My Father's Hands

"Into your hands I commit my spirit; redeem me, O Lord, the God of truth."
Psa. 31:5

Jesus quotes the first part of this psalm on the cross when he gives up his spirit at the moment of death. In his death, he has taken upon himself the sins of the world and the full weight of the fallen sin nature. It is in that state of spiritual heaviness that he gives his spirit into his Father's hands, for it is only His Father who can accept this gift as payment for the curse of sin and death that was put upon man long ago. Jesus, by quoting this verse, is referring to this need for man to be redeemed by God, and his prayer is not just for himself, but mankind. What he is really saying is, "Here I am, Father, burdened with sin, representing humanity, and I commit my spirit into your hands. Redeem me, representative man, from the Devil and death, for you are the God of truth and justice. Accept my payment for the indebtedness of mankind."

Each one of us also needs to commit our spirits into the Father's hands, not as payment for our sins, but in acknowledgement that we have been bought back by Jesus, and we now belong to the Lord. When we commit our spirits to Him, He, in turn, commits His spirit to us, and there is a spiritual bond that is intertwined for eternity. When we commit our spirits to Him, it is not just for the purpose of salvation. David goes on to say, "I trust in you, O Lord...my times are in your hands" (Psa. 31:14-15). We commit our spirits to the Lord because we trust Him with every part of our lives. Our times, events, circumstances, and hopes are put into His hands, for if He paid so much to buy us back, He must have a pretty good plan for what he wants to do with us in the future. We come to accept that everything that happens to us is not just a matter of chance or luck, but part of God's design. We accept the bad along with the good, for we know it all helps us to grow closer to Him.

Christ didn't see his death on the cross as a mistake or a failure. It wasn't a victory for Satan. Through Christ submitting his spirit to the Father to redeem mankind, Christ won the victory. Likewise, through our committing our spirits to the Father, we also have victory over the Devil. . We have been in the bondage of sin and death, but now we are redeemed and set free from the Devil's captivity. We are in the Father's hands, and we sense His tender touch, his warm comfort, his powerful strength, his safety and his leading. He carries us, lifts us up, caresses us, molds us and disciplines us with his hands, for we are His, and we trust our Father's hands, just as Jesus did on the cross. In our most awkward, trying moment, we know that the best place to be is in the same hands that created us. Then, even if we are asked to give up our lives for the sake of the gospel, as Jesus did, we can commit our spirits to him as we die, knowing that nothing has really changed, for we are already in his hands.

In Chains for Christ

"I am in chains for Christ." Phil. 1:13

It is human nature to feel sorry for ourselves if things don't go the way that we want them to. This is especially true when we feel that we have been victimized or treated unfairly, and we feel that there is nothing we can do about it. We even go as far as blaming God sometimes, for isn't it God who has allowed our suffering? Self-pity is a self-destructive time bomb waiting to explode into either anger or depression, which affects everyone else around us. It is especially destructive when our suffering is caused by our faith in Christ.

If we have taken a stand for Christ, and we are persecuted for our faith, the crucial element between victory and defeat is in how we respond. If we cannot partake of the crucified body of Christ without washing it down with a lot of "whine", then we end up carrying our own cross instead of the cross of Christ. All the attention is on our own martyrdom, instead of what Christ has done for us. What we need to understand is that even though our suffering can be a very humbling experience, it can also be a real ego trip if we put all the focus on ourselves instead of who we are suffering for. If all we do is feel sorry for ourselves, and try to get everyone else to feel sorry for us too, then we have taken our eyes off of Jesus, and like Peter, we have started sinking in the waves of self-pity.

What a contrast to Paul, who while he was in prison for his preaching Christ, never stopped lifting up the Lord in his suffering, and never stopped trying to lift up his brothers and sister in Christ as well. He says that because of his witnessing even in jail, that other Christians "have been encouraged to speak the word of God more courageously and fearlessly" (Phil. 1:14). In spite of all his suffering, he was able to turn what appeared to be a defeat into a victory, for in his greatest need, he didn't yield to the temptation of feeling sorry for himself. He continued to uplift the name of Christ, and his positive response gave others the courage to do likewise.

So, if we are down in the dumps, are we giving others directions on how to get there too, or are we helping the others who are already there to look up to the beautiful sky above us, so they can see the light that will set them free? If we have been crucified with Christ, then we need to learn to walk in his resurrection power, instead of smelling like the corpse.

I'm Not God

"Am I in the place of God, who has kept you from having children?" Gen. 30:2

Rachel was dearly loved by Jacob. After all, he had worked for fourteen years just for the privilege of marrying her. He had proven his love. Yet, Rachel wasn't happy, for she was unable to conceive, and her sister, Leah, had been able to give Jacob four sons. So Rachel became angry with Jacob and told him, "Give me children or I'll die." Jacob's response was the right one—"Am I in the place of God?" We can understand Rachel's frustration and even sympathize with her wanting someone to blame. Her biggest problem, though, is that she puts her husband in the place of God. In one sense, we could even call it a type of idolatry. Oh, she never bows down to her husband, or claims that he is God, yet she still worships him or puts him up on a pedestal where he doesn't belong.

We do the same thing at times. It might be a spouse, or a politician, or a pastor, or a movie star. It doesn't matter who it is or what it is, if they are put into a place of honor, where they are idolized or idealized beyond reality's limits, it is idolatry. The problem is that the world is full of people who either want to play God, or want to lift up others to play God for them. We aren't satisfied with just letting God be God. He is too aloof or distant for our liking. We would rather choose an individual to be our god for us. We put that person in a position where they are expected to be perfect—all knowing, all wise, all everything—and then we expect them to solve all of our problems, answer all of our questions, and meet all of our needs. Then, when they fail, which they will, we blame them for letting us down, instead of blaming ourselves for putting them on that unrealistic pedestal to begin with. We don't want to admit the truth or face reality, so we quickly move on to the next human victim of our idolatry, until they too let us down.

We need to stop expecting others to play God for us, and start seeking a closer walk with the real thing. God himself should be our main source of truth, hope, and love, not some human construct that we have built up in our imaginations. God created us in His image. We are not supposed to create our gods in our image by lifting up others to be our ideal. Remember that people are but statues of clay—odd mixtures of dust and water—mud pies of molecules—that God has chosen to empower with life and energy, soul and spirit. Without God, man returns to dust, and any man who tries to play God or is lifted up as a god, is nothing but a dirty joke.

March 31

I Have Had Enough, Lord

"I have had enough, Lord...Take my life." I Kings 19:4

Elijah had just completed one of the most miraculous days in history. He had challenged the four-hundred prophets of Baal to a test of power, called down fire from heaven, prayed to have it start raining again after three years of drought, and out-ran the horse and chariot of Ahab for twenty-five miles from Mt. Carmel to Jezreel in the pouring rain. This guy was a super saint—a bigger than life hero of the faith. What power! What courage! What communication and trust between God and man! Yet, when Elijah gets to Jezreel, he hears that Jezebel, the queen, is seeking his life for killing her prophets, so he runs away to hide, and cries out, "I have had enough, Lord...take my life."

Wait a minute. What happened to our hero? How can a person go from the highest mountain top experience imaginable to the deepest despair over night? How can a person have faith without limits one moment, then absolutely no faith the next? What happened? I believe that this is a perfect example of spiritual exhaustion or "divine depletion". He had been in spiritual warfare against the pagan demons of darkness, and he had prevailed. He went way beyond himself in each one of the miracles that were performed, relying completely upon the power of God, and he was personally on empty. It was like the feeling that pastors have on Monday mornings after pouring themselves into ministering to people all day on Sunday. There is a tremendous letdown, physically and spiritually, after a spiritual high, and depending on the extremity of the peak, the greater the fall. The Devil gets pastors to sin more on Mondays than any other day of the week. They have done their very best, with maximum effort, and now they can do no more. They let their defenses down and relax, and the Devil takes advantage of their weakness. It is like a prize fighter fighting fifteen rounds with a very difficult opponent and winning the victory, but then being beaten up by a little street punk while he is walking home because he is too exhausted and bruised to even fight back. Some of the greatest upsets in sports happen right after the hardest fought victories because they just don't have any reserves to keep going.

We have the same problem spiritually. We lack spiritual stamina. We are like spiritual fireworks. We go up to the sky in a blaze of glory, but then we cool off and disappear just as quickly into the darkness. The problem is that we look at our spiritual experiences as adrenaline rushes or drug fixes, and we have to go to church once a week to get high. What God wants is something more stable. He tells us to "abide in me, and I will abide in you. No branch can bear fruit by itself. It must abide in the vine" (John 15:4). He wants us to live in His power, day by day, moment by moment, drawing strength from Him alone.

I Can Hardly Breathe

"My strength is gone and I can hardly breathe." Dan. 10:17

There are times in everyone's life when life itself seems unbearable. We are overwhelmed by trials and worries, and the burdens that we bear seem so heavy that they seem to be crushing our spirits, making it hard for us to even breathe. We feel like we are being suffocated by the cares of the world, and even our faith seems to be like an anchor pulling us down rather than lifting us up.

Usually this feeling of breathlessness is associated with hopelessness, for we are trying to carry our own burdens instead of turning them over to God completely. Sure, we may have prayed for God's help, but have we really yielded the outcome of our problems to the Lord? We often want Him to handle the problems, but we want the outcomes to be decided by us. We don't often fully trust Him to work things out the way that we want them to be, so we hold on to some of the worry or burden just in case God doesn't come through for us.

When Daniel, though, comes to the point where his strength is gone and he can hardly breathe, it is not because of any selfish holding on to the lordship of his life. He "had set his mind to gain understanding and to humble himself before the Lord," and God had responded by giving him a vision of things to come. Daniel was "overcome with anguish because of the vision," and he was left feeling "helpless" and breathless in the presence of God's truth.

Have we ever felt this kind of breathlessness—not caused by the cares of this world, but a humbling closeness to the "I AM"? Where the anguish we feel is not for our own personal wants, but for the lost souls of the world, and the ultimate judgment of mankind? Daniel's prayer is a cry for mercy, not for himself, but for Jerusalem. Oh that we would pray that God would make us "breathless" for a vision from God that would make us anguish from His perspective rather than ours. Only then can he breathe into us a new breath of life that transcends all of our own little problems that tend to take our breath away.

How Long will you Waver?

"How long will you waver between two opinions? If the Lord is God, follow him; but if Baal is God, follow him." I Kings 18:21

One of the biggest complaints by women today is that they can't find a man who is willing to make a commitment. Men are like microwaves. They want everything quick and easy. They like fast cars, fast food, and fast women. They want the freedom to be flexible—to go with the flow. They don't like being tied down. Commitment in personal relationships is synonymous with bondage to the male mind. They don't mind being committed to their jobs, their favorite sports teams or their hobbies, but love is a four letter word. At least that is the male stereotype. Not all men are like that, just as not all women are loving and nurturing.

It seems, though, that Elijah here is talking to just the men of his community. "How long will you waver between two opinions?" When are you going to make up your minds? Why can't you make a commitment, one way or the other? You say you believe in God, but you also believe in idols. You can't have it both ways. "No man can serve two masters…He will hate the one and love the other" (Matt. 6:24).

You say that isn't true? You say that you love both God and the world at the same time. Not really. What you love is the part of God that you like. If you love the world and the things in the world, you don't love God as the sovereign Lord of your life and ruler of the universe. Your love for God is a religious rocking chair. It may be constantly moving, but it isn't getting you anywhere. James compares your faith to a "wave of the sea, blown and tossed about by the wind" (James 1:6). You are a "double-minded man, unstable in all" that you do.

Part of the problem is that many men are often just little boys in adult bodies. They don't want to grow up. The apostle Paul tells us, "Become mature" and "speaking the truth in love…grow up", so "we will no longer be infants, tossed back and forth by the waves, and blown here and there by every wind of teaching and by the cunning and craftiness of men" (Eph. 4:13-15).

Wavering back and forth between God and worldliness, then, is a kind of freedom—the kind that blows you wherever the wind may take you. Yet, if you are committed to finding truth and love in your life, freedom has to take a back seat to faith, and choosing God is the only decision that a "real man" can make.

He Restores My Soul

"He makes me lie down in green pastures, he leads me beside quiet waters, he restores my soul."
Psa. 23:2

Have you ever owned an antique car, an old house, or a prized painting, and you had the opportunity of restoring it to its original mint condition? What a cherished possession, for it is worth far more to you than if you had bought it new. You have poured your heart into it, not just your money, and all the effort that it cost you, the blood, sweat and tears, has only increased the joy at the finished product. It's more than just a restoration of something to its original form, it's a reflection of the character and creativity of the craftsman who recreated a masterpiece.

The same thing happens when God restores our soul. When God created man, he was created in the image of God, without the stain of sin, and walking freely and openly in fellowship with the Creator. When man sinned, however, he became a slave to sin and Satan, the ruler of this fallen world, and he lost communion with his maker. When Christ died on the cross for the sins of mankind, though, he made it possible for man to be restored to a right relationship with the Father. When we accept Christ's atonement for our sinful nature, we are born again—made like new—but far more precious to God than Adam and Eve in the Garden of Eden, for Christ invested his own blood, sweat and tears into our restoration. We are a reflection of our master's character and creativity, and we have his seal of approval, the Holy Spirit, to make sure that the restoration is complete. For, even though we have been restored in our spiritual connection to the Creator, we are in a continual process of being restored to the image of Christ throughout our lives. We still have a lot of the old dents and scratches of our old natures that have to be worked out, and occasionally even need a tune up or overhaul of our spiritual engines. Our spiritual energy or power sometimes gets sluggish, like we are trying to pull too heavy of a load with our antique chasse, or our spiritual oil gets clogged up with the cares of this world. It is then that the Holy Spirit works best as our "Mr. Good Wrench", and he cleans and restores us to our full power.

So, restoring our souls is more than just the initial rejuvenation or revival that happens when we accept Christ. It is also the refreshing renewal of our spirits when we, like Atlas, feel that we are carrying the weight of the world on our shoulders, and Christ, as our shepherd, takes us aside and tells us to rest in the green pastures of his nourishment, and drink from the still waters of his abundant life. He restored our souls once for all when we became his new creations, but he still enjoys polishing the shine every day.

He Knows our Thoughts

"Lord, you know everyone's heart." Acts 1:24

There was a movie that came out recently where a man somehow was able to hear the thoughts of other people. This gave him a huge advantage, for he knew what others were thinking about him, and that helped him to decide what kind of relationship he wanted to have with them. If he could tell they were being hypocritical, thinking one thing, but saying something else, he would act accordingly. This helped him at times, but actually made his life more complicated and chaotic at the same time. If he had used his "gift" wisely, he may have produced great good in the world, by helping others that he sensed were having problems. By focusing on his own selfish desires and fantasies, however, he only made things worse for himself and the others around him.

God is different. He too knows our hearts and minds, but He always has our best interests in mind. Yes, it is not always pleasant having a God around who knows everything. How would we like having a friend around who knew our every thought? It's intimidating and uncomfortable. With God it is the same way, for we know that we can never hide anything from Him. We can be sneaky and deceitful around others, but He always knows the truth. It's no fun being under a microscope all of the time. We want to be able to let down and hang loose sometimes, and its hard to do that when we have "company" around.

What it comes down to is trust. There are some things that we don't want others to know about us, except our closest friends. Well, God is our closest friend, and we can trust him with the innermost secrets of our hearts. Prov. 3:5 says, "Trust in the Lord with all your heart." Usually this is understood to mean that we just need to trust God more. Another way of looking at it is that we need to trust God with our hearts, in the sense that we have given our hearts to him to take care of. Our hearts are an open book to him, and we have entrusted them to Him in a very special way. It isn't just a matter of recognizing that He knows our every thought, so we might as well turn them over to Him. We are giving our thoughts to Him like treasures that we would give our best friend, knowing that He will guard them and cherish them as if they were His own. If our attitude is truly that of trusting God with our hearts moment by moment, the good, the bad, and the ugly, then gradually there will be a lot more that will be in tune with God's own heart, and then He may be more inclined to share His own secrets with us.

Hanging of a King

"Joshua smote them, and slew them, and hanged them on five trees." Joshua 10:26

Joshua and the Israelite army had gone from city to city, conquering each place without mercy. No one could stand in their way, for God was fighting for them (Josh. 10:25). Yet, they didn't just slaughter the kings of each place. They would capture them and hang them on trees for all to see. So, when five kings banded together to fight against the Israelites, all five kings were captured and hung on five trees, as symbols of the victory that the Lord was giving them, even over their greatest foes. They were pagan kings, and God wanted to make it very clear that these battles were not just physical wars, but judgment upon the paganism of their enemies. They were wicked, and they must be destroyed to keep them from poisoning the minds and hearts of the Israelite people.

It is no surprise, then, that Satan wanted to seek revenge. When the time was right, he took his opportunity, and he hung the King of Kings upon a tree, just like his kings were hung many years before, and he gloated in triumph over what he thought was his greatest victory. Hanging Jesus on the cross was to be a sign to the rest of the world that he had victory even over God, and that the rest of the world better beware. He was now king, and he would rule the world into sin and death.

Except that God had other plans. Jesus was hung on a tree, but he was never killed. He gave up His own spirit, and after three days, rose again from the dead, to conquer sin and death forever. Satan is merely a counterfeit, and every time he tries to imitate Christ, he fails, even in the hanging of a king.

God's Substitute Teacher

"Speak to us yourself and we will listen. But do not have God speak to us or we will die."
Ex. 20:19

So many times I have wished that I could have walked with God in the Garden of Eden, before the fall of man, and before other people telling me what God has said. I just wish that I could hear His voice and His truth without a depraved mind and without other depraved minds trying to interpret truth for me. I look forward to that day in heaven when we will see Him face to face, for "now I know in part; then I shall know fully even as I am fully known" (I Cor. 13:12).

It is hard for me to understand, then, why people would not want to talk to God personally. For the Israelites to ask Moses to speak to them, but not want God to speak to them seems like it is just a matter of fear. They are afraid they "will die." This could be a positive sign of worship and awe for the mighty God, yet I think there is more to it than that. The important aspect of their unwillingness to have God speak to them is not so much their fear, as much as their not understanding God's love for them. Basically, they just don't know Him. They grew up in Egypt, with pagan gods, who were all based on things that they were afraid of. Why should this God be any different? They didn't think that it was possible to have a personal relationship with God—to actually be a child or friend of God. Sure, they had seen His power in destroying the Egyptian army, and they were afraid they might be next. Yet, they missed the point—God loved them so much that he was willing to save them from their enemies. What was meant as an act of love was seen as an act of terror.

When we love God and have accepted His love for us, there is no more terror, for God is love. We don't need any "substitute teachers" for God to speak to us, for He has sent His own spirit into our hearts to teach us (John 14:26). That doesn't mean that He can't speak to us through others. It just means that that shouldn't be our preference.

God's Math

"Five of you will chase a hundred, and a hundred of you will chase ten thousand."
Lev. 26:8

Have you ever noticed how God loves numbers? Certain numbers have special significance to God, and they are used over and over again. For example, seven, forty, and twelve are used repeatedly. There is the command to keep the seventh day holy, and the seven seals of Revelation. There is the forty years of wandering through the wilderness, and the forty days of Christ's temptation in the desert. There is the twelve tribes of Israel and the twelve disciples, etc. etc. These numbers have special symbolic significance, and they all point to a master plan by God to control the universe and history beyond time and space.

Yet, there is one area where numbers don't seem to matter to God. That is the matter of how many there are on the enemy's side. It doesn't matter how strong the enemy's forces are, God is always stronger. After all, he is the creator of all things, and in an instant he could annihilate them all. It doesn't matter if they are principalities or powers in high places, his enemies could be destroyed with a touch of his little finger. So, when he promises to bless the Israelites as they conquer the Promised Land, the Israelites have no need to worry or despair. It doesn't matter if they are greatly outnumbered, as long as God is on their side.

When he tells them that five Israelites will be able to have victory over a hundred, and a hundred will have victory over ten thousand, then, it isn't a matter of God being poor in math. It doesn't matter how inadequate the soldiers are, or how afraid they are about the odds. When God is on our side, He will fight our battles for us (2 Chron. 32:8), and then the only number that counts is when He is number "one".

God's Good Intentions

"You intended to harm me, but God intended it for good." Gen. 50:20

It is amazing how God works behind the scenes to achieve His purposes. Joseph's brothers were jealous of his favored relationship with his father, and of the spiritual visions that he said that he had received from his heavenly Father, as well. They resented that his dreams implied that they, who were the older brothers, were going to have to bow down and serve their younger brother. It is no wonder, then, that they plot to have him killed, and then finally sell him to slavery. Even the brothers who did not want him dead, at least wanted him out of the way.

Joseph was blessed by God, though, so that even in his captivity, he rose to great power and glory. He became the greatest man in Egypt, second to only Pharaoh himself. From scripture, however, we discover that all this happened not just as some accident of fate, but as God's special plan to provide for His people in a time of great famine. If Joseph had not been sold by his family, his family probably would all have died by starvation. They intended to harm him, but "God intended it for good."

Yet, notice that it was not just for Joseph's good. We often like to focus just on ourselves, so when we read this passage, we like to apply it to just us. Someone has hurt us, and yet God has used it for good in our lives. That is fine, but it does not go far enough. What Joseph says is, "God intended it for good to accomplish what is now being done, the saving of many lives." He wasn't focused on what God had done for him, in spite of what his brothers had planned. He was focused on how God sees the whole picture, and how even when we end up getting the short end of the stick sometimes, His greater end of helping to save the many is still upheld. In other words, God's good intentions may use us for his ultimate plan, but they are never just about us.

God, the Master Chef

"You prepare a table before me in the presence of my enemies. You anoint my head with oil; my cup overflows." Psa. 23:5

Imagine for a moment being in the army of King David and fighting alongside the king himself in a ferocious battle against the king's worst enemy. Then, at the end of the day, you both take a walk back to the camp together, and the king spends the entire time encouraging you by telling you how great of a job you did in the battle. Then, when you get back to the camp, he takes the time to bathe you, to wrap your wounds, and to bring you a clean set of clothes. Then, while you are resting in the king's tent, he prepares a feast before you, anoints your head with his own precious oil, and fills your cup of wine to overflowing. He is your personal master chef.

King David knew exactly what this experience was like, for this is how he was treated when he came back from battle. He was the warrior King, and when he finished fighting he was still treated like royalty, even in the presence of his enemies. David also knew what it was like to be treated as royalty by the King of Kings and Lord of Lords himself. He knew what it was like to fight his spiritual battles with the Lord fighting by his side. He experienced first hand the encouraging words of the master after a hard won battle. He knew the gentle hands of the Lord cleansing his soul after the fray, and the healing touch of the Great Physician. He felt first hand the rest and peace in his heart that only the Lord can give. He watched in amazement as the Lord unselfishly prepared a spiritual feast before him to nourish his battle-worn soul, and then felt the tears role down his cheeks as the Lord's abundant mercy poured the oil of his grace upon his head, and filled the cup of his heart to overflowing with the refreshing power of the Holy Spirit.

What about us? Do we feel war-torn and beat up by the spiritual warfare all around us and within? Do we feel worn out and burned out by our Christian service, and we just need some time alone with the Lord? The Lord is waiting to take us aside to his tent of intimate communion and refreshing renewal. He can't wait to fix our favorite dish, just the way we like it. He is our master chef of spiritual food. He knows exactly what we need to give us strength and encouragement, one day at a time. We are not alone. He not only fights with us, but helps us recover along the way. He wants us to win. He is our king with a servant heart.

Do we have that same servant heart for Him? Hopefully, when we realize how much He has done for us, we will be refreshed enough to be willing to go back into the battlefield with renewed zeal and faith, always looking forward to the end of the day, when once again we will be allowed to eat at the banqueting table of the King, and the banner over us will be "Love" (Rev. 19:7-9).

God Owns Everything

"The Lord gave and the Lord has taken away." Job 1:21

Have you ever lost your shirt? Perhaps your company got downsized, or the stock market crashed, or you got replaced by a machine, but somehow you lost your job and weren't able to get another one right away. You ended up losing your home and car because you couldn't make the payments, you had to move in with your parents, and everyone in your family is angry with you for making them move away from their friends and starting over.

In times like these, the tendency is for people to drop out of church. They are too embarrassed to face people, they are turned off by the pastor's pat answers, and they are just plain angry with God for allowing all of this to happen. Satan knows the routine. If he takes away all of the good things in our lives, he can get us to turn away from God. That's the way that it usually works.

In Job's case, though, it didn't work that way. Satan was given permission by God to take away all of Job's possessions, including the lives of his children, yet when it was all gone, Job's response was, "Naked I came from my mother's womb, and naked I will depart. The Lord gave and the Lord has taken away; may the name of the Lord be praised" (Job 1:21). Job didn't just lose his shirt, he lost the lives of his loved ones, and he still didn't curse God.

How could someone be so callused, we ask, for it seems to us that he just doesn't care. Yet, before all of this happened, he went out and sacrificed animals for his children every day, just in case that one of them might have sinned by cursing God in their hearts (1:5). Trust me; he did care about his children. How, then, could he respond to this tragedy with such controlled sorrow?

There are a few principles that we can learn from this. First, if we fear God, and we realize that He knows our every thought, we are very careful that everything that goes through our mind and heart is subservient to the will of God. If anything even begins to enter in that doesn't belong there, we quickly get rid of it before it takes root. That includes any evil thought or doubt about God himself. It is our fear of God which causes us to shun evil, which means to get as far away from it as possible, even in our thoughts. That is one mistake that many Christians make. They are careful about their actions, but careless with their thoughts.

Second, we need to understand that everything we have is given to us by God. Even things we earn are still ours only by God's grace, not because we deserve them.

Last, but not least, God owns everything. We are only servants who have been given the responsibility to take care of the landlord's possessions. If He wants, He has the right to take them away from us and give them to someone else. They don't belong to us.

God is Knocking

"Here I am! I stand at the door and knock. If anyone hears my voice and opens the door,
I will come in and eat with him, and he with me." Rev 3:20

This verse is usually used in gospel tracts to illustrate the process of asking Jesus into our heart. This verse, however, is not talking about salvation. It is written to Christians in the church of Laodicea who lack real commitment. They are rebuked for being "neither hot nor cold, but lukewarm." God is trying to get them to repent, so they will be more on fire for the Lord. He is trying to make it clear that He is anxious and ready to forgive them and to have fellowship with them once again, but He is not going to force it on them. He eagerly waits at the door of their hearts and knocks, using the word, the Holy Spirit, and other believers, to convict them of their backslidden state, so He can abide with them and have close communion with them once again. He is speaking of the abiding that Christ speaks of in John 15, not of salvation.

If we, as Christians, refuse to repent of our lukewarmness, it says that God rebukes and disciplines those whom He loves (Rev. 3:19), and if we continue to harden our hearts, He will even spit us out of His mouth (Rev. 3:16). On the one hand, if we repent not, He will not abide with us. On the other hand, He will not want us to abide in Him either. He spits us out, as if we are a bad taste in His mouth. We think as Christians that it doesn't really matter what we do, for God will love us anyway. We take God's love and forgiveness for granted, but we fail to realize that even though God may forgive us, He may come to the point that He no longer wants to have fellowship with us. He doesn't like one-sided relationships any more than any of us. For now, He may be knocking, but He also may choose to just walk away. Are we up for company, or are we eating alone?

God Finishes What He Starts

"In the beginning God created the heavens and the earth." Gen. 1:1

Have you ever started a project, but just weren't able to finish? You started with all kinds of energy and excitement and a burst of creativity, but then you got distracted by something else or got bored or just discouraged because the project wasn't turning out the way that you wanted. So, you quit, and the project got shoved into a closet or a garage. You promised yourself that you would get back to it later, but that day never comes, and it ends up being forgotten, or even thrown away. What a waste.

God has made us in His image, and one of the ways that it is demonstrated is by our ability to be creative. Yet, we waste all that creative power throwing it to the wind, only to watch it come crashing down to the earth. Part of the problem is that we view creation as an act of an instant instead of as a process that continues on and on. We are really good at momentary impulses of imitating God's creativity, but we lack the perseverance of His power. God didn't just create the world and everything in it. He also continues to create by maintaining the process that He set in place. It says that "all things were created by him and for him. He is the initiator of all things, and in him all things hold together" (I Cor. 1:16-17). Creation for God, then, is never just a momentary thing, even though He may have started it all with a single word (Psa. 33:6).

Whatever God starts, He finishes, not only in the physical realm, but the spiritual as well. The Word promises us that "he who began a good work in you will carry it on to completion until the day of Christ Jesus" (Phil. 1:6). We have all heard the statement, "Be patient. God isn't finished with me yet." That means that God may have created man in His image a long time ago , but He is still creating us in His image now (Col. 3:10), and He won't be done until we are "Master pieces," or self-portraits, looking just like Him (Rom. 8:29). We may not look so good now, with dark globs of human nature hanging out all over, but the finished product is going to be glorious, and God never gives up till His work is done.

If we are going to be creative like God, then, we need to learn how to persevere. We can't just be satisfied with moments of inspiration that blow away like chaff in the wind. We need to think of ourselves as taking part in God's creation of our inner man. He is not going to give up on us, and neither should we. Paul compares this creative process to a race (Heb.12:1, 2). He says that we can't allow ourselves to get slowed down or distracted by "the sin that so easily entangles" us, but "fix our eyes on Jesus, the author and perfecter of our faith." As an author or creator, God is waiting to put the finishing touches on His creation as the "perfecter of our faith," but we keep trying to edit what He is writing. We need to just let him finish what he has started.

From Wild Beast to Holy Priest

"They have killed men in their anger and hamstrung oxen as they pleased."
Gen. 49:6

Who could this verse possibly be talking about? Who not only had the nerve to go around killing men, but mutilating animals? Who was so out of control that they were cursed by their father on his death bed? It was Levi and Simeon, two of Jacob's twelve sons. They were so violent, in fact, that neither one received any inheritance in the Promised Land. Their families were dispersed among the rest of the tribes, and their families received nothing. And yet, God, through His abundant mercy, took the descendants of Levi and made them the priests for all the children of Israel. He took their natural tendency toward bloodshed, and made them responsible for all the sacrifices to the Holy God. They had to take the blood that was shed at the tabernacle or temple, and pour it on the sides of the altar, for the atonement of all the people. They had to listen to the confessions and prayers of each person who came to them as their spiritual leaders. They had to receive all their food and provisions from the offerings of others, rather than following their natural lust for just going out and taking what they wanted. They had to be completely controlled by the letter of the law, and not make a single mistake; otherwise, it could bring down the wrath of God, and even mean their death (Lev. 10:1-2).

The totally uncontrollable, wild men became the most controlled of all, not because they were better or more holy than anyone else, but because God couldn't trust them to have the freedom to do whatever they wanted. Instead of rejecting them, though, he made them his right-hand men so He could keep a closer watch on them. Sometimes we get the impression that our spiritual leaders are the saints of the church, and we need to put them up on pedestals to bow down to. We forget, however, that they are just sinners like the rest of us, and that God may have called them to be preachers in order to keep them in the Word and out of trouble. Some of the best preachers are those who were the rowdiest teenagers, and they know the Word the best because God has had to apply it to their lives the most. So, if we feel the call of God, it is no reason for pride. It may be that we have a weak character, and God just knows that we need more scrutiny by others to keep us in line.

Forfeiting God's Grace

"Those who cling to worthless idols, forfeit the grace that could be theirs."   Jonah 2:8

The angels are wonderful creatures. We often picture them as having long white robes with wings and harps, and almost always as females. Yet, the scriptures paint a very different picture. All of the angels mentioned in the Bible have masculine names, not all of them have wings or harps, and some have eyes all over their bodies and four heads (Ez. 10:14). They would probably seem like monsters to us if we saw them, and not very "angelic" at all. Many of them are warriors, in fact, who are used by God to bring judgment on the earth (Rev. 6). Sure, they get to be in heaven with God, to live eternally, and to have great power, but we are not to worship them or pray to them, like many in our own culture do today. Angels are not the ideal that we need to aspire to. They are not perfect, for many, like Satan, have rebelled against God because of their pride (Ez. 28:12-19). Not only that, but they lack depth in their relationship with God. Even the ones who have not sinned have never experienced the forgiveness, grace and mercy of God firsthand, like we have. They are close to God in their physical being, for they live with Him in heaven, but can never "abide with Him" in the same sense that we can, for we have Him abiding in us, and we are His children, not just his messengers. After all, He died for mankind, not the angels, and the angels are only powerful spectators to God's grand design.

Unfortunately, not all people have experienced God's grace either. They are like the angels, yet different, in that, they have at least been offered God's mercy, but have refused the gift of salvation so they can continue to walk after their own gods. They "forfeit the grace that could be theirs by clinging to worthless idols".

What about us? Would we rather be like the angels, just spectators of God's grace as it abounds in others, or are we ready to experience the knowing of God in a deeper, richer way than even the most holy angel in the presence of the Almighty? The choice is ours.

For Such a Time as This

"Who knows but that you have come to royal position for such a time as this?"
Esther 4:14

Have you ever been put into a position of leadership or influence where it seems as though you have been picked up by the hand of God and placed in a certain spot, almost like Dorothy in the Wizard of Oz being picked up by a tornado and placed in a magical kingdom, wondering how on earth did I get here? It's as if God is playing chess and you are the bishop sitting comfortably right next to your own king, then all of a sudden you have been moved clear across the board, and you are challenging the king of the opposition. In an instant, you are moved from a place of safety, your comfort zone, and been asked to be on the offensive. You have been in the support group, but now you are the commander of the Green Berets challenging the front lines. What happened?

Esther found herself in the same position. She was just a poor orphan girl, living with her uncle Mordecai. She was a minority teenager living in the inner city, with absolutely no prospects or hope for success in life. Then some stranger comes along and takes her to the King's palace, where she is placed in the King's harem. She pleases the king so much, that he makes her his queen. Wow! From rags to riches in a moment.

If the story stopped there, it would be enough to capture our imaginations. She is the Jewish Cinderella. Yet, it isn't just a matter of settling in and enjoying heaven on earth. She is not living in a fantasy world. The king is going to kill all of the Jews. He doesn't realize that she is a Jew. She can keep quiet, and let her nation perish, or she can try to change the king's mind, and lose her head. Her uncle, Mordecai, convinces her that God has put her in that position so that she can save her people. If she refuses, God can raise up someone else to do the job, but she will miss out on the blessing of being used by God, and probably be killed for her unwillingness to submit to God's will. What a choice! She could die either way. Her only hope is that the Lord will honor her faith and protect her. She goes through with her plan, saves the Jewish nation, and has her faith memorialized in scripture for eternity. There is no fairy godmother, but this Cinderella has a God-Father, and He has transformed her into a queen for all times.

Are we in that same position right now? The place where God has put us for just a time as this? Where if we are self-sacrificial and obedient to what God wants us to do, there could be dramatic transformations of ourselves and others, and the miraculous, awesome God will be glorified? We shouldn't let fear keep us from fulfilling what God has planned. We are only a channel, and this is only a test. We shouldn't let self clog up the "test-tube".

Fighting Against God

"You will not be able to stop these men; you will only find yourselves fighting against God."
Acts 5:39

Occasionally, even the hard-hearted Pharisees came up with truth in their lips, even though they didn't understand the full significance of their statements.   In this case, the Pharisees were frustrated by the miracles and teachings of the apostles. They thought that when they got rid of Jesus, that would be the end to this untamable spirituality. Now they thought of killing the disciples also. If it wasn't for Gamaliel, a Jewish teacher, whom God raised up to be in the Sanhedrin at this very moment, they probably would have.

Gamaliel's premise is very sound. He says, "If their purpose or activity is of human origin, it will fail. But if it is from God, you will not be able to stop these men; you will only find yourselves fighting against God." It is a miracle that the stiff-necked Pharisees even listened to such wisdom, but they still flogged the disciples before setting them free. If killing God's messengers would have been wrong, wouldn't it also have been wrong to flog them? Either way, they would be fighting against God. Somehow this logic passed them by. What fools.

Yet, don't we do the same thing? We have certain sins that we consider "the bad ones," and we wouldn't think of doing them. God would be angry with us if we did those things, so we decide that it wouldn't be wise to fight against God. We do other sins, however, which we don't consider very bad. We have justified them in our minds and hidden them from our friends, so we think they are okay. As long as it doesn't hurt anyone, it can't be that bad, we think.

Well, it does hurt someone. It hurts God, others, and ourselves whenever we sin, no matter what the sin is. Sin breaks our fellowship with God, which, in turn, hurts our ability to be Christ-like to others, or to have peace, joy and power in our daily walk. Even the small sins are rebellion of the heart, and without even realizing it, we are fighting against God. When we are struggling with God's lordship of our lives, then, our purposes and activities are just of human origin, and they will fail. We can't be fighting the Lord with one hand, and then expect Him to fill the other one with His blessings. God wants our two-handed embrace, not the one in the Word, and the other fist in His face.

Excuses, Excuses

"They gave me the gold, and I threw it into the fire, and out came this calf." Ex. 32:24

From the beginning of time, men have been coming up with excuses for why they have rebelled against God. First, Adam blamed his sin on the woman. Then, the woman blamed the snake. Here Aaron used a very unique excuse. Moses was up on Mount Sinai for 40 days and nights, and the people were getting restless. They all thought he was dead, or at least hoped he was. They missed their pagan gods from Egypt, and they convinced Aaron to make them a new idol. Aaron did not have the respect of the people, and they were beginning to get out of control, so he gave in to them. He was trying to maintain control by making everyone happy, even though he knew it was wrong.

When Moses came back, though, he knew he couldn't make Moses happy with the truth, so he made up this far-fetched lie. No one in their right mind would believe that he just threw some gold in the fire, and "out came this calf". Yet, this lie was easier for Aaron to accept for himself, even though no one else would believe him. He just couldn't bring himself to admit that he just did a completely foolish thing, as well as totally losing any dignity or respect that the people might have had for him as their new priest.

His foolish act was responsible for 3,000 people being killed that day in punishment for his actions. Can you imagine living with that on your conscience for the rest of your life? Yet, he not only had to keep living, he had to continue being their leader and priest. Every time he sacrificed animals for the sins of others, then, he was also sacrificing for his own in his heart, for as a leader, he was without excuse—a good one, that is.

Enriched in Every Way

"In Christ Jesus…you have been enriched in every way—in all your speaking and in all your knowledge—Christ was confirmed in you." I Cor. 1:5-6

What do you get for someone who has everything? That is a question that you might ask if you are fortunate enough to know someone who is wealthy. You want to get something that they will really appreciate, but they already have everything they need and desire. What a dilemma. It is interesting to note that the Bible talks about us in the same way. It says that "in Christ Jesus…you have been enriched in every way." In other words, we have been made "wealthy" in Jesus. He has not only blessed us with His love, grace and salvation, but with every spiritual gift that we need to grow closer to Him and to help others to grow. We are rich—the King's kids, and our spiritual wealth is a confirmation that we are indeed the children of God.

Yet, wealth is worthless if it is never used. What good is a vault of gold if it just sits hidden away? When we are enriched in Jesus, it is not just a storage room. He also gives us the ability to share the wealth with others. That doesn't mean that we are all gifted speakers, but we all have been given the ability to reach out beyond ourselves in meaningful ways to share the love and truth of our Lord. We have been given everything we need to make a powerful impact upon the world around us when we are abiding in Christ Jesus.

Having everything, though, does not mean that there is nothing more. The word "enriched" doesn't just mean to be made wealthy. It also means "fertilized to increase productivity". In other words, we have been given everything we need, but it is given to us in the same way that Jesus was—as an infant. Jesus was perfect from the very beginning, but he still needed to grow before he could fulfill God's purpose for his life. Our spiritual gifts and blessings are all sufficient from the very beginning of our new birth, but that doesn't mean they don't need to mature. A fruit tree needs to dig and spread its roots deeper and wider into the rich soil to be able to produce more fruit. It needs to be watered, nourished, and fertilized. It needs to be pruned at the proper time.

The Lord, once again, has given us everything we need. He nourishes us, prunes us, and strengthens us so we can keep growing. Having something and using it, though, are two different things. What we choose to do with our wealth is up to us. We can hoard it, like spiritual Scrooges, cherishing our time alone with the Lord, but never sharing his blessings with others, or we can be sharing the wealth. The verse, "Freely you have received, freely give" (Matt. 10:8) does not apply to money. It is talking about using your spiritual giftedness to help others. What about you? Are you stingy in the Spirit, or are you a cheerful giver?

Don't Put Out the Fire

"Do not put out the Spirit's fire." I Thess. 5:19

Can you imagine going camping, and everyone is trying to keep warm by staying close to the camp fire? Yet, at the very same time, everyone is throwing buckets of water on the fire as fast as they can move. What is wrong with this picture? On the one hand, everyone wants the warmth and comfort of the fire, but on the other hand, they are trying to put it out. This doesn't make any sense, but this is exactly what is happening spiritually speaking every day. Every true believer wants and prays for the fire of the Holy Spirit to come upon them and to empower them and to comfort them in their time of need. Yet, they don't like the light of the Holy Spirit's fire exposing their sin. They want the blessings of God, but they don't want Him to tell them how to live their lives. They want the feeling of spiritual elation, but they don't want to feel convicted of their rebelliousness. So, they are constantly praying with one hand, but extinguishing the flames of God with the other.

According to I Thess. 5, we extinguish His fire by not being joyful or thankful in all things, by not praying continually, by not seeking God's will in our lives, by not believing or obeying His word, by not cherishing the good things of God, and by not avoiding every kind of evil. If we truly want the power of the Spirit's fire, we also must be willing to accept the purifying, purging aspect of that fire, and allow Him to cut off and burn every area of our lives which is not pleasing to Him.

Part of God's light is caused by His inherent Nature of goodness. Part of His light, though, is caused by His burning away everything in our lives which is contrary to His divine Nature. Are we ready for both kinds of fire?

Don't Give Up

"Let us not become weary in doing good, for at the proper time we will reap a harvest if we do not give up." Gal. 6:9

It is amazing how fast that construction workers can build a building when they know that if they don't make the deadline, they won't get paid. I have heard about a house that was built from the ground up in one day. It looked great, and was ready to move in. The problem was that when something is built that fast, the builders often take shortcuts, and they will use inferior products to save money besides. It still looks great, but in a short time, it starts falling apart. There are plumbing and electrical problems, and the windows and roof start leaking. There are cracks in the plaster, concrete and fireplace, and not a single wall is built square. They use a lot of molding to cover up the mistakes, but when any fixit work is done, the gaps become obvious. The builders get what they wanted—money—but the home owners have to pay for their sloppiness for the rest of their lives. On the other hand, when something is built with care by an expert, who takes all the time that they need to do the job right, a building can become a work of art.

The Bible makes a similar comparison. It says that when people do things just to bring themselves immediate, temporal pleasure, that whatever they do will just fall apart and be destroyed, for it wasn't made to last (Gal. 6:8). However, if someone seeks to please the Holy Spirit in all that they do, instead of their sinful nature, they will build things for eternity's sake, and they will be rewarded with eternal blessings (Gal. 6:8). The problem is that even though we start out doing things for the Lord, we often get sidetracked by our own ambitions or pride, and we want the glory instead of the Lord. Or, it takes such a long time to see real results, and to produce the quality that we know the Lord wants, that we get discouraged and just plain worn out before we complete our mission. We do well for a while, but then we give up before we reach the finish line. It's just too hard to keep going on to victory, we think, so we end up being failures not because we can't go on, but we just won't.

This is a greater tragedy than the first builders, who lived only for self, and had everything they built crash and burn. The tragedy for the second builder is that there was so much more potential, for eternity was built into the initial stages of the design. In the end, though, it became like a fallen temple that once housed the Lord, but now is only rubble. The Bible tries to encourage us by saying, "Let us not become weary in doing good, for at the proper time we will reap a harvest if we do not give up." We just need to keep going and doing what we know will please the Lord, and leave the results to Him. Rome wasn't built in a day, and eternity might take a little longer.

Don't Be Afraid of the Dark

"Moses approached the thick darkness where God was."
Ex. 20:21

Most people are afraid of the dark, to some extent. The dark represents the fearful unknown, the "boogieman" in our imagination that lurks in the darkness like a monster ready to pounce on us and devour us as a bedtime snack. We control our fear by putting up boundaries or walls around our "safety zone", thinking that at least in this spot of familiarity, the monster can't get us.

We have this same protective approach when it comes to God. We tend to walk with God only in areas where we feel comfortable and in control. As long as God appears as the tender Jesus, we are willing sheep following our loving shepherd. Yet, when He asks us, like Moses, to approach the thick darkness where God is, we shudder in fear, like the Israelites did, and we want someone else to go in there for us. We want the ministers or missionaries to be the pioneers, to test the waters or journey into the darkest jungles for us, and then tell us about their exciting adventures of being explorers for the Lord. We are satisfied with being spectators, while other more daring souls risk their lives and souls for the sake of eternity.

We can't learn to be a great athlete, though, by watching sports on TV, and we can't get closer to God at the top of the mountain by only watching others climb. We have to be willing to not only climb ourselves, but to enter the darkness at the very top where God is. Of course, after we go through the darkness, there is ultimate light, but He wants to know if we trust Him first before He reveals Himself to us completely. If we want to see God part the waters of the Red Sea, we have to be willing to step into the water first. If we want to see the light of God, we first have to be willing to follow Him even when His path seems to make no sense, walking in shadows more than in sunlight. Yet, there can be no shadows unless there is a light source somewhere, so we need to get our eyes off the darkness and sincerely search for the light. It doesn't matter if we can't see the next step ahead of us. We need to trust the Spirit to guide us to the throne of God—He's been there before.

Do You Smell?

"We are to God the aroma of Christ among those who are being saved and those who are perishing." 2 Cor. 2:15

The question, "Do you smell?" is a loaded question. It could be referring to your ability to use your nose, or it could be talking about the fact that others can smell you. It is also ambiguous about whether you might smell good or bad. For the apostle Paul and other followers of Christ, it actually means smelling good and bad at the same time.

Paul compares our walk with Christ as a triumphal procession, where He spreads us around the world as a "fragrance of the knowledge of him" (2 Cor. 2:14), as if we were the flower petals being thrown before the King after he has come back from a victory. It is a beautiful picture of our glorifying and pleasing our Lord and King.

However, not everyone appreciates this triumphal entry. Those who are perishing see it as a threat to their evil domain. Yet, what bothers them the most is the awful smell. Paul says that we are the "aroma of Christ among those who are being saved and those who are perishing." The difference is that to the saved, it is a sweet smelling fragrance that emanates the beauty of God's grace and love. To the perishing, who have never experienced the resurrection power of our Lord, all they can smell spiritually speaking is the crucified Jesus, and they know in their inner beings that they are guilty of his shed blood. To them, we stink, because we are a constant reminder of their guilt and their own sentence of death.

In addition, the closer we are to Christ in our walk, and the more crucified we are with Him, the more we stink to the unsaved world. They hate our spiritual stench. To those who believe, however, we are "the fragrance of life".

Divine Destiny by Default

"The scepter will not depart from Judah." Gen. 49:10

What an honor that was given to Judah. It was going to be through his lineage that King David would be born, and the King of Kings, Jesus Christ our Lord. One would think that this great honor would be given to one who had distinguished himself in holiness and devotion to God. In fact, according to the law and to Jewish custom, it seems that this honor and inheritance would have come to the first-born son of Israel, Reuben. Yet, it was given to Judah, who was Israel's fourth son. Why?

Well, the first son, Reuben, committed fornication with his father's concubine, so his father cursed him to a life of turbulence (Gen. 49:3-4). Then, his second and third sons, Simeon and Levi, were both murderers, and were cursed to be dispersed without an inheritance (Gen. 49:5-7). Israel, then, blesses his fourth son, Judah, to be the ruling tribe that would father kings and the holy messiah, not so much out of worthiness as by default. He was merely the next in line.

Although this may seem strange to us, this follows God's guidelines all along. It says in I Cor. 1:26-30 that "Not many of you were wise by human standards; not many were influential; not many were of noble birth. But God chose the foolish things of the world…so that no one may boast before him. It is because of him that we are in Christ Jesus," not because of any greatness or worthiness on our part. He chose the Jews as His chosen people, not because they were the greatest, but because they were a stiff-necked people that He could use as an example of His grace. He chose fishermen and tax-collectors (and us) to be his disciples for the same reason.

Consecrate Yourself

"Consecrate yourselves, for tomorrow the Lord will do amazing things among you." Josh. 3:5

The children of Israel were getting ready to enter into the Promised Land. They had to follow the sacred Ark of the Covenant into the Holy Land in order to fight a Holy War for the glory of a Holy God. They, too, then, needed to be holy in order to be used by God. They were told to consecrate or sanctify themselves for this holy mission. When Moses told the people to consecrate themselves before they received the law, they had to wash their cloths, bathe, and refrain from sex. Yet, whatever the external requirements were, I am sure that they also internally were suppose to make themselves right before God through confession of sins and purification of thoughts and hearts before Him. After all, God was going to perform "amazing things" among them, and use them in amazing ways. He needed them to be clean vessels ready to be used by the master, even though they didn't understand exactly what that meant.

God wants us to consecrate ourselves for the very same reason. He wants to do amazing things through us and for us, yet we must be ready, for God's miraculous power could be manifest at any moment. He tells us, "Be prepared in season and out of season" to preach the Word and to minister to others (2 Tim. 4:2). We need to approach each day with an attitude of great expectation, ready for anything the Lord sends our way. We need to be ready all the time, not just on Sundays or Holidays.

The word "consecrated" means "set apart for a special mission or purpose". The word "holy" also means to be set apart. In order to be consecrated, then, we must be holy in our relationship to God, and wholly dedicated to His purpose for our lives. The word consecrated is similar to the word ordained. Each believer is ordained by God to be a saint and a priest, regardless of what our spiritual gifts are. God may not ask us to preach a sermon, but we are still supposed to be ready to do whatever he asks us to do. He says, "Be obedient…Be ready to do whatever is good" (Titus 3:1).

Are we ready to be so filled by the Holy Spirit that we are overflowing into the lives of others? Are we pure enough to be able to see God's wonders with childlike eyes? Are we so empty of self that God can fill us with Himself, and be satisfied that He is the one who gets all the glory? If so, then we are consecrated enough to enter the Promised Land of God's blessings and victorious Christian living. Hold on to your hats, for here come the miracles.

Circumcision of the Heart

"The Lord your God will circumcise your hearts." Deut. 30:6

The ritual of circumcision was established by God for basically three reasons: purification, identification and confirmation. According to Jewish law, a woman who gave birth to a son would be unclean for seven days. That is why she has to wait until the eighth day to have her son circumcised. The circumcision, in one sense, then, was a purification ceremony for both the mother and the child, and the father was the one who performed the ritual.

The same thing happens on a spiritual plane. When someone becomes a Christian, they are still greatly influenced by their sinful natures. They are born again, but they are "unclean" in many ways. So the father waits for a while, until the new spiritual child is ready, and then He circumcises their hearts through the cutting away of the old fallen self. It is a painful process, just as the physical circumcision, yet it must be done so we may be purified.

The sexual organ passes on seed so that new life can be produced. The circumcision of the heart is also necessary so we can be pure enough to reproduce our spiritual seed into the lives of others. For a while after we are born again, when we are still struggling with sin, our mother, the bride of Christ, the church, is also made unclean by our sins, but when Christ circumcises our hearts, the bride is cleansed as well.

The second reason for circumcision is identification. When a child is circumcised, it identifies that child as a Jew, as one of God's chosen people. It is like a physical and spiritual brand, identifying the child as belonging to the master. This is such a distinguishing brand, that during different times, like the holocaust, Jewish men actually had the ritual undone through surgery, so that their enemies could not identify them as Jews. The circumcision of the heart is meant also as a form of identification. There should be such a change in our lives and attitudes, that the world should be able to tell that we are Christians. Sometimes Christians try to undo their circumcision of the heart so that the world will not know they are Christians, and they become like unclean children again.

The third reason for circumcision is confirmation of the covenant made between God and His people. God had made a promise to the Jews that they would be His people for eternity, and that through them, He would bless the world by sending the messiah to atone for their sins. The circumcision would be a reminder of the covenant and also a symbol of the promise. After Christ died on the cross, his disciples compared the crucifixion to Christ's circumcision, for it was through his painful physical death that the sinful nature of the world was cut away and condemned (Col. 2:11). So, have you ever been circumcised from the inside out?

Childlike Evil

"Every inclination of his heart is evil from childhood."
Gen. 8:21

Oh to be young again—to live in dream lands of innocence and wonder, full of fun and not a care in the world. That is the ideal, or so we are told. Even the Bible tends to give this impression, with childlike faith being the very essence of salvation. Yet, childlike faith cannot save someone unless they first acknowledge their childlike evil. One of the basic tenets of Christianity is that we are born with a sinful nature. That is why we need a savior. That means that even as children, we are bent and twisted in the wrong direction.

Society or our environment is not the reason for our sinfulness. We are not lost because of any individual sin that we have committed, the friends that we have, the rotten schools that we have attended, or any other external cause. According to scripture, "Every inclination of [man's] heart is evil from childhood". It doesn't say that a child is primarily a little angel, with a little spot of evil on one of its wings. It says "every inclination" is evil.

Self-centered "meism" is dominant from birth, and is only mellowed by nurturing parents or caregivers who teach the child the value of love. Even this mellowing, though, is still motivated by what makes "me" happy. I will be kind, but only because I receive positive reinforcements and encouragement when I do. We are like Pavlov's dogs. We are nice to others because we get rewarded when we are, and punished when we are not. It's in our best self-interest.

Even the idealistic childlike faith, though necessary for salvation, is also the means by which we are pulled into our greatest sins. We are naïve as children, and we are gullible followers of anyone who promises us a good time. We want to be liked, and we are pulled like magnets toward those who offer "friendship" to our hearts or to our bodies, even though our souls might be jeopardized. Our childlike faith when directed toward God is a window to heaven. When it is directed toward the anti-Christ's of this world, it is a window to hell.

It is our job as adults to take every opportunity to direct and build our children's faith and love in God as their savior and Lord, knowing that it is their very nature to do just the opposite. If they have childlike innocence, it is not because it is their nature to be that way, but only their lack of experience. Their nature is evil from birth, and unless they are born again, their childlike faith will be in the Devil, even if they never know him by name. He is the "unknown god" that most people bow to, who is hidden in the mirrors when we look at ourselves. Childlike faith is blinded by childlike evil, unless the Lord reaches down in His grace to open their eyes. Are we willing to be the Lord's healing hands in helping the blind to see?

Can You Compete with Horses?

"If you have raced with men on foot and they have worn you out,
how can you compete with horses?" Jer. 12:5

When I was a child, I heard about the great Olympian, Jessie Owens, challenging horses to a race in the one-hundred yard dash, and winning. I don't know about the truth of that story, but it was based upon the premise that a very fast man can beat a horse in a short sprint, for it takes a while for the horse to get up to full speed. In a longer race, however, there is no way that any man could beat the strength and endurance of the horse. Spiritually speaking, though, God does expect us to be able to compete with the horse's endurance and power. We are to persevere through even the greatest trials, as well as the very taxing daily grind, with victorious attitudes and joyful hearts.

Unfortunately, most of us have a hard enough time racing against feeble men, let alone the chariots of heaven. God wants us to be thoroughbreds, and we can't get past being stubborn mules. We wear ourselves out because we are "racing" with our own strength, and we whine more than we whinny. "I can't do this." "This is too hard." "Find someone else to do the hard stuff." "I just want to enjoy the lush green clover."

Jesus wants to mold us into His glorious image, but we are just stuck in the mud. He wants to use us to ride victoriously into battle, while we are satisfied with just rolling in the hay. We have blinders on all right, but they are not the blinders of a race horse. They are the blinders of self-centeredness, which keeps us focused more on our "heavenly fodder" than our Heavenly Father, and instead of becoming champions for Christ, we are just put out to pasture.

An Undivided Heart

"I will give them an undivided heart and put a new spirit in them;
I will remove from them their heart of stone." Ezekiel 11:19

Have you ever played tug of war--two sides pulling in opposite directions, using every ounce of energy to win the battle? Finally, one side becomes so weary, that they can't fight any more, and the stronger side always wins. Our hearts are the same way. We all have sinful, selfish natures that are pulling us one direction, and we have a conscience which pulls us the other way. This is true of Christian and non-Christian alike. However, the Christian has another dimension to deal with. He has a new nature with a "new spirit" in them, and the Holy Spirit to teach, encourage, and empower. The two natures still battle with one another over who will be the lord of our life, but when the Holy Spirit is in complete control, and we have the mind of Christ, the new nature is so much stronger than our sinful nature, that the Christian can walk victorious, with "an undivided heart" and a confidence in the power of our Lord.

It is like having a debate, and the judge decides on the victor before anyone even speaks. The victory has already been won through Jesus Christ, and no matter how much Satan would love to try to pull us back into the battle, all we have to do is to acknowledge that the Devil has already lost, so there is no longer any need for further debate. It doesn't do any good to argue about who should be president after the election is already over. It also doesn't do any good to let Satan pull us down and try to discourage us, as if we are the ones who are the losers, when we know that we have already won in Christ.

A heart that is divided is one that isn't quite sure who the winner is, or even who we want the winner to be. One thing for sure: if we continually let Satan win the spiritual skirmishes, our hearts will no longer just be divided. They will become "hearts of stone" that are too hardened to even respond to the gentle Holy Spirit speaking.

Can we imagine standing along the road when Jesus had his triumphal entry into Jerusalem, with all the crowd singing and shouting "Hallelujah", and us with our heads hanging low in depressed silence? It is time to give up our defeatist, pessimistic attitudes and to start claiming the victory that we already have in Christ. If we don't, even the stones may cry out.

A Spare Room in Heaven

"I am going there to prepare a place for you." John 14:2

I don't know what your image of heaven is, but I grew up dreaming of a mansion in heaven and streets of gold. Somehow it seemed to balance out all the misery in this world, if someday I would inherit a palace of my own, and be treated like the child of a king. Part of this interpretation of the future was based on the King James Version of the Bible, which says, "In my Father's house are many mansions" (John 14:2). In the original language, however, it doesn't say mansions. It says "rooms" or "dwelling places". This is a very different concept. Instead of my getting my own personal palace as a reward for my faithful service here on earth, I'm getting a spare bedroom in the King's own house. Not only that, but Jesus promised to prepare a room for each one of us. Not to be disrespectful, but the image I have in my mind is that of a housekeeper going to spruce up a room before the guests arrive. Nothing in the palace will belong to us. It is still the "Father's house". We have merely been invited to live there with him.

Yet, ownership and property isn't going to be as important to us up there as it is down here. Even the crowns that we get as rewards for our faithfulness, we are going to give right back to the King because we recognize that all the honor and glory belongs to him. We aren't going to be jealous, though, for in heaven our real reward is never being separated from God for eternity. Nothing else will be important. We won't need our own mansions. We will get to live with Jesus, and eat at the banqueting table of the Lamb of God. We will no longer have to go to the house of God on Sundays. We will be living in the house of God, and every day will be holy.

A Harmless Holiday?

"She had made a repulsive Asherah pole. Asa cut the pole down and burned it."
I Kings 15:13

It is hard for Christians to know what holidays to celebrate. There are the obviously pagan holidays, such as Halloween, that many Christians shun, yet others celebrate because it is fun, and there is so much peer pressure. Then, there are the traditionally Christian holidays, such as Christmas and Easter, yet, even these seem to have pagan traditions that go along with them. So, some Christians just try to avoid holidays all together in order to avoid controversy, except for May Day, which seems harmless enough. What could be wrong with celebrating the beginning of spring, taking flowers to our loved ones, and dancing around a Maypole with flowers in our hair and songs in our hearts?

The problem is that even May Day, with all of its simplicity and beauty, is also a pagan holiday. It is in honor of the goddess of the sea and fertility, Asherah. She was the prostitute or mistress of the god, Baal, and she was pictured as riding a lion, with a lily in one hand and a snake in the other. She was the goddess of every thing that was wild and untamed. The lily she carried was a symbol for the female sex organ, and the snake was a symbol for male sexuality. The wooden Asherah poles that were built in her name were also phallic symbols, or representative of the male sexual organ. On May Day, all of her followers danced around the Asherah poles, or May poles as we call them today, dressed in animal costumes and having sexual orgies in honor of their goddess and the season of fertility. According to ancient texts, though, it didn't stop there. She was a Sadist, and would often kill or torture her sexual partners while she was having sex with them. She was the original black widow, who mates and then kills her husband.

What was even more appalling in Old Testament times was the fact that these Asherah poles were built side by side with the Jewish altars that were used to sacrifice animals to God, Jehovah. It would have been bad enough if the Jews had just become idolaters, but they worshipped the Lord and the goddess at the same time. They celebrated the festivals of the Lord, but also celebrated the rituals of pagans.

Yet, don't we do the same thing? Some churches that I know actually have May Poles built on their church property right next to the cross. What on earth are we doing? While we dance and laugh around the Maypole, in "harmless" ecstasy, the Devil dances and laughs "at us", for we are blind fools and ignorant idolaters without even knowing it.

A Garden Before, a Desert Behind

"Before them the land is like the garden of Eden, behind them, a desert waste." Joel 2:3

This passage is dealing with the judgment of God. Before He comes, the land is like a beautiful garden. Yet, after He is finished, it is a wasteland. Of course, God doesn't always come in judgment. He also comes in blessing, turning deserts back into gardens. The problem with many people is that they are stuck in the first destructive mode, and they never get to the part where things are turned around for the better. God offers them so much, and they can see and taste the delights in the distance, but they can never quite get there. They are always seeking, but never finding; or, if they find the garden, they leave it trashed and ruined, instead of taking what they have, and expanding the blessing even more. Adam and Eve were like that. They didn't know or appreciate what God had given to them, so they trashed the garden by bringing death and sin into it, and God, the land Lord, kicked them out of their home for being poor tenants.

Instead of always asking God for more, what about asking Him to search our hearts, to see what we have done with what He has already given us? Have we taken His garden and turned it into a desert waste, or have we allowed Him to cultivate in us a Master piece of His design? The natural state of land is barrenness, and the only thing that grows naturally is weeds. If we have done nothing with what God has given us, it will revert back to its natural fallen state, and people will be able to tell where we have been by the devastation left in our wake. All of us make mistakes, for no one is perfect. Yet, even in our mistakes, we can be creative, like God, who can take the worst desert and turn it back into a beautiful garden. Instead of giving up and moving on to the next disaster, we need to yield to the Master Gardener, and watch Him create new life out of our dust.

May 2

Blasphemy of the Heart

*"Because he has despised the Lord's word and broken his commands,
that person must surely be cut off." Num. 15:30*

Blasphemy isn't something we usually talk about in our churches because we don't really believe that it applies to us. After all, Christians aren't the ones who are committing blasphemy. It's only those pagans on the outside. Right? Unfortunately, no. In fact, blasphemy probably happens far more in the pews than in the pubs.

What do I mean? First, it is necessary to understand what the word blasphemy means. Some people think that it just means using the Lord's name in vain. Others believe that it happens when a person says something really bad against God, his Word, or his truth, proclaiming heresy, or even claiming that God's miracles happen through the power of Satan. All of these definitions are correct, in a limited sense, but they are actually only naming the symptoms rather than the disease.

Blasphemy is not something that comes out of our mouths. It is something that takes place in our hearts. The Bible says that "anyone who sins defiantly…blasphemes the Lord…because he has despised the Lord's word" (Num. 15:30). Blasphemy, then, can happen even when a person never says a word. If a person knows what God wants them to do, and they defiantly refuse or disobey, they are blaspheming God in their hearts. They are showing that they despise God's word and God's authority in their lives. It is a spiritual "double negative". God says "don't", and they say "no".

Although this defiance can happen anywhere and anytime by anyone, it happens most often in church because that is where most Christians hear the word on a regular basis. Since most Christians do not read the Bible at home, they wait to be spoon-fed the scriptures by the hired man. It makes the Bible much more impersonal that way, so they can think in their mind that the preacher is talking to someone else. What they are doing, though, is committing blasphemy, for they are defiantly refusing to really listen or obey what the Bible is saying, which shows that they despise both God and his message.

It is true that this defiance sometimes comes out in the form of what they say, so others know they are blasphemous, but the blasphemy occurred in their hearts long before any word came out of their mouths. Many people believe that as long as you don't say it or do it, you haven't sinned. Jesus taught differently. He said that if you even think about something in your heart, you are guilty of committing the act also (Matt. 5:28).

So, have we committed any blasphemy lately? Unfortunately, most of us have blasphemed far more than we would like to admit, and some of us even as we read this devotional right now. Are we defiant? Do we despise what the Lord is trying to say to us right now? Blasphemy!

Bargaining with God

"Deal bountifully with me, Lord, and I will live and obey your commands."
Psa. 119:17

The problem with this idea of God's dealing bountifully with us is that of expecting reward because we feel that we deserve it. When we have lived a life that we feel is close to God, we can get a feeling that God owes us something. We say in our hearts, "Look, God—I've given up all these things for you, I've served you faithfully, and I don't have any known sin in my life—therefore, I expect some special blessings in my life." Out of our spiritual arrogance or self-righteousness, we make bargains with God. "If you treat me right, God, I will do what you want. If you answer my prayers the way that I want, I will live the way you want me to."

We turn the Word upside down by quoting the verse, "We love him because he first loved us" and changing the meaning to "I'm not going to show my love to you until you first show your love to me." It isn't enough that God already proved his love for us on the cross. We want more proof. We want him to be our spiritual Santa Claus and to give us all the gifts that we have listed on our "Most Wanted List." We are not satisfied if God is just providing our basic needs. We, like David, want him to "deal bountifully" with us. We not only want more, we expect more.

Sure, we were saved by grace alone, but we think rewards after salvation are different. Aren't we God's children now—part of the royal family? Didn't Jesus say to seek His kingdom first, and then he would give us all the other things that we want as a reward? That is how many Christians read into these passages. "God, if you give me what I want, then I'll obey you."

They don't understand that seeking the kingdom of God first means that they want Him not as some magical gift giver who supplies their every fantasy, but that they want him to be the Lord and master of their lives. They must submit their wills and desires to God, and be content with whatever God does or does not give them. Obedience must be absolute and unconditional, expecting nothing in return but what God's grace determines is for our best.

We are all sinners, fallen far short of the glory of God. What right do we have, then, to ask for heaven to be handed to us on a silver platter when we only deserve the broken pottery of the lowest hell? We shouldn't let our pride deceive us into thinking that we can even be in a bargaining position with God. If we think we can stand toe to toe with God, our God is too small.

At the End of my Rope

"I led them with cords of human kindness, with ties of love." Hosea 11:4

Freedom is cherished very highly, especially in western cultures. Children are brought up with the idea that freedom from the rules of their parents, teachers or any other authority figure is the ideal, and they can't wait to get out on their own. They want to be their own person and to do their own thing without any limitations except for the limits of their own imaginations. They push, shove, and pull at the boundaries to see how far they will stretch. They are diametrically opposed to the word "no", and will often do just the opposite of what is asked just to show their independence. Those who dare to put boundaries on them are looked at as the enemies, who are too old to understand that I just want to be "me".

At least that is what they think. They forget that their parents were young once too, and that they know by experience that life without boundaries only brings chaos and destruction. In fact, our human nature seems absolutely determined to destroy us before we are mature enough to understand what we are doing. That is why we need nurturing adults who will guide us along the way and keep us from diving off the nearest cliff just for the fun of it.

God, too, is a loving parent, who seeks to lead us "with cords of human kindness" and "with ties of love." The cords or ties of God are meant to give us as much freedom as possible, limited only by the protective spirit of God's love. He is not the enemy, any more than our parents, teachers, or the law, but is just trying to keep us going in the right direction so we can turn into productive, creative, fulfilled adults who find that real freedom or liberty only comes through knowing and obeying the Lord. We never have to try to escape the "ties" of God, for He only wraps us with His loving arms, and we are only bound by His love. If we ever feel that we are at the end of our rope, that's a good place to be, for that is where God is.

Are you a Doubting Thomas?

"Unless I see the nail marks in his hands and put my finger where the nails were, and put my hand into his side, I will not believe it." John 20:25

Have you ever done anything stupid, and because of that one foolish act, you now have a reputation that is built upon that one mistake? Maybe you got drunk once, and made a fool of yourself, and now people call you the town drunk. Or perhaps you were chubby when you were growing up, and now if you even put on ten pounds, people make fun of you as being the fatty again. People can be so cruel. Most of the time, though, people only make fun of others who are still alive.

In Thomas's case, however, I really doubt that the other disciples ever made fun of him for his lack of belief. It just happened that Thomas wasn't there when the resurrected Jesus first appeared to the other disciples. He wasn't the only one who doubted the risen Lord. When the ladies came back from the empty tomb and told them what the angels had said, none of them believed. They were all doubters. Yet, because Christ told Thomas, "Stop doubting and believe," Thomas has been labeled the doubter ever since, and anyone who even questions God today is given the derisive label of a "doubting Thomas" in his dubious honor.

If the truth be known, not only didn't Thomas doubt any more than any of the other disciples, he was one of the most committed and courageous of the disciples besides. Before Christ's crucifixion, Jesus had fled to the other side of the Jordon with his disciples because the Pharisees were seeking to kill him. When he heard about his friend, Lazarus, being sick unto death, he was going to go back to Judea to heal him. The disciples tried to talk him out of it. They said, "But rabbi, a short while ago the Jews tried to stone you, and yet you are going back there?" (John 11:8). When Jesus responded that he had to go because Lazarus was dead, and he was going to wake him, the disciples continued to try to dissuade him, except for Thomas, that is. Thomas boldly said to the rest of the disciples, "Let us also go, that we may die with him" (John 11:16). There was no doubt in his mind here. He was willing to die for the Lord, if necessary, and he was brave enough to try to talk the other disciples into laying their lives on the line as well.

In other words, doubting Thomas was not really a doubting Thomas after all in his day by day walk with the Lord. He was a totally committed Christian who actually had more faith than even the other disciples. If he doubted even the one time, he was not doubting Jesus, but the word of his friends. He didn't just blindly follow them when they tried to talk Jesus from going to heal Lazarus, and he didn't just believe them about the resurrection either. He wasn't a doubter. He was an independent thinker, who trusted Jesus completely, but questioned everyone else. We should seek to be more like him instead of making fun of him, and give him the honor that he is due.

Premeditated Sin

"If I had cherished sin in my heart, the Lord would not have listened."
Psa. 66:18

Cherish is a word that we usually use only when we are talking about a loved one or a precious treasure. The treasure may be a material object, like jewelry, a nostalgic keepsake, or something immaterial, such as a memory or special moment. The idea in either case, though, is one of attributing great value to something because of what it means to us personally, even if it means nothing to everyone else. For us to cherish sin, then, means to value it so highly that we would rather give up anything else, as long as we can keep our sin. It is like the pearl of great price, where the man sold everything he had in order to buy the field where he found the pearl. Nothing else mattered.

Christ uses this parable to talk about the great value of the kingdom of heaven, yet people also do the same thing for the kingdom of this world. Their sin is so precious to them that it is like an addiction, and no matter what others say, or how damaging it may be, they are not willing to give it up. For the non-believer, in fact, sin could be their whole lifestyle.

For the Christian, though, it is usually just one sin that we have a hard time giving up. For each one of us, it is probably a different sin, and even for ourselves, it probably will be a different sin during different periods of our lives. Yet, there is something about that one sin that is almost human to us. We are in love with it, and we have cherished it to the point that it has actually become a part of us or one with us, as in a marriage. We can't imagine living without it.

The second meaning to the word cherish goes along with this. It means to aim at something as a primary focus or goal. The kind of sin that we cherish, then, is not just any sin that we might commit along the way, even without thinking about it. This sin is so special to us, that we set it as a primary goal in our lives. We think about it all the time and even make elaborate plans on how we can indulge in our pleasure. We are like criminals planning out a crime, doing everything we can not to get caught. Our favorite sin is premeditated, willful, and devious. God and others may have spoken to us about it, if we have been discovered, but we refuse to give it up, or even to acknowledge that we have a problem. Just like the alcoholic, we are in denial.

Whether we like to admit it or not, we are slaves to our sin. We are in bondage, blind to the fact that we are even in jail. We are imprisoned, but not like someone who has been arrested against their will. We have willingly walked into the prison, locked the door, and said, "I think I like it here".

A Father to the Fatherless

"A father to the fatherless, a defender of widows…
God sets the lonely in families." Psa. 68:5-6

Loneliness is one of the biggest problems in the world today. Whether we are an orphan, a widow, or just feel like one, many people feel isolated and alienated from the world around them. We feel like tiny islands in the middle of turbulent oceans. Well, God understands that sense of isolation. Even Christ on the cross felt abandoned and alone when he cried out, "Father, father. Why have you forsaken me?" When we feel abandoned, though, God has promised to always be there for us. He will never leave us or forsake us.

That is hard to comprehend when we live in a world where parents often leave their children at home alone while they go to work or go on vacation, or even leave them with friends or relatives, and just don't come back. How can we relate to God being our heavenly Father when our own parents have neglected us or abused us? Yet, God patiently and tenderly draws us to himself, knowing that we might have trouble trusting Him because people around us have been untrustworthy. He gains our confidence through His consistent, faithful love, forgiveness and provision for our needs. Even when everyone else lets us down, we learn that we can depend on Him. He is a father to the fatherless, a husband to the widows, and a friend to the lonely.

One of the provisions that He has made for our loneliness is by adopting us into his own family. We not only have a Father in heaven, we have brothers and sisters here on earth. The church is our family. Just as we don't always get along with our natural families, there are going to be conflicts with some of our spiritual family as well. Yet, warts and all, they are still part of our family. We need them, and they need us. Even though we may feel like being more independent, God wants us to belong. He tells us not to forsake the bonding times that He wants us to have with our spiritual brothers and sisters (Heb. 10:25). He has placed the lonely into families so they can be encouraged and strengthened by the power of unity that is often lacking in individuality.

Even if we are not lonely, and we don't feel that we need anyone else, there are others who need us. The Bible tells us that "Christ came not into the world to be ministered unto, but to minister" (Matt. 20:28). The same thing should be true of us. When we join a church fellowship, it should not be with the motivation, "What can I get out of this?" It should always be, "Lord, how do you want me to use my spiritual gifts to encourage and build up this body of Christ?" If our emphasis is reaching out to meet the needs of others, our own needs will be met, and God will bless us with spiritual riches that we never would have received if we just sought to meet our own needs. We are part of God's family, and every meeting should be a family "re-union".

The Majestic Mule

"Praise be to the Lord, to God our Savior, who daily bears our burdens."
Psa. 68:19

Picture for a moment the Israelites, with David as their king, marching out into battle. They all have their weapons, their clothes, their food, their tents and cooking supplies. They need to travel long distances to fight their enemies, and they need to plan for being gone for a long time. They can't carry all of their supplies themselves for they are too heavy and the journey is too long. If they tried, they would be too tired to fight. So they use pack animals. They use horses and mules, and maybe even some camels, and they march off to war.

In one sense, this is what happens with us each day. We are in a spiritual warfare. Every day we get our marching orders for where he wants us to fight the battle. Yet, we cannot do it alone. We need the help of other believers standing with us, and we need the help of the Lord. In Psa. 68 it portrays a majestic picture of God riding into battle with thousands of chariots at his command. He scatters the enemy, and the earth quakes before Him. It is a picture of power and royalty. Yet, at the same time, it says that He bears our burdens for us.

Wait a minute! How can He be pictured as a king and mighty warrior one moment, and then as a servant or pack animal the next? It seems like a terrible contradiction. Yet, this is exactly what happened when Christ came to the world. He offered Himself as the king of the Jews, and then offered Himself as the sacrifice for the entire world. There is constantly the paradox of his joint divinity and humanity—his right to rule, but his submission even unto death—his being the king of kings, but coming to serve and minister to others. He is the majestic mule. He both leads the way through the treacherous terrain, and carries our burdens for us.

We are weak, and He is strong. Yet, His strength is not just in His fighting our battles for us. It is in His loving, unconditional servant's heart toward us. He is willing to do anything for us to help us to win. He will fight beside us, lift us when we fall, give us nourishment to keep us strong, give us encouragement and guidance on how to do our best, and even carry the burden of all of our needs while we fight. He fights with one arm, and carries our tent and backpack with the other. He is God, our savior, who also carries our burdens. He is the owner of the hotel, and the bellboy at the same time.

He is also our best example. It is so easy to get puffed up about who we are, or how important we are, and pastors or church leaders are no exception. Regardless of our position in the church, we are given our spiritual gifts to help others, not for self-glorification. We may be children of the king, but we are also meant to be his servants. We need to be willing to be ministering mules, just like the Master.

Carefree and Condemned

"This is what the wicked are like—always carefree." Psa. 73:12

The world holds up the ideal of being carefree as if it is the highest goal that man could attain. Just think about it—no worries, financial freedom to do whatever we want, money to burn, time to relax—a fantasy existence of heaven on earth. It seems, in fact, that there actually are people who experience this fantasy. We see them all the time in the media—driving around in fancy cars, living in mansions, power, fame, and always a smile on their faces. It makes us both envious and confused. We can't understand why they have all this, and we don't.

How can someone who doesn't know God seem to be happy and successful? Is it just an act, where they are pretending to be happy, but they are really miserable inside? Although this is probably true in many cases, it is also true that many are really happy. How can this be? Shouldn't non-believers be miserable and guilt ridden? We as Christians often think so, yet this is not the case. The truth is that many non-Christians are happier and more content with their lives than the believers. Although some feel guilty from time to time when they do something wrong, a truly evil person feels no guilt at all.

The reason they are so carefree is that they have "callous hearts" (Psa. 73:7). They don't care about anyone but themselves, and are completely oblivious to any hurt that they have done to others. "They scoff and speak with malice; in their arrogance they threaten oppression" (Psa. 73:8). They have "zombie souls", where there is a lot of activity, but no life or feelings. Their pride is so great, that they think they are invincible and omnipotent. They think that they can do whatever they want and get away with it. The Bible says, "The evil conceits of their minds know no limits" (Psa. 73:7).

Unfortunately, these wicked, heartless people are not just outside the church. This passage also says that they often claim to be believers, but their god is really their possessions and the power they have in this world. It says, "Their mouths lay claim to heaven, and their tongues take possession of the earth…They say, 'How can God know?'…This is what the wicked are like" (Psa. 73:9-12). They are so arrogant, that they think they are good enough for heaven, at the same time that they don't even believe that God knows what they are doing. The problem at church is that these people are often the leaders, who always have a smile on their face, because they are carefree, and we think it is because they are close to God. We are fooled by people's appearances, but their true hearts are revealed by the way that they treat others.

The Bible says that we shouldn't be discouraged by these people. It says, "When I tried to understand all this, it was oppressive to me till I entered the sanctuary of God; then I understood their final destiny" (Psa. 73:16-17). They may be carefree now, but their destiny is condemnation. They won't be smiling forever.

A Doorkeeper for Christ

*"I would rather be a doorkeeper in the house of my God
than dwell in the tents of the wicked." Psa. 84:10*

Being a doorkeeper sounds like an official position, like a security guard posted at the door to keep undesirables out. In fact, there were such people assigned to that duty at the Old Testament tabernacle (I Chron. 15:23-24). They were there to protect the arc of the covenant and Holy place, to make sure that no one entered without permission, or defiled the temple in any way. Yet, the meaning of the word "doorkeeper" here is not talking about this position. It means someone who lies down at the threshold. This would not be the temple guard, but the misfit who was not allowed in to the temple. They were the beggars seeking handouts from the people as they were entering the sanctuary.

This reminds us of the woman who came to Jesus asking him to heal her child. At first, he said no because she was a Gentile, and he only came to help the Jews (Matt. 15:27). However, when she said that even the dogs get crumbs from their master's table, he healed the child. When the psalmist tells us, then, that he would rather lie down at the threshold of the temple than to dwell in the house of the wicked, he is saying that even the spiritual crumbs that he might get as an unworthy beggar at the temple would be of far greater worth than any pleasures that he might get from living in sin. He might be a misfit in the eyes of the world, but God in His mercy still reaches down to him in love and compassion.

He is not just talking about the value of going to church. Some Christians feel that they have to be in church every time the doors are open, but this verse is not saying that. We get so program-centered and activities-centered in our churches, that we place guilt trips on our members if they don't show up all the time. The important thing here is not the temple, but it is where the presence of God is. God's presence actually came down into the Holy of Holies to speak to the High Priest. People came there to make themselves right with God. It wasn't about meetings for the whole family, or social activities for everyone. It was about meeting the Lord, asking forgiveness, and seeking Him.

Dwelling at the threshold, then, was a special place, for that was as close as many people ever got to God. Today, our hearts are the Holy of Holies, for we have the presence of God within us. We don't have to stand outside begging at the door, hoping for just a morsel of bread. We have an intimate connection and oneness with the High Priest, Jesus Christ. He is the bread of life, and we have partaken of Him. Yet, we still need to come to Him with the same urgency and longing that a beggar might, with open hands and hearts, anxiously waiting even a word of wisdom from our Lord. Hearing that one word, or sharing in one moment of fellowship with the Lord at His threshold, should be more valuable than anything in this world.

A Good Conscience

"I have fulfilled my duty to God in all good conscience to this day." Acts 23:1

Unfortunately, there are not many people who can make this statement. They may have lived a good life, and kept their actions under control, but when it comes to the internal conscience, that is a different story. One problem is that the conscience is not always reliable. It can become calloused from sin, and no longer be sensitive to the conviction of the Holy Spirit. It can also be misleading, making us believe that what we are doing is right, when it is really wrong.

For example, the Israelites often rebelled against God, even though they knew what they were doing was wrong. However, they also sinned by "doing what was right in their own eyes", even though it was contrary to God's will (Judges 17:6). They thought they were doing the right thing, their conscience was clear, but there was no one in leadership at the time to tell them any different. They were like sheep without a shepherd, wandering wherever they wanted. Someone can have a clear conscience, then, because of ignorance. It has nothing to do with being right with God. They just don't know any better.

It is possible, though, for someone to be very knowledgeable about the things of the Lord, and sincerely seeking to follow Him, and yet still be sinning. It is called spiritual blindness. The Apostle Paul was an example of this kind of blindness. He was raised a devout Jew, had studied the scriptures thoroughly, and was completely committed to serving the Lord by aggressively seeking to weed out heresy. His conscience was clear, but he was absolutely wrong. He was fighting against Jesus and his followers because he thought they were heretics blaspheming the law of God. He was zealous for God at the same time that he was fighting against Him, without even knowing it.

God set him straight, though, by healing his spiritual blindness, and making him a spokesman for the truth instead. Having a clear conscience wasn't good enough. He had to have his mind and heart transformed, so that the Holy Spirit could guide his conscience, instead of just his own natural sense of right and wrong. Once he gave his heart to God completely, he was able to say that he did everything with a clear conscience, for he always had. Yet, now it was from God's perspective and not just his own. Of course, the religious leaders of his day were appalled by the fact that Paul would even say such a thing. They lived in a realm of rigid laws and rules made by men. No one, from their perspective, could have a completely clear conscience, even though they self-righteously felt they had come pretty close.

One of the joys of being a Christian is that in spite of the fact that we are not perfect, we are forgiven, and we can have assurance from the Holy Spirit that we are right with God. What more could we ask for?

Vile Things

"I will set before my eyes no vile thing." Psa. 101:3

Usually we think of vile things as things which are immoral, such as pornography. Yet, the word "vile" is not limited to just immorality. It can also refer to anything that is worthless, foolish, or wicked. Considering the TV programs, supermarket tabloids and magazines that we have today, we would almost need to walk around with bags over our heads to avoid seeing "vile things". In fact, there is so much around us that is just plain worthless or foolish, we have become desensitized to it. It doesn't bother us the way that it should because it is so commonplace.

Yet, this verse is not talking about just "seeing things". We cannot live in this world without seeing things that we shouldn't. God doesn't want us to be hermits. He wants us not to set things before us which are vile as goals or ideals to imitate. They are not to become idols, things which we value more than God. They are not to become the focus of our lives. Anything which pulls us away from our focus of following God is vile.

In sports we often hear that an athlete didn't catch or hit a ball because he took his eyes off the ball. The same thing happens spiritually speaking when we take our eyes off Christ and divert our attention to seeking something else instead. This is not just an act of ignorance or not knowing any better. To be vile implies wickedness, which involves willful choices to rebel. We know something is wrong, worthless, or foolish, but we pursue it anyway. It could involve greed, envy or lust of something that we know we shouldn't have because its power over us is stronger than our desire to obey the Lord. It is degrading because it pulls us down into the depths of our depravity, and makes us a slave to things that we would be embarrassed about if someone we loved or respected knew about it. Yet, we ignore the fact that God knows about everything. We need to ask ourselves not only, "What would Jesus do?", but "What would I do if Jesus was standing right here watching me?", for he really is, whether we see him or not.

We idealize freedom in our society so much that we think that means that we should have the freedom to watch whatever movies we want, read "beach blanket books", and watch endless hours of TV which may be completely worthless, all in the name of entertainment. What we don't think about is that all the hours that we waste seeking worthless pleasure or empty escapism could have been spent doing things which would actually draw us closer to God.

The Bible says, "All things are lawful for me, but not all things are edifying" (I Cor. 10:23). We should be looking at things which build us up, not tear us down, especially since the Hebrew word for vile is also the root for "villain", and it is used in the New Testament to speak of the Devil, himself, with the name, "Belial". To think vile thoughts, then, is to be focused on Satan, the greatest villain of them all.

The Prayer of Perdition

"May his prayers condemn him." Psa. 109:7

There are some things in life which are meant to be very special and should be treated with respect and honor. An example of this is the physical bond between husband and wife. In its proper context, in holy matrimony, as an expression of love and unity in Christ, it is a beautiful, consecrated thing. If we take it out of this context, however, it is not only immoral, but condemned. According to the law, people who commit adultery are to be executed (Lev. 20:10). It is not considered just a "moment of indiscretion" or "meaningless mistake" as it often is today. It is a capital offensive worthy of death. I wonder how many Christians would be on death row right now if this was still the law of the land.

Yet, there is another sin which is considered even worse than this by the Lord. It is the prayer of the wicked. Don't misunderstand me. The Lord wants sinners to pray when they are repentant and seeking forgiveness. The prayer that is condemned is the prayer of the wicked person who comes before the Lord in all of his arrogance, hypocrisy and hard-hearted rebellion as if he is facing God as an equal, rather than as his Heavenly Father. This kind of prayer is denounced by Christ, himself, when he gives the parable of the Pharisee and the tax-collector (Luke 18:10). Here the Pharisee gets up in the middle of the marketplace and boldly proclaims, "God, I thank you that I am not like other men—robbers, evildoers, adulterers—or even like this tax collector." Jesus denounces his self-righteous egotism and the foolishness of his prayer. We never, even as Christians, have the right to come before the Lord in our pride as if we were worthy enough to stand before Him. On the other hand, we always have the privilege of coming to Him in prayer when we are humble before Him. The wicked person has no such humility. Instead, in his arrogance, he never thinks "of doing a kindness," but hounds "to death the poor and the needy and the brokenhearted" (Psa. 109:16). He loves "to pronounce a curse" upon others, but finds "no pleasure in blessing" those in need. He is heartless, self-centered, mean, cruel and hateful. Yet, he has the arrogant nerve to pray to God as if they are old friends on good terms. It is his prayer that condemns him, even more than his actions towards others.

We know that it is blasphemy to curse God. It is also blasphemy to pray to him from a wicked, non-repentant heart. It is using the Lord's name in vain, for the Lord will not answer his proud plea. Yet, it isn't just a matter of God not listening. God hears his every word, but condemns him for his blatant unholy prayer. It is not a prayer of repentance, but a prayer of perdition, for it is authored by the son of perdition, himself, Satan. It is the Devil's disguise to try to get his own way, thinking that he can lie to God by hiding behind the prayer of one of his followers. It is a prayer designed in hell.

Godlessness and Wickedness

"The wrath of God is being revealed from heaven against all the godlessness and wickedness of men who suppress the truth by their wickedness." Rom. 1:18

At first glance, Godlessness and wickedness seem to be the same thing. In some ways they are very similar, tied together by a common cord of evil. Yet, in other ways, they are far apart. Godlessness means they have left God out of their lives. There is a vacuum there. God is a non-entity. They don't think about God anymore than we, as Christians, might think of a pagan god. To them, he is just a figment of our imaginations. So, they live their lives devoid of God in every way. They never even consider what God might think about their actions, for he doesn't exist.

On the other hand, the wicked person knows that there is a God, but he has purposely rebelled against his authority. As the scriptures tell us, "Although they knew God, they neither glorified him as God nor gave thanks to him" (Rom. 1:21). In this case, it is not a matter of ignorance or just omission. The wicked person "knows" God, but has rejected Him. He is an anti-God or an anti-Christ. They know the truth, just as Satan knows the truth, but they refuse to accept it or obey it. "They exchanged the truth of God for a lie" (Rom. 1:25).

Why would someone willingly reject something that they know is true? Just as is true with Satan, the problem is pride. They do not want to be accountable to anyone but themselves. They want to be their own god. Why, then, would they want to build idols to worship? The Bible says that they "worshiped and served created things rather than the Creator." They "exchanged the glory of the immortal God for images made to look like mortal man and birds and animals and reptiles" (Rom. 1:23). The wicked person has a desperate desire for God, at the same time that he rebels against him. So he creates his own gods, whether actual images or just materialistic pleasures, as substitutes for his need for the divine. He "exchanges the glory of the immortal God" for something that he has created himself, making him the creator or god of his own world. His idols are created in his image, just as we are created in God's. They reflect who he really is, lifeless and meaningless. They are flaming fires without light, always devouring, but never giving.

What happens when a person becomes wicked and totally denounces God? The Bible says that their thinking becomes futile and their foolish hearts become darkened (Rom. 1:21). They become blinded by the dark shadow of their own inflated ego. They are rushing toward hell, but are excited by the wild ride. The result is that God gives them over to their sinful desires, and there is a downward spiral into greater and greater sin (Rom. 1:24). On the other hand, the Godless person might actually be a good, moral person. It is possible, then, for a person to be Godless without being wicked. A wicked person, though, is bent on going to hell, and can't wait to get there.

Sow in Tears

"Those who sow in tears will reap with songs of joy." Psa. 126:5

Imagine for a moment being an Israelite and being torn from your home by the enemy. You are taken to a foreign land where you become a slave to a pagan ruler, with no hope of every seeing your homeland again. You know in your heart of hearts that you are in captivity as a result of your sin, for not only you, but your whole nation has fallen into idolatry. You have abandoned the faith of your fathers, and now you are reaping the consequences. There is much weeping and gnashing of teeth, but it does you no good. Your tears are tears of feeling sorry for yourself, not of repentance, so you wallow and whine in your self-pity, but God looks the other way. Finally, God melts your heart through your hardships, and you fall on your knees before Him. You confess your rebellious heart, and make yourself right with God.

All is forgiven, yet the consequences of your sin are still there. You still have to get up every morning and serve a godless master, and your tears of remorse and prayers for help seem to no avail. Then, at the very point when you are broken to despair, you hear the news that you are being set free. You are no longer going to be a slave. You are free to go home. What exuberant joy! You want to dance, sing, and shout from the highest mountain! "Praise God, from whom all blessings flow!" In spite of your sin and idolatrous blasphemy, God's mercy has given you another chance. You know you don't deserve it—just the opposite. Yet, God's grace has not only forgiven you, but set you free to live in peace and harmony with Him. You have a future with God because He has wiped the slate clean from your past. This is the first day of the rest of your life. That's all that matters. You have sown in tears, but God, through his mercy, has allowed you to experience a joy that only the forgiven can know.

Not everyone is this fortunate. Some people have to live with the consequences of their sin for their whole lives. They have been forgiven, but they are still in captivity to their guilt or the natural results of self-destructive behavior. They just can't seem to break away from the grip that their pasts have upon them. It is here also that tears need to be sown, not just by the individual who is suffering, but by others in the body of Christ who feel their pain. They know what it is like to be enslaved and set free, and so they pray earnestly for the souls of the broken-hearted. They reach out to the wounded spirits, and tearfully pray for their spiritual healing. When one of these "bruised reeds" finally finds peace and freedom to grow past the past, there is a joy that surpasses even the joy that we feel for ourselves. What an exciting privilege to know that our tears have helped to water the flowers of joy in another, and brought forth a great harvest that keeps on producing. Can we pray for others and cry for them too? Their peace and joy may depend on it.

The Three Roads to Eternity

"Those who turn to crooked ways, the Lord will banish with the evildoers."
Psa. 125:5

Imagine that you have a long trip to take, and you need to plan out the journey. You can either take the interstate freeway, which is wide and well-paved, or a very narrow, rough road, which is also very straight. Which would you take? Most people would take the freeway because it is easier. The same thing is true about the journey of life. Jesus tells us to "enter through the narrow gate. For wide is the gate and broad is the road that leads to destruction. But small is the gate and narrow the road that leads unto life, and only a few find it" (Matt. 7:13, 14). Most people choose the wide road because it is easier. It doesn't matter that their destination is hell. They are living for the here and now.

The Bible, though, talks about a third road to eternity. It's also a narrow road, like the road to heaven, but this one goes to hell. There aren't very many people on this road, for it is the old highway that winds and twists its way up the steep mountains, sometimes merging with the new, wider freeway, but most of the time off on side roads, through dark tunnels and deep caverns. It is the road of true evil or wickedness. There are a lot of people who are lost, but only a few who choose to be wicked. They are the anti-Christ's of this world. The Bible calls this the "crooked path", for there is something terribly twisted about this pathway and these people. They want to bring down as many people as they can with them. They are not just lost. They are the enemy.

The Bible is our war manual. It helps us to identify our enemy, and trains us how to fight against them by avoiding the pot-holes and land-mines that they leave in our paths. Here are some of the words that are used to describe those on this crooked road—"warped" (Deut. 32:5), "evildoers" (Psa. 125:5), "devious" (Prov. 2:15), "perverted" (Prov. 8:8), "unjust" (Isa. 59:8), lack integrity (Prov. 10:9), and "depraved" (Phil. 2:15). Do we know anyone who is on this path? Perhaps we work with them, or even live with them.

The Bible says, "To the pure, show yourself pure, but to the crooked, show yourself shrewd" (Psa. 18:26). In other words, be wise, be cautious, and be on your guard. Jesus tells us to be "shrewd as snakes, and innocent as doves" (Matt. 10:16), for we are like "sheep among wolves". The crooked path is like a twisted chain, and those who are on it will try to use it to bind us, trip us, and beat us up. Being on the straight and narrow path does not protect us from their attacks. It makes us their targets. That is why we need to be wearing the "full armor of God" (Eph. 6:11).

All roads lead to eternity. It's just that some lead to eternal life and others to eternal death. Unfortunately, there are a lot of intersections where the roads cross paths along the way, and there are a lot of tragic collisions. It is our job to keep from being one of the casualties, and to keep our eyes on the road ahead.

The Rising Sun

"The path of the righteous is like the first gleam of dawn, shining ever brighter till the full light of day." Prov. 4:18

Everyone loves a beautiful sunset. It is a perfect ending to a romantic evening, as the glory of God is splashed across the sky in vivid colors. The poets and song writers love to sing of its praises. Yet, there isn't the same enthusiasm about the sunrise. Maybe that is because not as many people see the sunrise. They are still in bed dreaming and reliving the wonderful time they had the night before, or procrastinating having to deal with the new day ahead. One of my favorite times, though, is the dawn of a new day. I get up long before the sun rises because I can't wait for it to start. Then, the light of the sun gently diffuses the darkness, starting slowing, then quickly filling the entire sky.

Although we might wish for a sunset to last a lot longer, extending the pleasure of a magic moment, we are glad when the dawn rushes into full daylight. Dawn is just a spark, and we can't wait for the full flame. In fact, we would be greatly disappointed if the dawn lingered, and the sun decided to stay in bed a little longer.   We are anxious for the light and its warmth to fill us. We can even check the newspaper to find out the exact moment when the sun will rise, and we expect it to be on schedule. No tardiness is allowed.

Our Christian walk is supposed to be the same way. The Bible says, "The path of the righteous is like the first gleam of dawn, shining ever brighter till the full light of day." Before we became Christians, we were living in darkness. We could see some light, the stars of the Christians around us, but our own dark souls overshadowed their radiance. Then, God's light dawned within, and new truth was illumined before us. We could see and understand things that we were blind to before, and the cold, deep darkness of our hearts was gently replaced by the rising Son, Jesus. It is resurrection morning all over again, and we are risen with our precious Lord.

Yet, the dawn is supposed to continue "shining ever brighter till the full light of day." Many of us never seem to get past the dawn. We are holding on to the darkness of the night, reluctant to give up any pleasures that we had hidden in the veil of the shadows. We straddle the horizon, with one leg still in yesterday, and the other stepping into today. We are supposed to be moving on, growing, "ever shining brighter", but we are stuck on being just "dim". God wants us to be glowing examples of His love and grace to the world on the mountain tops, but we are satisfied with just being a fading twinkle of what might have been.

It's time to move past the fireworks of the sunsets, or the falling stars of the night, and press on to the new day of walking with the Lord in the light of His love and truth, ever seeking to share that light with others.

Foolish Fire

"Can a man scoop fire into his lap without his clothes being burned?" Prov. 6:27

Occasionally we hear about people who have accidentally spilled a cup of hot water or coffee on themselves and been badly burned. It's a tragedy that can happen to young and old alike. If the hot liquid is not wiped off immediately and ice put on it quickly, the heat will continue burning deeper and deeper. No one in their right mind would spill hot fluid on themselves on purpose. One would have to be crazy.

King Solomon compares this situation with someone who has fallen into the snare of a prostitute or had an affair. It is compared to pouring a scoop of fire into one's lap. It may be a blazing adrenaline rush, but it is going to have disastrous consequences. We can't expect to play with fire without getting burned. It is just common sense. Yet, when it comes to areas of morality, we sometimes test the limits. We want to get as close to the flame as possible, hoping for the heat, but thinking we can pull back fast enough before we become engulfed by the flames. We don't like limits to our freedom, so we constantly try to stretch the boundaries, thinking we can get away with it, even if no one else can. We know there are dangers, but life without risk is no life at all, we think to ourselves. We are thrill seekers, and a certain amount of danger is desired. We know there must be limits, but we want to be the ones who set them. When the Bible tells us, then, "You will reap what you sow", we don't care. So what if we have to learn the hard way, we say, as long as we experience the excitement of life on the edge. It will be worth it. At least we think this way when we are young. When we become older, we become a little bit more cautious. Yet, even in old age, we can become bored with life, and we start stretching the boundaries again.

When will we ever learn? There are negative consequences to sin. This doesn't just apply to sexual immorality. Any kind of sin is like a spark that could start a forest fire of self-destruction. It might be a single lie that could cause us to lose our job or destroy our reputation. It might be only one time of excess at a bar that leads to a drunk driving death and a prison term. It might be only one unwise sexual encounter, and a lifetime of suffering from a sexually transmitted disease or an unwanted pregnancy. Little sins build up to bigger flames, and before we know it, they can consume us. We can become addicted to them, or calloused to them, and we need more and more to get the same thrill. They can not only burn our clothes, but our souls, and the souls of others who are close to us.

Is the magic of the moment really worth the years of torment that may follow? Whether we like to admit it or not, we are not invincible. It is only by the grace of God that we have not paid more dearly for the foolish fire that we have already set ablaze in our lives. If we take His grace for granted, our faith may go up in smoke.

It's Refreshment Time

"A generous man will prosper; he who refreshes others will himself be refreshed."
Prov. 11:25

Everyone is working hard, or attending classes or meetings, and then we discover, its refreshment time or break time. It may not be more than a few minutes, a cup of coffee or a donut, yet it is looked forward to by us all. It gives us the rest, or the energy, or the stress release that we need to continue on. It is a mini-vacation, of sorts, and we feel cheated if we are asked to miss it for the sake of the business. We are possessive of "the pause", and we are psychologically dependant upon it, as much as, if not more than, the need for physical rest.

The same thing is true spiritually speaking. This is one of the reasons that we were given the Sabbath day as a day of rest. We need a day of spiritual refreshment. Yet, we also need the moments of "time out", as well. We need times of quiet meditation, prayer, scripture reading, and listening to God to be refreshed by His spirit, so we can have the strength to carry on. We can't afford to just commune with God once a week. We need the spiritual refreshment breaks throughout the day. When we are caught up in the rat race, we need to take time to listen to the maker of the rats. A marathon runner doesn't just drink water at the end of the race. He takes deep drinks periodically throughout the race, knowing that his body needs refreshing while he is exerting energy, not just when he is finished.

The one who wins the race, though, is not the one who only seeks refreshment for himself. It is the generous man who will prosper, for "he who refreshes others will himself be refreshed". The King James Version puts it this way: "The liberal soul shall be made fat". The word liberal here is not talking about politics. It means "generous" or "giving". In other words, if our emphasis or focus is on serving others and meeting their needs, then our own needs will be met in abundance. The word "fat" here does not mean bodily stoutness. The purpose of fat is stored energy and heat, so that in times of severe cold or hunger, our fat can provide the nourishment and warmth that our body needs to survive. Spiritual fat is the same way. We need to have storehouses in our souls that are filled with spiritual energy and power, faith and truth, so that when we are tested by the trials of life, we can respond with wisdom and strength.

Ironically, the more we share with others what God has given to us, the more He trusts us with, so we can be ready for the next time. We give refreshing waters of blessings to others, like a lake giving forth water through evaporation, and then we receive even more in return when God multiplies the blessings as He rains His love and goodness upon us. His showers of blessings cool us down and fill us up, so we can, in turn, share them with others. If water is just stationary and self-contained, it only becomes stagnant. So do we.

Chasing Fantasies

"He who chases fantasies lacks wisdom." *Prov. 12:11*

One of the attractions at Disney Land is "Fantasy Land". It is filled with fairies, Tinker Bell's, Cinderella's, and dreams. It is not meant to be a picture of reality. It is a world of make-believe, the imagination, and the idealistic. It is what we might wish the world to be like if we could stay children all of our lives. Unfortunately, many of us do stay children all of our lives, for we refuse to grow up. We would rather stay in our fantasy worlds of escapism and pleasure, rather than being the responsible, mature adults that we should be.

In the Midwest, there are people called "tornado trackers" or "storm chasers", who instead of running from the storms, actually head toward them so they can live the excitement of the moment. They aren't scientists studying natural phenomenon, they are adrenaline rush addicts. They want to be like Dorothy in the *Wizard of Oz* and be caught up in a mystical tornado of magical self-realization and fulfillment. It doesn't matter if they are dashed to the ground in the process. They want to enjoy the wild ride.

Not everyone, though, is a thrill seeker. Many people who chase fantasies are just unrealistic. They attend college, even though they know they are not good students, just so they can get away from home and continue their adolescence for a while. They buy enormous quantities of things that they don't really need on their credit cards, thinking that having it all means happiness. They go from one sexual relationship to another, confusing physical intimacy with true love. They move from job to job, or church to church, always thinking that utopia or perfection is just around the corner. In other words, they are chasing fantasies that do not exist in the real world. Instead of having "wis-dom", they are just plain "dumb".

First of all, the beginning of true wisdom is the fear of the Lord. When we fear God the way we should, we don't waste our time living for the frivolous. Fairy fluff and frou-frou just don't match up to the fulfillment of faith. The only reason that people chase fantasies is because their relationship with God is either totally lacking, or so shallow that their fantasies seem like upgrades to the real thing. The world offers all kinds of substitutes for a real relationship with the divine, from drugs to the occult, yet none of them truly satisfies or meets the need. We think we need a fairy godmother, and what our soul needs is the Heavenly Father. What we want to be is Peter Pan searching for eternal youth, yet, we end up being another Peter, who denies Christ every time the stress gets too great.

What we hope for is a life full of fun and games, where everything goes our way, and God is Santa Claus showering gifts on us all the time. What we get is a God who loves us enough to die for our sins, and who demands that we take up our cross and follow Him. God wants disciples, not dream-catchers.

Beware of the Gull-Catchers

"A simple man believes anything." Prov. 14:15

It's very frustrating when you go out and buy a new carpet, or a new couch, or new clothes, and then, that very same day, to spill some food on it which leaves a permanent stain. Now-a-days, we have chemicals that we can spray on to the fabrics to keep them from absorbing the stains. What a blessing! They look the same, but they are now less vulnerable to damage. As people, we need the same kind of protection. Some of us are particularly vulnerable because we are tenderhearted and impressionable, which makes us super-sensitive and super-absorbent. We come into contact with another person, and their character rubs off on us. We want to be like them or to be liked by them. We are people pleasers.

If this describes us, we are probably often confused, frustrated and hurt. In our mind, being tenderhearted is a good thing, which it is. Unfortunately, it can also mean that we have no backbone. We have a hard time saying, "No". The problem is not in the softness of our heart, but the softness of our brain. We are not thinking things through carefully enough, for we follow our heart instead of using good judgment. If it feels right, we decide that it must be right.

This makes us easy targets for those people in the world who love to manipulate others. They are the con-artists of the world. They are the magicians of the emotions. They can put words into our ears and pull out of our hearts anything they want. We want to please them, so we yield to their charming personality, and we become the rabbit that they pull out of the hat. We are the "simple man" or woman that the Bible talks about who "believes anything".

The word that we use today for this is "gullible". This word means that we can easily be mislead or deceived because we want to believe in others to the point that we trust them too much. We are taken advantage of over and over again, even by the same people, because we want to believe that they are really good people, and the first times must have just been mistakes.

Besides being called con-artists, these people are also called "gull-catchers". Their main goal in life is to "catch the gullible" off-guard so they can use them and abuse them for their own pleasures. They may be charming, but they don't really care about us. They are taking advantage of our tender hearts to fill their own stomachs. In other words, if "Brother John" on TV asks us for money so he can send food to the starving children in Africa, but he looks as if he has eaten enough for the whole orphanage, we might want to reconsider giving away our inheritance.

It is more important to trust in God and to please Him than it is to please the smooth talking salesmen of the world. Be wise. Be cautious. Beware of the gull-catchers. They'll eat your heart out.

The Carpenter Family

"Unless the LORD builds the house, its builders labor in vain." Psa. 127:1

Everyone knows that Jesus was a carpenter, for his earthly father, Joseph, was a carpenter. This is one of the reasons that the Jewish leaders were thrown off guard, for they expected the Messiah to be a priest who would rise in power, save them from their enemies, and become king of the Jews (Zech. 6:13). Of course, from our perspective, looking back with the help of scripture, we can see how Jesus did fulfill this prophecy, and was both priest and king. Yet, they were confused by his earthly vocation. Jesus just didn't seem to match the pedigree. They were looking for someone who was more majestic and godlike, not just a commoner.

Jesus, however, was just following in his father's footsteps—not only Joseph's, but the Heavenly Father's. The Bible talks about God the Father being a carpenter too. It says, "Unless the LORD builds the house, its builders labor in vain." The word for LORD here is Yahweh, which refers to God the Father, not the son. God the Father set the example from the beginning, and the Son followed His steps.

Even Zechariah, when he prophesied about the coming Messiah, not only said that he would be a priest and king, but a builder, as well. He said, "He shall build the temple of the LORD" (Zech. 6:12). The Messiah was supposed to build his Father's house. This is interesting because Solomon was the one who wrote the psalm which says, "Unless the LORD builds the house, its builders labor in vain." He, as the son, was the one who was able to build the temple that his father, David, had always wanted to build. David built the temple, then, through his son. Yet, Solomon knew that it was really the LORD who was building the temple. God was the foreman, and he was just one of the workers, or one of the tools in God's hands.

God the Father also is building his church today through His Son, Jesus. Yet, he is not using wood, stone, or nails. He is the chief cornerstone, the foundation, the door and the capstone himself, and we are the bricks and mortar that he has molded and fired with the heat of adversity, into a building not made with hands, but with the power of the Holy Spirit (Eph. 2:21). We, the church, are the temple of God, and His dwelling place, as well as God's fellow workers who are to build the church (I Cor. 3:9). We are to be carpenters, just like Jesus, and His Father, and build each other up (I Cor. 14:12). This is why we have been given spiritual gifts, just as the builders of the first temple were given spiritual gifts to build it (Ex. 31:3).

This makes the Holy Spirit a carpenter also, for He is the one who taught the craftsmen how to build the tabernacle, and He is the one who teaches us how to build the church. Being a carpenter, then, runs in the family of God, and we are part of that family. So, we need to get our tools--the Word, prayer, and the gifts of the Spirit—and start building. The reputation of "Yahweh and Sons" is at stake.

Self-Help Gurus

"There is no wisdom, no insight, and no plan that can succeed against the LORD."
Prov. 21:30

It is amazing what people will do in the name of "self-help". They will attend seminars, read books, go on diets, join health clubs, do Yoga, go on pilgrimages—you name it, they'll do it. Why do people put themselves through all of this? One reason is the media. There is such an emphasis on the glamorous in our society, where the beautiful, happy people are constantly paraded before us as the standard to live by, that we naturally join the parade. Yet, we feel so inadequate when we can't live up to this standard that we often end up feeling worse off than when we began. So, we attend more seminars or read books on how to overcome our insecurities that were caused by our failure to live up to the other self-help guides. We keep searching for the one magical answer that will be the key to success that will make us happy and fulfilled.

Yet, we end up going down one dead end road after another. The problem, according to one self-help guru, is that we need to focus just on the positive—think only happy thoughts, and we will be happy. Another guru says that we need to look within ourselves to find the divine light that is within us all—we don't need a God outside of who we are. Be your own god—then you can decide what is right and wrong, and what defines happiness. If you aren't happy, then just change the definition.

I hope that it is clear that these self-help gurus are really anti-Christ's. Christ said, "I am the way, the truth, and the life. No man comes to the Father but by me" (John 14:6). If anyone, then, tries to get to the divine in any other way, they are going against the teachings of Christ. We cannot get closer to God through our own self efforts. We can't make ourselves good enough for God. We cannot redefine what it means to be good so that we will always fit the description. The Bible says, "For all have sinned and fallen short of the glory of God" (Rom. 3:23). No matter how hard we try, we will always fall short of God's standard. There is only one way to reach God, and that is by admitting that we can't reach Him. We have to come to Him in humility, acknowledging that we can't help ourselves. We need God to save us by His grace and according to His plan of redemption (Eph. 2:8-9). We have to come to realize that "There is no wisdom, no insight, and no plan that can succeed against the LORD".

If anyone offers us a different wisdom or plan, it is not really "self-help"—it is self-destruction. Remember, if the best things in life are free, then why are the gurus charging us money for them? Is it possible that they may be more interested in filling their bank accounts, than they are in filling our souls? The only self-help they know is helping themselves to our money. God's plan is free. Yet, the hardest thing for some is to do nothing.

Iron Sharpening Iron

"As iron sharpens iron, so one man sharpens another." Prov. 27:17

Do we ever feel kind of dull? Do we have any dull friends? The word "dull" can mean different things. It can mean stupid or mentally challenged. I really doubt that this description fits us, or we wouldn't be seeking God's wisdom. However, the word can also mean sluggish, lacking life or spirit, slow to hear or see, blunt, or not burning brightly. Perhaps one of these words or phrases fits us more accurately. That's okay. Even the most intelligent people can feel dull in some ways at some times.

The Bible, however, gives us a solution. It says, "As iron sharpens iron, so one man sharpens another." It is other people around us who are there to sharpen us up. Sometimes, if someone's iron is burning brightly, just being close to them can heat up our own flame. Their vivacious spirit is contagious, and we are drawn to their fire. We feel enlivened and on fire for the Lord when we are around them. Dullness doesn't dwell with a dynamo.

There is another kind of sharpening that takes place, though, when iron goes against iron. It involves either great pressure or friction. Think of the blacksmith pounding out a horseshoe with his iron mallet, or a swordsman sharpening his sword by rubbing iron against iron. Sometimes people sharpen us in the same way. They can put a lot of pressure on us to change or to move in the direction that they want us to, or they can cause a lot of friction or tension when we don't respond the way that they want. If this kind of pressure or friction comes from a friend or a spouse, at least we know that their motives are good. Yet, sometimes it comes from people that we work with, neighbors, or even people in power that we don't like or even respect. This is more difficult to put up with because we resent the source. We may even view these people as our enemies, and ask God to remove these sources of friction from our lives.

God, however, looks at things a little differently than we do. His main goal is to help us to be conformed into the image of Christ—to be more Christ-like in our actions and attitudes. He knows that we would rather just get into a comfort zone, where we are satisfied with who we are, and stop growing. In other words, we become dull, sluggish, and stagnant. God, then, allows us to be around people who rub us the wrong way, to cause friction, so we can be sharpened and more useful to Him.

Yes, even the bad guys in our lives can actually be tools in the Master's hands to sharpen our senses and spirits. Sometimes God has to be blunt with us so we won't be "blunt" for Him. He wants us to be alive and sharp, even if He has to pound some truth into our thick skulls. He is the divine blacksmith, using iron against iron, man against man, to mold and sharpen us, the two-edged swords that He needs for the spiritual warfare. Are we strengthened and shaped by the fire, or do we just melt away?

Tested by Praise

"Man is tested by the praise he receives." Prov. 27:21

Most of us think about being tested as having to put up with hardship. Our patience is being tested, or our strength, perseverance or character. We have to put up with the criticisms of our mother-in-law, or the nagging of our spouse, or the bullying of our boss, or the temper-tantrums of our teenagers. As the tensions rise, we keep telling ourselves, "This is only a test. This is only a test. This too shall pass."

Yet, it isn't just the negative that tests our character. It is also the positive. God wants to know what we are going to do with the good things that happen to us, as well as the bad. Are we going to take all the credit for what we have achieved, or are we going to glorify and thank Him? Are we going to get proud and big-headed, as if we deserved everything we have and more, or are we going to be able to humbly acknowledge God's grace in our life? Are we going to look down upon others who maybe don't have as much as we do, as if we are better than they are, or are we going to give to others as freely as we have received?

In some ways, being tested by the praise that we receive and the blessings of your life is actually more difficult than being tested by the hardships. When we go through tough times, it tends to make us more dependent upon God, and sympathetic toward others. When we have everything going for us, we don't think that we need God, or that we must be something special to God, so we look down upon others. The hardships often bring us closer to the divine, but the praise often causes a great divide. In fact, if we serve the Lord just to get the praise of others, the Bible says that that will be the only reward we ever get (Matt. 6:1-2).

The praise of men can become more important to us than the praise of God (John 12:43). In other words, it can become idolatry, for we actually worship the praise, rather than God. When we are tried by hardship, we may get discouraged, and may even struggle with our faith. When we are tried by praise, we are tempted to put our faith in ourselves, and we become like Lucifer, feeling that we deserve to be at the right hand of the Father instead of Jesus. Remember, "Pride goes before destruction, a haughty spirit before a fall" (Prov. 16:18).

The Lord told his disciples that if they wanted to be honored, they needed to become servants with servant hearts. If we seek honor now, we will be humbled in heaven. What is more important to us—having a parade in our honor down Broadway, or being welcomed by God in His fiery chariots, and riding with Him in honor down the streets of gold? The true test of praise is time—do we want it "right now, or else!" or are we content to know that it will be ours for eternity?

Righteous Boldness

"The righteous are as bold as a lion." Prov. 28:1

Meekness is often thought to be the ideal of Christianity, for Christ, himself, said, "Learn of me, for I am meek and lowly in heart" (Matt. 11:29). Meekness, though, is sometimes associated with weakness in our minds. We think of a meek person as a milk toast who has no backbone, who must be sitting all of the time because, in our minds, he doesn't stand for anything. The word "meek", in fact, comes from the word "muck", and means fluid or flexible. Who wants to be stuck in the muck? Yuck! Yet, being fluid and flexible are good things, for they imply that we are not rigid or stiff-necked. We are giving and forgiving.

There can be a great amount of strength, then, associated with meekness. It takes a great amount of moral strength and integrity to turn the other cheek at times, and walk away with humility, instead of fighting back with bitterness and revenge. Meekness is not "cowardess". It is confidence in God instead of self. It is an assurance that our relationship with God is alright, and that is all that matters. We don't need to defend ourselves, for our mission in life is not about us. We have a higher calling, one that goes beyond human understanding. Everyone else may think that we are weak, but God gives us an inner strength in our tenderness. We have the courage to be submissive in spite of the ridicule that it might bring.

Ironically, it is out of this meekness that righteous boldness comes. Anyone can be bold—daring, courageous, confident—but not everyone can have righteous boldness. Righteous boldness is based on a right relationship with God. It requires that we be completely in tune with the leading of the Holy Spirit. In our humility we are able to hear the still small voice of God, and we are totally submissive to His will. Yet, His will may be to go into battle, fighting with all that we have, not giving an inch, for we are confident that we are doing the will of God. We are not afraid of the consequences, for God has given us our marching orders, and there is no turning back. It is a conviction that we must fight, must stand up for the truth and against the darkness, even if it means our death.

Righteous boldness is total abandonment to the will of the Father, with no thought for ourselves. It is taking up our cross and following Jesus. It is being crucified with Christ, yet having confidence in the resurrection power of the Almighty. It is fearing God, but having absolutely no fear of man. It is a solid resolution that we are nothing apart from God, but with Him, we can conquer the Goliaths of the world. We can be meek as lambs and bold as lions at the same time, for Jesus is our example, and in his submission unto death, he actually conquered death itself. He had the boldness to use his meekness to win the victory.

The Eternal Heart

"He has set eternity in the hearts of men." Eccl. 3:11

What does it mean to have eternity in our hearts? Some people think that it just means that we will live forever. However, immortality is different than eternity. Immortality only moves forward. Eternity involves past, present and future. It always has been, and always will be. Only God is eternal. So, for God to set eternity in our hearts means that He has put His own personal stamp on our souls. There is a part of Him in every person, not just believers. We are all created in the image of God. Even in our fallen state, we still reflect who He is in a limited sense.

What is that limited sense of the eternity in each of our hearts? First of all, we know through looking at creation that God is powerful (Rom. 1:20). Yet, we are not talking about external observations here. We are talking about what our heart tells us about God. The core belief in our hearts has to go beyond creation. It has to be convinced that "from everlasting to everlasting, [He is] God" (Psa. 90:2). Even when our minds don't come to this conclusion, our hearts must sense this truth in our very depths to make all men everywhere keep searching for the source of that divine echo that keeps shouting from the mountaintops of our spirits. Although most men try to ignore this spiritual voice within them, it is the echo of eternity, and it will not be silenced.

Along with this echo of God's eternal nature within us is the revelation that He deserves to be on the throne in our hearts (Psa. 93:2). It isn't just a matter of knowing that God is God. We sense that He deserves to be our God. He has a divine right to rule us and to hold us accountable. Man doesn't like this, for he likes to rule his own life, but he is very conscious of God's right to rule. This is why his conscience is able to convict him of sin. If there was no one that he had to be accountable to, why feel guilty? Yet, he knows that he has failed God, and even as a non-Christian can feel convicted about his sins. If this sense of God's kingship was not there, man would never feel the need for God's forgiveness and salvation.

In addition to believing that God is King of Kings and Lord of Lords, there also must be a belief that God is always right in order to feel a conviction that we have been wrong. We must sense that God's standard is the right one to make us feel guilty that we just haven't measured up. The Bible says, "His righteousness endures forever" (Psa. 111:3). That means God's holiness has always been the standard, and always will be. Our hearts tell us that, even if we don't like it.

It is true that our hearts can become calloused, and we can become insensitive to the speaking of the Holy Spirit. Yet, when God set eternity in our hearts, He gave us everything we needed to know Him. He gave us the ability to respond to the eternal nudge on our spirits, and to know that it is God who is drawing us to Himself. If we search our hearts, we will find the divine.

Don't Be an Extremist

"The man who fears God will avoid all extremes." Eccl. 7:18

Extremists are often made fun of, or ridiculed as being out of touch with the common man. There are the right-wing extremists, the left-wing extremists, religious extremists, extreme sports athletes, extreme hairdos, and extreme feminist radicals. To every belief and cause there is an extreme. So what does it mean, then, when the Bible tells us to "avoid all extremes"? Are we supposed to be middle-of-the-roaders, moderates, or vanilla personas just so we don't offend anyone?

I don't think so. Jesus was an extremist. The rightness or wrongness of extremism depends upon the standard that we use as the "norm". If we think of ourselves as the norm, then anything or anyone who goes against our standards is an extremist. If we are Christians, then the Muslims are extremists. If we are Muslims, then the Christians are extremists, etc.

According to the Bible, though, God is the standard. He is the norm that He wants everyone to compare themselves to. That is why it says, "The man who fears God will avoid all extremes." Fearing God requires a proper recognition of who He is, and who we are in relation to Him. What He wants is for us to be as close to Him as possible, actually becoming one with Him. We become "Norm-El" when we accept Elohim as the norm. Anything that is contrary to God, then, is extremism from His point of view.

From the world's point of view Jesus was an extremist. When Jesus on the cross became the central focus of all human history, though, he redefined extremism on his terms. He became the standard, and all history revolves around Him. We are either B.C. or A.D. from that point on. We are redefined based on who we were "before Christ", or "after death" of Christ became our focal point. We are to fear God, and to do nothing which would separate us from Him.

According to God, the pagans of the world are the extremists. Yet, so are the Christians who turn their backs on God as their norm. It is alright to be an extremist from the world's point of view. Daniel, Shadraq, Meshach and Abednego were extremists from the King's perspective. The Apostle Paul was an extremist by the Jew's standard. Joseph was an extremist from his brothers' point of view. Jesus told his disciples that the world would persecute them and kill them because they would see them as extremists.

Being an extremist is not wrong, then, if we take a firm stand against the Devil as the norm. If we turn away from God, though, and become our own standard for norm, we will become "norm-ill" instead of "Norm-El", and the worst kind of extremist is the one who is extremely separated from Him in hell.

Wrestling with God

"You have wrestled with God and men and have overcome." Gen. 32:28

How on earth could a man actually wrestle with God in a human form all night long and still overcome? God, in any form, could have wiped Jacob off the map without even lifting his baby finger. Yet, God allowed Jacob to struggle with Him, like two friends in a backyard, testing strength for strength, and revealing Jacob's weakness. Jacob knew at the end that he could not succeed without God's blessing, and he was a different man from that day forward. He was no longer a momma's boy. He was now the Father's man. God signified the moment by changing his name from Jacob to Israel, which means "he struggles with God".

Struggling with God can be a negative thing if it is out of rebellion and prideful resistance prevails. Yet, it can also be a growing experience, where a lesson is learned, and submission to God's will is the final product. Even a baby struggles as it is being born. So the adult often has to struggle, even with God, before it can often see the light of day.

There is another kind of wrestling with God, however, that I believe is even more beneficial to the human soul. It is wrestling with God as a teammate instead of as an opponent. The Bible says, that "we wrestle not against flesh and blood, but against …the spiritual forces of evil in the heavenly realms" (Eph. 6:12). Can you think of any one that you would rather have as a tag-team partner against the Devil than the Lord? He knows the enemy's every move before he makes it, and He empowers us with faith, hope and a holy boldness that can bring even the demons to their knees. We know that Satan is not going to give up and say "uncle" to the very end, but maybe the beginning of Satan's torment in hell is not going to have to wait until after Armageddon. We can bring him great pain and suffering every time the Lord helps us to be victorious over the Devil's evil schemes. Just when he thinks he has us pinned, we do a reversal, and the gold medal goes to the Lord's team every time.

So, how do we do most of our wrestling with God—as the opposition or as a teammate? We can grow either way, but staying in His corner is always better than being merely carried into His heavenly dressing room, beat up and bruised at the end of the match.

The Weakling and the Warrior

"Let the weakling say, 'I am strong'." Joel 3:10

Joel starts this passage by saying, "Prepare for War"(3:9). Although there are a lot of men out there who would jump at the chance to prove their manliness, there are also many who are pacifists, or who would love to fight, but hardly have enough strength to lift a sword, let alone try to swing it at someone. When the Declaration of Independence says that we are all created equal, it definitely wasn't talking about physical prowess or natural abilities. There are some who are born to be gladiators, and there are others who are better suited as librarians. That isn't something to be ashamed of. God has given different gifts to each one of us, and we should be thankful for who we are, not try to be something that we are not.

In the spiritual realm, though, it is a different ballgame. Sure, we still have different gifts, for we are different parts of the body of Christ, and the thumb should not be slighted because it doesn't have the strength of the arm. Yet, no matter what part of the body we are, and no matter how weak we are compared to other parts, we have one thing in common—we are all warriors in spiritual warfare. It doesn't matter how much of a pacifist we are, or how much we would rather just sit on the sidelines and watch others do the fighting, God has chosen us as one of His warriors. There isn't any way to avoid it or escape it. Even if we choose not to become a Christian, thinking that will be a way of escape, we are wrong. All that means is that we have chosen to be on the other side of the war.

There are no sidelines or spectators, though many Christians act as if there is, coming to church like going to a theater, expecting to be entertained and fed spiritually, but not willing to give of themselves. Yet, what they do not realize is, that by just sitting there and vegetating, they are losing a battle. There is no place in the spiritual realm that is called "stationary" or the "status quo". We are either winning or losing. We are either going forward or backward. We are either for the Lord or against Him. There is no third choice.

The Lord tells us, even if we are weaklings, to say that we are strong, and to charge into each battle, expecting victory. For God promises us, that His strength is made perfect in our weakness (2 Cor. 12:9), and that we can be "more than conquerors through Him who loves us" (Rom. 8:37). So, stop whining about the battle, and start trusting in the Captain of our faith.

What is your Legacy?

"A little folly outweighs wisdom and honor." Eccl. 10:1

As a boy, I remember watching a parade on New Years Day. It was a glorious occasion, with lots of beautiful floats, clowns, and people everywhere. The thing that I enjoyed the most, though, was the horses. There was a group of horses that not only looked majestic, but pranced in synchronized formations. They were powerful, yet completely controlled, and every movement was a lesson in dance. They were muscular, yet graceful, and I was in awe.

Then I saw the unthinkable. One of these royal animals deposited its excrement on the street. Not only was it shocking to me, it caused a huge problem for the marching band that was following. They were supposed to be marching in unity and focused on excellence, but now their attention was diverted by having to step over or around a mess that threatened to disrupt all of their hard work and training. Some were laughing, others expressed anger, but all were upset. It didn't matter how beautiful or masterful the horses were. As far as the audience and the band were concerned, it is what they left behind that counted.

The same thing is true with humans. We can live a wonderful life, full of service and good deeds, yet one indiscretion can ruin a person's reputation for ever. In our minds, it shouldn't matter that much. We have these huge weight scales in our minds where we place our deeds, good and bad, on different sides, and we are happy as long as the good outweighs the bad. After all, no one's perfect, we think, so it doesn't matter if there are a few mistakes in judgment now and again. Just keep our balances right, always countering any bad with more good, and we will be alright.

According to scripture, though, that is not how it works. It says, "As dead flies give perfume a bad smell, so a little folly outweighs wisdom and honor." Have we sat down to eat a good meal, but had to throw it all out because there was a fly in our soup? It doesn't matter how good the soup was, or how many hours that it might have taken to prepare this wonderful feast, one fly can ruin the appetite and spoil the broth. The same thing happens to perfume. It might be the most beautiful perfume in the world, yet dead flies in the fragrant liquid will spoil the entire smell. Even though we don't like it, and it goes against what we think is fair, the same thing happens with our lives. One act of folly, one poor choice of words, one act of anger, or one immoral moment can ruin a person's reputation for the rest of their lives and damage any memories of the good they have done even for generations to come. They can be filled with wisdom and honor, and be used by God in mighty ways, yet be remembered only for the Delilah or Bathsheba episodes of their lives. They, like the horses in the parade, may be beautiful, majestic, and powerful, but only be remembered by the mess they left behind.

The Flower of Faith

"I am a rose of Sharon, a lily of the valleys." Song of Songs 2:1

The "Song of Songs" is a beautiful love song between a poor shepherdess and her shepherd/king. He is powerful and majestic, and she is lowly and humble. Yet, there is a romantic bond between the two that breaks down any economic or cultural barriers. It is a Cinderella story where the poor waif is swept off her feet by her prince charming. She can't believe that it is happening to her. She says in amazement, "I am a rose of Sharon, a lily of the valleys". Even though we see this as a beautiful picture, it is rather a description of her lowliness. The rose of Sharon, you see, isn't really a rose. There weren't any roses in Israel during the time of Solomon. They were not introduced into the Holy Land until much later. The translators merely put rose because the next verse talks about thorns. The British translators of the King James Version inserted their own cultural bias based on their European gardens.

Sharon is the lowland along the coast of the Mediterranean Sea below Mt. Carmel. It is covered with grasses for their sheep, and Crocuses, a beautiful meadow flower that sprouts up through the grass during different times of the year. It would probably be a favorite for the poor shepherdess, but she knows that it is only a common flower. It is a wild-flower, not a rose or a lily. It is a bulb that reproduces under the cold, winter earth, and comes up early to blossom in the first sign of spring. The shepherdess understands her lowly state, and humbly calls herself the wildflower of the plains.

The shepherd/king, however, seeks to build her up by comparing her to the other women. He says, yes, you are a common flower, but you are "like a lily among thorns is my darling among the maidens" (S.of.S.2:2). He is not saying that she has thorns. The maidens are thorns in comparison to her delicate beauty. He knows that she comes from poverty, but in his eyes, all that he sees is his love blossoming before him. He is not blind, but he has chosen to focus on the beauty of her present petals instead of the lowliness of her past.

Our relationship with Christ, our shepherd/king, is the same way. We are nothing apart from Him. Our bulbs, or hearts, are buried in the cold earth of spiritual winter, but he has raised us up in the warmth of His love, and helped us to blossom in ways that would be impossible without Him. We may be surrounded by others who are thorns in our spiritual sides, but He helps us to grow in spite of the pain and persecution that the weeds and briars might bring. He knows that we are just common plants of the pasture, but he has chosen to focus on what He has done through us, instead of our environment or heredity. In His eyes we are flowers of faith transformed and regenerated by the springs of His eternal life. He left the Garden of Gethsemane and entered His Garden of Grace, and we lift up our petals in praise to the Master Gardener, our shepherd/king.

The Secret Garden

"You are a garden locked up, my sister, my bride." Song of Songs 4:12

Wine makers, I'm told, often keep the best wine for themselves. They have their own private reserve, and every year they add to it the choicest fruit of their labors for their families and friends. The wealthy often do the same thing with their gardens. They have flowers and trees all over their estates, but they will set aside a small section as a private, special garden where they have their prized plants with unique qualities or rare beauty reserved just for themselves. They often are surrounded by tall walls with wrought-iron gates to keep others out, including the animals that may want to nibble at their prized possessions. The walls keep others out, but they also serve to give the owners a feeling of enclosed intimacy with their gardens, as if there is a special communion they have with their flowered-friends. There is a sense of solitude, meditation, and openness to listen to the quiet voices of Nature and to one's own soul.

When the shepherd/king in the Song of Solomon, then, compares his bride to his private garden, it is a beautiful metaphor describing his relationship with his beloved. She is his own "private reserve" meant just for him. She is cherished for her rare, unique qualities, her inner, as well as external beauty, and he longs for the quiet, intimate moments that they can share. He will care for her, just as a gardener would take care of his prized plants, showing special attention to their every need. He will protect her by surrounding her with his arms, like walls with iron gates. His love for her will help her to feel secure and safe from those who will seek to devour her, and he will nourish her with the water of his compassion and care.

In the same way, God cares for us. We are His secret garden. We, as Christians, belong only to Him. We are His bride, and He cherishes the quiet moments of fellowship and communion that we share. There is nothing more intimate than the Holy Spirit communicating with our spirits. There is nothing more private and personal than the thoughts that we share. He knows our deepest feelings, motives, and subconscious responses to His still small voice whispering in our ears. He knows our futures, as well as our pasts. We are His children, His brothers and sisters, His bride— we are family. We have a special bond, and He wants to cultivate even a deeper bond. He wants to nurture us with His Word, remove the weeds around us with His Spirit, fertilize us with His encouragement, and fumigate us with his gentle rebuke. He will prune us when necessary, and support our branches when the fruit gets too heavy.

God is the Master-Gardener, and He takes pride in His secret gardens. We are all part of His huge estate, but separated by the walls of His intimacy, in our own special space with the Spirit. We still may get aphids of evil or gophers of grief that may sneak into our gardens, but the gardener is there to exterminate them away.

The Devil's Dyslexia

"Woe to those who call evil good and good evil, who put darkness for light and light for darkness, who put bitter for sweet and sweet for bitter." Isa. 5:20

One of the learning disabilities that often goes unnoticed is dyslexia. Students can go through their entire education without even knowing that they have the problem. They just know that reading and spelling are really difficult for them, and they are often branded as being "dumbies" at an early age because they get so frustrated, they just give up. Well, the problem, as we know, is not a matter of being dumb or mentally retarded. It is a problem with how their eyes send the wrong messages to their brains. Their eyes tell the brain that they are seeing a "d" instead of a "b", etc.. In other words, they are seeing things backwards. There are a lot of theories of why this happens, from birth defects to mind-control, from mental illness to child abuse. Regardless of the cause, people with this problem can retrain their brains to see correctly, or to compensate by consciously telling their brain to interpret things just the opposite of what they see.

In the spiritual realm, this problem also occurs. I will call it the Devil's Dyslexia. The Devil causes people to see things backwards, or the opposite of what they really are. They "call evil good and good evil", confuse "darkness for light and light for darkness", and exchange "bitter for sweet and sweet for bitter." Everything is just the opposite of what God intended. It is really an act of rebellion, for the followers of Satan refuse to accept God's standards of measurement or value. Yet, it isn't just rebellion. The Devil's children literally cannot see correctly. He has warped their minds and hearts to the point that whatever they see is twisted inside, and they are really blind to the truth. Everything is disguised and masked by the Devil's darkness, so what they see is definitely not what they get. It is a mental and spiritual masquerade or Mardi Gras, and everyone is fooled to believe that the disguises are the reality. It is like going through a maze of mirrors, never knowing for sure which are the real images and which are merely the reflections of other reflections.

The Devil doesn't want us to know the truth about anything. He is a master at mind-control and deceit—the grand magician, whose slight of hand is faster than the mind can comprehend. He has the world hypnotized by his charm, so when he snaps his fingers, and tells us that we are seeing "good instead of evil", we believe him.

The apostle Paul, though, gives us some hope. He says of the Devil, "We are not ignorant of his devices" (2 Cor. 2:11). We do not need, then, to "let Satan get an advantage over us." We can "be transformed by the renewing of our minds" so we can prove the validity of God's will and standard for truth in our lives (Rom. 12:2). We don't have to be brainwashed by the Devil's Dyslexia. We can see things from God's perspective, for He is Truth.

Unclean Lips

*"'Woe to me!' I cried. 'I am ruined! For I am a man of unclean lips,
and I live among a people of unclean lips'." Isa. 6:5*

Imagine standing before the throne of God, with angels all around singing, "Holy, holy, holy is the LORD Almighty; the whole earth is full of his glory"(Isa. 6:3). What would be going through our minds at that moment? Would we fall on our faces and start asking forgiveness for all our sins? Would we start begging for mercy? Would we start singing in praise along with the angels?

It is interesting that the one thing that Isaiah says in that circumstance is, "I am a man of unclean lips, and I live among a people of unclean lips." Why that? Why not confess his thought life, or the way that he treated people, or his negligence in obeying God? We might guess that Isaiah must have had a problem with lying, so he was convicted of that. Yet, he says that everyone else has the same problem. It is the only sin that he mentions. He could have picked a thousand other ones. Why this one?

For one thing, Isaiah was appearing before God so that he could be ordained as a prophet. He was going to be God's spokesman, so the angel had to purge his lips with a hot coal, to purify the messenger for the message. God was going to use him to proclaim the voice of the Lord, so God had to impress upon him first that he was inadequate for the job. His lips were unclean and incapable of proclaiming the truth without God's intervention. Once he was purged, he could say with boldness, "Here am I. Send me."

Yet, how does this apply to us? We're not all called to be prophets or preachers, are we? Well, as a matter of fact, we are. The word "prophet" means not only those who can foretell the future, but those who forth-tell the truth. All of us are commanded to do that in the great commission. It says, "Go and make disciples of all nations, baptizing them in the name of the Father and of the Son and of the Holy Spirit, and teaching them to obey everything I have commanded you"(Matt 28:19-20). This applies to us whether we go to Africa, China, or San Francisco. Wherever we are, no matter what our job is, no matter what spiritual gift that we have, we are commanded to tell others about Christ, and to take the time to make disciples of those who believe. We don't have to be gifted speakers, we just have to share what God has done for us.

Yet, if we are going to be sharing the truth of God with others, then we need to have our lips purged, just as Isaiah did. That doesn't mean that we have to have a vision of heaven, or have an angel touch our lips with a hot coal. It does mean, though, that God does need to cleanse our hearts and minds, so that when words come out of our mouths, they come from the Holy Spirit within us, and not just from our own ideas. We need to be clean channels of His truth, where self doesn't get in the way of God speaking through us. Purge me, O Lord!

Don't Confuse Me with the Facts

"Give us no more visions of what is right! Tell us pleasant things, prophesy illusions." Isaiah 30:10

On television now-a-days, we have what is called "Reality TV". It is based on real people just living their lives, instead of seeing actors portraying roles. The idea is that people are more interested in seeing the real thing than just make-believe. They are supposedly able to relate to real people better than fantasy characters. Of course, at the same time, they are also spending millions of dollars on going to movies such as "Spiderman" and "Batman", as well as spending hours playing fantasy games such as "Dungeons and Dragons" and "Pokemon". They want the freedom to know it all, without limits, as well as to fantasize without limits.

The one area that they don't want to know about is accountability to God. So, even if they go to church, they want the preacher to focus on positive things, such as love and feeling good about ourselves. They don't want him meddling in their lives or telling them what they can't do. According to Isaiah, "They say to the seers, 'See no more visions!' and to the prophets, 'Give us no more visions of what is right! Tell us pleasant things, prophesy illusions." They may want Reality TV, but they don't want Reality Spirituality. They don't want to be told they are sinners who need to humble themselves before God. They want an easy religion that pats them on the backs and sends them on their way. If someone tries to tell them the truth, they become very defensive, as if the messenger is the enemy. They say, "Leave this way, get off this path, and stop confronting us with the Holy One of Israel" (Isa. 30:11).

People don't like being confronted with the truth about themselves. They just want to know all the dirt about others. It helps them to feel better about their own weaknesses when they see other people struggling. It really is an ego trip because they are building their own self-esteem by exposing the faults of others. "At least I'm not that bad", they think. Unfortunately, there are many ministers out there who are willing to play along with the game. They are willing to give the audience what it wants, instead of sharing the hard-hitting truth. After all, if they are too hard on the people, they will stop coming, and then who will pay for their salaries and fancy buildings? We think, how foolish these people are.

Yet, are we the same way? When we read the scripture, what do we spend our time reading? Do we like reading the Psalms or Proverbs, but tend to shy away from reading the Law and the Prophets? Do we like reading the story of baby Jesus, but skip over his no-nonsense preaching to the Pharisees? Do we like the story of Ruth, but completely avoid Revelation? We need to get to the point where we approach God with the attitude of a court bailiff, who asks for and expects, "the whole truth and nothing but the truth."

Quietness and Trust

"In quietness and trust is your strength." Isa. 30:15

We all have our problems. It doesn't matter if we are rich or poor, intelligent or uneducated, beautiful or plain. The test of our character is how we respond to those problems. If we get stressed out, irritated, frustrated, depressed, moody or worried, we probably are not going to be able to cope with our trials very well. We will overreact, lose our temper, say things we shouldn't, make poor decisions, seek to escape or hide, and basically become someone that we don't really want to be. In other words, we are out of control, like a stunt plane doing a downward spiral, and unable to pull ourselves out of the "crash and burn".

Actions are not the only things that are self-destructive. Attitudes can also destroy us. The Israelites are perfect examples. They had enemies on all sides, and problems within. They became fearful and desperate, but instead of going to God for help, they sought the protection from Egypt. God rebukes them and asks them, why are you taking all your wealth to Egypt to buy her help instead of coming to me? Why do you go "to Egypt, whose help is utterly useless?" (Isa. 30:7).

When we get into trouble, we do the same thing. We try to solve our own problems, sometimes even through elaborate schemes or plans, seeking to dig our way out of the mess we are in. We fight and struggle against others who we see as the enemies, we isolate ourselves from our friends, and we pull our hair out trying to deal with the stress of it all. We drink more coffee or alcohol than we should, we eat more than we should, we sleep less than we should—In other words, we are a nervous wreck.

What happened? How did we get in this mess? Is it just spiritual warfare, and there is nothing we can do about it? According to scripture, it is because we are "children unwilling to listen to the Lord's instruction" (Isa. 30:9). We think we know better than the Lord how to solve our own problems, and don't seek his help until we get way over our heads. God is our last resort instead of our first response.

What is the instruction of the Lord that we tend to ignore? "In repentance and rest is your salvation, in quietness and trust is your strength" (Isa. 30:15). What we fail to realize is that when we worry and fret and stress about everything, it is an act of rebellion against the Lord. We are saying, "I want to run my own life my way. I know better than the Lord." What we need to do is acknowledge worry for what it is—sin—and repent. Then, we need to rest in the Lord's ability to handle our problems in complete, confident, quiet trust. Our strength is not in how hard we fight or how much we struggle. It is in yielding and submitting to the power and authority of the Lordship of Christ. Only He can calm the stormy seas. He says, "My power is made perfect in your weakness" (2 Cor. 12:9). Stop trying to swim across the Red Sea. Stand back and watch Him separate the waters instead.

True Nobility

"The noble man makes noble plans, and by noble deeds he stands." Isa. 32:8

The idea of nobility is often misunderstood, for it is often associated only with the upper class in society, where people pride themselves in somehow being above the commoners. The concept of nobility, however, has nothing to do with one's social rank. It has to do with the distinctiveness of one's character. The reason for the confusion is that it is assumed that people who have had the best education and training would also have noble characters. This is the reason for our educational system today, which assumes that if people are well-educated, then they will be better people. This, as we well know, is a false assumption. Nobility of character is not based on how much we know, but upon our moral values. It is not based on just filling the brain. It involves the dignity of the mind and spirit. It is that which elevates the soul to such virtuous endeavors as bravery and selfless generosity. It isn't satisfied with the mediocre, but always strives for excellence. It values the conscience as the most sacred of all property, and has contempt for anything that might degrade or dishonor one's character.

Does this sound like any "princely" people that we know? Are those who are considered "noblemen", really noble men? The Bible says that true noble men make noble plans and are able to stand on the genuineness and integrity of their noble deeds. They have a reputation for their dignity, honesty, and strength of character. People know that they can be trusted. If they promise to do something, we know they will do their absolute best to fulfill their promise. Their handshake is as good as a signed contract, for we know that they mean everything they say.

There is absolutely no deceit in a true noble man, so if he is our friend, we know he will be the most loyal friend that a person can have. We would trust him with our life or with our wife. His virtue has been tested and proven reliable. There isn't anything phony about him. He is genuine through and through. He is Christ-like in actions and attitudes, for he knows that others are looking up to him as an example or role model.

Why are others looking up to him? He is the child of the King, the ruler of the universe. He is of noble birth, for he has been born again into the King's family. He is a prince with principles. The word "principle" means first cause or origin. It is the foundation or core value of everything that follows. As Christians, our core value or principle is that we are all lost or fallen by nature. There are none who are naturally noble, no not one. Yet, when we are born again spiritually, through the atoning blood of our Lord Jesus Christ, we inherit the noble spirit of our Lord, himself, and are gradually transformed into his character. We become truly noble only when we become truly like Him, for He is the standard for all that is good and generous. He is truth and love, and nobility is the unity of both.

Bruised, Broken, and Burning

"A bruised reed he will not break, and a smoldering wick he will not snuff out."
Isa. 42:3

When we hear the word "bruise", we picture in our minds bruises that we have had over the years. Perhaps we have banged our shin on a coffee table, had a black eye from a boyhood battle, or been bruised and battered from playing a friendly game of football. When we read about a bruised reed, though, it probably doesn't mean a whole lot to us, except we know that it has been damaged somehow. It's hard to be sympathetic about a wounded plant.

However, the Bible is talking about much more here than bruised botany. The reed is a symbol for people who are submerged in the problems of life. The reed grows in water, much too much water for nourishment purposes. If it was any other plant, in fact, it would probably be drowning. Yet, this plant thrives in this environment. It is tough enough to endure, in spite of the poor conditions. Some people are like this as well. They are used to being up to their knees in trials, so instead of drowning, they are growing stronger and wiser.

Yet, in spite of their strength, they still get bruised and beaten up by the storms of life. It would be easy for someone to come by, looking for strong reeds to make a basket, something useful, to conclude that they are too bruised and damaged to use. Their first response might be to just break off the reed and to throw it away, making more room for the young and vigorous. The Lord, however, doesn't look at people that way. He sees the value and wisdom of the bruised reeds, and he patiently heals and nurtures them back to health.

The word "bruised" here is not just talking about a superficial wound. It means "cracked to the core". It is broken as well as bruised. Others would probably discard it, but the Lord uses the splints of the Spirit to hold it together until he can heal it from the inside out.

The Bible passage also says that a "smoldering wick he will not snuff out." The wicks of this time were made out of flax, which is a kind of reed, made of a lot of fibers, which are separated and made into a variety of things, such as wicks and threads as fine as satin. The flax is cut, pulled apart, and isolated from its others parts in order to make it more useful. Sometimes people are the same way. We are used to the strength that we have in numbers, with the encouragement and support of others. Yet, sometimes God allows us to be separated, even torn apart, because He wants us to grow more dependent on Him rather than other people. Our flame may grow dimmer for a while because we are pulled apart from the other flames, but He promises to keep our fire going until we can be reunited with the others. It doesn't matter, then, whether we are bruised, broken, or burning. He never gives up on us.

From Reject to Redeemer

"He was despised and rejected by men, a man of sorrows, and familiar with suffering." Isa. 53:3

The world wants a super-hero. They want a glamorous movie star to play the role of savior of the world. They want someone who is a combination of Hercules, Gandhi, Elvis, and Mother Theresa. Well, Jesus just didn't fit the mold for a super model or a super hero. The Bible says, "He had no beauty or majesty to attract us to him, nothing in his appearance that we should desire him" (Isa. 53:2). So, forget about the handsome portrayals of a muscular messiah that we have seen in pictures or movies. Jesus was an ugly misfit-reject that only a mother could love.

Why did the Lord choose to come to us in this way? Why didn't he come as a shining prince on a white horse? Someday He will, but His first appearance was not meant to appeal to the masses. He wanted people to be drawn to Him because they recognized that their souls were lost, and that He was a man of sorrows who would understand their need.

Jesus never sought popularity, even though his miracles made him the talk of the town. He, in fact, told people not to spread the word about their healings, for he didn't want to be a pop hero. He had a mission to perform. He knew he was going to be rejected and killed, and he accepted that from the very beginning. He wanted people to be drawn to Him personally, not to his looks, not because of his miracles, and not because of some political agenda. He knew people would be offended by his message, but he didn't try to water it down to make it more appealing, like a politician would have done.

He was "like one from whom men hide their faces. He was despised, and we esteemed him not" (Isa. 53:3). Can we imagine actually hiding our face from the Lord because we didn't even want to look at him? Can we imagine being so disgusted and disillusioned with the Lord because he didn't live up to our expectations, that we were ashamed of him? That's what happened when Peter denied the Lord three times, and the other disciples fled in shame. Are we sure that we wouldn't have done the same?

Not only wasn't Jesus very appealing to look at during his life, but he was even worse off through his time of torment. The Bible tells us that "his appearance was so disfigured, beyond that of any man, and his form marred beyond human likeness"(Isa. 52:14). He looked so bad that he didn't even look human. He looked like some Frankenstein monster—a bunch of flesh and bones just hanging together. Yet, this ugly bag of bones, thrown out with the trash by mankind, "took up our infirmities and carried our sorrows…was pierced for our transgressions…was crushed for our iniquities" (Isa. 53:4-5). He was a nobody, a misfit. Yet, this reject became our redeemer, so that we would not be rejects for His Father. The "loser" became Lord.

Hide and Seek

"Seek the Lord while he may be found; call on him while he is near." Isa. 55:6

When we are children, we play a fun game called "Hide and Seek". Even as adults, we sometimes play this game with our children or grandchildren. We like the challenge of being able to find a place to hide that no one else can find, or being a Sherlock Holmes and finding the deeply hidden. In one sense, there is this same joy when we search for God. I'm not saying that God is playing games with us. He does, however, sometimes hide from us, and He waits for us to come find Him.

Why does He hide from us? Doesn't He want us to find Him? I believe there are three main reasons why God hides. First, He is hidden in the sense that He is infinite and we are finite. We are only human, so our intelligence and ability to understand the complex things of this world, as well as the spiritual world, is beyond our limited comprehension. The Bible says, "Where then does wisdom come from? Where does understanding dwell? It is hidden from the eyes of every living thing… God understands the way to it, and He alone knows where it dwells" (Job 28:20-23). God is wisdom and truth, and He has hidden himself by making us incapable of understanding Him fully. There can only be one God.

The second reason that He hides from us that He has a plan, and we have to wait for His perfect timing before He reveals himself to us. It wasn't in His plan to reveal the truth to the Pharisees, or even most of the people. Instead, he taught in parables, and took his disciples aside to explain the deeper meanings. He hides himself from us until He knows that we are ready to receive Him more fully, and when it is in His plan to teach us or use us in a new way. We are completely at His mercy when this revelation is going to happen. We cannot do something, like shout, jump up and down, or pray harder to make it happen. We just have to be yielded completely to Him, and then wait for His timing.

We are told to "Seek the Lord while he may be found; call on him while he is near" (Isa. 55:6). This is because of the third reason that he hides himself—our sin. When we rebel against God and turn our backs on him, He withdraws His fellowship from us, and He hides from us until we decide to repent and come back to Him. The Bible says, "Your iniquities have separated you from your God; your sins have hidden his face from you" (Isa. 59:2).

So, if we are seeking God, and we are having a hard time finding Him, it may be that we are living in sin, and He is hiding from us. It may also be that it just isn't God's timing yet, and we need to wait patiently for His plan for us. Finally, it may be that we just need to accept the fact that God is God, and that we will never reach that level of perfection. We need to learn to be content with the hidden manna that He gives to us, and not complain when He doesn't give us the prime rib.

Light a Candle

"Spend yourselves in behalf of the hungry and satisfy the needs of the oppressed, then your light will rise in the darkness, and your night will become like the noonday."
Isa. 58:10

It is amazing how much we are dependant upon light. We don't realize it until the power goes out, and we are left in complete darkness. We grumble and complain as we grope through the house looking for a candle and some matches, stumbling over things, perhaps sticking our hands in wet, slimy things that we don't recognize, and maybe saying a few swear words under our breaths. Finally, someone finds that candle and lights it, and the overwhelming darkness is brought under control. We are able to laugh about our fumbling, and any fear that we might have had quickly vanishes away.

The same thing happens in life when we face the darkness in people's souls. We face spiritual warfare every day, and the dark side is often overwhelming. Our first response is usually a combination of fear and anger, and we want to fight back against the Darth Vader's of the world. We start seeing villains and vampires behind ever corner, and we become so defensive and negative, that we become dark ourselves. The Bible says that the best way to fight the darkness is to "do away with the … pointing finger and malicious talk", and "spend yourselves in behalf of the hungry and satisfy the needs of the oppressed. Then your light will rise in the darkness, and your night will become like the noonday".

In other words, the best way to fight the darkness is not to just point our finger at people we don't like or to talk maliciously about them, but to help those who are oppressed and in need. We overcome evil with good, not by becoming evil ourselves. The world says fight fire with fire. The Bible says fight darkness with light. The secret of success is to do exactly the opposite of what the dark side wants us to do. If evil people are trying to trigger us into a fight, the best response is patient love. We need to focus our attention and energy on helping others who are oppressed by the Evil One, instead of using all our strength to fight against the oppressors.

Jesus could have called ten-thousand angels to wipe out all of his enemies. He chose instead to lay down his life in love to save the world. The power of love is far greater than the power of hate and revenge. We need to stop fueling our thoughts with anger at the bad guys of the world, and start feeding the flame of encouragement, nurturing care, empathy, and setting the captives free. Let the Lord fight the Goliath's of the world. We are called to be torchbearers, not mercenaries. We need to set our light upon a mountain top for all to see, instead of letting it be buried under the oppression of negativity.

Remember, it is better to light a candle than to curse the darkness, and one candle can be used to light many others. Believe it or not, candles are more useful in spiritual warfare than swords. Need a light?

Faithless or Unfaithful

"Faithless Israel is more righteous than unfaithful Judah." Jer. 3:11

Satanism, paganism, atheism—surely these are the worst of the worst. They are Godless and anti-Christ. They are evil and working for the Evil One. They are against everything that we stand for as Christians, and they are against us. They are the enemy, plain and simple. Yet, according to scripture, there is something worse than these. It is believers who are unfaithful to the Lord. The Bible says, "Faithless Israel is more righteous than unfaithful Judah." That's right. Someone who has no faith at all, the pagan, the atheist, and the Satan worshipper, are actually considered more righteous than a believer who has committed spiritual adultery against the Lord. That means that if we have accepted Christ, and then turned your back on Him, we are worse than an unbeliever.

In one sense, it is like a parent trying to deal with different aged children. If we have a baby, and they accidentally knock over a vase and break it, we are not going to punish that child because they didn't know any better. On the other hand, if we have an older child who is wrestling in the living room, even though we told them not to, and they accidentally break that vase, we have to discipline them because they knew they were doing wrong, but did it anyway. We have to deal with each child according to the truth that they understand, and hold them accountable according to the level of their submission or rebellion against that truth.

Someone who knows the Lord, then, and has tasted of his grace and forgiveness, is more accountable than someone who just lacks the faith to believe. It is possible for someone to be an unbeliever just out of ignorance. A believer who has been unfaithful to the Lord does not have that excuse. He should know better. How the Lord chooses to deal with such unfaithfulness is up to Him, for only He knows the heart, and what it would take to bring that person back to Himself. Yet, would we want to be in the shoes of the one who was considered less righteous than an unbeliever?

It is easy for Christians to look down on the unbelieving world with a self-righteous attitude, thinking that it doesn't really matter what we do, because we are saved, and that is all that matters. Not true! If we are saved, and yet we are willfully living in sin, turning our backs on God and everything that we know to be right, we better get ready to face the wrath of God. Yes, God is merciful, but even if we won't go to hell someday, God may put us through hell right here if we keep rebelling against His authority. If we don't fear God, our love for God doesn't mean a whole lot. God doesn't want just a gooey, fuzzy feeling for him. He wants total submission. If we have accepted him as savior, but reject him as Lord, we are worse than an infidel, for we are the bride of Christ, and we are acting like a whore. Heaven is not a brothel, and Christ is not a pimp.

The Habit of Sin

"Can the Ethiopian change his skin or the leopard its spots? Neither can you do good who are accustomed to doing evil." Jer. 13:23

What are our habits? We all have them. They are things we do all the time because we are used to them or feel comfortable with them. Maybe we always eat our meat first, watch a certain TV show, dress a certain way when we go to church, drink a certain espresso drink, or use the same expression when we greet a friend. We are creatures of habit. We tend to fall into patterns of behavior, and we tend to get stuck in a rut. Once we start going in a certain direction, our momentum keeps us going.

The word "habit" means "to have and to hold", which is the same phrase we use when we get married. When we have a habit, then, it is like getting married to that practice. We are one with it. It is now a part of us. It affects everything we do.

Another meaning for the word "habit" is clothing we put on all the time. This is why a priest's robe or a nun's robe is called a habit. It is worn all of the time, so it becomes a part of that person's identity. When we see that person, we know what they stand for.

A third meaning is a dwelling or habitat where we live. It is where we have settled in and called home. It is where we feel that we belong.

Although most habits are harmless, some are self-destructive, such as driving too fast, drinking too much alcohol, smoking, procrastination, or being late all of the time.

The Bible says that the problem with bad habits is that they keep us from forming good ones. We are so captivated or controlled by the negative practices, that we don't have the time or inclination to do the good. In other words, we become addicted to the bad, and we just can't stop. We become addicted to sin.

The Bible says that trying to change our bad habits is almost impossible. It says, "Can the Ethiopian change his skin or the leopard its spots? Neither can you do good who are accustomed to doing evil" (Jer. 13:23). We may know that we are doing wrong, and may even want to change, but it's just too hard. It's like being overweight, but working as a cook in a restaurant. When we are around it all the time, it is hard to fight the temptation. Sin is habit-forming. We need to treat it like an addiction. If we are an alcoholic, then we can't spend time in a bar. If we have the habit of being critical, we need to seek positive friends. If we have a problem with our thought life, then we need to discipline ourselves to focus our minds on virtuous things, and stay away from movies, magazines or books that we know will bring us down.

Yet, it is going to take more than just discipline. To change a leopard's spots, it takes the hand of the Creator. To change evil habits, it also takes the Lord's hands, for we cannot do it by ourselves. We are slaves to sin, and we need to be set free. We need to put on a new kind of clothes—the garments of praise—a wedding gown of holiness to meet our bridegroom.

Passing the Torch

"His word is in my heart like a fire, a fire shut up in my bones. I am weary of holding it in; indeed, I cannot." Jer. 20:9

Have you ever had a lot of money, and you couldn't wait to spend it? I remember as a boy having some money that I earned, and my father saying that I acted as if it was going to burn a hole in my pocket. I couldn't wait to spend it on a new toy. Jeremiah talks about the word of the Lord in the same way. It is like a fire in his heart, and he can't hold it in any longer. He has to share it with others. He is not free from its burning until he gives it to someone else.

So often, though, we don't have that same burning. The Word of God has become so common place that it is boring to us. It doesn't excite us anymore. It is same-old, same-old. Why is that? One of the reasons is that we don't share what we have learned. The Word of God was never meant to be a hidden treasure in our hearts. It was meant to be a torch that is given to us, so we, in turn, can give it to someone else. Think of the Olympic torch, which is passed from one person to the next, until it reaches its final destination. What would happen if one of the torchbearers decided to just keep the torch for himself? The whole process would be stopped, and it would rob many others of the chance of carrying the light themselves. It would be self-centered and wrong to hide the light, and to just keep it for oneself.

The same thing is true with the Word. God gives it to us, and then we are supposed to hold up the light of it, and then pass it on to the next person. The light of God is only a spark when it is given to us, and can only grow into a full flame when it is shared with other flames. The excitement of the word comes not only in knowing how it has changed our own lives, but in seeing how it changes the lives of others around us. The glow is magnified and glorified when passed to others, as if the wind of the Holy Spirit fans it brighter as we pass it along.

Another thing, though, that keeps the word from shining brightly is the sin in our lives. If we are so used to sin being there, that we have become insensitive to the Holy Spirit speaking to us, then when the flame of the Word comes to us, we are calloused to it, and it doesn't burn our hearts the way that it should. We douse the flames with our self-centeredness and stubbornness because we don't feel like sharing the Word with others when it doesn't seem to have any effect on us. We are trying to ignore the pleadings and urgings of the Spirit, so we naturally would avoid talking about them to our friends. We have heard the saying, "The buck stops here." Well, we need to add, "The torch stops here." If we are not feeling the burning of the Word in our heart, so much so, that we just have to share it with someone else, then that is exactly what happens. Don't douse or hide the flame. Be a torchbearer, and pass it on.

Standing in the Gap

"I looked for a man among them who would build up the wall and stand before me in the gap on behalf of the Lord so I would not have to destroy it, but I found none." Ez. 22:30

When our children were young, we would take them on many long hikes and adventures. Sometimes we would come to a break in the path, where it was necessary to jump or stretch a long distance to make it to the other side. This is where my long legs and arms came in handy, for I could stretch the distance easily, then help the others across. In my mind, this is what it means to stand in the gap—being a human bridge to help others get through obstacles that they wouldn't be able to make on their own.

However, there is another kind of standing in the gap that is mentioned here. The children of Israel had rebelled against the Lord, and they were worshipping idols, committing incest and adultery, murdering strangers, and oppressing the widows and orphans (22:1-12). God was filled with wrath, and He was ready to wipe them all out. It says that He looked for a single individual who would stand in the gap on their behalf, and be a mediator between God and man. In the past, God had found such a man—Moses. When the Israelites were in the wilderness, God was going to destroy them for their idolatry, but Moses begged for mercy (Psa. 106:21-23). He "stood in the gap" between the Lord and the people, and the Lord saved the people because of Moses' faith, in spite of the people's rebellion.

The same thing happened again later, except this time it was the grandson of Aaron, Phinehas, who bridged the gap. God sent a great plague upon the people for bowing down to foreign gods and marrying foreign women. It wasn't until Phinehas took a spear and killed one of the guilty men and his foreign wife that God stopped his fury. The Bible says that God accepted this act of Phinehas as an act of atonement for the sins of the people because "he was zealous for the honor of his God" (Num. 25:13). He stood in the gap, and he kept God from destroying the people.

At times, maybe we have had to do the same thing. We are aware of the sins of our children, or our friends, or our nation, and we have pleaded with God for His mercy. We know that the others are struggling with their faith, and probably deserve God's wrath, but we stand in the gap, and hope that our faith and prayers will be sufficient. Even though this works, at times, we know that ultimately, as far as salvation is concerned, only Jesus can be the mediator between God and man. He stood in the gap on the cross, and took upon himself all of the wrath of God. Yet, when it comes to the day by day rebelliousness of our hearts, sometimes God allows us to stand in the gap for those we love. So, the greatest warriors are often the prayer warriors, who sitting, standing, or kneeling, can bridge the gap to God for someone we love.

Seaweed Wrapped Around My Head

"Seaweed was wrapped around my head. To the roots of the mountains I sank down." Jonah 2:6

Everyone knows the story of Jonah. He was told by God to tell the people of Nineveh to repent so they could be saved. He refused, and he ran away from God. A great storm came, and the men on the boat had to throw Jonah overboard to save their own lives. Then God sent a huge fish, probably a whale, to swallow Jonah so that he would not die. Three days later he was thrown up onto the shore, and he ended up preaching to the people after all. All of this we know, for we have heard this story since the time we were children.

Yet, there is a part of this story that we usually are not told. What happened to Jonah when he was thrown overboard? We picture in our minds the whale hovering near the surface and catching Jonah in its mouth the moment he entered the water. Unfortunately, this is not the case. Jonah tells us the rest of the story from inside the whale. While he was in the belly of the whale, he prayed, "You hurled me into the deep, into the very heart of the seas…The engulfing waters threatened me, the deep surrounded me; seaweed was wrapped around my head. To the roots of the mountains I sank down…When my life was ebbing away, I remembered you, Lord" (Jonah 2:3-7).

In other words, the Lord didn't save Jonah the moment he was thrown off the ship. He let him sink down as low as he could go without dying before he saved him. He made him feel the slimy seaweed around his head, the turmoil of the raging sea, and the darkness of the deep, clear to the roots of the mountains. One can't get any lower than that this side of hell.

Why did God let him sink so far before he helped him? Sometimes God helps us immediately, but sometimes he waits for us to reach the depths of desperation. He knows that our needs sometimes go much deeper than the surface problem that we are dealing with. We are looking for a band-aid and a kiss on our "owie", and He is trying to cure the cancer of our souls. We don't understand that many of our problems are results of our own sins, and that God wants us to learn a lesson before He comes to help us. He wants us to struggle first so we won't be tempted to fall into the same mess again. Jonah rebelled against God, and was foolish enough to think that he could run away from Him. God had to teach him that He was in control. Jonah waited till he hit bottom before he acknowledged the Lord, and even when he was rescued, he looked a mess. After all, he was being digested for three days before he was vomited by a smelly fish. Even when God rescues us, we still may have seaweed around our heads and puke in our nostrils. We may be saved, but our past may still cause us to stink. Unconditional love is the kind of love that loves a lot even though it knows a lot and has to hold its nose a lot.

The Spice of Life

"You are the salt of the earth." Matt. 5:13

In modern culture, salt is used primarily to add taste to different foods. So, when we read in the Bible that we are suppose to be the salt of the earth, we look at it as a positive thing. We are supposed to add spice to life. We are supposed to make the trials of life easier to swallow because of our kindness, love, and generosity.

Salt, though, is used for other things besides taste. It is also a preservative. Before refrigerators, in fact, salt was used as the main way of preserving meat. As Christians, we too are supposed to be preservatives—preserving the principles and truths of God's Word in our pagan world. How are we supposed to do that? Salt is a compound of acid and some other base mineral. There are over 2,000 different kinds of salt based on what the base mineral is, but the one common in all of them is acid. Though we think of acid as a harmful thing, it is actually what helps to preserve the food. It eats away at the bacteria that forms on food, so that the food will not be harmed. Christians are supposed to have this acidic part to our natures which seeks to destroy or control the spiritual bacteria in the world.

Salt is a corrosive as well as a preservative. If put on grass, for example, it will actually burn the grass. When used in the right quantities, however, salt is really a fertilizer that helps things to grow. The problem is that many Christians are too acidic or corrosive, and not enough useful fertilizer. We do an overkill on the bacteria around us, and we end up harming the good plant life that we are supposed to be trying to help. We are so negative or anti-everything, that we leave a sour taste in everyone's mouth whenever we are near. Jesus is our example of what salt is supposed to be like. He is the perfect blend of acid (truth) and taste (love), and we need to follow his ideal balance of the sweet and sour of life.

Besides being used to preserve that which is good, salt is also used to purify that which has gone bad. It is used by the prophet, Elisha, for example, to purify a pool of water for the people to drink (2 Kings 2:20). The presence of Christians in any group should help to purify any evil that has crept in. We should have such a positive impact on the attitudes, goals, and actions of the group, that we should be able to turn even the most bitter of circumstances into a much more mellow experience.

Salt is created when the heat of the sun evaporates the water and leaves the crystallized compound behind. The salt of the Christian is created the same way. We gain our saltiness when we go through the heat of our trials, and we come out the other side more purified and ready to purify. We are able to add spice to life because we are actively working against everything that is dead—sin, idolatry, Godlessness—not just by being against things that are bad, but by being a sweet, smelling savor to every thing we touch. We don't destroy, we transform.

Where is your Treasure?

"Do not store up for yourselves treasures on earth, where moth and rust destroy, and where thieves break in and steal. But store up for yourselves treasures in heaven...For where your treasure is, there will your heart be also." Matt. 6:19-21

This is a very hard doctrine to follow, especially for Christians in our western civilization who base much of their time and energy on working hard so they can have more things. They want a bigger house, a nicer car, a fancier TV, a boat, an RV, a cell phone, new furniture, a hot tub, more and more gadgets and toys, and the list goes on and on. We live in a materialistic world where having lots of things is a priority. It doesn't matter to us that there are starving children in Africa, or families that live in cardboard boxes in Mexico. We are proud of our prosperity, and even justify it as God's blessing upon a Christian nation. It is our Christian work ethic that has given us all these things, we think, so there is no reason to feel guilty about how much we own. We've earned it, and God has blessed us with it, so what's the problem?

There are several problems actually. The first has to do with priorities. What is the most important to us? The Bible says, "Seek first the kingdom of God and his righteousness, and all these things shall be added unto you" (Matt. 6:33). There is nothing wrong with having things. In fact, God promises to give them to us. However, He wants us to put Him first in our lives. If having things is more important than having Christ as the Lord of our life, then the things are too important. When anything is more important to us than God, it is idolatry. When the rich young ruler came to Jesus and asked him what he needed to do to be saved, Jesus told him to "Sell everything you have and give to the poor, and you will have treasure in heaven" (Luke 18:22). This is the test. We need to ask ourselves, if God asked us to give up everything we own and give it to the poor, would we be able to do it? This is hard. We have spent our lifetime getting these things. They are our treasures. Yes, but are they more important to us than our relationship with God? Also, if we have more than we need, shouldn't we be willing to be generous with our abundance? Are we hoarding up a lot of extra for our own future use, or are we giving to the poor and less fortunate than ourselves?

First, we need to acknowledge that everything we have is a gift of God, and not just things that we have earned. They do not belong to us, they are merely loaned to us by God for good keeping. Second, when God gives us things, he expects us to be generous with them. In other words, he gives them to us to give away, not to keep. The Bible says, "You will be made rich in every way so that you can be generous" (2 Cor. 9:11). If our treasure is here on earth, and that is the most important thing to us, then it is the only treasure that we will ever receive. Yet, if our treasure is the Lord's presence, it will be a treasure forever.

Why Worry?

"Do not worry...Who of you by worrying can add a single hour to his life?"
Matt. 6:25-27

Everyone worries at one time or another. It is so common, in fact, that someone might get worried about us if we didn't ever worry. Yet, whether we like to admit it or not, worry is a sin. The Lord commands us not to worry, and the Bible says that, "Whatever is not of faith is sin" (Rom. 14:23). We cannot be filled with faith and worry at the same time.

Besides this obvious truth, there are also some negative aspects to worry that we need to be aware of. First, the word "worry" means to irritate. When we work real hard without gloves, we are probably going to get blisters on our hands. The shovel or pick that we were using caused an irritation on our skin. Yet, what happens when we work hard over a long period of time? Those blisters turn to calluses, and they don't bother us any more. The same thing happens spiritually speaking. Worry irritates our souls. It causes troubling blisters on our hearts. They are warnings that we shouldn't worry any more. Yet, when we continue to worry anyway, we can develop spiritual calluses, and we get to the point that worrying doesn't bother our conscience any more. We just accept worrying as part of life, instead of the sin that it is.

The second definition of worry is "a plague". A plague is different than just an illness, in that, it is highly infectious. It spreads to others easily. When we worry, we usually share our worries with others. We spread the disease of the heart, and we get others to worry also. We are generous with our germs of the soul. It irritates others until they too become calloused, and we all become insensitive to the Holy Spirit's telling us, "Don't worry. Trust in the Lord." It's easier to just worry, we think.

The third definition of worry, though, makes it a little bit harder to deal with. It means to harass. Actually, it means to harass like a dog biting at our heels, constantly barking, never letting up. It won't go away. It just keeps eating away at us until we don't have a leg to stand on. It consumes us.

Worry, then, is not just a sin. It is self-destructive, and harmful to those around us. It is like an acid that burns into the depths of our inner self, and takes over our whole being like leprosy. Not only that, it is an insult to God. Think about it. Every time that we decide to worry, we are basically telling the Lord that we don't trust Him. We would rather hold on to our feelings rather than our faith. We would rather feel sorry for ourselves than to move forward with the hope and assurance that God is sufficient to carry us through. The only thing we need to worry about is the fact that we worry too much. We need to recognize this for what it is—sin—and turn our problem over to the Lord. Trust and obey, and He'll show the way. Why worry, when we can pray?

A Double Standard

"Do not judge, or you too will be judged. For in the same way you judge others, you will be judged." Matt. 7:1

Have you ever attended a sporting event where you felt that the referees were prejudiced in favor of the home team? Every time the opposing side even looked at the ball wrong, they got called for a penalty. On the other hand, every time the home team committed a flagrant fowl, the referees were purposely looking the other way. If you are rooting for the home team, you might notice the oversight, but you have no complaints. Yet, if you are for the opposition, you feel like charging onto the playing field and pouncing on the judge. It is unfair, you cry. There shouldn't be a double standard. Everyone should be judged the same. At least this is our opinion when we feel we have been wronged. If we are in the wrong, then all we want is mercy. We too have a double standard.

Well, believe it or not, God has a double standard also. He has his own standard, of course, which is based on his own holiness and character, but he also judges us by our standard. What do I mean? The Bible says that "in the same way you judge others, you will be judged". That means that He not only judges us by His standard, but by the standard that we use to judge other people. In fact, sometimes our standard even preempts God's. For example, if our standards are very low, and our philosophy of life is "live and let live", then we probably don't judge others very often. God's standard is always there, though, and we will be accountable to his values, not ours, if our conscience is so insensitive that we feel no guilt for our sins, or no acknowledgement of the sins of others.

However, if God has chosen to be merciful to someone, but we come down hard on them because they don't live up to our standards, then God will not be merciful to us. He, instead, will judge us with the same standard that we use to judge that other person, without grace. Have we ever, for example, judged someone for being lazy and wasting time at work, and yet we slack off sometimes ourselves? Then God will judge us in the same way that we judge the other person. Have we ever judged someone for being dishonest, and yet we have lied or stolen whenever it suited our need? Why is it right or justified when we do it, but wrong when someone else does it? Basically, this is hypocrisy, when we judge others for something, when we do the same thing ourselves. We want God to come down hard on them, but look the other way when it comes to us. We want God to have a double standard--One for us, and one for everyone else.

Well, He does have a double standard—His own, and ours, and we will be held accountable for both. The only way that we can avoid this is if we don't judge others. If, however, we continue to look down on others, we will be hit with a double-edged sword—ours and God's.

The Golden Rule

"Do to others what you would have them do to you." Matt. 7:12

Most people have heard some version of the Golden Rule. Even other religions, such as Buddhism, Confucianism, etc. have their versions. The version that I usually heard when I was growing up was after I had done something mean to one of my siblings. My mom or dad would say, "Is that the way that you would want to be treated?" This rule has an appeal to justice or fairness. It is used both to subdue negative behavior, and to encourage the positive.

Yet, even though most people know this rule, most people are unaware of where the name, "The Golden Rule", came from. The Bible doesn't call it that. It actually isn't called by this name until the 18th century. It is derived from a rule of arithmetic called "The Golden Rule". This rule is the rule of proportions. It states that "A is to B what B is to C." For example, 1 is to 4 what 8 is to 11. It is a rule of equal comparisons. In the early schools in America and Europe, Christianity was taught side by side with reading, writing, and arithmetic. The teachers didn't just teach specialized subjects. They taught them all. In doing so, they often made connections between the subjects that we often miss today. They would tie together principles that were learned in history to philosophy, science to psychology, writing to relationships, and yes, even arithmetic to religion. Just as in math, they reasoned, the way that we treat one another should be based in proportion to how we want to be treated. There should be a direct correlation.

Even as the second greatest commandment states, we should love others in the same way that we love ourselves. Although this is a good principle, for it promotes fairness , equality, and sensitivity, it really falls short of God's ultimate standard. Yes, Jesus gave the Golden Rule, so it is God's standard, but it is only meant to be the bare minimum, not the ultimate. The ultimate standard or the ideal actually reaches beyond this. It is based on the life of Jesus himself. It isn't based on equal proportions, but in self-sacrifice. Jesus states it this way: "If someone wants to sue you and take your tunic, let him have your cloak as well. If someone forces you to go one mile, go with him two miles" (Matt. 5:40-41). This goes beyond equal proportions. We are to go way beyond what anyone would ask or think. We are to go the extra mile. Isn't this what Jesus did? We are to love others with no expectations of any return.

In today's pessimistic world, if someone is nice to us, our first response is, "What do you want?" We can't imagine someone being nice without wanting something in return. This is the twisted Golden Rule—being nice so they'll give you what you want. God wants us to get past our selfish motives for doing good. That's fine for a child who is just learning to be kind, but we need to love because it is part of our Christ-like character, not just as a means to an end.

Faith like a Mustard Seed

"If you have faith as small as a mustard seed, you can say to this mountain, 'Move from here to there' and it will move. Nothing will be impossible for you." Matt. 17:20

Although the emphasis here seems to be on the size of the mustard seed and how little faith needs to be in order to accomplish great things, we can also learn some other things about faith from this small seed. For example, the word "mustard" itself actually means "strong scent". As a seed it doesn't really smell that much, but when the seed is crushed, the scent carries far and wide. It can dominate and fill a room easily. The same thing is true with Christians. It is only when we are crushed or broken that we really learn to trust in God, and our faith can spread to others like a sweet smelling fragrance as they see us respond to the trials of life.

The mustard seed is also a diuretic, which means that it helps our body to rid itself of excess fluids and toxins in our system. Our faith should do the same thing, for it helps us to stop trusting in our self, and to put more of our trust in the Lord. It helps us to get rid of the spiritual toxins of fear and doubt, and replaces them with faith and hope.

The mustard seed is a stimulant as well. It makes our body organs work harder and more efficiently. It is so easy for Christians to fall into a comfort zone, where we become spiritual couch potatoes or voyeurs of what others are doing, but we are not willing to become active ourselves. We put money in the offering as sort of payment for the entertainment, expecting others to do the work for us. The Lord wants us to have the faith of a mustard seed so we can be stimulated to action, energized by the inspiration of the Holy Spirit.

Faith is compared to a seed here for a purpose. It is meant to grow. The mustard seed, even though it is the smallest seed that is used in the gardens of the Holy Land at this time, can grow into a tree that is ten to fifteen feet high, big enough for birds to make their nests in. Even though faith may begin small, it is evidence of great potential. It can give shade to other weaker plants that would wither in the full sun. The mustard plant, on the other hand, thrives in full heat when well-watered. Our faith, too, is meant to help us even through the toughest times, as we rely on the nourishment of the Word and the comforting springs of the Spirit.

One other use for the mustard seed is to make a poultice or mustard plaster, which is applied to the skin, like a moist heating pad, to sooth away aching muscles, and to relax and cleanse the skin. When we have faith in God, it should have the same effect upon our souls. We should be able to relax and rest in the Spirit, and it should sooth away and heal the pains of our broken or bruised hearts. If we have the faith of a mustard seed, then, we should not only be able to move mountains, but smooth away all the jagged crags in our souls as well.

He Must Increase

"He must increase; I must decrease." John 3:30

John the baptizer was a pop-icon. He had crowds coming to him from all over. At the peak of his popularity, in fact, it says that "the whole Judean countryside and all the people of Jerusalem went out to him" (Mark:1:5). When Christ came on the scene, though, a lot of the attention was shifted away from John to Jesus. John's disciples, his groupies, got a little jealous, and they wanted John to protest somehow. They thought that John might be the Messiah until Jesus came, so it was a let down when John's influence started fading. They wanted their man, their hero, to receive glory so they could be pulled along by his coat-tails into that same glory. It was like a political campaign, and they were hoping their guy would win.

John, though, would have none of it. He wasn't in it for the popularity or glory. He knew exactly what his role was—to prepare the way of the Lord. He knew the Messiah was coming, and he knew it was his job just to sweep the path for the King. John's disciples were hoping he was going to be the king, but John knew that he was just the spiritual custodian or janitor getting ready for the royal procession. John wasn't jealous at all. He says, in fact, that now that the Christ has come, his joy is complete. His goal has been fulfilled—mission accomplished. He says, "He must increase; I must decrease."

We, too, need to come to this same conclusion. Our lives, our ministries, our mission fields, our goals, our families, our possessions—aren't really "ours" at all. It's not about us. It's not about how successful we can become, or how many converts we can win, or how many baptisms we can do, or how many people we can get into our churches, or how many TV channels or radio stations we can broadcast on. Our churches and ministries have become another extension of our competitive society, and we are competing with other ministries for people and money. We need to come to the same place as John, and tell our disciples, "Hey, folks. I'm not the messiah. Stop focusing on me, and focus on Christ.

Even if we are not in the ministry, but just trying to walk with the Lord each day, the emphasis needs to be on Him, not ourselves. The primary focus of our prayers, our thoughts, our desires, our goals, and our dreams should be on Jesus, not just our own self-centeredness. Our question always should not be, "What do I want?", but "What does the Lord want?" "What would Jesus do in this situation?" "Is this glorifying to the Lord, or am I just seeking my own glory?" "Am I doing this because I want more rewards in heaven or more blessings here on earth, or am I doing it without any expectation for anything that might benefit me." John was willing to lose his popularity, his followers, and even his head for the sake of lifting up Christ. He learned the secret that we can't become more until we first are willing to become less.

The Truth Will Set You Free

"You will know the truth, and the truth will set you free." John 8:32

I attended a secular university once where the library had this verse engraved on the entry way. Of course, it didn't identify where the quote came from, and I am sure that it didn't mean the same thing to them that it means to us. To the secular world, education is the answer to society's problems, and knowledge will set you free from any self-destructive or society-destructive behavior. In their thinking, once a person knows the truth, they will no longer have any reason to do wrong, for prejudice and evil are only products of ignorance.

This verse, however, is not talking about the value of education. It is talking about the value of knowing Jesus. It is only when we know Jesus that we will know the truth, for Jesus is "the way, the truth, and the life, and no man comes to the Father but by [Him]" (John 14:6). Before we know Jesus, we are slaves to sin, not because of ignorance, but because of our sinful, fallen nature. We need a savior, not an education, to free us from our bondage. The world can only offer a superficial kind of freedom and a shallow truth. If we accept Christ, however, we can experience true liberty. "If the Son sets you free, you will be free indeed" (John 8:36).

There is more to this freedom, though, than just knowing Jesus. The context of Jesus' teaching is, "If you hold to my teaching, you are really my disciples. Then you will know the truth, and the truth will set you free." Knowing the truth is never just an intellectual thing. It is always based on obedience. If God has revealed his truth to us, and we have obeyed that truth, then he will reveal even more truth to us, and that truth will set us free. If, on the other hand, we reject or disobey the little truth that we have, God will not set us free from our sins, nor will he reveal any more to us. We, in fact, become even a deeper slave to our sin, because we have turned away from the light that God has tried to give to us. The truth of God will only set us free if we accept it and obey it. Those who disobey it, no matter how educated they are, are really slaves to the Devil, who is the Father of Lies, "not holding to the truth, for there is no truth in him" (John 8:44).

Of course, the scholars would say, "Don't insult our intelligence. We don't even believe in the Devil." Yet, if we were to ask those same scholars, "Doesn't truth stand alone, totally apart from whether anyone believes it or not?", they would have to say, "Yes". Truth has to stand alone, apart from faith, for Jesus is truth, and he cannot stop being truth just because we don't believe in him. Truth is not just a characteristic of Jesus, like a piece of clothing that he can put on or take off according to the fad of the day. It is an essential quality of his essence. It is part of the eternal "I AM". If we know that essence, and become one with it, then that truth becomes part of our essence, and that obedient truth will set us free.

June 25

I Have Overcome the World

"In this world you will have trouble. But take heart! I have overcome the world."
John 16:33

What a powerful promise. We don't have to worry about the trials of this life, for Christ has already overcome the world. His victory gives us hope. We have already won because He has already won. Yet, when exactly did Jesus win? When did He overcome the world? At the crucifixion, when he died on the cross for the sins of the world? At the resurrection, when he had victory over death, and gave us the hope for immortality? Actually, Jesus makes this statement, "I have overcome the world", before He is even arrested.

How on earth did Jesus overcome the world even before his death and resurrection? First of all, he survived being born. Joseph could have accused Mary of adultery when he found out she was pregnant, and he could have had her stoned. Second, Jesus could have been killed when Herod had all the baby boys be killed in Bethlehem. Third, Jesus lived thirty-three years on this earth without sinning. Fourth, he was tempted by the Devil, himself, for forty days in the desert, yet he did not sin. Fifth, he was attacked by God's worst enemies, the religious leaders and the demon possessed, and he still acted with integrity, wisdom, and compassion. Sixth, he was able to cast out demons, heal the sick, raise the dead, and forgive sins, all by his own authority. Seventh, he was able to escape being killed by the Jews numerous times, not being crucified until he was ready, until the time was right. Satan, death, God's enemies—no one and nothing had any power over him. He had victory over them all, even before his death and resurrection.

Yet, he chose to do it all through the power of the Holy Spirit, instead of his own power, so that we too would know that we also could have that same victory. We can be "more than conquerors through Him that loved us" (Rom. 8:37), "for everyone born of God overcomes the world. This is the victory that has overcome the world, even our faith" (I John 5:4). Yes, we will still have trouble in this world, even as Jesus did, but we are to "take heart" and not give up. If Jesus could do it through the power of the Spirit, then so can we.

One of Satan's greatest temptations is to make Christians think that we can't make it, that we are losers, and that there is no way to win over his ultimate powers. This is a lie. Satan has already lost, he just doesn't know it yet. It is our job to educate him. Every time that he tempts us to have a panic attack, to get discouraged, or to give up, we need to help him get his facts straight. We need to say, "Satan, I think you are mistaken. You have it all backwards. You are the loser. You are the one who doesn't have a chance against the power of God. Jesus has already won.

Divide and Conquer

"On that day a great persecution broke out against the church at Jerusalem,
and all except the apostles were scattered." Acts 8:1

One of the great chants of the civil rights movement of the sixties was "United we stand, divided we fall." Everyone recognizes the fact that there is strength in numbers. One of Satan's greatest tools is to split the church so it will be less effective. If he can cause a division in the church, where Christians are fighting or arguing with other Christians, he can destroy the faith of many people at one time. Even in the early church, when thousands were becoming Christians in a single day, Satan knew that he needed to get them separated in order to have victory over them. United they were just too strong. So he caused great persecution. If Satan can't bring a church down from within, he will bring it down from without. He will cause whole communities to rise up against certain congregations, passing laws against too much noise, or too much traffic congestion. Building codes are sometimes changed to discourage construction or growth, and some churches are forced to move just so they can continue to grow.

Yet, even though all of this persecution seems so bad, and we all know who the source of the irritation is, we also need to recognize that God allows this persecution for a reason. For example, when the early church was persecuted, it was scattered across the known world. What was the result of this forced division? "Those who had been scattered preached the word wherever they went" (Acts 8:4). It would have been easy for the early Christians to get too comfortable back in Jerusalem, where all the apostles were, where there was always good preaching, and lots of miracles. Why go anywhere else? Yet, what about the rest of the world? Well, leave that to someone else. God had other plans. He wanted them to go into all the world to preach the gospel, even if they didn't really want to go. So, he allowed the persecution in order to spread out the Christians, so that the power of the good news would be shared with others who needed to know the way.

We have similar situations in our lives, where we look at circumstances as being bad, yet they are really used by God to redirect our lives. We want to stay in our comfort zone, but God wants us to move on, to grow, and to be used somewhere else. So, He allows us to lose our jobs, get sick, be ostracized by our families, be divorced or abandoned by a spouse, and we are devastated. Instead of getting discouraged or defeated, though, we need to accept the situation as allowed by God for a purpose. We need to ask the Lord what he wants to teach us, be receptive to whatever he tells us, and go wherever he leads. Satan may have designed the catastrophe for our harm, but God allowed it for our good. Good conquers evil even in the midst of division, for when we are separated from others who give us strength, we are forced to rely more on God.

Be Not Ashamed

"I am not ashamed of the gospel because it is the power of God for the salvation of everyone who believes." Rom. 1:16

Have you ever gotten caught with your hand in the cookie jar? When you are a child, being caught taking a cookie when you have been told not to can be a devastating experience. It is embarrassing being caught red-handed. You can't deny it or excuse it. You are filled with shame for you know that you are guilty, and others know it too. If you are just a child, the shame probably won't last too long. You may get punished, but then it's over. You get over it. As an adult, it is different. Getting caught often means long-lasting consequences. It may mean the loss of a job, getting divorced, going to jail, or losing a reputation that you have been trying to build all of your life. It can all be over in a minute, yet the consequences last a lifetime.

Being ashamed, then, is usually thought of as being degrading and disgraceful in the sight of others. Why, then, would Paul say, "I am not ashamed of the gospel"? Is the gospel something that people are ashamed of? The gospel is not something bad. Why would someone be embarrassed about it? I think part of the explanation lies in the root for the word "shame". It is "sham". It means a lie or deceit that you have been caught in. It means you have been a phony, and others have found out the truth.

Unfortunately, this is why we are sometimes embarrassed about people knowing we are Christians. Christianity has been given a bad name by a lot of people who claim to be Christians, but who live ungodly lives. Sometimes they are worse than the non-Christians. They are judgmental, bitter, hypocritical pretenders of the Way, and many Christians are ashamed or shy about proclaiming their faith because they don't want to be associated with "them".

It is interesting that the pagan word "shaman" comes from this same root. The shaman is the magician or witchdoctor of the pagans. Ironically, even he is derided by the non-believing world as being just a trickster who is able to deceive people through his ability to create illusions. We, as Christians, are often put into the same class of people, con-artists, who will do anything and say anything just to get more power and more money. We are phonies, and the world knows it.

In spite of the phonies, though, it doesn't change the validity of Christianity itself, and those, like Paul, who are genuine in their faith, have every reason to stand boldly for what they believe, with confidence in the truth of "the power of God for the salvation of everyone who believes." There is no reason to be ashamed of something that has passed the test of time. Jesus was no shaman, and Christianity is not a sham, so we don't need to be ashamed of the power of Christ. Only be ashamed if we say that we believe, but don't live it.

Producing Hope

"Hope does not disappoint us, because God has poured out his love into our hearts by the Holy Spirit, whom he has given us." Romans 5:5

Everyone recognizes that hope is a good thing, and that we need more of it. Yet, who can explain how we can get more hope? Is it just a gift of God, and we just need to pray and ask for it? Well, the Bible tells us where it comes from, but you aren't going to like the answer. There is a process that we need to go through. The Apostle Paul tells us, "we know that suffering produces perseverance; perseverance, character; and character, hope" (Rom. 5:4).

That's right—hope starts with suffering. That's just the opposite of what we might think. In our minds we are more hopeful when everything is going our way. Doesn't suffering tend to destroy hope, not build it? To a certain degree this is true. There are different levels of hope. The first level of hope is similar to happiness, in that, it depends on circumstances. If everything is going in a positive direction, just the way we want it, then we are happy and hopeful for even better things.

However, happiness has a deeper level called joy. Joy is not based upon circumstances. It is based on our relationship with the Lord, and our peace and confidence in who He is, not what we are going through. Hope also has a deeper level. It is still called by the same name, but it is not based on good times. It is produced, in fact, through suffering—not just any kind of suffering, but suffering for the name of Christ. Other kinds of suffering can actually rob us of our hope, but suffering for Christ can build it.

What happens is that when we take a stand for the Lord, and we are persecuted for it, we are being tested to see how much our faith really means to us. This kind of suffering produces perseverance, and builds strong character. Our strong character helps us to stand firm upon the Christian principles that we believe in, and God blesses us for our perseverance and faith. He pours "out his love into our hearts by the Holy Spirit", which gives us the hope to carry on. It is the kind of hope that is borne on the wings of affliction because it has seen the power and strength of the Lord in action, and knows that his grace is sufficient. It is the kind of hope that is built on the solid assurance that God will provide "all our needs according to his riches in glory" because of who he is, not because we happen to deserve it.

Like it or not, we can't just get this kind of hope as a gentle gift, like manna from heaven. We have to learn it the hard way. We have to fight in the trenches of spiritual warfare, and experience the victory that can only come through humbly trusting in the power of the Almighty. If we don't have the guts to persevere, it means that we have a weak character, and we may need to suffer more in the spiritual boot camp of life before the Captain of our Faith will have any hope for us.

When Even God is Speechless

"The Spirit intercedes for us with groans that words cannot express."
Romans 8:26

We have all heard the statement, "A picture is worth a thousand words." Well, here is a new one: "A groan is worth ten-thousand words." If the groan is from the Holy Spirit, that is. The Bible tells us that there are times when the Holy Spirit doesn't pray for us in words. He prays for us in groans. I don't believe this is always the case. It is only during those times that we are so over-whelmed with life that we too have to pray with groans because we don't know how else to pray. The problems that we are facing are so complex that there just doesn't seem to be any right answer. We just know that we need help or we are going to drown. We are going under for the last time, and there just are no words that can express the lonely desperation that we feel. One last groan and then gurgle, gurgle to the grave.

The Holy Spirit feels our pain. He is the comforter, the healer, and the intercessor, so he prays for us by groaning with us. His groans are groans of empathy, not because he doesn't know how to pray, for he knows exactly what our needs are. His job is not just to intercede for us by expressing our conscious thoughts and needs, but the deepest cries of our souls. Our minds may be speechless for nothing makes sense on the logical plane, but our spirits are being tormented or torn apart, and the Holy Spirit, who dwells in this tortured temple, grieves, growls, and groans with our spirits, so that even our inner, sub-conscious prayers may be heard. This gives us hope, for we know that He understands our pain.

We know that we don't have to find the words to express our agony. It isn't necessary for us to understand what is going on, or what the solutions need to be. In God's way and in His timing, we know that "in all things God works for the good of those who love him, who have been called according to His purpose" (Rom. 8:28). It is enough for us to know that He has a purpose or plan for us because he loves us. It isn't necessary for us to understand the plan, or for it to even make sense. We may need to just keep groaning while were growing, until God fulfills his plan.

Even though we may feel like we are taking our last breath before it's all over, from God's perspective, it is really the first breath of the rest of our lives. It is the gasp for air of a new child coming into the world, every time that we grow into a new level of spiritual maturity. It doesn't matter how old we are, or how long we have been Christians. Growing in our faith is like a progression of painful rebirths. Every time that we are set free from the bondage of a particular area of our lives, it's like starting fresh, except with a greater wisdom than before. Our groans and the groans of the Holy Spirit, then, are good groans, for they indicate the breaking free from our old selves, and the Spirit's groans are just labor pains.

If God is for Us

"If God is for us, who can be against us?" Romans 8:31

This is one of those rhetorical questions where there is an obvious answer—"No one, of course." Yet, if we look past the obvious for a moment, it isn't that simple. In fact, the answer could be just the opposite—"everyone", and still be accurate. For it is exactly because God is for us, that everyone else could be against us. God has a lot of enemies, and we have those same enemies by association. There is the Devil and all of his demons. There are all the unbelievers who have sided against the Lord in their hard-hearted unbelief. There are also all the Christians, who at times can be used by Satan to thwart the cause of Christ in their actions, attitudes and words. Remember Christ's rebuking Peter, "Get thee behind me, Satan." Yes, even Christians can be the worst enemies of Christ and other Christians, for Satan can often do more damage to the church from within, than from without. Then there is ourselves. Sometimes we are our own worst enemies. Our sinful natures often work havoc in our lives, suppressing the truth, and cherishing idols within our souls. If God is for us, then, it is probable that everyone, including ourselves, will be against us, just as they were against Christ. When we become Christians, in fact, it is like painting a huge target on our chests, saying "shoot here". We are asking for trouble.

We don't like this answer, though. We would rather go back to the rhetorical, "obvious" answer, "no one can be against us". Maybe we need to reword the verse a little, with all apologies to the Apostle Paul, in order to get to the truth that is there. Maybe it should say, "If God is for us, no one has a chance in standing against us. There will be many who will try, but all attempts will be futile." Considering the context of this verse, I don't think this interpretation is out of line. Paul's point is that Christ has paid the price for our sins. We are justified and sanctified because of his death on the cross. It doesn't matter if Satan or anyone else in the universe attacks us, then, for our sins will not be held to our account. It isn't that we are perfect or sinless. We are just forgiven and pardoned. The crime of sin has already been wiped clean. Christ has paid the penalty of death, so we can have eternal life. We can't be tried again for the same crime, for that would be double jeopardy. We have already been declared innocent. If God, then, is for us, we have both the judge and the defense attorney on our side, so the Devil, or chief prosecutor, doesn't have a chance. He can do all the accusing and attacking that he wants, and he will, but he is the only one who will have to pay for his spiritual assaults. He has already been tried and found guilty of fraud, pride, idolatry, and a thousand other crimes, so the judge will throw out his testimony against us, not only because of Christ's death, but Satan makes an unreliable character witness.

Nothing Can Separate Us

"Who shall separate us from the love of Christ?"   Romans 8:35

We live in a very fluid world. It is constantly changing. We live in several houses during our life. We have many different jobs. We buy new clothes to go with every fad. We have to have a new car every five years or so. Even our relationships fluctuate. It used to be that people married for life. Now, they have prenuptial agreements, preparing for the inevitable divorce. Nothing seems permanent. There is so much instability in life, in fact, that many people are seeing therapists on a regular basis just to be able to cope with all the stress of uncertainty.

When we hear the question, then, of "Who shall separate us from the love of Christ?", we tend to put it into our modern context. From our perspective, love is just as temporary as everything else. So, the answer to the question would probably be, "Just about anything." We sin every day, so it seems logical to think that Christ would grow tired of us very quickly. Besides, he is God, which means he doesn't need anyone or anything. He could walk away without blinking an eternal eyelash. Yet, does he?

The Apostle Paul tells us, "I am convinced that neither death nor life, neither angels nor demons, neither the present nor the future, nor any powers, neither height nor depth, nor anything else in all creation, will be able to separate us from the love of God that is in Christ Jesus our Lord" (Rom. 8:38-39). Nothing can separate us, then. That is right. Nothing.

Why would God maintain a relationship with people who are so unfaithful to him? We have to go back to the reason why the relationship began in the first place. It certainly didn't start because we deserved it. The Bible makes it very clear that God saved us "while we were still his enemies", and that his love for us is based on grace alone (Eph. 2:8-9). If God loved us enough to die for us, then, in spite of the fact that we are so stubborn and self-centered, why would he abandon us later just because we sin? He knew that we would be unfaithful to him before he even claimed us as his bride. There are no surprises here.

Yet, he has a plan for us that extends past our present lives. He didn't just marry us. He is busy transforming us. We are a work in progress. It is like the taming of the shrew. What we are is not important. What he is changing us into is the priority. We are being transformed into "the likeness of his Son" (Rom. 8:29). It is our destiny, and nothing can change that plan. God is not someone who starts something, but then changes his mind. He has set his seal of ownership on us (2 Cor. 1:21-22), and his "gifts and call are irrevocable"(Rom 11:29). We shouldn't judge God according to our own standards. Just because our faith in him fluctuates like a feather in a tornado, doesn't mean that he loses his faith in us. He knows that we will turn out alright eventually, for he is the author, and he knows how the story ends.

False Expectations

"Who shall separate us from the love of Christ? Shall trouble or hardship or persecution or famine or nakedness or danger or sword?" Romans 8:35

There is nothing that can separate us from the love of God (Rom. 8:38-39). However, that doesn't keep Satan from trying to put wedges between us. If he can't separate us, at least he can make us feel like we are miles apart. He will cause all kinds of problems in our lives just to make us feel that God doesn't love us. He is a master illusionist or magician. It doesn't matter if it's real or not to him, as long as he can make us believe that it is real.

One of the reasons that we fall for his tricks, though, is our own fault. We have false expectations of what being loved by God means. We think that if God loves us, and we are right with him, then God will bless us, and everything will work out in our favor. After all, if we are the good guys, and God is on our side, then shouldn't we be the winners? So, if we are in a job situation that is abusive, and we are the victims, then we assume that if we pray about it, God will punish the abuser, and we will be vindicated. How do we respond, then, when we end up getting persecuted or fired because we have taken a stand against the abuse, and the abuser gets a raise? What went wrong here? What happened? Doesn't God love me anymore? Satan just won the battle.

The real spiritual battle is not the persecution that we receive when we stand up for Christ. That is only the surface attack. The real test is how we respond to the attack. If we respond by getting discouraged and giving up hope, and then doubting if God is real, or if his love is real, then we have just lost the battle. Yet, if we are expecting the attacks as part of being a disciple of Christ, and we realize that God only allows them so we can grow in our faith, then we can turn the attacks of the Devil upside down, and we can be victorious even while the world is rejoicing in our defeat. Remember Stephen, who was stoned for his faith, yet he was able to look up into heaven with joy in his heart and see the Son of God at the right hand of his Father. He may have suffered in a moment of time, but he was rewarded with eternity.

If we are true disciples of Christ we should expect the inevitable—Satan is going to do everything in his power to make our lives miserable, so that we will doubt God and his love, and just want to give up. Defeated Christians, then, can become his weapons to defeat other Christians, for we may belong to Christ, but still be used by the enemy. The Bible says that for the sake of Christ, "we face death all day long; we are considered as sheep to be slaughtered" (Rom. 8:36).

So, we need to take off our rose-colored glasses of false expectations and expect the worst. We are at war. Yet, don't get discouraged when it seems like we are losing. Even the death of Christ looked like a defeat, but ended up being the greatest victory. He is God. What did you expect?

Talking Back to God

"Who are you, O man, to talk back to God? Shall what is formed say to him who formed it, 'Why did you make me like this?'" Romans 9:20

Have you ever complained to God? Oh, I'm not talking about complaining about your job, or your spouse, or your miserable circumstances. I'm talking about grumbling to God about the way He has treated you or about decisions He has made. When you think about it, it is like a child talking back to his parent when the parent asks him to do something, or tells him, "No!". Being submissive to someone in authority is hard, even as a child. We want our own way. It is even harder as an adult. We think we know best.

Part of the problem is that sometimes we actually do know best when we are dealing with human authorities. We don't trust their opinions because they have made mistakes in the past, and we may not even agree with the values or priorities that they use to make their decisions.

When we are dealing with God it is the same way. We don't always have the same values or priorities that God has. So, we grumble when he makes decisions that go against what we want. Sometimes we can't understand his decisions because we thought we knew what He wanted, but He chose just the opposite. It's like a man buying a toaster for his wife for their anniversary, when she really wanted a diamond necklace. Sometimes we jump to conclusions on what God wants, and he ends up wanting something completely different. Then we get mad at him or frustrated because we guessed wrong on what He wanted, and it seems like He let us down. We complain and we argue with him, as if we could change his mind by our "solid logic".

Who do we think we are arguing with God? Are we spoiled spiritual teenagers who talk back to God when we don't get our way? The Bible says that we are nothing but lumps of clay that God has decided to make something out of. He is the potter, and if he wants, he has the right to just cast us aside as junk. We have no rights to even exist, let alone to challenge the decisions of the Creator. If we have a smart mouth with God, he could choose to have us get throat or tongue cancer so that we would never talk again. He can do whatever he wants, whenever he wants, without our permission. He is God, and we are nothing but maggots on the dung heap of the world. If it wasn't for his grace and love, he would probably destroy the world and just be done with all of our obstinate, back-talking, self-centered, immature temper tantrums.

So, we need to back off, and let God be God. His resume at being God is probably a lot more complete than ours, even if our spouse or mother thinks we are divine. We may be heavenly, but that doesn't give us the right to sit on the throne, or to tell the one who does how to do his job. The one who talks back to God will never move forward, for his spiritual vision will be stuck in reverse, and his power will be in neutral.

Zealous for God

"They are zealous for God, but their zeal is not based on knowledge."
Romans 10:2

The idea of zealousness is often confused with enthusiasm because they are very similar in some ways. They both deal with great passion in support of some person or cause. Yet, zeal is different, in that, it also has a negative side. To be zealous is to be so supportive of something that we become jealously protective of it. We become so angry and intolerant of anyone who seems to be against our cause, that we are willing to do anything to subdue them or oppress them, for they are the enemy. It is an irrational emotional response that far exceeds what is justified.

So, in one sense, the Christians killing the Muslims during the crusades, the Germans killing the Jews during the Holocaust, and the Jews killing Christ at the crucifixion were acts of zealousness. They believed so strongly for their cause, that they needed an enemy to attack in order to express all of their enthusiasm. It's like the politician who believes that people will lose their patriotic spirit if they don't have some enemy to fight against, so they pick some target and start a war, just so the people can appreciate their citizenship more. It's like they feel that unless we are strongly against something, we won't be strongly for something.

Having an enemy helps us to feel more like a victim, and more like a hero when we fight against the bad guy. It doesn't matter who it is, fighting back helps us to feel more alive. This is why there is such an emphasis on competitive sports today. It isn't enough to just be for a team or individual. We have to be adamantly against all the rest. It gets our blood flowing, and we feel like gladiators, even if we are just in the bleachers, or watching TV at home.

Yet, such enthusiasm often gets out of hand, and the spectators sometimes start attacking the other spectators, or throwing things at the referees, or becoming violent in the streets after a great victory. Zeal is not just being excited. It is irrational, self-righteous, and out-of-control. The Apostle Paul speaks of the Jews as being "zealous for God, but their zeal is not based on knowledge." He explains this by saying that, "Since they did not know the righteousness that comes from God", they "sought to establish their own." The problem is that they weren't really zealous for God at all. They were zealous for the idea that they were God's chosen people. It was an ego trip, and they thought they were something special. So, they started adding their own regulations to the law, and put themselves on pedestals to bring everyone else into submission. It was a power play, as zeal always is.

So, be enthusiastic for the Lord, for the word enthusiasm means "moved by the Spirit", but save the zealousness for the fanatics who always go overboard, even when they aren't even aware that their ship is sinking.

Practice Hospitality

"Share with God's people who are in need. Practice hospitality." Romans 12:13

Hospitality is a lost art in Western Culture. Very few people even have their close friends or relatives over to their homes anymore, except for a special occasion or holiday. Yet, the idea of hospitality goes far beyond just entertaining the chosen few. The word hospitality comes from the same root as the word hospital. The emphasis is on meeting the needs of hurting people, who are treated as special guests, even though they are only strangers. When was the last time that we had a stranger in our home, and we treated them as if it was our main priority to meet their every need?

The Bible says, "Share with God's people who are in need. Practice hospitality". The closest thing that we have to this concept is often the European hospice, which welcomes strangers, and treats them like family. Maybe if we started inviting people over to our homes for dinner who were visitors to our churches, instead of just the cliques that we have formed over the years, our churches would be more vital and effective, and we would have people coming back, instead of just church hopping.

Another aspect of hospitality is the realization that the church is like a hospital filled with sick people, instead of pretending that we are all super-saints. We are all sinners, struggling to just survive, let alone to grow, and we need one another's encouragement and help. There are no prima donnas in the body of Christ. We are all in need of TLC. We need to have empathy for those who are suffering, instead of looking down on them as inferiors.

The Bible says, "Rejoice with those who rejoice; mourn with those who mourn" (Rom. 12:15). It also says, "Love must be sincere" (Rom. 12:9). It isn't enough just to pretend that we understand the pains and joys of others. Our love for those who are hurting must be genuine, not just some phony display of smiling at everyone who comes to church. The reason that we are not more hospitable is that we don't really care about anyone but ourselves and those closest to us. Caring for others requires too much sacrifice, especially the needy ones. It's too draining. We just don't have the energy or desire to give that much of ourselves. We are too worn out by life, by work, by our families, by all of our daily responsibilities to even want to be hospitable. We don't even like it when someone else tries to be hospitable to us. We just want to be left alone.

Unfortunately, with this kind of attitude, the body of Christ stops functioning as a body, and we exist only as dysfunctional body parts on the cold slab of our local, holy morgue. The church was given spiritual gifts to help one another to grow into the likeness of Christ, yet most Christians don't even know what their spiritual gifts are, let alone want to use them. The result is that the body of Christ resembles a Frankenstein monster carelessly sewn together more than the beautiful bride that God intended.

The Debt of Love

"Let no debt remain outstanding, except the continuing debt to love one another."
Romans 13:8

Almost everyone today is deeply in debt. It didn't use to be that way. Before credit cards, people paid with cash or in barter. If we didn't have it, we just learned to live without. Today, we are convinced that we have to have certain things now, even though we may be paying for them for the rest of our lives. This concept is totally foreign to Biblical principles. It clearly states, "Let no debt remain outstanding." Sure, there are times when borrowing is necessary, but it is our duty to pay off the debt as quickly as possible, and not just accept debt as a way of life.

The only area where we are supposed to have continuing debt is "to love one another." This sounds confusing, for it implies that the only time I have to love others is if they first give me some, and then I need to repay them. However, the scripture teaches us that we need to love even those who aren't very loving or lovable. Where, then, is the indebtedness? The fact is that our indebtedness is to God, not to other people. Since He loved us, even while we were yet sinners, we owe him our love and our lives. Yet God has so ordained his plan that we are suppose to pay him back by showing love to others.

Notice what it says in Ephesians 4:32-5:1: "Be kind and compassionate to one another, forgiving each other, just as in Christ God forgave you. Be imitators of God, therefore, as dearly loved children, and live a life of love, just as Christ loved us." Christ is our example, and he is the standard. We are to love others in the same way that he loved us. That means we can't wait for others to show love first. Jesus didn't. That means that we have to love others even though we have every reason to not even like them. Jesus did. That means that love needs to be a way of life for us, not just the exception. Jesus was love.

We don't like the concept of love as a debt or a duty. We believe in romance, so love is suppose to be spontaneous, and filled with exciting fireworks of powerful feelings, and total passionate abandon. God, though, isn't in to romance or one night stands, or even honeymoons. Love, for God, is commitment—total, one-hundred and ten percent commitment, that keeps going through life because it is not based on just feelings. It is a debt or a duty—a clear-cut contract with God, family, friends, church and community.

That doesn't mean that the feelings can't be there also, but feelings or no feelings, the debt must be paid. Even the mornings when we don't feel very loving, it doesn't take away from the fact that we are still married. Christ is our bridegroom, and we have promised to love, honor and obey him as long as we live, for better or worse, for richer or poorer, in sickness and in health. How we feel at the moment is irrelevant. We owe our love letters to God, and everyone else is supposed to get a copy.

The Mind of Christ

"Who has known the mind of the Lord that he may instruct him?
But we have the mind of Christ." I Cor. 2:16

What does it mean to have the mind of Christ? We struggle so much with our thoughts, that our pea brains just seem incapable of thinking anything divine, let alone having the mind of Christ. Yet, it doesn't say that we need to pray for the mind of Christ. It says that we already have it. How can this be? I don't know of even a single human being who always has Christ-like thoughts. Does this mean that "sometimes ya' got it, and sometimes ya' don't"? That's not what the Bible says. It doesn't say that we have the potential for having the mind of Christ. It doesn't say that we have it only when we are good, but lose it when we are bad. It says, pure and simple, "we have the mind of Christ." This isn't just wishful thinking. This is fact.

So, it is important that we understand exactly what this means. The Bible says, "No eye has seen, no ear has heard, no mind has conceived what God has prepared for those who love him—but God has revealed it to us by his Spirit" (I Cor. 2:9-10). Humanly speaking, our minds are incapable of thinking divine thoughts. The finite cannot comprehend the infinite. Yet, through the indwelling power of the Holy Spirit, we have the ability to receive divine revelation from God. The Bible says that "no one knows the thoughts of God except the Spirit of God"(2:11), and "The Spirit searches all things, even the deep things of God" (2:10).

The astonishing thing about Christ is that, even though he was God-incarnate, he did not rely on his own power to think, to do miracles, or to fight the spiritual warfare that he was constantly fighting. He chose to subdue his power, to submit to his Father, and to rely completely on the power of the Holy Spirit (Phil. 2:6-8)(Acts 10:38). The mind of Christ, then, was a human mind, indwelt and empowered by the Holy Spirit, just as ours is, and we have the ability to understand the inconceivable thoughts of God through that Spirit.

"The man without the Spirit does not accept the things that come from the Spirit of God, for they are foolishness to him, and he cannot understand them, for they are spiritually discerned" (2:14). Yet, we have the mind of Christ, the ability to discern spiritual truths, for we have the Counselor within us, who has been given to us "to teach us all things" (John 16:13). Unfortunately, we also have our fallen sinful nature, which confuses and twists the truth into unrecognizable gobblygook. We have the mind of Christ, which is like a powerful antennae, capable of receiving even the still small voice of God, yet the enemy is also transmitting his messages and jamming the spiritual radio waves, so we aren't always sure exactly what we are hearing. What we need is not only the mind of Christ, but the heart of Christ as well, so that whether we understand the truth or not, our heart will know it.

The Scum of the Earth

"We have become the scum of the earth, the refuse of the world." I Cor. 4:13

When something is purified through extreme heat, such as liquor, all of the impurities rise to the top where they are removed, leaving just the finished product. These impurities are called the scum. They are worthless and thrown away. The Apostle Paul refers to himself and the other apostles as the refuse or garbage of the world, or the "scum of the earth" because he can identify with this purification process. The church, the bride of Christ, is being purified through the extreme heat of testing and persecution, and the scum has risen to the top. They are the apostles. They are in a position of prominence, like pastors are today, where their lives are on display to the world. So, as the congregation is struggling with their own personal demons of immorality, greed, backbiting, etc., the people can often hide in obscurity, while the pastors or shepherds of the flock usually take the heat. They are standing in the gap for their people, and they end up bearing the brunt of the criticism from the community. "It is the pastor's fault that the church isn't more alive and effective. They are our representatives to reach the world for Christ. Let them take the heat if the church is failing."

As in Paul's case, though, it isn't the leader's fault that the church is floundering. The people are just immature, still needing to be bottle fed, when they should have grown up a long time ago. He rebukes them by saying, "Stop thinking like children. In regard to evil be infants, but in your thinking be adults" (I Cor. 14:20). The pastors, though, are the easy targets. They get blamed by the church itself for not being effective, and they get ridiculed by the world because they are standing up for the ideal in Christ, when in reality, the church is falling apart, hypocritical, and insensitive to the needs of the world. It's as if they are the generals in front of an army, and they are getting fired on by the enemy, as well as their own men behind them. They can't win.

It's no wonder that the majority of pastors leave their churches after three or four years, discouraged and defeated by the overwhelming pressures coming at them from all sides. They are treated like the scum of the earth, and are thrown out with the trash. Paul also compares the leaders to "men condemned to die in the arena" as "spectacles to the whole universe" (4:9).

Why would God let his leaders be treated like this? He wants the spotlight to be on the best gladiators, so everyone can learn by their example how to fight the war. Everyone needs to see how they will respond to all of the negativity, so they will know how to deal with all the trials in their own lives. They need to be able to see if Christianity really has the power over evil that it says it has, and the leaders are the test models. How does Paul respond to the heat. He says, "We are brutally treated", but "when we are cursed, we bless; when we are persecuted, we endure it." Sounds like Christ.

July 9

Shadow Boxing

"I do not run like a man running aimlessly; I do not fight like a man beating the air."
I Cor. 9:26

Do you ever feel like a zombie, like a body that is just going through the motions, but there is no life there? Sometimes we get like that, where we get up to the alarm, go to work, do our duties, come home, watch TV, and go to bed. We are like robots who are programmed for certain activities, but nothing has any meaning. We have no purpose or focus in our lives but to survive, and we are not even sure why we should do that.

The Apostle Paul says, "I do not run like a man running aimlessly; I do not fight like a man beating the air." In other words, he has purpose and meaning in his life, and everything he does is pointed in that direction. He compares himself to the athlete who is competing in a race. He says, "Run in such a way as to get the prize. Everyone who competes in the games goes into strict training" 9:24-25).

The problem is that competition is hard, and training is hard, and we just want to take it easy. We have found a comfort zone where we feel safe and secure, and we have settled into a routine where even thinking is not required. We can just go through the motions and float through life, hoping that we can get through to the end of the road without too many potholes to slow us down. The problem is spiritual laziness. Oh, there is plenty of activity, but we are running aimlessly, or shadow boxing—pretending at life, rather than really living it.

We need to be more purpose- driven, goal-oriented, and disciplined to be disciples of Christ. It's true that when God called us, we were just sheep, and all we had to do was graze all day, meeting our own needs. Yet, as we mature, God helps us to see that the pastures are really battlefields, and we are really soldiers in sheep disguises. We have a war to win here, and we can't afford to just sleep by the still waters. There are very real enemies out there, wolves in sheep's clothing, who are trying to destroy us every chance they get. We can be sure that they are well-trained, and their evil schemes and war strategies are always in ready alert to pounce on the sheep who are too comfortable in their Christian lazy-boys. We need to know how to use our swords, the Word of God, have the breastplate of righteousness, the helmet of salvation, and the shield of faith (Eph. 6). We can't afford to have any holes in our armor, for Satan will always attack at our weakest point.

Unfortunately, the weakest point for many of us is just not being prepared for battle because we are too lazy to even put on the armor. We are sitting around in our spiritual boxer shorts seeking the calmness of mediocrity, when God is wanting us to be champions for Christ. We need to stop being spiritual couch potatoes, and roll up to God's prayer window and say, "Super Size Me". I want the best, and I know that God wants the best for me. Why settle for less?

Be Careful

"If you think you are standing firm, be careful that you don't fall." I Cor. 10:12

It happens all the time. The best team in the country ends up losing to the underdog. The seasoned politician loses to the newcomer. The vice-president of the company, who has been with the firm for thirty years, is laid off to make room for the Boss's nephew from Timbuktu. What happened? I know that life isn't fair. Yet, sometimes there is more to it than just life. Sometimes God is trying to teach us something.

For example, "Pride goes before destruction, a haughty spirit before a fall" (Prov. 16:18). Sometimes our pride makes us feel over-confident, so we take our prosperity for granted. We assume that we will always be victorious, so we let down our defenses, and we get ambushed and beaten by a lesser opponent. We might think that we are "standing firm", but then the ground gives way underneath us, and God makes us realize how vulnerable we are. He wants us to depend completely on Him, not our own strength or ability, so we need to be careful that we don't become too self-assured. Even if we are on a mountain top, we are only one step away from falling off a steep cliff.

The proud person "boasts of the cravings of his heart" and "says to himself, 'Nothing will shake me; I'll always be happy and never have trouble" (Psa. 10:3,6). Unfortunately, this is true of many Christians, as well. We are serving the Lord, and He is blessing us abundantly, and we assume that it will always be that way, as if we somehow deserved it as a child of God. Sometimes we need to be humbled a little to help us realize that even as children of God, we are also his servants. God loves us, but he doesn't want us to become spoiled brats. He will shower blessings on us, but he will also keep us in line. The Lord giveth, but he also taketh away.

Part of the problem is our understanding of ownership. We think that when God gives us something, then it belongs to us. This is a false perception. When God gives us something, He merely puts it into our possession to use for His glory. We are merely stewards or servants in charge of God's property. He is the landlord. We are merely the groundskeepers or custodians. This includes spiritual gifts or abilities. They are not really ours. They are merely tools of the trade which are owned by the company that we work for. If we think that we are indispensable to a ministry, and that it would not be able to exist without us, we can be sure that God will set us aside for awhile, whether in sickness or other difficulty, just to show us that God can do his work without us. He doesn't really need us. He just chooses to use us so that we can be drawn closer to Him by depending on His strength. He can always get someone else to do our jobs if we get too full of ourselves that we don't feel that we need Him any longer. The problem with pride is that we are standing firm on quick sand, and we are soon over our heads in the muck of self.

The Faithful Filter

"God is faithful; he will not let you be tempted beyond what you can bear. But when you are tempted, he will also provide a way out so that you can stand up under it."
I Cor. 10:13

Nowadays we have computer filters which parents can have installed in order to filter out any material from the Internet which might be offensive or harmful to their children. This feature gives the parents more control over what affects the impressionable minds and hearts of their young ones. It also gives them the flexibility to have different controls for different aged children in the family, as well as others for themselves. These filters can be adjusted or completely removed as the children mature, according to whether the children have shown themselves to be responsible or more rebellious. More freedom can be given at times, to test the children's ability to handle this liberty. If they prove themselves to be responsible, then they might be given more freedom. If they take advantage of their freedom to explore their evil desires, then this freedom can be taken away.

Of course, just as with computer viruses, no matter how sophisticated our filters, there are those who are out there who are determined to get through any blockades, and adjustments have to be made continually to stop any new attacks. Parents cannot assume that just because they have a filtering system, that it will always be effective. It constantly has to be updated. Their children also learn from their friends on how to get around the filters to see what they want to see, so the computers have to be monitored closely to make sure that the children are not getting around the system.

It's tough being a parent in our world of technology. There is a whole world of temptation and predators on the Internet, who are waiting to pounce on the innocent, and all done without even leaving the house. We, as parents, are protective, and want only what is best for our children, but it is hard to keep up with all the new weapons that are being used by the Devil to destroy the innocence of our youth.

Fortunately for us, there is another kind of filter that is available to us that can help us in our battle against the Devil's schemes. It is the Lord. He has promised to be our faithful filter, and to not allow us to be tempted above what we are able to bear. Although this is comforting, this isn't enough, from our perspective. We wish as parents that God's filter would just eliminate all temptations from our children. We want a one-hundred percent shield that doesn't allow anything through. God doesn't promise that. He only promises to keep us from more than we can handle. He knows our hearts better than we do, and he makes the judgment call on how much we can take. No matter what the temptation, though, he always provides a way of escape. He may not stop a virus from entering, but he can always keep it from spreading.

Bad Company Corrupts

"Bad company corrupts good character." I Cor. 15:33

Most of us are around "bad company" on a regular basis. We work with non-Christians who tell dirty jokes or use the Lord's name in vain. We have neighbors who argue loudly and have wild parties. We may even live with someone who is morally corrupt or warped in their philosophy of life. Does that mean that we are being corrupted by them? Not necessarily. The word "company" here does not mean just an acquaintance, or even someone that we are around all of the time. It means "companion", "close contact", or "friend". It implies communion, fellowship, or oneness.

It is possible, then, to be around bad people without becoming bad. However, if we accept them into our heart and mind, or open ourselves up to them, then we are easy prey to be manipulated by their values. This is one of the problems with "friendship evangelism", which tries to lead people to Christ by becoming friends with them first. It's possible that they might be influenced by our faith and love to the point that they may choose to be a Christian. Yet, it is also possible to be influenced by them to follow a worldly lifestyle, just so we can keep their friendship. Wanting to be friends with someone is a powerful force that pulls us into the desire to become like them or to be accepted by them. When that happens, it is not just our behavior which is compromised. It is our character.

The word character means a permanent mark which has been engraved in stone which distinguishes that stone as being distinct or different than others. When it applies to people, it is talking about the distinguishing qualities of our inner being which make us unique and which identify what kind of person we are morally. When we dabble in sin with a friend, then, we are not just experimenting with life, we are leaving deeply engraved marks on our impressionable soul.

The soul is like a soft wood table. We may take a piece of paper and write something on it while we are sitting at the table, thinking that we are just writing on the surface of the paper. However, when we pick up the paper, we can see that we have also left an impression into the wood. When we follow after our friends into sin, we are doing the same thing. We may think that we are just having fun, and on the surface we are right. Yet, when God picks up the tablet of our life, what he sees is the impressions that our sins made on our heart.

When we yield to a companion in sin, there is an internal change that takes place. The word companion implies communion, which is the same as when we partake of communion in church. We take the bread and the wine and we internalize them. They become a part of us. As Christians we should want to internalize the Lord, by digesting His word, and letting Him live through us. When we try to internalize our friends, though, their values sometimes end up digesting us.

Tough Love

"Be on your guard; stand firm in the faith; be men of courage; be strong.
Do everything in love." I Cor. 16:13

We live in a gender-oriented society, where different roles are assigned to men and women. The men are supposed to be the tough ones, and the women are supposed to be more tender or sensitive. These lines, of course, become blurred in the work place, for the women often feel that they have to be tough to compete with the men, and the men feel like they need to at least act more sensitive around the women just to keep from offending them. It's a constant game of walking on egg shells, trying to impress others by pretending to be something that we are not, just to become more successful in reaching our goals.

Well, we may reach our career goals, but we often end up being a different kind of person than we intended. We become strangers to ourselves, and may not even like who we have become, but at least we keep getting those promotions. What often happens, though, is that we end up having a mid-life crisis, wondering if it has been worth it all. So, we seek some kind of escape like alcohol, drugs, a job change, an affair, or weekly therapy, just to cope with the pressure of living according to the expectations of others, instead of just being who we really are.

As teenagers we may cry out, "I just want to be me", because we already feel the pressure by the adult world to conform. When we become adults, we still have that same desire, but we give in to the conformity because we want what the world has to offer—a good job, nice house, status in the community, etc. We make choices, and we often choose success and prosperity over peace of mind.

What we need to do is to set aside the expectations of the world, and to ask ourselves, "What kind of person does God want me to be?" He gives the answer in His word—"Be on your guard; stand firm in the faith; be men of courage; be strong. Do everything in love." This kind of person is not male or female, but Christ-like. They are tough in the principles that they stand for, but tender in how they deal with people. They are strong in their faith, but soft in their heart. They are fearless in standing against the Devil, but loving and patient with all those who have been wounded by the evil one.

It is a perfect blend of strength and sensitivity that only God can produce. When the world tries to manufacture this mixture, they get it all upside down. Their "toughness" isn't standing up for their beliefs. It is "looking out for number 1". It is self-centered, not God-centered, and only self is glorified. The only tenderness is hypocritical and self-serving, used for manipulation, rather than genuine concern. God wants us to be both tough and tender, but only on His terms. He wants us to become like Him, not just a shallow impersonation of what it takes to be popular or accepted. We will never be happy with who we are until we become who He wants us to be.

With Unveiled Faces

"We, who with unveiled faces all reflect the Lord's glory,
are being transformed into his likeness with ever-increasing glory." *2 Cor. 3:18*

When Moses saw God's glory on Mount Sinai, he came down from the mountain with his face literally shining (Ex. 34:29). The people were afraid to come near him, so he put a veil over his face. Yet, the real reason for the veil was not to shield the eyes of the Israelites from the bright light, but to hide the fact that the light was fading (I Cor. 3:13). He wanted people to think that he was still gloriously filled with God's presence, even though the closeness was long gone.

We do the same thing in our Christian communities. We wear superficial halos of joy when we are around people that we want to impress, even though inside we may be depressed and struggling with our faith. We veil our hearts because we don't want people to know how weak and needy we are. We want to give the impression of strength and power, not vulnerability.

The Israelites wear this same veil over their hearts (2 Cor. 3:14). They want to hold on to an illusion or appearance of holiness through the law that doesn't exist within. The veil is not removed until someone turns from their sinful ways, and turns toward the Lord, for it was when Moses faced the Lord that his own face shown. It was not the glory of Moses. It was a reflection of the light of God.

When we come to Jesus, we too will reflect his light (2 Cor. 3:16) if our hearts are not veiled by self or unbelief. If we allow him to transform us into his likeness, though, then the light of God shines brighter and brighter instead of fading. When we are walking a life of sin, however, we don't really want God's light to shine through us, for we don't want him to expose our darkness. We just want to give the impression of light to others so they will think more highly of us than they should. Instead of holding up the light of the Son, we hold up cheap florescent bulbs, which are just filled with electrically charged gas. In other words, our Christian light is filled with hot air, but no real substance. We hold a veil in front of it, like a magician holding a cape in front of his tall hat before performing a trick. Yet, because the source of the light is hidden instead of direct, we end up giving a lot more shadows than we think, and sooner or later, others can tell it's all just a phony light. Even Satan is an angel of light, but his light is different than the Lord's. His light burns and leaves scars, while the Lord's light enlightens and heals.

If we are wearing a veil on our heart, we can't be taught new truth or be touched by the Spirit. The veil becomes a shroud that not only hides, but buries a corpse. Isn't it time for us to let the Lord take that veil from our soul? We can't hide our true self from God, so why keep pretending? The only veil that we need to wear is the bridal veil, as we present ourselves humbly to Christ, our beloved bridegroom.

Jars of Clay

"We have this treasure in jars of clay to show that this all-surpassing power
is from God and not from us." 2 Cor. 4:7

It is interesting that our bodies are called jars of clay, for this isn't really something that we can relate to today in the same way as the early church. In the time of Paul, jars of clay were used for a lot of things. They were used by rich and poor. They were used for common things, such as water , cooking oil, flour, and wine. They were also used to contain valuables, such as jewelry, important documents, and even copies of scripture. Today, the only clay jar that most people have is a flower pot. Plastic has taken the place of pottery in modern culture, but we can still probably understand the concept that is being portrayed. God has chosen to place the precious treasure of Christ and salvation into the hearts of mere, frail humans, so that there would be no way for man to get the glory for the supernatural in his life.

Yet, there are some other lessons to learn from this analogy as well. First is the way that a clay jar is created. We can't just use any kind of soil to create a pot or jar. It has to be clay. The Lord tells us that our hearts are like different kinds of soil, and only the good soil is receptive to the gospel. Well, not only does the soil have to be receptive, it has to be moldable and durable under heat. It has to be molded into a certain shape by a master craftsman, and then put in an oven to dry and be hardened before it is usable. We, too, have to be molded into the image of Christ, and then learn to endure the heat of persecution and trials that are associated with being Christ-like. We can't really be used by God effectively until he knows that we can take the heat.

Second, the clay is porous, so it tends to soak up or take on the qualities of the thing that it contains. So, if we stored wine in a jar, we probably wouldn't be able to use it for flour or water later on. They would smell and taste like wine. We also take on the qualities of the One who lives within. He seeps into our spiritual pores, and we start to smell and taste a lot like the bread of life and the wine of the new covenant.

Third, in order to be molded into the desired shape, there has to be the proper pressure from both without and within the jar. Paul says, " We are hard pressed on every side, but not crushed" (4:8). The Lord knows how much pressure to apply from within, and how much stress to allow from the outside world in order to conform us into his image. His goal is not to crush us, but to strengthen us so that we can pass the test of time. Paul goes on to say that "we are persecuted, but not abandoned" (4:9). Even when we are tested from the outside, God does not abandon us. He doesn't discard the pot just because it has some chips or dings in it. The more abused it looks, the more it looks like Jesus. The Bible says, "We always carry around in our body the death of Jesus" (4:10). Our jars are also meant to carry his life.

The Indescribable Gift

"Thanks be to God for his indescribable gift." 2 Cor. 9:15

Why would something be indescribable? Usually it is because a person hasn't really experienced something, so they are ignorant of what they are trying to describe. Maybe they are physically blind, so they have never seen the object. Another reason, though, is that there is nothing in that person's experience that they can compare it to. Their experience is genuine enough, but there is nothing remotely similar to what happened to relate it to. We often describe things by comparing them to other things. "You are as beautiful as a rose", or "My love for you is wider than the ocean".   We use metaphors or similes because they help us tie together two apparently disassociated objects as if they are twins. Yet, if there is nothing to compare it to, then we are at a loss for words, or the words that we think of seem too inadequate.

Part of the problem with trying to describe the gift of God is that it is incomprehensible. It goes so far beyond anything that a person would do, that it seems irrational and like a fairy tale. Since it is inconceivable, it seems unreal and unbelievable. It goes way past the realm of the probable or believability quotient, so our minds just won't register to it, let alone try to describe it. It seems like foolishness to the non-believer, so the Christian has a hard time trying to tell the story and explaining its meaning without stumbling over words and concepts that can be understood logically speaking. It just doesn't work. Everything seems upside down and backwards. "Jesus is God's gift to us, but Jesus is God, so he really just gave himself. He submitted himself unto his Father, but he really is the Father at the same time (Isa. 9:6-7), so he was just really agreeing with himself. He was born in a manger, but he really has always been. He created all things (Col. 3:16), yet he lived inside a woman's womb for nine-months, then confined himself to living quietly in a small village for thirty years doing carpentry work before he performed a single miracle. He allowed himself to be beaten and crucified, and then waited to rise from the dead until 3 days later, just so people would know that he was really dead."

Even just telling the facts sounds so far-fetched that it is almost embarrassing to admit that we believe in their validity. "Christianity must be just for the ignorant imbeciles or delusional in our society" is the cry of the unbeliever. "No one in their right mind would believe this nonsense." Yet, some of the brightest minds in history have proclaimed their faith, and all the mystery and incomprehensibility only adds to their belief. They may not be able to explain it or even describe it in such a way as to make others believe or understand, yet it is a truth that is so real that millions of people around the world, from all different cultures and educational levels, feel a bond of love for God and each other, even when only a few have ever even met. It's indescribable, yet who would want to believe in a God who could be confined in a box of easy description?

Don't Make God Unhappy

"Do not grieve the Holy Spirit of God." Eph. 4:30

What would you do if you were allowed to be God for a day? Wow! That seems like it would be fun. We could do all these miracles, get rid of all the bad guys, be a Santa Claus and give gifts to all our family and friends. It seems like we would also want to use the opportunity to read people's minds, get rid of diseases, see what it was like in heaven, and enjoy every pleasure that is possible in the universe. Maybe we would even travel through the galaxies to other universes. There would be unlimited possibilities. After all, we would be God.

Why, then, would God ever be unhappy? He can do whatever He wants. Nothing ever happens without his permission. In fact, the Bible talks about God rejoicing with the angels every time someone repents and turns back to him (Luke 15:10-32). He must be happy all the time, for someone is always repenting. Yet, in spite of all this, the Bible says that the Holy Spirit grieves.

Why would we think that the Lord of Lords would grieve? Idolatry? Atheism? Unfaithfulness? Wrong. It is "bitterness, rage and anger" toward other believers (Eph. 4:31). What bothers him more than anything is the way that we treat our brothers and sisters in Christ. There is "brawling", "slander", and "every form of malice" within the family of God (4:31). In other words, in spite of the fact that he is the best Father in the world, his kids are brats. Instead of working together in unity as the body of Christ to win the world for Him, we are spending all of our energy being angry with each other, judging one another, and doing everything we can to get back at others for the things they have done to hurt us. We are so bitter that we turn everything and everyone around us sour. The world can't possibly see the light of God in us because we are filled with so much darkness in our spirits.

It doesn't do any good to say that we love God, but are just angry at people. Our anger at others cancels out our love for God (Matt. 6:14-15). Instead, we are commanded to "Be kind and compassionate to one another, forgiving each other, just as in Christ, God forgave you" (Eph. 4:32). We are to "be imitators of God," "as dearly loved children, and live a life of love, just as Christ loved us" (5:1). We are supposed to be like children, and follow the example of our Father. We are not supposed to be like children in the fighting and bickering with our siblings of the faith.

It doesn't matter who said what or who did what first. It doesn't matter how inconsiderate, irresponsible, or inconsistent they have been, we need to forgive them and try to build them up in their faith so they will be stronger the next time they are tempted to let us down. The cause of Christ is too important for us to let Satan tear apart His body. Don't let our hurt feelings keep us from embracing God's family members. It grieves the Lord more than we will ever know.

Children of the Light

"You are light in the Lord. Live as children of light." Eph. 5:8

God is light, and we are his children. We are supposed to be like him. Yet, what does it actually mean to live as children of light? First of all, it means the opposite of darkness. In other words, we are not to live in sin. The Bible tells us that people who live in sin seek darkness because their deeds are evil, and they don't want to be exposed (John 3:19). We, on the other hand, should be so filled with God's light, that we should want people to see us, so that God's righteousness and truth will be praised (Matt. 5:14). There should not be anything hidden or devious about our lives that we would be ashamed for anyone to know.

Second, we need to share God's light, the gospel, with those around us. Jesus tells us, "I am sending you to [the unsaved of the world] to open their eyes and turn them from darkness to light, and from the power of Satan to God" (Acts 26:18). We help them to turn from darkness to light by being lights ourselves. They need to see Christ in us. One way that we can do that is by living according to the principles of the light of God's Word. His Word is a lamp for our feet, and a light for our path (Psa. 119:105). We need to demonstrate to the world the validity and genuineness of that light by showing its transforming power to change lives. We need to let it change us first, and then be a good example.

The Word tells us that we need to "become blameless and pure, children of God without fault in a crooked and depraved generation, in which you shine like stars in the universe as you hold out the Word of Life" (Phil. 2:15). The reason that we can see stars so clearly is that when it is very dark outside, there is such a sharp contrast between the lights and the darkness, that their beauty sparkles beyond measure. One star by itself doesn't make that much of a difference, but a lot of stars in a constellation or galaxy can make an enormous impact. It is important, then, that not only one or a few Christians are lights to the world. We need a united effort—a perpetual meteor shower of heavenly lights crashing through the atmosphere of people's minds and hearts—sinking deeply into the lamps of the world's souls.

It takes light for things to grow. That's why the Bible says "the fruit of the light consists in all goodness, righteousness and truth" (Eph. 5:9). Just as there is the fruit of the Spirit, there is the fruit of the Light. When we let God's light shine through us, watered by the Living Water of Christ, and nurtured through the power of the Holy Spirit, we have a divine garden that is unequaled. Everything that is good grows there. Everything that is true to God's standards of truth blossoms in this light, and the fruit is meant to share with others. We need to pick the fruit in the light of day, and then give it to those who are in the shadows of the night. We can't afford to wait for them to come to the orchard. Take the fruit of light to them.

Making the Most of It

"Be very careful, then, how you live—not as unwise but as wise, making the most of every opportunity, because the days are evil." Eph. 5:15

It's amazing how tragedy in one's life changes one's priorities. We are going along fine, living through the daily routine, surviving and coping by using normal methods of stress reduction, and feeling fairly comfortable or secure. Then, something traumatic happens, such as an accident, a divorce, one of our unmarried children getting pregnant or in trouble with the law, losing a job, or having a mentor, like a pastor, experience a moral downfall. All of a sudden, our world seems to fall apart, and we have to reevaluate our values and priorities. Nothing seems the same. Everything has been turned upside down. Those things which seemed important before just don't mean anything now. We have lost our moral frame of reference, and our world view got knocked off of its axis. Where do we go from here?

First of all, we need to realize that if a tragedy has been able to knock us that far down, it's probably because we were off balance to begin with. Boxers and martial arts experts tell us that victory over an opponent is often achieved not because of greater strength, but the ability to knock the opposition off balance. The same thing happens in the spiritual realm. If we are a well-balanced individual, with our priorities right and our head on straight, we can't be knocked down by the enemy as easily. Or if we do get knocked down, we are able to bounce back up more quickly.

The problem is that our lives are out of kilter even before the tragedy hits. We don't see this, for everything seems normal, so we are blind-sided when the tragedy hits. "What happened?" we think. Let's be honest with ourselves for a moment. What is really important to us? I'm not talking about some theological cliché. What do we really value? Realistically speaking, this can't be answered truthfully unless we take into account how we spend our time and our money. How much time do we spend each day or week on entertainment, leisure, or pleasure? On a average, most Americans spend five hours a day just watching TV. Then there is work, plus the commute time to and from, plus lunch hour, taking up another eleven hours a day, at least. Then there is sleep for eight hours a day. That makes up a total of twenty-four hours a day just being a couch potato at home, a hot dog at work, or a mattress muffin in bed.

It sounds like a menu of life that may be filling but not very fulfilling. Where is the spiritual nourishment? Where is the time alone with the Lord to listen to what he has to say to our heart? Where is the reaching out to the needy of the world, our community, or even our family? Where is the quality time of sharing and listening to those we love? The Bible tells us to be wise, and to make the most of every opportunity for the Lord, not just the leftovers.

Intoxicated or Inspired?

"Be not drunk with wine, which leads to debauchery, but be filled with the Spirit."
Eph. 5:18

When people get drunk, it has different effects on them. Some become free-spirited and uninhibited, while others become depressed and drowsy. Some become happy and super friendly. Others become angry and anti-social. Some have a loose tongue and will say just about anything. Others become totally withdrawn and silently isolated within themselves. Regardless of its physical, psychological or social effects, though, its spiritual effect is always the same. We cannot be drunk with wine and be filled with the Holy Spirit at the same time.

In fact, we can't be drunk with anything and be filled with the Holy Spirit. It doesn't matter if it is drugs, sex, or even love. Drunkenness implies being out of control. It means being overwhelmed or overpowered by something which is stronger than we are. So, if we are intoxicated by love or passion, addicted to sex or drugs, or even a compulsive eater or spender, we are not acting in the power of the Spirit because we are being controlled by something else. God cannot fill us with his power if we are already overpowered by the demons of drunkenness. "A man is a slave to whatever has mastered him" (2 Peter 2:19). We cannot serve two masters. Either we choose to serve whatever it is that gets us drunk, or we choose to yield to the power of the Holy Spirit.

Either way we are yielding to something, but when we yield to God, we never give up our ability to change our mind. When we are intoxicated, we give up that right. We are no longer able to make our own decisions, for something else is controlling our thoughts. We are experiencing temporary insanity when we are drunk. We are not in our right mind.

On the other hand, when we are filled with the Spirit, he helps us to clarify our thoughts, and leads us to wisdom, instead of debauchery. One of the fruits of being filled by the Spirit, in fact, is self-control, just the opposite of drunkenness. We can't be filled with the Spirit and be angry, depressed, anti-social, or rebellious. We are calm, at peace, joyful, and purpose-driven. We can love deeply, but in constructive, edifying ways.

Drunkenness is self-destructive and hurtful to others, as well. It is co-dependent and abusive, insensitive and self-centered, and almost completely focused on the immediate need, with no regard for the consequences. When we are filled with the Spirit, in contrast, we are able to put Christ first, others second, and ourselves last. We are able to empathize with the pains and joys of others, and be sensitive to the fact that we have grieved the Spirit when we only think of self. All of our senses are heightened, for we are acutely aware of the Creator and everything that he has made, and awesomely grateful for it all.

So, are we intoxicated or inspired? We can't be both. It is our choice.

Poured Out for Others

"I am being poured out like a drink offering on the sacrifice." Phil. 2:17

When we think of Old Testament sacrifices, we naturally think of sin offerings to atone for the trespasses of the Israelites. Yet, there were other kinds of sacrifices, as well. One type of sacrifice which has special significance for the church is the burnt offering, for the sin offering could only be given for the Jews, but the burnt offering could be given for the Gentiles also. In fact, even Caesar Augustus had the Jewish priests offer burnt sacrifices on his behalf, even though he believed in many gods. He just wanted to cover all of the bases.

He missed the point, though, because the purpose of the burnt offerings was complete submission and dedication to God, which you can't do while you're worshipping pagan deities. For us as Christians, though, it has special significance because it means that God desires and allows us to have fellowship with him, in spite of the fact that we are not part of his chosen people. Even before Christ's atonement for our sins, God opened the door for those who had faith to become part of his family, regardless of ethnicity. It did, however, require total commitment. For the sin offering, only a portion of the animal was actually burned, while the rest was eaten by the priests. For the burnt offering, though, the entire animal had to be burned. It meant complete abandon and surrender to the Lord of Lords.

Along with this burnt offering, there were also two other kinds of offerings which were given at the same time—the grain offering and the drink offering. These symbolized the first fruits or the best of what man can produce for the Lord. The grain was ground up into flour and mixed with olive oil, and the grapes were crushed and purified and made into wine. Then they were both poured onto the burnt offering as a dedication of everything they are and have to God.

The Apostle Paul compares himself to this drink offering which is being poured on the burnt offering of the Christians. The believers are dedicated to serving the Lord completely, but they haven't really been tested yet. Paul, on the other hand, has been crushed and purified like the grapes, and he has been willing to be poured out or emptied of himself for the sake of the church.

We, also, need to come to the place where we are willing to be drink offerings for the sake of others. We need to realize that our lives should not just be spent meeting our own needs and desires, but pouring out our best to help others to be more dedicated, through encouragement, edification and prayer. Even our prayers need to be drink offerings for those who are struggling in their spiritual warfare or fighting the good fight of faith. Our offering of dedication is poured onto their offering of dedication, like the wine on the burnt offering, and the combination is a sweet smelling savor to the Lord.

Knowing Christ

"I consider everything a loss compared to the surpassing greatness of knowing Christ Jesus my Lord." Phil. 3:8

Theoretically speaking, every Christian would probably agree that knowing Christ is more important than everything else. Whether we actually put him first in our lives is a different matter. Even when we are at church, Christ often isn't the main priority. We are more concerned with seeing our friends, being entertained, being busy doing our duty, and taking care of our family needs than really growing closer to the Lord.

Yet, he thought that I want to dwell on here is not about priorities. It is about knowing Christ. If knowing Christ is supposed to be our priority, what does that mean? Certainly it has to be more than just salvation, even though this is vitally important. The question here is what does it really mean to know Christ individually, not just as a doctrine, a messiah, or as a deity? What does it mean to know anyone on a personal level?

So often we spend our lives living or working with people, and yet we still don't know each other. We have certain things in common, areas where we feel comfortable with one another, and yet other areas that we completely ignore or avoid because of possible tension or fear of disapproval. Maybe we have tried to share at one time or another, but we sensed irritation or intolerance, so we put mental blockades around the danger signals, and we are never able to share openly again. Our relationships are like mazes that we carefully have to wind around to avoid the walls that we have built up. We decide that survival is more important than intimacy, and perseverance more important than personal fulfillment.

Unfortunately, we have the same approach when it comes to knowing Christ. We love the Lord, but we don't really want him to get too close. We have a comfort zone that we allow Christ to dwell in, like a guest bedroom in our house, but most of the house is off limits. We don't really want him to know us too well, for we are self-conscious about the stuff that we have hidden in the closets of our minds and hearts. We also don't want to know him very well, for he is so perfect that he would make us feel bad by comparison.

To know someone intimately means to understand and be one with their thoughts and feelings. Even without saying anything, we know what that person is thinking, and how they are responding to certain circumstances. We have to be completely open and honest in order to achieve this kind of oneness. Communication is necessary for communion, yet pride and pretense get in the way. Like it or not, the surpassing greatness of knowing Christ cannot be experienced without first surpassing self so we can focus on him.

Rejoice in the Lord

"Rejoice in the Lord always. I will say it again: Rejoice." Phil. 4:4

Joy is a wonderful thing. It far exceeds happiness, in that, happiness is dependent upon favorable circumstances, and joy is not. Joy is a gift of the Spirit. It isn't something that can be drummed up by the individual by his will or his efforts, although churches, sometimes, try to imitate it through lively worship, thinking that singing joyfully will somehow produce the real thing. Joy is a fruit of the Spirit (Gal. 5:22). It is something that only He can produce. Happiness, by comparison, is just a sugar substitute—an artificial joy, that many people settle for because the real thing never seems to come. The real thing, of course, is dependent upon peace with God, which even many Christians do not possess.

It is one thing to believe in God and have the assurance of salvation. It is something completely different to feel one with the Lord in mind, heart, and will. Many Christians love the Lord, in that, they appreciate all that he has done for them. Yet, they still struggle with Him about the trials of their lives, not fully trusting Him, or even agreeing with Him on many things. So, they carry around their own burdens, as well as the burdens of their loved ones, and the world itself. They are so frustrated at life and God's allowing their trials that they can't possibly feel any joy that God has to offer. It's like the Spirit is trying to produce the fruit of joy in us, but we keep burying the tree with manure, so it can't possibly grow. We need to let go of our burdens and let God be God.

However, even if we don't have real joy, we still have the command to "Rejoice in the Lord always". It doesn't say to rejoice only when we feel like it. Yet, how can we rejoice if we have no joy? Is God asking us to be hypocrites? No. God is not commanding us to feel joy or to pretend that we feel it. The word "rejoice" means to express joy "with" someone. Imagine that we are on a team with our best friend. We are both excellent players, always giving it our best. When the end of the season comes, our friend is rewarded with the Most Valuable Player Award. Although we are disappointed in not winning the award ourselves, we still are happy for him.

Ideally, in our Christian walk, we should be able to let go of our burdens, have peace with God, and experience genuine joy. However, even if we can't, we still should be able to be happy for those who can. We still should be joyful that others have found that peace, hope, and love in the Lord. We need to take our eyes off of ourselves, and be thankful on behalf of every little victory that others experience in their spiritual journeys. We also need to appreciate and share in the Lord's own joy for the victory that he achieved on the cross and through his resurrection. He won over death and the Devil. Can't we be happy for his sake, even if we can't be for our own? Rejoice "with" the Lord always, and again I say rejoice. He's earned it.

The Gentle Giant

"Let your gentleness be evident to all. The Lord is near." Phil. 4:5

When I was growing up, I remember that whenever I hurt myself, I was told to repeat an old saying, "I'm okay. I'm rough and tough and used to hardships". I'm not sure where this saying came from, but the same sentiment was expressed in our culture in general. "It is wrong for boys to cry or to express their emotions. We need to be strong, and feelings are for females." When we are presented, then, with an image of a gentle Jesus, who wept for a lost friend, had compassion on the multitudes, and didn't fight back when others attacked him, we are faced with a dilemma. How can "manly men" follow a "female faith"? How can I be a "he-man" when my "hero" is so "humble"? "I want to be a warrior, not a wimp."

First of all, Jesus was no wimp. He was a manly carpenter who easily gained the respect of even the toughest fishermen. He was a man's man. Yet, he chose to show his strength in different ways than most men. In fact, gentleness, when understood correctly, can be seen as a very manly characteristic. It means cool, calm, and collected. It means under-control. It takes a lot of courage and strength to be self-controlled.

Gentle humility does not mean weakness. It means being so confident and assured of who we are and the power that we have within us, that we don't need to react defensively whenever we are being attacked by the enemy, or things don't go our way. We just continue in our quiet purposefulness, and we don't let the winds of turmoil ruffle our feathers. It means "soft", in that, we can absorb the blows from the outside without being hurt by them. They just bounce right off us. It means "smooth" or non-abrasive. We don't have to be like sandpaper which rubs people the wrong way. We don't irritate people whenever they have contact with us. Instead, we are able to smooth out difficulties and be a peacemaker because our "gentle answer turns away wrath" (Prov. 15:1).

It takes real strength of character to not seek revenge through words or actions when someone abuses or oppresses us in some way. We want to stand up for ourselves and fight back. Yet, that is the easy way. Fighting back actually shows that we are intimidated by the oppressor, so we feel like we have to defend ourselves against the enemy. Gentle confidence doesn't need this defense mechanism. It can walk away without being fazed by the onslaughts, for there is a deep peace in one's soul, even when there is turmoil all around. Gentleness is able to be tender to the needy, for the gentle person doesn't spend all of their energy feeling sorry for their own victimization. They can move forward with the positive because they aren't focused on the negative.

The true "gentle-man" is not feminine. He is just a focused force of persistent, positive power and inner strength, who doesn't feel the need to be "macho" in order to be a man.

Sufficient, or Just Satisfied

"I have learned to be content whatever the circumstances." Phil. 4:11

I recently heard a missionary tell of a remote tribe in Africa which was isolated from other cultures, and completely devoid of any modern conveniences. Their lives were at the mercy of the elements. During the rainy season, they were flooded and greatly limited in what they could do. During the dry season, there wasn't even enough good water to drink, let alone to water any crops, so they often became sick, and child mortality was extremely high. Yet, they were content with their lives. They were satisfied with what they had for they had just learned to accept all their trials as part of life, so why try to fight it? "Que sera, sera. Whatever will be, will be."

Sometimes we as Christians feel that this should be our attitude as well. "Everything is controlled by God, so we might as well just accept it." "We are supposed to be content in all things, so don't try to change anything". "Just go with the flow, and don't make any waves." Religion is looked at as being the "opiate of the masses", which makes us so content and placid that we won't resist any oppression, or complain about any hardship. We are internally controlled by our contentedness, so we don't need external controls.

The word "content", though, doesn't just mean satisfied or pacified. In fact, it is possible to be content and not satisfied at the same time. The primary meaning of the word content is "sufficient within, even when the externals are not". The idea of sufficiency is far different than just satisfaction. It is the confidence that I have the power within me, that of Christ and His Spirit, to overcome any obstacle that I may face. It is not just the matter of accepting the obstacle as unavoidable fate. It is knowing that God's grace is sufficient to meet all our need. Even a pagan can be satisfied. Only a Spirit-filled Christian can be sufficient.

The apostle Paul went through all kinds of persecution and hardship, and he learned through it all to be content. That doesn't mean that he just threw up his arms and said, "Oh well. I'm happy anyway." It means that he knew that with God, all things are possible, and that he could have peace with this God, who even knows the number of hairs on our heads. It doesn't matter, then, what the obstacle or trial is, whether poverty or riches, pleasure or persecution, God is able to empower us and to bring about great victory and growth.

Paul, therefore, is not just submitting pacifly to whatever happens. He is walking boldly forward, inspired by the Holy Spirit to take on whatever challenge comes his way, because he knows that he "can do everything through him who gives us strength" (4:13), Jesus Christ, our Lord. Being just satisfied is a lazy man's way of excusing non-action and non-involvement. Being sufficient in the Lord is the warrior's battle cry as he takes on the principalities and powers in high places, knowing that the victory is already won.

Devoted to Prayer

"Devote yourselves to prayer, being watchful and thankful." Col. 4:2

Can you imagine an Olympic athlete staying up partying the night before his event, eating a huge meal, getting drunk, getting beaten up in jail, and then running ten miles to the stadium right before he has to run the marathon? Usually elite athletes are more dedicated than that, and they are able to stay focused on their goals enough to keep distractions from hindering them. However, occasionally, you do find a really gifted "Adonis" who thinks they are invincible, and they can do whatever they want, and still be better than anyone else. They are similar to the student who never studies, but still gets straight "A's". We would say that they are foolish, that they need to get their priorities straight, and that they should do their best to live up to their potential, instead of just being satisfied with the least that is necessary.

Unfortunately, this same problem happens in the lives of many Christians. They are just coasting through life, either being satisfied with mediocrity, or thinking they are the greatest super-saints without even trying. They are constantly being distracted by the things of this world, and they come to church too worn out to even close their eyes in prayer without dozing off. The apostle Paul says that we are supposed to be like athletes, who are pressing "toward the mark for the prize of the high calling of God in Christ Jesus" (Phil. 3:14). There needs to be that same level of dedication that an elite athlete has toward improvement and perfection.

One area that particularly needs improvement is our prayer life. The Bible says that we are to devote ourselves to prayer. The word "devote" comes from the same root as "to make a vow". When someone took a vow in the Old Testament it meant self-denial, sacrifice, dedication, consecration and being set apart for a certain period of time, with God as our witness. Some vows, like the Nazarite vow, were sometimes even meant for life. Paul tells us that prayer needs to be that kind of commitment.

If we are going to be prayer athletes or prayer warriors, we can't afford to just pray when we feel like it, or when there is an emergency, or when others are around, such as church or at meals. We have to make prayer a priority—the priority of our Christian walk. It is our source of power, wisdom, direction, and access to God. Everything else, including studying scripture, preaching, sharing the gospel, and spiritual gifts are useless and powerless without prayer.

Yet, we treat it like a tie or corsage that we might add to an outfit, instead of the crown that is closest to the head, Jesus Christ. We need to be praying without ceasing throughout the day, in constant communion and communication with the Father, whatever we are doing. We need to be students, priests, soldiers, athletes, champions and children of prayer. Prayer is not supposed to be an hors d'oeuvre before a meal. It is meant to be the main course.

What is your Ambition?

"Make it your ambition to lead a quiet life, to mind your own business,
and to work with your hands." I Thess. 4:11

What is your ambition in life? Is it to be rich and famous? Is it to be successful in your career? Is it to have a nice house, a fancy car, a good spouse, or superior kids? Or perhaps it is to make a difference in the world by working toward positive change in your community or environment. How many of us, though, would choose the above verse as our guide for an ambition? In fact, ironically, it almost seems like it is saying to make it your ambition not to have any ambition.

Ambition to us seems to imply wanting more and stretching to get it. Here it implies that we should just be content with what we have, and to purposely limit our influence on those around us--Just do our job, keep quiet, and leave everyone else alone. Live and let live—that's all.

Our first response to this might be, "This must be a cultural statement that only applies to the nomadic or simplistic tribes of Paul's time. Our lives are too complex today to live this way. Unless we go live on a farm someplace or become hermits, this just isn't practical."

First of all, Paul didn't minister to nomads out in the wilderness somewhere. He went around to the main metropolitan areas of the Roman Empire. He was talking to very busy, educated, culturally complex individuals along well-traveled trade routes. They were business men and women, seeking prosperity and good fortune, like everyone else. So how does this verse, then, apply to us? The same way that it applied to them—Slow down, simplify, and settle for less.

In other words, much of the complexity of our lives is not a necessity. It is caused by wanting too much, wanting it now, instead of waiting, and wanting too much from others, as well. We have it fed to us by society and the media that we need all these things to be happy. We need just as much, if not more, than our neighbors or friends, to make us feel good about ourselves. Our self-esteem is based on comparison and competition. It isn't enough to just keep up with the Jones. We need to try to be a little better. We can't wait until we actually have the money to buy things. We have to have them now, so we buy things on credit, get further and further into debt, and never seem to quite get over the hump of what it takes to feel that we have actually arrived. We build our self-images by putting other people down, criticizing them for not living up to our expectations or standards, and judging them when they fail. God tells us very plainly—Stop! Do whatever we can to simplify our lives—give up our worldly goals—seek peace and quiet with God and others instead of trying to compete with them—and build others up instead of tearing them down. Keep it simple. Make it our main ambition to be more like Jesus.

Guardian Angels

"Guard what has been entrusted to your care." I Tim. 6:20

When we hear the word "angel", we usually think of celestial beings. Sometimes, though, we apply the term metaphorically to small children or angelic women. In this context, the word means innocent, beautiful, gentle and caring. The primary meaning of the word angel, however, is messenger. Angels are God's messengers to mankind. In this light, then, ministers can also be considered angels, for they are the messengers of God's truth to their congregations.

This doesn't mean that people have to go through their pastor in order to hear or understand the Word. God dwells in the heart of every believer, and the only mediator we need is Christ. However, God has also given spiritual gifts to some to be prophets, pastors, evangelists and teachers. They have been asked by God to be angels or messengers of His truth, and have been given the ability to make this truth clear and simple for others to understand. They are stewards of God's revelation of Himself to mankind, and they are told to treasure this truth, and to guard it with their lives.

In this sense, they are guardian angels—messengers of God, whose main mission is to guard His truth. What does it mean to guard God's truth? First of all, it is to cherish its special source as being divine, and not just the words of men (2 Tim. 3:16). The Devil constantly tries to attack this principle, wanting us to disbelieve or doubt the inspiration of scripture, because then he can attack the validity of its truth. He offers to us, instead, all kinds of "falsely called knowledge" (I Tim. 6:20), trying to cloud or confuse our thinking with his deceptive lies. Our pastors are our guardian angels, in that, they are to guard the Word against such attacks.

If there is any part of scripture which can be discredited, then the whole thing can be thrown out, for it is then open to every man's interpretation, and each individual becomes his own judge of what is truth. When this happens, the Apostle Paul calls the result, "godless chatter" (6:20). When man takes God out of the equation, and promotes the idea that the Bible is just man's wisdom or historical traditions, then the Bible itself becomes nothing but Godless chatter.

The messenger of God's truth needs to guard against this heresy with all his might and dedication. If the minister loses this battle, he might as well give it all up, for everything else that he believes in is based on this foundation. If the Bible is just a good story book or man's mythology, then what are we left with but man's intuition, intellect and imagination? Each man, then, becomes his own god, creating his own reality, his own standard of right and wrong, his own idea of heaven, and his own hell.

We need to all be guardian angels against this blasphemy, and jealously guard the treasure that has been entrusted to us. Without the Word, we have nothing more to say.

Fan the Flame

"Fan into flame the gift of God which is in you." 2 Tim. 1:6

Every person in the body of Christ has been given a spiritual gift to use in the building up of other believers (Eph. 4:11-13, I Cor. 12:7-11). However, many Christians are completely unaware of what their spiritual gift is, or they have chosen not to use it. Imagine going downstairs on Christmas morning, seeing all of the presents, but no one ever bothering to open them. Imagine how we would feel if we spent a great deal of money to buy one of those presents in order to show someone how much we loved them, and then when they opened the gift, they just put it on a shelf and never used it. Think about how much God had to pay with the death of Christ on the cross in order for us to have a spiritual gift. How do we think He feels about our neglecting the gift he has given to us?

The Bible compares our spiritual gifts to flames, but they start out only as sparks. They need to be fanned into flames. There has to be movement in order to fan a flame. We can't just sit still and do nothing. Our spiritual gifts must be developed through usage. They are like muscles that do not grow unless they are stretched, strained, and strengthened. If a muscle is not used, it atrophies, or becomes totally useless. Spiritual gifts are the same way. We either use them, or we'll lose them.

If we want a flame, then we need to start fanning. We need to discover what our spiritual gifts are through serving others in any way that we can. We will soon learn where our giftedness is through the results of our ministry. Then we can fan the flame until it grows and grows, giving forth light and warmth to all around.

Flames can not be fanned without wind, and wind is a symbol for the Holy Spirit. Fanning the flame of our spiritual gift cannot, then, just depend upon our human efforts or activities. We have to allow the Holy Spirit to move within us, to empower us, and to lead us in the direction that he wants us to burn. If we just try to fan our own flame, we will burn out quickly, and all our enthusiasm and effectiveness can be consumed in a moment's time.

There is a lot of excitement when there is a big flame, but big bonfires eat up the wood in a hurry. They need to be constantly refueled in order to maintain their glory. Spiritual gifts also need to be refueled constantly, digging deeper and deeper into our store piles of God's Word and prayer in order to fan the flame. Our goal should be to help the fire grow bigger and bigger so that others can benefit from the flame. Paul tries to encourage Timothy because he was timid and wasn't using his spiritual gift the way that he should. Paul tells him, "God did not give us a spirit of timidity, but a spirit of power, of love and of self-discipline" (1:7). In other words, get out there and start fanning the flame. Others need to see the light.

Mentoring Teachers

"The things you have heard me say...entrust to reliable men
who will also be qualified to teach others." 2 Tim. 2:2

The word "mentor" comes from the story of Ulysses, where Mentor was the friend and advisor of the hero. He traveled with Ulysses on his adventures, and taught by example, as well as words of wisdom. Being a mentor, then, is more than just being a teacher, who may keep his distance from the students at a more professional level. The mentor is a traveling companion, who experiences the joys and heartaches of a friend, and encourages the friend to keep focused on moving forward in the journey.

Yet, the mentor is not just dedicated to helping an individual be successful. His goal is to train his friend in such a way as to make him a mentor also. He sees beyond the here and now to the future needs of the church. He wants Ulysses to realize that he can't just be satisfied with being a hero himself. He must want to help others to be heroes too.

The apostle Paul was a mentor. It would have been much easier for him to just have traveled by himself, for he would have had less to worry about. Yet, he chose to always travel with a group of followers, assistants, or students, who learned from his teachings, as well as his example. He was not just instructing them. He was training them, so that they could go out and mentor others.

Timothy was one of those trainees. When Paul felt that Timothy was ready to take on a leadership role, he sent him to Ephesus to be the pastor there. His mission was to find reliable men whom he could teach and train to be mentors. This should be the goal of every pastor or church leader. So often, the pastors of a church become our paid professional Christians, and we are just the spectators, applauding their victories. The preachers pour out some spiritual food to us, we digest what we can, and we wait for the next meal.

The pastors, though, should not just be proclaimers of the truth. They need to be trainers of teachers, and every church needs to be a "teachers' college". They need to be teaching more than facts. They need to be teaching how to teach, how to encourage, how to shepherd, or how to mentor. Every leader in a church should be mentoring someone.

Every mature Christian should be taking younger Christians under their wings and helping them to mature. We should all want to be Christ-like, and Christ was a mentor. We should all have our disciples that are following our examples, and we should all be willing to share the truths that God has taught us with others who are still learning. We need to be looking beyond ourselves and what we can get out of church.

In the world of fish aquariums, those fish that settle for the occasional food that drops down to its lowest level are the "bottom feeders". God doesn't want us to be just bottom feeders, settling for the leftovers. He wants us to rise to the top, and to seek to bring others up with us. Be a mentor. It isn't an option. It's a command.

Boundaries, but No Bondage

"God's word is not chained." 2 Tim. 2:9

The apostle Paul was imprisoned several times for preaching the gospel. Part of the Word of God, in fact, was penned by Paul while he was a prisoner. Yet, the Word of God and its spiritual power in the lives of others can never be bound. It can have boundaries put on it, for certain countries may even outlaw it, but it can never be in bondage. Paul had boundaries on him in a jail cell, but God still used him to lead people to the Lord in prison, and allowed him the opportunity to preach even to Caesar when he was in captivity. God is not bound, for He will achieve His purposes no matter what the circumstances or obstacles put in His way.

God is not bound, but He does have boundaries. He cannot go outside the limits of the circumference of His character. He cannot sin. He cannot do anything that would be contrary to His divine Nature, holiness or truth. Within that circumference, though, He has no limits.

Therefore, within that same circumference, His Word can have no limits. It cannot be contrary to God's character. It cannot be pornography or mythology. It can only reveal God, for Jesus is the Living Word (John 1). Yet, within that parameter, the Word is never bound. It has boundaries, but never in bondage, for it sets the captives free, and makes hearts soar to the heavenlies.

This is why Paul could be in bondage physically, yet still feel free in the Spirit. This is why they could stop Paul from traveling, but could not stop his message from spreading far and wide. This is why we too should not accept the boundaries that society places on us when it tries to oppress the Christian message as a defeat. They may have the legal right to establish boundaries, or to even put us in jail for standing up for our beliefs, yet they cannot bind the power of God. In fact, the more that the Devil tries to suppress the truth and limit its influence, the more that God is glorified by breaking the chains that bind us.

God specializes in the impossible. If Satan tries to bind God, like Delilah tried to bind Samson, the Lord will overcome. If Satan tries to bind us through making us captives to our temptations, then God will provide a way of escape (I Cor. 10:13). We don't have to be afraid of boundaries set by the world. They are merely bridges to miracles. God is not bound, His Word is not bound, and we are not bound in the center of God's will. Those who have obeyed God have walked on water, lived through a fiery furnace, praised the Lord in a Lion's den, walked through the Red Sea on dry ground, and killed a giant with a pebble and a sling. The heroes of the faith are those who refuse to accept the boundaries of the world as limitations to the Spirit, and who are willing to die to prove their point. That which is immortal can never be martyred, for it can never die.

A Form of Godliness

"Having a form of godliness, but denying its power." 2 Tim. 3:5

Paul was not only an apostle, he was a prophet. God revealed to him what the world was going to be like during the end times. He foretold that "People will be lovers of themselves, lovers of money, boastful, proud, abusive, disobedient to parents, ungrateful, unholy, without love, unforgiving, slanderous, without self-control, brutal, not lovers of the good, treacherous, rash, conceited, lovers of pleasure rather than lovers of God" (3:2-4). What a list. What an exact description of our own age. What a condemnation of our own self-centered society.

Yet, the most condemning characteristic of our times is none of the above. It is that we have "a form of godliness", but deny its power. All of the rest of the things listed are obviously sinful. If someone did these things, they could easily be identified as being worldly and of the Devil. They are advertising the fact that they do not know the Lord. Yet, those who have a form of godliness are more deceptive. They are wearing a mask, and pretending to be something that they are not. They are counterfeits, and they don't always realize that they are not the real thing. They can go through their whole lives thinking that they are going to heaven, without a clue that they are already in hell.

Hell is not just a future home of Satan and his followers. It is spiritual separation from God, and those who think they are the closest, may actually be the furthest away. Those who are openly living in sin, can be made aware of their sinful ways, and turn to God as their savior, for they see the need. Those who are living good lives, on the other hand, may not realize that they need the Lord. In their minds, they are already good enough through their own efforts. They don't need God. This is unfortunate, for they are blind to their own sin.

What is even more unfortunate, though, is when this verse applies to Christians. Yes, it is possible for a Christian to have a form of godliness, but deny its power. They know the Lord, but they do not trust Him in their daily lives. Their Christian walk is all done manually, with no reliance on the power of the Holy Spirit. They go through the motions of religion and being good, but inside there is no flowing of God's presence. They are satisfied with doing it on their own. They are stagnant. There is no growth taking place because they are already content with who they are. They are proud, but disguised in religious piety.

These people can do more damage to the name of Christ than those who openly live in sin. Even Christ spent more time criticizing the hypocritical Pharisees than he did the prostitutes and thieves. He knew that there was great danger in godliness that was just a form without life, for it is just like idolatry, worshipping a lifeless form. What is worse than an empty church? A church full of empty Christians. What is worse than living in the dark? Having a light, and never turning it on.

Tragedy or Triumph?

"It was fitting that God, for whom and through whom everything exists, should make the author of their salvation perfect through suffering." Heb. 2:10

In Greek drama, there is a form called "heroic tragedy". In this kind of play, there is an idealistic, heroic protagonist who has great potential and glowing qualities. He has giftedness in heroic proportions. Yet, he also has some tragic flaw which keeps him from reaching his full potential. He starts to rise like the sun, yet crashes quickly like a falling star before he can reach his peak of glory. This is considered a tragedy because of the sharp contrast between the brightness of what could have been, and the depths of the darkest downfall. We are shaken in our sensibilities and sense of justice because our hopes and expectations are shattered. We wanted a hero, and we got an outcast or a loser instead.

Jesus is often portrayed in this same light. The Jews were looking to him as a possible Messiah, a political-religious savior who could save them from their enemies and restore the glory of God's chosen people. He had great promise, with all of his miracles and wisdom, but then he was martyred before he had the chance to fulfill his mission. What was his tragic flaw? Maybe it was that he dared to challenge the established religious leaders. Maybe if he just kept quiet about their hypocrisy, and focused on doing good to the poor, he might have had a chance. Who knows? Maybe he could have become another Mother Theresa or Dr. Switzer if he had just kept his mouth shut.

Of course, I hope you know, that this is all foolishness. Jesus is not just a tragic hero, who had the potential of being great, but blew it in the end. He didn't have any flaws which kept him from reaching his goals. He was perfect and without sin. His suffering and death did not keep him from reaching his potential. Quite the contrary. He came to die for our sins, not to save us from our political enemies. His goal was spiritual, and his death was an important step in our salvation. It was not a failure, but a victory. He planned it all and was in control of every plot and subplot in this wonderful story. He even chose the villain who would betray him, and the moment that he would give up his own spirit to save the world.

Yet, the climax of the story is not the crucifixion, but the resurrection. The world likes to stop at the crucifixion because it likes to think of Jesus in human terms only, as the epitome of human perfection. Yet, we believe that Jesus was not just perfect man, but God incarnate, who died and rose again, because human perfection was not good enough to save man. Jesus was the "author" and finisher of our faith, but he did not pen any tragedies. He has written into our stories the same victory that he had at the resurrection. We don't have to have tragic endings if we trust in Him. The only real tragedies are those who have heard the truth, yet have turned the other way

Fix Your Thoughts on Jesus

"Fix your thoughts on Jesus." Hebrews 3:1

We complain about the hard life that we live—all the bills, responsibilities, and problems. Fix your thoughts on Jesus. We dwell on our past, and feel burdened by all of our guilt and pain. Fix your thoughts on Jesus. We worry about the future, afraid of all that might happen, expecting the worst. Fix your thoughts on Jesus. We look down on others, and blame them for all of our problems. Fix your thoughts on Jesus. We criticize others for not living up to our expectations or standards, even though we often fail ourselves. Fix your thoughts on Jesus. We hold anger and bitterness in our hearts for years against people that hurt us long ago, even though we might not even remember how. Fix your thoughts on Jesus. We see others sinning around us, and we can't wait to tell others what we saw. Fix your thoughts on Jesus. The Devil reminds us of something we did a long time ago, and we can't forgive ourselves, even though God has forgiven and forgotten. Fix your thoughts on Jesus. We see others who are from other countries or races, and we try to fit them into boxes or stereotypes where we can control them because we fear their distinctiveness. Fix your thoughts on Jesus. We are tempted to lust with our eyes and heart, thinking that it doesn't matter, as long as we don't do the act. Fix your thoughts on Jesus. We judge people who belong to other denominations as being either unsaved or heretical, even though we are not really sure what they believe. Fix your thoughts on Jesus. We look down on the poor, homeless and dysfunctional of our society as if they were to blame for their unfortunate state. Fix your thoughts on Jesus. We lift ourselves up on pedestals of pride, thinking that we deserve God's blessing and the praise of men. Fix your thoughts on Jesus. We are easily led astray by all of the distractions of this world, having our time consumed by meaningless, mediocre, mundane and materialistic dung heaps of the imagination. Fix your thoughts on Jesus. We study the Word, but we focus on argumentative, problematic, controversial or subjective interpretations, and we get all tangled up with logical lunacies. Fix your thoughts on Jesus. We become plagued with doubt and unbelief because we haven't seen any miracles in our life, or Christianity just hasn't lived up to our expectations. Fix your thoughts on Jesus. We have become disillusioned with the church because a priest or pastor has fallen into immorality, and every Christian we know is a hypocrite, including ourselves. Fix your thoughts on Jesus.

Only Jesus is constant. Only Jesus is always true. Only Jesus is the same yesterday, today, and forever. Only Jesus is forever. Only Jesus could have died for our sins. Only Jesus is unconditional love. Only Jesus is the way, the truth, and the life. Only Jesus is worth focusing our thoughts, our hearts, and our goals on. Fix your thoughts on Him.

The Double-edged Sword

"The Word of God is living and active. Sharper than any double-edged sword, it penetrates even to dividing soul and spirit, joints and marrow; it judges the thoughts and attitudes of the heart." Heb. 4:12

The word "active" here means energized and energizing. It is not only alive, but gives life and the power to live life. Our souls are like rechargeable batteries, and every time we plug into the Word with our hearts and minds, we are storing up spiritual energy to face our trials.

Besides this powerful, positive potential that we gain from the Word, we are also told that it is used by the Lord to perform spiritual surgery. It is compared to a two-edged sword that penetrates and cuts away or prunes away parts of our lives that are dead or unproductive. The Bible says that it "penetrates even to dividing soul and spirit". It doesn't say that it divides soul "from" spirit, for this might imply even physical death. It divides soul "and" spirit. The soul represents the will of man, and the spirit his emotions. In both of these areas, the Holy Spirit uses the Word to prune away things that do not belong there. In the area of the will, the Spirit often has to deal with us on who is the Lord of our life, our ego, and obedience. With the emotions, we are often struggling with fear, anger, doubt, and love. The Word penetrates these areas, and with double-edged intensity, makes us feel the pain and grief that we often cause the Lord when we rebel or lack faith.

Sometimes the Lord uses the Word gently, like a goad or prod, to nudge us back to the right path. Sometimes, though, he thrusts the Word into our very core being, as if to cut out the cancerous sin from our souls. The word for "sword" here is not the long sword used in battle, but the shorter dagger, which requires the one bearing it to be much closer to the recipient before the attack. When the Holy Spirit plunges the Word into our hearts, then, he is not striking haphazardly from a distance. He is embracing us with one arm while thrusting with the other. He is tenderly loving us and holding us up, so that when the blow comes, he is there to catch us.

The dagger of the Divine also penetrates the joints and marrow. The joints are those areas of our lives that help us to move and be active for God, and the marrow is that which keeps our spiritual bones alive, strong, and growing. Sometimes sin causes calcification and arthritis of the spirit. The Word helps to cut away any hindrances to growth or movement, helping us to be more fluid and flexible in our ministry with others. God doesn't want us to have "petrified or paralyzed personalities". He wants us to be able to dance with the Divine, letting Him take the lead. He doesn't want to dance with a stiff corpse. He wants us to be alive and vibrant, growing and bursting with spiritual energy. Before he can light our fire, though, he has to cut away the dead wood, and then use it to start the flame.

He Speaks with Forked-Tongue

"The Word of God is alive and active. Sharper than a double-edged sword." Heb. 4:12

In early America, the Native Americans often criticized the white men as speaking with a "forked-tongue"--saying one thing to them when making a treaty, but saying something completely different when they were with their own people. It was as if their tongues were split in half, like a snake's, with one half making promises, and the other half denying the whole thing.

A similar phrase is used in the Bible when it talks about the revelation of God. It says, "The Word of God is ...sharper than a double-edged sword". From first glance, it just seems like the Word has two sharp edges, so it can penetrate your heart easily. This, however, is just the surface meaning. The phrase actually means "double-mouthed sword". It comes from an old saying which refers to a fork in a river or a road, where a single river or road all of a sudden is divided into two. In other words, it is like saying that God speaks with forked-tongue, but in this case it is not implying hypocrisy or being two-faced. The revelation of God is just divided into two streams of thought, one of justice and the other mercy. On the one hand, God is a holy God who demands holiness from us. Since we are all sinners and have fallen short of God's standard, we must pay the penalty of death. There are no exceptions. However, the other stream of thought is based on God's mercy and love. In His wisdom, He knew that we would all be condemned to hell unless He provided a perfect substitute for our sins, who could die in our place, and take the punishment for us. That way His justice could still be appeased, and yet his love could also be fulfilled.

This two-fold message, though, is like a double-edged sword, for it can cut both ways. The justice of God has condemned us all for our fallen, sinful natures, and the mercy of God condemns us if we reject it. It's like being twice-cursed—once in ignorance and once in rebellion. The thrust of scripture is to help us to understand our double jeopardy if we reject Him, or the grace that is ours if we accept Him. These two messages are mouthed time and time again throughout the Bible, not just the New Testament. God's justice and grace are intertwined from eternity past and wind together throughout history like a double-helix, identifying the divine genetic makeup of our Creator. They work together to convict man of his need for a savior, and to cut away the dross, in order to transform us into the image of Christ.

We have to be conformed to Christ's image because God's justice demands that only Christ deserves to live. So, unless we are bonded together with Christ, so that when the Father looks at us, all he sees is Jesus, then the double-edged sword is only for judgment. If we are Christ-like, though, God uses His sword like a mirror, to show us how much we look like Him.

Milk, Meat and Maturity

"Though by this time you ought to be teachers, you need someone to teach you the elementary truths of God's Word all over again. You need milk, not solid food."
Heb. 5:12

When a mother nurses her baby, she is not only giving it food. She is also passing along antibodies to keep the child from illnesses or allergies. She is sharing love, and bonding with the child in a way that only a mother can understand. She is also healing her own memories of pain from childbirth, for the warm milk that flows from her breasts seems to sooth her own heart more than it fills the baby's stomach. Her tenderness touches the child's soul, and he learns that he is loved.

When we become Christians, we are like this little baby. The Lord feeds us the milk of the Word, the tender touches of his grace and love, and we are bonded with Him in a special way. He passes along spiritual antibodies or principles to keep us from becoming sinfully sick, and he provides the Holy Spirit, like a nanny, to be our comforter and guide.

A mother knows when a baby is ready to be weaned. She gradually makes the transition to solid food because she knows that just a sudden stop would cause pain for both her and the child. The Lord also is sensitive to our readiness to grow up. As we begin getting our spiritual teeth or ability to chew and digest truths from His Word, He gently gives us more and more as we hunger for Him. He is like the mother bird, who chews up the worms before she gives them to her babies to make them easier to digest. God tenderizes his truth, and gently feeds our souls.

His goal, though, is to have us grow strong, and to be able to digest even tougher lessons to learn. He wants us to be able to understand and internalize the meat of the Word. Unfortunately, some of us never grow up. We are like Peter Pan who would rather stay a child all of his life rather than facing the hardships of reality. Our fantasy worlds are easier to live in because we make the rules, and we can escape anything through our imaginations, rather than having to deal with them. This is true both emotionally and spiritually. Sometimes we hold on to childhood because it seems like a safer place. We have been exposed to pain or trauma, and it scares us. Our fear keeps us from moving forward, so we hold on to our "sandbox spirituality", where we can just sit and play and make-believe. God tries to feed us meat, but we cry for our bottles instead. God tries to move us on into more challenging, life-changing experiences, but we throw a tantrum, and refuse to budge.

God wants us to grow up so we can help him take care of the other children. He wants us to start being teachers as soon as we have learned a new truth. He wants to train us how to train others, but we are stuck in the dirty diapers of our self-centered ways, and we can't look past the end of our pacifier—"At least I'm saved". It's time to grow up.

The Hands of the Living God

"It is a dreadful thing to fall into the hands of the living God." Heb. 10:31

Palm readers tell us that they can read a person's life just from looking at our hands. They say that they can tell how long our life will be, if we will get married, how many children we will have, etc. I believe that there are only two things that a palm reader can determine from looking at our hands: how fat our wallet is, and how gullible we are.

Yet, I do think that there are some things that we can tell by a person's hands. We can usually tell if the person is a manual laborer or desk clerk by how calloused or soft their hands are. We can also tell something about their personality by how they shake our hand, whether with gusto, or very timidly.

God's hands, though, are the most revealing. The Bible says that in "the beginning you laid the foundations of the earth, and the heavens are the work of your hands" (Psa. 102:25). Yet, his hands are not just limited to creation. They are involved with the discipline and forming of each individual's spiritual growth. Sometimes God has to chasten us by allowing physical hardship to test us. The Word tells us that "he wounds, but he also binds up; he injures, but his hands also heal" (Job 5:18).

This is contrary to our normal way of thinking. We assume that Satan does the injuring, and then God steps in to heal us. According to this passage, God is the one to inflict pain, and then he heals. It is like a parent's spanking a child to correct bad behavior. When God inflicts wounds, it is to correct someone that he loves. He wants us to fear Him as well as love him because he knows that it will keep us from destroying ourselves. He wants us to feel the full force of Paul's statement, "It is a dreadful thing to fall into the hands of the living God". However, he wants us to know that it is only dreadful if we have fallen into sin.

We can believe in his full strength and power, and tremble at his wrath, yet feel comforted by his mercy, patience and healing hands. We can say with the psalmist, "Into your hands I commit my spirit" (31:5) because we know that he loves us. We know that his hands will uphold us and protect us, embrace us, and draw us to himself. "In his hands are strength and power to exalt and give strength to all" (I Chron. 29:12). That means that his hands are not only strong, but they give us strength as well.

It is easy, then, for us to say that "Our times are in your hands" (Psa. 31:15), for we know that whether his hands are used to discipline us or to comfort us, wound us or heal us, they are always being used to empower us to become more like him. Jesus, himself, had wounds in his hands, but he was able to touch people's lives with them in ways that no one else could. The hands of the living God are nothing to dread, unless we also dread to live for Him. He would rather give us the right hand of fellowship.

Trying to Please God

"Without faith, it is impossible to please God." Heb. 11:6

Have you ever tried to make someone happy, and yet, no matter what you did, they always found fault in it? Some people are just really hard to please. It's like they believe that the world needs to be more balanced, so when someone does something nice, or tries to be cheerful, it is their responsibility to balance it out by contributing the negative. From their perspective, everyone else is looking at life through rose-colored glasses, so it is their job to set them straight, or to help them be more realistic. They think that others are too naïve, so it is their job to tell "the rest of the story", which is always criticism. You just can't please them. They are determined to be miserable, and they want everyone else to be miserable too.

Sometimes we think that it is too hard to please God also. We picture God as an old, miserable grouch in heaven, who isn't happy, and he doesn't want us to be happy either. That's why he gave us so many rules, because he doesn't want us to have any fun. This, however, is just the typical adolescent view of authority figures. It doesn't matter whether it is a parent, a teacher, the police, or God—adolescents resent being told "No!". When a person grows up, though, they realize that the world is not about them, and that there is a lot more to life than just having fun.

Personal fulfillment and joy come from serving God by serving others, not by putting one's own needs and desires first. The problem with old grouches is that they have reverted to being self-centered teenagers again, but at the other end of the spectrum. Teenagers just want to have fun, and old grouches don't want anyone to have any fun. Yet, they are both looking for the same thing—attention upon themselves. God, though, knows that we can never be really happy as long as we are focused on self because self is depraved, dead and ugly. There is nothing beautiful there to look at. It is like looking at the reflection of ourselves in a cesspool, or using our septic tank as a wishing well.

Our spirit, however, can become beautiful if it is transformed by trusting in Christ. When we look outward instead of inward, then we can see life from God's perspective, and he is no grouch. He wants us to have life, and to have it more abundantly (John 10:10). He wants us to find joy and peace. He just doesn't want us to waste our time looking in all the wrong places. He knows that we will only be happy if we put our faith in Him, so why look elsewhere?

The plus side is that our faith not only makes us happy, it makes God happy too. "Without faith, it is impossible to please God." That means that with faith, we are both happy. Pleasing God is not a matter of "trying" but "trusting". We need to put our faith in him, and not in what we can do for him. Trying to please God actually achieves just the opposite. God isn't interested in a flurry of activity. He wants our faith, not our flurry.

Make Level Paths

"Make level paths for your feet, so that the lame may not be disabled, but rather healed." Heb. 12:13

I love to go hiking in the mountains. The fresh mountain air, the breathtaking views and the challenge of an invigorating walk all pump my adrenaline to its peak. I love to walk fast, climb over large boulders, and wade through rushing streams. It stretches me to the limits, and I feel mystically closer to the divine. When I am leading others on a hike, though, it changes everything. I have to slow down, take shorter strides, and stay on the well-worn path more so that I don't lose anyone, or go beyond their ability levels. I am more focused on their enjoyment than my own, and the emphasis is on group bonding more than individual growth or enlightenment.

The same thing happens with our spiritual walk. When we are alone with the Lord, we can leap and bound with the inspiration of the Spirit as our guide, feeling exuberated by the closeness and freshness of God's majesty in our individual growth. We can wrestle with God in the raging streams of Mount Sinai, dig desperately for living water in the deserts of our lives, or stretch over the boulders of our base humanity, barely grasping the ledges with our fingers of faith. Yet, when we are guiding others who are weaker than ourselves, we need to be careful that our lust for the limits doesn't scare off the novices of the faith that we are trying to mentor. We sometimes assume that if something excites us, then it should interest others also. Yet, we have to remember that not everyone is ready to climb Mount Whitney. If we push them too quickly, we can burn them out, and we could be creating drop-outs instead of disciples.

Leaders should never just go at their own pace, and expect everyone else to keep up. The Bible says, "Make level paths for your feet, so that the lame may not be disabled, but rather healed." It says this not for our benefit, but for those who are following us. Sure, we could probably take a harder, more challenging road if we were on our own, but we are being watched. People are trying to follow our example, just like children trying to imitate their parent. They are trying to step in our footsteps, and their spiritual legs are a lot shorter than ours.

So, slow down, take it easy, keep it simple, so the lame, the wounded, the broken-hearted, the immature, can grow at their own pace, instead of yours. Don't' be in such a hurry to push your spiritual children into adulthood by throwing the depths of your apologetics   or scriptural controversies at them, just because you think it will help them to grow up. Forcing a baby to eat steak doesn't help them to get bigger faster. They could choke and die. The same thing is true spiritually speaking. You can be profoundly wise and simple at the same time. Keep the paths level. If people peak too early, the only place left to go is down.

The Disgraceful Choice

"He chose to be mistreated along with the people of God rather than to enjoy the pleasures of sin for a short time. He regarded disgrace for the sake of Christ as of greater value than the treasures of Egypt." Heb. 11:25-26

When we read the story of Daniel being thrown into the lion's den because he was commanded not to pray to God, but he did it any way, we applaud his civil disobedience. It is better to obey God than man. When we read about Shadrach, Meshach, and Abednego refusing to bow down to an idol, and being thrown into a fiery furnace as punishment, we cheer their divine rescue, for it affirms their rebellion against evil authorities as being blessed by God. Each one of these men stood up for their own spiritual rights, with no regard for the consequences, and God honored them.

Moses, however, was different in his rebelliousness. He didn't stand up for his own rights, but the rights of others. He saw his people, the Israelites, being oppressed and abused, and he decided to take a stand. He could have just looked the other way, and enjoyed the privileges of a prince in Pharaoh's court, but his conscience wouldn't let him just carelessly enjoy life while others were suffering. He chose to step into a situation that wasn't really any of his business, interfering in a battle between an Egyptian and an Israelite, and he ended up killing the Egyptian as the only way to end the struggle. The result was that he had to flee from the law, give up his status in society, and become a poor shepherd in a foreign land. From the community's perspective, he was a disgrace. He had broken the law. Yet, in his heart of hearts, he felt that he had done the right thing. He had made a disgraceful choice according to society, but his conscience told him that it was of greater value to follow God than to enjoy anything that the world had to offer.

God honored his choice by making him the leader of his chosen people. God needed a shepherd who was willing to lose it all for the sake of his sheep. This is amazing all by itself, but what is even more amazing, is the motivation behind Moses' decision. It says that "He regarded disgrace for the sake of Christ as of greater value than the treasures of Egypt." Yet, how did he even know about Christ if the Bible wasn't even written yet? This was before Moses wrote the Pentateuch. This was before the books of prophecy. Moses, in fact, had made this choice before God had spoken a single word to him personally.

Yet, God had spoken to him through his Jewish mother while he was being nursed, probably his first four years, and she inbred in his heart the divine destiny of the chosen people, the rich heritage of oral history and God's providence through the years for Israel. God used godly parents to instill in his future leader the principles that would be necessary to give Moses the motivation, dedication, and vision to put it all on the line for the sake of the coming Messiah and his people, in spite of what the world might think.

No Bitter Root

"See to it that ...no bitter root grows up to cause trouble and defile many."
Heb. 12:15

The word "bitter" usually refers to either a bad taste or a bad attitude. The word, however, is not limited to just these two. It also means sharp, piercing, painful or poisonous. Eating hot salsa, then, could be considered bitter because of how much pain that it causes our lips and tongue, even though some people actually like the sensation of sacrificing their mouths on the altar of machismo. When it comes to emotions and relationships, though, it refers to anything, like anger, jealousy, envy, or pride, that causes trouble or defiles many. It is anything that serves as a poison or cancer within the heart, that eats away at the soul, and destroys relationships with others.

It is compared to a root here because roots are usually underground, hidden from sight. Our own bitterness usually starts out being hidden as well. We don't want people to know how upset we are or how we really feel, so we play the pretend game. Roots, however, have a way of producing things above the surface too. They can be as little as grass, or as tall as a Redwood tree, but they all start as roots. Then they grow to their full height if we continue to feed them and water them. Bitterness may only start with a seed, but the roots help it to grow if we keep feeding it with our prideful, hurtful thoughts. Every time we dwell on what we are upset about, or the person who offended or hurt us, we fertilize the roots. They spread out like tentacles that wrap around and suffocate the roots of the good plants around us, and choke out any fruit that the Spirit is trying to produce.

The word "root" means "ray", like a ray of light. Just as rays of light spread out from its source, so the rays or roots of a seed spread out searching for nutrients to strengthen the plant. They are meant to be something positive to promote growth and stability, to keep the plant from blowing over in the wind. Unfortunately, sometimes roots spread out into diseased soil, and a plant may grow into full height, but then wither and die. The same thing can happen to us spiritually. We may be growing in the Lord, but then the spiritual climate or soil that we are in becomes diseased or poisoned by either ourselves or others, and we start to wither. The bitter root can wrap itself around the other good roots, and the cancer of the soul spreads.

Our root as Christians is supposed to be Christ (Col. 2:7), and we are to be rooted in the soil of love (Eph. 3:17), so that our rays of light can be spread to all those around us to help them to grow as well, instead of choking them out with our dark, brooding spirit. Our roots can either give us stability in the Lord, or they can make us weak and wobbly by eating away at the plant that they are supposed to be nourishing. Our roots can either produce good sap for the body, or make us into a sap. It's our choice.

Worship God with Reverence

"Worship God acceptably with reverence and awe, for our God is a consuming fire." Heb. 12:28-29

Have any of you been to a worship service lately? I mean, a service where worship was the main focus of the meeting, and not just a momentary expression in a multi-faceted, multimedia event. It seems that modern churches have become so experiential in nature, that the focus is on our feelings about God or about each other, rather than on the character of God himself. The so-called "worship" segment of our services is little more than a spiritual aerobics class, intended to pump up our feelings of emotional well-being, so that we feel better about ourselves. We feel encouraged by the singing because the tunes make us tap our feet or dance to the rhythm, which is fun and invigorating, but has nothing to do with spirituality.

The word "worship" has nothing to do with feeling good about ourselves. It's not about us. It means "worth-ship", or feeling fear, reverence, and awe toward God because He is worth our respect and honor. "God is a consuming fire", not a video game that we can manipulate and control for our entertainment and happiness. Yet, we act as if God is not even there. We are there to see our friends, or to be seen by them, we chit-chat during the sermon instead of listening to the Word of God, we think about what we are going to do the rest of the day, we think bad thoughts about people we see, and we judge the sermon on its entertainment quotient, instead of the message from God.

The Bible says that we are to worship God with awe. The word "awe" means to be so astonished and amazed by God's presence and character, that we are afraid of his discipline because we don't live up to his standard. When was the last time that we stood in fear and trembling in the presence of God? Some people feel that we don't need to fear God unless we are living in open sin. Most of us are just average sinners, in our minds, so we aren't any worse than anyone else. So, what's there to be afraid of? "I'm doing my best!" Worship, again, is not about us. It has nothing to do with how good or bad we are, or what spiritual gifts we have, or how long we have been serving the Lord. It isn't about us. I repeat--It isn't about us. We need to take our eyes off of ourselves and glorify God alone.

If we haven't focused on who God is—his majesty, his character, his worthiness—we haven't worshipped him. Yes, we can feel good about the fact that God loves us, but only in contrast to the fact that we know that we don't deserve it. God's love without God's grace doesn't exist. God is worthy—we are not. We have become too complacent about God's love and our salvation. We take God for granted, and even our hymns of praise are lip-synced, for our mouths move, but the words are not coming from our hearts. We are hypnotized by the repetition of words, but don't have a clue what they mean.

Entertaining Angels

"Do not forget to entertain strangers, for by so doing some people have entertained angels without knowing it." Heb. 13:2

There have been several movies about angels, and there is a whole cult following of the divine beings, from Christians and non-Christians alike. The non-Christian followers like the concept of angels because they long for the spiritual in their lives, but they don't like being accountable to God. An angel is less offensive, almost like an invisible friend who just takes care of them. They are Pixies or Fairies, like Tinker bells, cute and lovable, or they appear in human form, because they are really just humans who have died, and they are sent back to the earth to make amends or earn their way into heaven. These are humanistic and pagan ideas, of course, for they have no connection to any teaching in scripture.

The Bible says that angels are God's messengers. They are spiritual beings, who were created as angels, not men, and their purpose is to glorify God and to carry out His purposes. There are fallen angels, too, who may become our "friends" by giving us power to do evil, but it is only at the cost of our souls. God may send an angel to help us through a particular trial or help us fight the spiritual warfare we are in (Acts 5:19-20), but he is not meant to be our buddy or spirit guide that we can rely on or communicate with like a confidant. The Lord gave us the Holy Spirit to be our guide and comforter. If we glorify angels, we are replacing the Holy Spirit with substitutes of our own choosing.

Some people feel that the above verse means that any stranger could be an angel, so we need to be careful how we treat them. God may have sent them as a test to see how we will treat them. We are supposed to treat strangers carefully and with respect, but that doesn't mean that any stranger could be an angel. For example, if we see a bum sitting on a curb, in a drunken stupor, using the Lord's name in vain, and swearing at us when we don't give him any money, he wasn't an angel. How do I know? Well, first of all, an angel wouldn't swear or use the Lord's name in vain. Second of all, the only times in scripture where God sent an angel in human form to man, where he didn't know that he was angel at first, was when God sent them as messengers to call someone for service (Gideon) or to prophesy about his coming judgment or blessing (Abraham).

It is possible that God may send an angel to us in human form also, so we need to treat strangers kindly, but if he is an angel, he will make himself or herself known by the message that he brings, or the blessing that he bestows. If it is an angel, and he tells us to do evil, or anything contrary to the Word of God, we can know he is not from God. If he appears as a human, though, and he gives us supernatural help or guidance, when only a miracle will do, and he gives the glory to God alone, we can be assured that we were entertaining an angel, and angel food cake might be appropriate as a token of our hospitality.

August 14

The Monotony of the Messiah

"Jesus Christ is the same yesterday, today and forever." Heb. 13:8

America is called the melting pot of humanity because we have so many cultures represented in our society, and they all seem to blend together, like a stew or soup. Yet, people hold on to their cultural identities and traditions, and even ways of cooking remain unique. We have Chinese food, Italian food, Mexican food, French pastries, German chocolates, and Swiss cheese. We have our favorites, but we also like variety, so we take advantage of the opportunity that we have to try them all. Even though the menus are varied, though, we expect a certain regularity of quality. Every restaurant has to conform to certain safety and health standards, as well as standards of acceptable taste. We want the tastes to be varied, but the standards uniform.

With due respect, Jesus is a lot like a good menu at a restaurant. In other words, he has a lot of variety that he offers to each individual, according to our own personal needs and maturity levels, yet he always has the same standard of excellence. He offers a "kiddie meal" for those young in the faith, a well-balanced variety of choices for the adult believers, and senior citizen meals for the more mature. Yet, in spite of his dealing with us as individuals, in very eclectic ways, He always remains the same. "Jesus Christ is the same yesterday, today, and forever." That doesn't mean that he is monotonous, in the sense that he never changes his tone, or that he is boring. He is monotonous, though, in the sense that he always stays the same, without variation in his character or essence.

He cannot change who he is, but he will change the way that he handles our souls. He is the Great Physician, who knows how to treat each illness differently, and our sinful natures are like illnesses or diseases. They have caused our spirits to be deformed and crippled, and God is the only one who can reach into our hearts with his loving, healing hand, and remold our defects into his image. Our sinful natures, though, are unique, like fingerprints of the soul. We all have them, but they are individualized according to the temperaments, intellects, and divine imprints upon our hearts. God created us in his image, with his characteristics, but sin has distorted them into twisted shapes. We are like the mirrors in a fun house or carnival that distort our image to make us look short or tall, thin or fat, or just twisted out of shape.

God is always the same, then, but as he is reflected in each one of us, we don't always do him justice. God's nature is a uniform light, but his revelation of himself is a varied rainbow, and then our reflection of him is even more varied. God's character may be monotonous, but his characteristics are a kaleidoscope of never ending changes, as he appears new and fresh to us all the time. He is the perfect paradox—always the same, yet in new ways.

Fire and Brimstone

"The tongue also is a fire...It sets the whole course of [man's] life on fire, and is itself set on fire by hell." James 3:6

Every year there are forest fires that ravage the trees, kill the wildlife, destroy homes, and take the lives of many people, all started by careless individuals who happened to throw a cigarette into some dry grass, leave a campfire burning unattended, or recklessly play with fireworks in a hazardous area. It is amazing how much devastation and heartache can be caused by a single spark.

The Bible compares the tongue to this spark of fire. It too can cause great devastation and hurt, far beyond the original intent. A person says something, maybe even in jest, and yet that word is spread by others, like a whirlwind, way beyond the control of the person who started it. It may be a nasty rumor, gossip, lie, backbiting, criticism, slander, or sarcastic humor, but its effects can ruin the lives of the person who started it, the one whom the rumor or lie is about, and those who hear about it and spread it to others.

The words that come from our mouths can be like a disease or plague that spreads to people's hearts and brains, and eats away their souls like a cancer. The Bible says that "No man can tame the tongue. It is a restless evil, full of deadly poison" (James 3:8). The Bible says that the tongue "is itself set on fire by hell". The Devil is the one who puts evil thoughts into our hearts and minds, which causes us to say things that we know that we shouldn't say. The Bible says that hell is filled with fire and brimstone (Rev. 19:20). It's as if this fire and brimstone, then, bubbles up from hell like lava from a volcano and consumes everything in its path.

Sulfur is a very brittle mineral, which is very combustible. When it burns, it gives off a very pungent odor. When it is mixed with water and diluted, however, it is useful in hot springs to sooth away aches and pains of the body. Sulfur, then, is a lot like our feelings. Christ is compared to the living water, and when we are one with him, our feelings are transformed into the fruit of the Spirit—love, joy, peace, longsuffering, etc. We are like the soothing mineral hot springs that others long to be embraced by. When we are separated from the Lord, though, because of sin or self-centeredness, we become dry and brittle and combustible. When some one says something hurtful to us then, we become defensive, and our tongue lashes back like whips of fire, seeking revenge for the hurt that we have endured. Our anger consumes us, and our tongue ignites a wildfire of rage, bitterness, and discontent. Our whole being becomes like fire and brimstone, and our life becomes a living hell. We live in Hades, so we want everyone else around us to feel our pain. This kind of life, like Sulfur, stinks, and no one wants to be around us.

We need to douse the flames, jump back into the Living Water, and use our heat to sooth instead of to singe those around us.

Faith, Hope, and Love

"Now these three remain: faith, hope and love. But the greatest of these is love."
I Cor. 13:13

What is the best way to lead someone to the Lord? By being the kind of leader that someone would want to follow. The Apostle Paul says, "Remember your leaders, who spoke the word of God to you. Consider their way of life and imitate their faith" (Heb. 13:7). It doesn't matter if we are leading someone to the Lord, into salvation or into deeper sanctification, we need to be a good example to lead the way. Paul says, "Follow my example, as I follow the example of Christ" (I Cor. 11:1). People are watching us. What do they see when they observe our way of life? What can they tell by our words, our actions, and our attitudes that would make them want to follow us? Are we so Christ-like, that if someone were to follow us, they would find Him? Is our faith, hope and love so strong and powerful that there wouldn't be any doubt as to what we stand for and who we represent? Would they be able to know the validity of our faith by the validity of our life?

The Bible says that "without faith it is impossible to please God" (Heb. 11:6) Yet, even if we have faith, we cannot please God unless we also have works (James 2:17). Faith that doesn't work is useless. It is incomplete, like a blueprint to a house (James 2:22). The design may be perfect, but unless someone takes the time to build it, what good is it? Christianity is not about just saving us from hell. It is about pointing people to Christ by being Christ-like ourselves. That means we can't just stop with faith. Our life has to be an example or out-working of what that faith means in day by day life. The word "hope" means a sure, definite, firm expectation that something is going to happen. In other words, if our faith is genuine, there should be a firm expectation that it is going to be demonstrated in our life. Hope means that we are sure something that we believe in is going to really work because we have put it into practice. Our life is a practical illustration of our faith. People can see that we practice what we preach.

Yet, even with both faith and hope, these are still not enough to please God. The Bible says that "If I have a faith that can move mountains, but have not love, I am nothing" (I Cor. 13:2). In other words, even a faith that is demonstrated through good works is not good enough, unless it is motivated by love. Faith, hope, and love, then, are not just three good things that we should want to have. They are the recipe for becoming Christ-like and for leading others to Him. If we leave out any of the ingredients, it is useless, because we would be leaving out an important quality of Christ's character for people to imitate. When it says that love is the greatest of these three, it is not talking about importance. It is saying that love is what makes the others complete.

The Horse Whisperer

*"When we put bits into the mouths of horses to make them obey us,
we can turn the whole animal." James 3:3*

There is a movie call *The Horse Whisperer*, where a man is able to train even the most stubborn, wild horses through talking to them gently. He doesn't have to whip them, or break them. He gains their confidence and friendship, so they <u>want</u> to obey him, instead of being forced to. This is how the Lord tries to deal with us as well. He speaks to us with a still, small voice, and whispers to our spirits (I Kings 19:12).

Yet, some of us are used to running wild with the range stallions, and the pounding of the hooves of the herd drown out any sound of the Savior's voice. Our nostrils are flared, our blood pumping wildly, and the adrenaline rush of sin makes our rebellious stampeding with the crowd an intoxicating whirlwind of earthy, sensual excitement. We don't have time to listen to a soft word from the Horse Whisperer. We are too filled with life to listen to the giver of life himself.

When it talks about putting a bit in a horse's mouth, then, we are impressed that such a small thing can control such a big animal. Yet, the horse, if its spirit is right, can be handled with much less. It is only the horse that is a bit on the wild side that even needs a bit at all. God would much rather just have to whisper into our hearts to get us to go the right direction. He uses the bit, a little bit of pain or trial, to get our attention or encourage our submission only when he has to. He's hoping that it won't be necessary.

The unfortunate thing about using a bit all of the time is that a horses' mouth can become calloused, and it won't respond to the bit anymore. The same thing is true of us, especially if we keep resisting the leading of the Lord. Stubbornness in a horse can lead to its master using the stirrup or the whip to get it going where it is supposed to be going. We don't see any stirrups or whips for show horses. They can dance and prance, go forward and backward and sideways, just with a gentle gesture or word from the owner.

That's the key—it knows who the owner is. Wild horses keep wanting to run wild. They want to be free from any owner. The call of the wild is just as strong for people who have once tasted their wild oats. They have a hard time recognizing the Lord as their owner or master. They want the Lord to be their savior, the one who saves them from the wolves, bears, and lions of the world who seek to devour them, but they still want to be able to run free. This kind of horse, or person, isn't good for much more than the glue factory, as far as the Lord is concerned. Yet, He continues to work with us, patiently waiting and hoping that we will yield our wild spirits to Him and stop fighting His will for our lives. He hopes that we will come to the point where we can prance with joy to his whisper, instead of being led to the green pastures "bit by bit".

Three Kinds of Wisdom

"Who is wise and understanding among you? Let him show it." James 3:13

A wise person is not just someone who knows a lot. The word wisdom implies an exceptional degree of skill in putting into practice what we know to be true. This could apply to a lot of different areas of interest. We could be a wise doctor, a wise lawyer, a wise mother or father, a wise minister, etc. We don't have to know it all. We just have to be able to practice what we preach.

The Bible talks about three different kinds of wisdom: worldly wisdom, demonic wisdom, and divine wisdom. Worldly wisdom is something that anyone can have. We have learned through education and experience that certain things are true, and we have agreed to live according to those principles. We are a wise person. Yet, this kind of wisdom is humanistic because it is limited to those things that we can learn through our own efforts and insights without any help from supernatural sources. It is "knowledge so called" because it is based only on the brain and the heart, without any help from the spirit and soul (I Cor. 1:20-21).

Worldly wisdom can never lead someone to Christ. In fact, it is only by recognizing how inadequate that human wisdom is that man can come to God. Worldly wisdom is a lot like trying to drink salt water when we are adrift on a life raft. It may fill our stomach, but it doesn't quench our thirst. In fact, it makes us even more thirsty for pure water. Human wisdom may fill our thirst for knowledge for a while, but it doesn't fill our spiritual God-shaped vacuum. In fact, the more we become filled with human wisdom, the less satisfying that it becomes. It just wets our appetite for the real thing, which we cannot have apart from the divine.

Some people come to realize that human wisdom is inadequate, but they refuse to acknowledge God in their lives. So, they seek the supernatural from other sources. They may call it by different names, such as the New Age Movement, Astrology, Kabbala, Mysticism, Gnosticism, Channeling, or the occult, but whether they will admit it or not, it is demonic wisdom. Any movement or belief system that seeks supernatural powers or insights apart from God is demonic (Deut. 18:10-12; James 3:15).

The only kind of wisdom that meets man's need is divine wisdom. It is a gift from God, and He has promised to give it to all those who seek it (James 1:5). Yet, even here, it is important that we are not just seeking wisdom in and of itself, because even the search for divine wisdom can become an ego thing. What we need to be seeking is God himself, not the gifts that he can give us. If we seek him first, then he will give us wisdom as part of the process of conforming us into his image, so we can become more like him, not so we can become more gifted. Wisdom is not meant to be a trophy that we put on our shelf of spiritual attainments. Humility comes from wisdom, not bragging rights (James 3:13).

Friendship with the World

*"You adulterous people, don't you know that friendship with the world
is hatred toward God?" James 4:4*

The word "friend" is derived from the word "free". It means to feel free around someone, and to love someone enough to set them free. Unfortunately, the world takes this to mean that if you are my friend, you will give me the freedom to do or say whatever I want without judgment. "Live and let live". In other words, being a friend means the same thing as toleration and acceptance, regardless of how obnoxious, hedonistic, evil, self-centered, anti-social or anti-God I might be. "If you really love me, you will accept me the way that I am, not try to change me."

Realistically, though, this kind of friendship only seeks permission to sin, and only seeks friendships with others who want to sin also. It is not willing to tolerate or accept anyone who seeks to follow God or his commandments. True friendship, however, is based on true freedom, not just the license to sin. True freedom, or liberty, in fact, is freedom from the slavery of sin. Whereas, the world's standard of freedom alienates people from God, true freedom is being set free to be friends with God. Where freedom to sin is self-destructive and hurtful of those around us, liberty in Christ gives us spiritual wings to reach heights that we would never be able to reach without him.

We seek friendship with the world because we long for the excitement or pleasure that it promises, but we don't really consider the consequences of our actions. It is like diving off of a cliff and enjoying the wild flight, without thinking about what will happen when we hit the bottom. What is the result of seeking friendship with the world? We become an enemy of God (James 4:4). Do we understand what that means? Sometimes we have the naïve feeling that it doesn't really matter what we do. We can do whatever we want, as long as we go to church one hour a week, or say an occasional prayer to wipe the slate clean. Such mediocre lip service to God is an insult to the Heavenly Father. In fact, the Bible says that He considers friendship with the world, "hatred toward God".

We might think, "I don't hate God. I just enjoy pleasure." Yet, He sees it differently. It is similar to a person trying to say something in a foreign language, yet he doesn't say it right, so it comes out meaning something completely different. Maybe we don't intend to express that we hate God, but we are speaking a foreign language to God, and He interprets it totally contrary to what we wanted to get across.

Doesn't God judge us according to our motives? Doesn't God know what we mean? Absolutely. He understands our motives better than we do. We justify ourselves or excuse ourselves because we think we are basically good people with good motives. God knows the "real us". He knows when we love the world more than him, and he calls it adultery.

How to Make the Devil Run Away

"Submit yourselves, then, to God. Resist the Devil, and he will flee from you." James 4:7

A lot of people are afraid of the Devil. He is portrayed as the big, bad boogieman of the world, and people tend to deal with him with kid gloves because they are afraid of what he might do to them. Well, the Bible says that there is something that we can do to make him actually run away from us. There are seven steps that we must take to make the Devil run, and they are all found in James chapter 4. The first is "Humble yourselves before the Lord, and he will lift you up" (vs.10). According to Prov. 16:18, "Pride goes before a fall." In contrast, humility goes before being lifted up. Pride is what makes us sin and fall into the hands of the Devil. Humility lifts us up out of the Devil's reach, and into the hands of Jesus. Humility, then, must be the first step to get the Devil to run.

The second step is built upon the first. It is repentance. The word repentance comes from the word "pain", meaning that we are to feel the same pain about our sinfulness that the Lord feels. The Bible tells us to actually, "grieve, mourn, and wail" because of our sins (vs. 9). It is not just talking about going through the motions here. It is talking about suffering in our souls because of the grief that we have caused the Lord.

The third and fourth steps are based upon this one. They are purification through confession of both the actions and the heart. It says, "Wash your hands, you sinners, and purify your hearts you double-minded" (vs. 8). It isn't enough to just confess our deeds. We also must confess our motives or desires that lead to the deeds. Of course, purification is not something we do through human effort. God has to cleanse us, forgive us, and transform us. Our hearts and minds have to be purged from our double-mindedness through the grace and power of God alone.

The fifth step is to "Come near to God, and he will come near to you" (vs. 8). When we have been living in sin, we are too ashamed to come near to God. Yet, once the sins have been taken care of, and the lusts which caused those sins, we can be assured that we can humbly approach him. He wants us to be near Him.

Once we are near Him, and abiding in Him, we need to do the sixth step, and that is "submit yourselves, then, to God" (vs. 7). We need to be willing to do whatever he asks us to do. We not only have to leave our sins behind, we have to be willing to yield to the Lord's guidance as we move forward into maturity. Then, and only then, can we do the seventh step, and that is "Resist the Devil, and he will flee from you" (vs. 7).

We cannot resist the Devil unless we have done the other steps first. Yet, if we are humbled to the point of feeling what Jesus feels, clean enough to be close to the Father, and yielded completely to the leading of the Holy Spirit, it is no wonder that the Devil takes off running. He sees the Trinity.

Powerful Prayer

"The prayer of a righteous man is powerful and effective." James 5:16

Most Christians wish that their prayer life was more effective. Sometimes it is just a matter of discipline because we don't spend enough time actually praying to make a difference. We are too lazy or too busy to make the time to pray, and even when we take the time, we are not in the right frame of mind to talk to God. Our minds are racing about everything else going on in our lives, and we can't seem to quiet our hearts long enough to listen to what God has to say to us. So, we say a quick one-liner, like "Help, Lord!", and we are on our way.

Yet, let's just say for a moment that this doesn't apply to us. We are disciplined, and we do take the time to pray each day. Yet, our prayers still do not seem to be very effective. We seem to be on a different wavelength from God, and whenever we ask for anything, it seems that God just tunes us out. What's missing?

First of all, we must have the faith to believe that God will answer our prayers (James 5:15). It doesn't take a lot of faith, for even if we have faith as small as the mustard seed, we can move mountains (Matt. 17:20). Yet, it has to be unwavering faith (James 1:6-7). It must be a faith without any doubt.

Second, we must be right with God. There cannot be any sin in our life. The Bible says that the "prayer of a righteous man is powerful and effective". Are we righteous? That doesn't mean that we have to be a perfect saint. No one is perfect or sinless. Yet, it does mean that we have to have all known sin confessed and cleansed before we come to the Lord asking him for anything. Otherwise, he will not listen to us.

Imagine going to your boss just after you have had a heated argument with him, and asking him for some extra time off to go see a ball game or a concert. Your boss may even fire you for having the gall to ask such a thing right after fighting with him. We should expect the same response from God. If we are living in sin, why should he answer our requests? We'll be lucky if he doesn't smack us on the side of our head for even asking for anything under those conditions.

The third thing that we need for effective prayer is fervency. The word "prayer", in fact, in this context means "fervent prayer", and the King James Version translates it, "The fervent prayer of a righteous man avails much." The word "fervent" means burning like a white hot coal. In order for coal to burn that hot, it has to be in the hottest part of the fire. It has to be in the center and burning bright. We, too, must be "white hot" in our fervency, for fire is a symbol in the Bible for the power of the Holy Spirit. If we are in the center of the Lord's will for our lives, and we are abiding, moving and growing in the power of the Spirit, then our prayers will be his prayers, and they can't help but be effective. The Bible says that when two or three pray together, God will answer. How much more so when He and you are the two?

Test the Spirits

"Do not believe every spirit, but test the spirits to see whether they are from God, because many false prophets have gone out into the world." I John 4:1

Have you tested any spirits lately? What kind of test would you give to a spirit anyway? Multiple choice? True or False? Fill in the blank? Essay? We need to give them a true or false test, and there is only one question. The Bible even tells us what the question is--Do you believe that Jesus Christ came in the flesh? (I John 4:2). Wait a minute. There are a lot of people, even non-Christians and atheists, who would acknowledge that there was an actual historical man named Jesus. This is a well-known fact. How can this be a test of the spirits, then, when everyone would give the same answer—"True"?

Yet, there is more to this question than meets the eye. First of all, we must understand the true meaning of the words in the question. The name "Jesus", for example, means "Jehovah, our savior". That means that what one must acknowledge is not only that a man named Jesus lived on earth, but that that man was God, Jehovah, in human flesh, come to save the world.

To reinforce this idea, Jesus is also given the title, "Christ". The word "Christ" is the Greek form of the Hebrew word "Messiah". The Jewish teachings about the Messiah were very clear from scripture—the messiah was to be God incarnate—God in human flesh, come to save the world. The prophet Isaiah foretells the coming of the messiah, and he says, "For unto us a child is born, unto us a son is given, and the government will be on his shoulders, and he will be called Wonderful Counselor, Mighty God, Everlasting Father, Prince of Peace. Of the increase of his government and peace there will be no end. He will reign on David's throne" (Isa. 9:6).

From this prophecy, several things are very clear. First, the messiah was going to be born as a human. Second, he was going to be God Almighty, the Everlasting Father, in human flesh. Third, he was going to rule an eternal kingdom. Jesus the Christ or Messiah, then, was not just some Jewish carpenter who happened to live a long time ago. He was God the Father in a human body. The Apostle Paul says it this way: "He is the image of the invisible God…For by him were all things created; things in heaven and on earth…all things were created by him and for him" (Col. 1:15-16).

The one question test, then, to see if a prophet or teacher is from God or not is, "Do you believe that Jesus was God, the Everlasting Father, who created all things, and who came to the world in human form to save man and to rule eternally? There are many prophets and religions today that do not believe this. They teach that Jesus was only a carpenter, or perhaps a good teacher, or maybe even the son of God, but not God himself. The Bible says that such teachers are anti-Christ's (I John 4:3), and that we should not believe them, for they are not from God. It's time to turn in your tests. The exam is over.

Jezebel, Judaism, and Jesus

"You have this in your favor: You hate the practices of the Nicolaitans,
which I also hate." Rev. 2:6

Ahab was the king of Israel, but he rebelled against God, and he became an idolater. In his defiance, he married a pagan priestess from Phoenicia, Jezebel, and she led him into even greater sin. She was a priestess of Baal and Asherah. Baal was the main male god of the Canaanites, and Asherah was the main goddess. They were gods of fertility, so sexual immorality played an important part in their rituals. They had male and female prostitutes who helped the people worship them. The worshippers, though, were often killed by the prostitutes in the act of sex as the highest sacrifice that they could give to their gods.

Jezebel had 450 priests of Baal and 400 priests of Asherah serving under her power, for she was the high-priestess, and she gained spiritual power from the Devil every time one of her priests sacrificed another human to their deities. She claimed to have special, secret knowledge and magical skills, supposedly making her invincible and immortal. At her peak, there were only 7,000 Jews left out of the millions that were in Israel that had not bowed down to Baal or danced around the Asherah or May poles. She had killed all of the prophets of God, except for Elijah, and she was doing everything she could to kill him.

Even though she is eventually killed, her moral depravity and pagan influence continued to plague the Israelites through the time of Christ and the early church. Gnosticism was a derivative of this pagan heresy, for it continued the idea that they had some secret, hidden knowledge that no one else had access to.

The Nicolaitans also followed suit, teaching that it was alright for Jews and Christians to live immoral lives and participate in pagan rituals, along with their other religious practices. They taught dualism, or the belief that there are two different worlds, the physical and the spiritual, and what you did in the physical world had no impact on the spiritual. Therefore, you could live in immorality without it affecting you spiritually.

The Lord praises the church in Ephesus because they hate the practices of the Nicolaitans, just as he hates them. The Lord hates it when Christians feel that it is alright to live worldly, sinful, immoral lives, as if what they do with their bodies in their spare time is totally irrelevant to their belief or worship of God. They have dissected their everyday lives from their "Sunday life", and they don't see any problem with it. Without even knowing it, in the midst of their pleasure, they are being sacrificed to Baal or Beelzebub, Satan, himself, and those who are seducing them into their lives of sin are gaining spiritual power every time they slay another believer. We cannot dance around the pole of Asherah and bow down at the tree of Calvary at the same time. There is only one tree of life.

A Portrait of Jesus

"His head and hair were white like wool, as white as snow, and his eyes were like blazing fire."
Rev. 1:14-16

Many people have tried to paint pictures of Jesus based upon their imaginations and their relationships with the savior. Sometimes he is pictured as a strong, masculine man's man, and sometimes as a meek, mellow momma's boy. Some people paint him to match their own cultural heritage, whether white, black or brown, so they can identify with him better. In a sense, they are creating God in their own image, or how they want him to be. Jesus, however, is not limited by our perceptions or the box that our comfort zone might seek to place him in. Even John's vision of what Jesus looks like is inadequate, for he speaks in similes and metaphors, desperately trying to compare Jesus to things from his own experience.

Jesus is not limited to our experiences, or to anything that is human or even physical. He is a spirit with a spiritual body that transforms the material world and our finite concepts of the divine. Yet, he has chosen to reveal himself to John in this vision in physical terms to demonstrate his character and his majesty. He is the living Word, and every part of his glowing description speaks volumes about who he is.

First, his head and hair are white like wool and snow. White is a symbol for purity or holiness, and white hair speaks of his eternal wisdom as the "Ancient of Days". Wool points to the fact that he was both the lamb that was slaughtered for our transgressions, as well as the shepherd who loves and guides his sheep. Snow not only represents purity, but the fact that God's love covers over a multitude of sins. He transforms even the most barren life into a glorious wonderland of refreshing beauty.

He is not just cold and lifeless, though, for his eyes are like blazing fire. He is able to pierce through even the toughest exteriors of our souls and purge our deepest sins. He knows everything, and his fiery eyes melt our hearts.

His feet are like bronze glowing in a furnace. Bronze is an alloy or combination of tin and copper. Tin is more flexible and common, whereas the copper is more firm and gloriously shiny. The tin represents the flexible mercy of Jesus and the copper his firm judgment and righteousness. The two sides of the Lord are constantly being heated and blended and molded together into one perfect whole.

His voice is like the sound of rushing waters, for he is the Living Water that gives forth life. He holds the seven stars, or ministers of the churches in his hands, because they are his spokesmen. They are going to help him proclaim the double-edged sword, the Word of God, which comes from his mouth, and his face shines with the glory of the sun.

Jesus is not just the lowly carpenter that used to walk, eat, and catch fish with his disciples. He is God, and this is the last picture he wants in our "family album".

God Sees You Naked

"You say, 'I am rich. I have acquired wealth and do not need a thing.' But you do not realize that you are wretched, pitiful, poor, blind and naked." Rev. 3:17

Why do you do what you do? What motivates you to go to work each day, to get married, to buy the things that you buy, to have the relationships that you have, to worship God, or to go to church? What keeps you from doing the things that you refrain from? What keeps you from stealing, killing, committing adultery, abandoning your family and friends or lying? When we have abnormal feelings or actions, one of the first things we do is to seek help from either a professional counselor or trusted friend to help us sort out why we are acting or feeling this way. Yet, shouldn't we also be asking ourselves why we do the "normal" things?

When we think about it, many of us are motivated by trying to please others. It might be our parents, our spouse, our friends, our pastor, our neighbors or our co-workers, but we are very much focused on what would impress those we care about. There are many things, in fact, that we wouldn't think of doing ourselves if it wasn't for trying to make a good impression on others. We walk on egg shells much of the time, trying not to offend anyone by what we say or do, because we want them to like us or accept us or respect us. We go home at night, our castle, where we can let it all hang out, and just be ourselves, where we think that it doesn't matter if we are self-indulgent slobs because we have already given all that we can at the office.

Probably our greatest motivation, though, whether we admit it or not, is trying to impress God. This is true of non-Christians, as well as Christians. Non-Christians, who have an in-bred God-consciousness, try to impress God in the same way that they try to impress people—either by how good they are, how successful they are, or how "cool" they are. Christians tend to emphasize just the first two. Yet, what happens in both cases is that people try to get to the place where they don't need God—where they are good enough or successful enough without his help.

We are like children trying to learn how to ride a bike, with our parent holding on to the back, and our crying out, 'You can let go now. I can do it by myself'. Unfortunately, God is not impressed. For, no matter how prosperous we are, and no matter how much we have been able to impress other people by our fancy clothes, cars, houses, and accomplishments, God always sees us naked. He sees our bare-bones hearts and nude souls. Everything external is just clutter to God. From our perspective we may be "rich", but from his perspective we are "wretched, pitiful, poor, blind and naked". We may be able to fool some of the people all of the time, but God is never deceived. He knows every wart and wrinkle of our thoughts and lives, and he isn't impressed by the religious girdles and support-hose that we are able to fool others with. He knows the bare facts.

Created in the Image of God

"Then God said, 'Let us make man in our image, in our likeness, and let them rule...over all the earth." Gen. 1:26

What does it mean to be created in the image of God? First of all, it is important to note that it says, "Let us make", and "in our image". There seems to be a plurality here. Yet, we know from other passages in scripture that only God created all things, and that there is only one God (Col. 1:16). The only explanation that I believe is supported from scripture is that each person in the Trinity played a role in the creation (Deut. 32:6; Heb. 1:2; Job 33:4).

To be created in the image of God, then, is to be created in the image of the Trinity. Man, himself, is a trinity, in that, his inner self is divided into three essential components. These are illustrated by Jesus when he tells us that the greatest commandment is to "Love the Lord your God with all your heart and with all your soul and with all your mind" (Matt. 22:37). No other created being has the ability to love God with these three things in the way that man can. It is these three things, in fact, that make us unique.

Even angels, with all of their intelligence, power and ability to feel admiration and fear, are not able to feel love. No where in the Bible does it say that angels love God or man or each other. They do not know love because they have never experienced first hand mercy, grace or forgiveness, which are essential elements of love. Animals, also, are limited. They have nurturing instincts and feelings of loyalty and fear, but love is beyond their capabilities.

Only man has the heart (the complex depth and range of emotions that are necessary for love), the soul (the spiritual threshold that makes it possible to be connected and bonded together with God and other people in a spiritual dimension), and the mind (the ability to make rational decisions, choices, and commitments that are necessary for true friendship, love, and oneness).

In other words, being created in God's image is being given the ability to love Him and others. This is why Satan spends so much of his time trying to disrupt and destroy the three main elements necessary for love. He tries to distort and confuse our thoughts, entangle and wrench our emotions, and block any spiritual access to God and others through his own spiritual interference or jamming our spiritual receivers. His one main goal is to undo or mangle the image or portrait of God in our lives so badly, that we will not be able to love or choose God.

Satan doesn't want our love. He just wants our obedience. He knows that the only way that he can get that is if our hearts, minds and souls are filled with fear and anger instead of love, for fear and anger are the only emotions that he can feel, and he wants us to be recreated into his image, instead of God's.

Mediators of Mercy

"Please forgive their sin—but if not, then blot me out of the book you have written."
Ex. 32:32

Have you ever made something with your children, where you let them do as much as possible by themselves, but then you came behind to touch up or finish what needed to be done? It is the parent's natural desire to want the best for their children. Sometimes that means giving them support and encouragement when they need your strength or help. Yet, it also means protecting them from the negative experiences that you feel might hurt them or even destroy them. So, you stand in the gap, you might say, to be a bridge over troubled waters, to help them through the tough times, or to pick up the broken pieces when all goes wrong. You would do anything to protect them from the bad guys of the world, even if it means sticking your own neck out, or becoming vulnerable so that they can stay safe.

Yet, it isn't just the bad guys that we need to protect our children from. We also need to protect them from God. Wait a minute! Before you throw this book in the fire as kindling or use it to line your bird cage, hear me out. The Bible makes it very clear that there is only one mediator between God and man, Christ Jesus, our Lord. There is no question about the validity of this truth, as far as salvation is concerned. Jesus is the "way, the truth, and the life. No man comes to the father but by" him (John 14:6). There is another kind of mediator, though, that the Bible encourages us to be—mediators of mercy. For example, Job's children were adults, and they would often have parties. Job would go to their homes the next day after a party and purify them by offering sacrifices for them, just in case, in their drunkenness, they might have cursed God (Job 1:5). He knew that God probably had every reason to be angry at his children, and that they probably deserved to be punished, but he stood in the gap for them to protect them from God's wrath. Instead of judging them, he did everything he could to save them—to be a mediator of mercy.

We can understand this kind of unconditional love from a parent's perspective, for a loving parent would even be willing to die for their children. Moses, though, had this same kind of love for the children of Israel. They had just offered sacrifices to an idol, and God was ready to destroy them all, but Moses stood in the gap for them, even though they were a stiff-necked, rebellious people, who didn't respect or love him. He pleaded with God for mercy, even if it meant losing his own salvation on their behalf.

Are we willing to protect even our enemies from God's wrath through intercessory prayer? That is the kind of mediator that God wants us to be—willing to accept the wrath of God that others might deserve, so that they might be saved. After all, isn't that what Jesus did?

Dews and Don'ts

"Let my teaching fall like rain, and my words descend like dew." Deut. 32:2

When we think of the Old Testament writers, we usually associate Moses with the law and David with the Psalms. Moses is the historian and David the poet. Yet, near the end of Moses' life, the patriarch wrote a beautiful song, and he stood before the Israelites and sang his heart out. We don't know what kind of voice Moses had, but listen to God's heart strings as they are played upon the lyrics of this psalm of the desert. "Listen, O heavens, and I will speak; hear, O earth, the words of my mouth. Let my teaching fall like rain and my words descend like dew, like showers on new grass, like abundant rain on tender plants. I will proclaim the name of the Lord. Oh, praise the greatness of our God! He is the Rock, his works are perfect, and all his ways are just" (Deut. 32:1-4). Even David couldn't have said it better.

Yet, the second stanza of this psalm isn't quite as beautiful. Moses rebukes the corruption and shame of the Israelites. He says they are a "warped and crooked generation" (32:5). He asks, "Is this the way you repay the Lord, O foolish and unwise people? Is He not your Father, your Creator?" (32:6).

What just happened here? Moses started out wanting to refresh the hearts of the people of Israel, with his own heart filled with poetic praise, but all of a sudden his gentle rain and peaceful dew turned into a thunderous uproar of reproach and disgust. He wanted to give them the dews of heaven, but ended up giving them the don'ts of earth. What happened is that Moses came to understand the Israelites from God's perspective. God, too, came to His chosen people with open arms and tender thoughts. He shielded them and cared for them, "like an eagle that stirs up its nest and hovers over its young, that spreads its wings to catch them and carries them on its pinions" (32:11). He wanted the best for his people. He nourished them "with honey from the rock, and with oil from the flinty crag" (32:13). Yet, they "abandoned the God" who made them and "rejected the Rock", their Savior. "They made him jealous with their foreign gods", and "sacrificed to demons" (32:15-17). He wanted the best for them, but they chose the worst.

Instead of refreshing rain and dew, then, God was stirred to send forth his flaming anger. The Bible says that "a fire has been kindled by my wrath, one that burns to the realm of death below…and sets afire the foundations of the mountains" (32:22). God's rain of love and grace has been turned into a volcano of rage. Jesus later reaffirms this same sentiment when he says, "How often I have longed to gather together your children, as a hen gathers her chicks under her wings, but you were not willing" (Matt. 23:37).

God comes to us, as well, with open arms, ready and willing to comfort and care for our every need, longing to draw us closer to himself, yet we often choose the excitement of the storm over the peace of a calm, Spring rain.

Ready for the Amazing

"Consecrate yourselves, for tomorrow the Lord will do amazing things among you." Joshua 3:5

In the Boy Scouts, they have a motto which says, "Always Be Prepared". This is a good principle to live by, whether it applies to family, work, adventure, emergencies, or ministry. Yet, how do we prepare for the tragedies that happen to so many of us—the death of a child, rape, war, or getting fired? Many times we are left feeling completely devastated and on empty, without any reserves, energy or wisdom to deal with the pain that we must endure. God promises us, though, that in these times of weakness, his grace and strength are sufficient (2 Cor. 12:9), if we trust in Him, instead of trying to work through the problems ourselves. We can't always control the circumstances of our lives, but we can control how we respond. We may not be expecting tragedy, but we can be prepared for it, in one sense, by having our hearts in a right relationship with the Lord, yielded to His will, no matter what happens.

Tragedies, though, are not things that most of us have to deal with on a regular basis. They are the exception. We have problems many, tragedies few. The same thing is true on the other end of the spectrum. We have many blessings, but few miracles. Just as the tragedies catch us off guard, the miracles seem to sneak up on us, as well. We believe in the power of God, and that he loves us, but when he steps into our lives in a moment of crisis, he raises the bar of our expectations and spiritual awareness. When that happens, all we can say is, "Wow!" "Praise God!" "Thank you, Jesus!" "I am unworthy!" The truly miraculous just blows us out of the water, just as the truly tragic knocks us off our feet. In our humanness, we just aren't expecting or prepared for the extremes. They knock us off balance, and we are left in the moral dilemma of "How then should we live?" "If life is this bad, or God is this good, what difference should it make in my life?" "What should my priorities be?"

We think that we know the answers to these questions before the tragedies or miracles happen, but the traumatic tends to open our eyes to new levels of awareness never approached before. We feel that we have been knocked down to the ground, and we have to learn how to walk all over again. What we need to do each day is to consecrate ourselves, to present ourselves a living sacrifice, where our will and desires aren't important (Rom. 12:1-2). If we can come into each day completely yielded to God's will, then we should expect both the tragedies and the miracles as part of the norm. We should be ready for both the spiritual warfare and the spiritual victories. When we view ourselves as soldiers in God's army, we should expect some wounds. We should also expect the amazing. Miracles and mayhem are two sides of the same coin. They are both part of learning to trust in God.

August 30

Liable to Destruction

"They have been made liable to destruction. I will not be with you anymore unless you destroy whatever among you is devoted to destruction." Joshua 7:12

The Israelites had just crossed the Jordan River on dry ground, had completely routed Jericho, and had been promised by God that they would be able to conquer all of their enemies as they claimed their inheritance in the Promised Land. They had every expectation of success. When they sent an army to the next city, though, they were easily defeated. Joshua and the priests fell on their faces and cried out to God, "Why did you ever bring us over the Jordan if you were going to just let the Amorites destroy us?" In other words, "What went wrong? We did everything you told us to do, and we still lost? That's not supposed to happen."

What Joshua didn't realize was that not everyone had obeyed God's commands. One man had taken some treasures from Jericho for himself instead of giving them to the Lord. The result was defeat for the whole army because God could not bless them as long as there was sin among them. This seems kind of harsh, since it was only one man, and the whole group had to pay the consequences, yet we need to understand what was really going on here. This isn't just about a man deciding to steal a few trinkets for himself. This is spiritual warfare in major proportions. The Promised Land was Satan's territory. The people in this land were so pagan that they were offering their children as sacrifices to the Devil, turning their sons and daughters into temple prostitutes to their gods, and practicing all kinds of sorcery and divination, demonstrating complete access to Satanic powers. God was not just sending the Israelites into this land so they could have an inheritance. He was using them to purge this land of demonic evil and destruction. They were going to be part of a holy war, God's army versus the Devil's, and it was extremely important that every member of God's army be selflessly consecrated to being willing to die for the cause, if necessary. Selfish interests could play no part. They needed to move through the land as a united front, as if one soldier in complete armor, united in minds and hearts to serve the Lord. When one man was tempted to use the opportunity for his own personal gain, it was like taking off part of that united armor, and leaving the whole soldier vulnerable to the attack of the Devil.

The same thing happens today when one person within a church or Christian organization poisons and robs the effectiveness of the entire group because of their selfish interests or ego trip that they are on. The same thing happens on an individual basis when we think that we are okay because we only have one sin that we have allowed into our lives. The truth is, when the armor is down, the Devil's darts can enter, and all it takes is one to destroy and defeat everything else the Lord wanted to do for us and through us.

The Other Law of Moses

"Be very careful to keep the commandment and the law that Moses the servant of the Lord gave you: to love the Lord your God, to walk in all his ways, to obey his commands, to hold fast to him and to serve him with all your heart and all your soul." Joshua 22:5

When we think of the law of Moses, we think of the Pentateuch, or all the laws, regulations, and rituals that were given to Moses by the Lord. There are a lot of Christians today who view this law as only an historical curiosity that has no relevance to them in our modern context. They view the Israelites as a bunch of Pharisees who were so wrapped up in legalism or the letter of the law that they were nothing more than a group of puppets being controlled by God, the Grand Puppeteer, through meaningless motions done only out of fear.

Yet, when Joshua was getting ready to send a group of Israelites back over the Jordan, because they were going to get their inheritance outside of the original Promised Land, and they had already helped the other tribes be victorious, he wanted to make it very clear that obeying the law was not just a matter of following a bunch of regulations. It never had been. Joshua summarized what the law meant to Moses and the rest of the Jews.

First, he tells them "to love the Lord your God". The word "fear" is not even mentioned as a motivation for obedience. Following the law was a matter of relationships, not just rules. If you love the Lord with your whole heart, mind, and soul, you aren't going to want to do anything that would hurt your relationship with him. You are going to want to "walk in all his ways" because you will not be able to think of anything that you would rather do than to walk in his steps, or to be like him. Obeying his commands, then, is nothing more than holding "fast to him", so that your actions are in unison with his will. Your main goal or priority is to "serve him with all your heart and all your soul", so anything that he asks of you is never meaningless motion, but seeking to remain in tune with the Master, or seeking to please your beloved bridegroom's every desire. There is no sense of being controlled by a distant, unattached force, or of being an unfeeling, wooden Pinocchio.

The Pharisees were just one faction of the Jews during the time of Christ, who lost their relationship with God, so the rules were the only thing they had left to hold on to. The Israelites at the time of Moses and Joshua, though, understood that it was never just about the rules. When Joshua sent the tribes away, he didn't send them with complete copies of the Pentateuch. He sent them with the feeling that if they kept their hearts and minds focused on loving and holding fast to God, that they could maintain a right relationship with him, regardless of what side of the Jordan they were on. God would always be near.

September 1

Naomi and Mara

"Don't call me Naomi", she told them. "Call me Mara, because the Almighty has made my life very bitter." Ruth 1:20

Everyone is familiar with the story of Naomi and Ruth, but how many know the story of Naomi and Mara? Naomi was a typical woman from Bethlehem, who got married, had two sons, and did her best to be a good wife and mother. She probably had the same dream of most women of her time, that of settling down near her family and friends, and having a good life. Yet, when the famine hit, everything started falling apart. She was forced to leave her home town and everything that was familiar, and travel to a foreign land, just to survive. Then to make matters worse, soon as she got to the foreign country, her husband died, leaving her alone with her two sons.

Fortunately for her, her sons were old enough to take care of her, and to make the best of a bad situation. They married two local women, and survived the best they could for ten years. Yet, there were no grandchildren for Naomi to love and care for. Then, both of her sons died, and her state of mourning deepened. She was too old to get remarried, and she had no means of supporting herself or her daughters-in-law. She was destitute, lonely, and discouraged.

She knew that her only hope was to travel back to her homeland, and to fall upon the mercy of her relatives. Completely broken, she tells her daughters-in-law to go back to their own families, and to leave her alone in her misery. She tells them to call her "Mara", instead of Naomi, "because the Almighty has made my life very bitter." The word "Mara" means "bitter", and "Naomi" means "pleasant delight". Her heart has become burdened down with a heaviness so deep that she feels that she has nothing left to give to anyone. She is on empty emotionally and spiritually, and in her mind, God is to blame. She tries to send her daughters-in-law away, not out of kindness to them, but because she just wants to be left alone in her misery. The Lord has taken her family away, so she might as well throw away the rest. She is drowning in self-pity and bitterness, and has allowed herself to be transformed from Naomi into Mara because in her mind, God has let her down. She feels like she has been cursed by God, and she doesn't want that curse to pass on to her daughters-in-law.

She is surprised, then, when Ruth says that she not only wants to go with Naomi, but wants to follow her God as well. She must have been puzzled, "Why on earth would you want to follow a God who has done so much harm to our family?" Yet, she took Ruth along with her, back to Bethlehem, and you know the rest of the story. God blessed Ruth and Naomi, and Naomi's bitterness was turned to joy. God had never abandoned or cursed Naomi. He only closed a door, so he could open an even better window.

Don't let the past keep you from enjoying tomorrow. Start with today.

The Bodyguard

"David put him in charge of his bodyguards." I Chron. 11:25

King David was a mighty warrior. His exploits, from killing Goliath to killing lions with his bare hands, are well known. Yet, in spite of his apparent invincibility, he still needed bodyguards. He had lots of enemies, and he knew that he needed lots of help. We can always tell the quality of a leader by the quality of those who are closest to him—those that he trusts the most.

On a spiritual plane, David trusted Nathan, the prophet, the most. David knew that Nathan always spoke from God's perspective, and he listened, even if it meant that Nathan had to rebuke him for his sins. On a physical level, though, he trusted a group of thirty warriors to lead his army, for he knew that they were blessed by God and knew no fear.

On a more personal level, he had a group of bodyguards who were around him constantly. You might say that they knew him better than any of his wives or concubines, for David only saw the women when he wanted them. The bodyguards were always there. They heard his every conversation, knew his every decision, watched his every mistake, were aware of his every vulnerability, and they were as loyal as a best friend.

David had to be very careful about who he chose as his bodyguards. David was particularly careful about choosing someone to be in charge of his bodyguards, for he knew that person would have to set the standard of excellence. He chose a man named Benaiah. He was a valiant warrior who was famous for his exploits. He had jumped down into a pit on a snowy day to kill a lion. He had struck down an Egyptian who was seven and a half feet tall by grabbing a huge spear out of his hand, and stabbing him with his own weapon. In fact, "he was held in greater honor than any of the thirty" fighting men that David chose to lead his army (I Chron. 11:25). His honor was to be the chief of David's bodyguards, the inner circle of David's personal protection. Yet, who has ever even heard of Benaiah? He was a quiet presence, always there, always loyal, always trustworthy, always capable—in fact, so quietly capable as to be hardly noticed at all. He wasn't there to bring attention to himself, for selfish ambition, or to prove how great he was. Amasai, the chief of the thirty warriors, put it this way: "We are yours, O David!...Success to you, and success to those who help you, for your God will help you" (12:18).

Benaiah, and all of David's best men, were willing to follow David because they believed that he was God's man. It isn't hard to be a follower, even if you are a born leader yourself, if you believe that the person you are following is following the Lord. There is a sense of connectedness. As Christians, we all have power, but some are meant to be generators, and others just extension cords.

Purge the Pulpits

"You must purge the evil from among you." Deut. 13:5

So often we hear about churches that just aren't very loving. They are cold cathedrals, and the deacons need defrosters just to warm up enough to smile. Yet, the opposite is also true. Some churches are too loving. How can that be true? Doesn't the Bible say that they shall know we are Christians by our love?

Part of the problem is that Christians confuse love with tolerance. For example, how are we supposed to respond when someone within our church falls into sin? Well, many would say that the loving thing to do is to just look the other way. After all, who am I to judge? Yet, the Bible makes it very clear that we are to rebuke those brothers and sisters in the faith who have fallen by the wayside (2 Tim. 4:2). Even Christ tells us to rebuke those who are living in sin (Luke 17:3). This command from the Lord, though, is often ignored, for we feel uncomfortable about confronting people. We tend to practice the Golden Rule here. We wouldn't want someone confronting us, so we don't confront them.

It is true that confrontation must be done in the right spirit, and that we must make sure that our hearts are right first. Yet, it cannot just be neglected. If it is, all kinds of problems occur. If we just let sin happen, without comment, it will continue, and become even worse. We know as parents that we just can't ignore the bad behavior of our children. Why, then, just ignore the bad behavior of our Christian family? This is particularly important if the person who is sinning is in a position of authority within our churches. The pastor is no exception. We cannot afford to just look the other way if the pastor is having an affair, is robbing the church offering, or is drinking too much of the sacramental wine to even walk straight down the aisle.

Most churches would take some kind of action against a pastor who would do such things. Yet, what about the pastor who is not preaching the Word, or who is preaching false doctrine? This is sometimes a more difficult thing to pin down because we assume that the pastor is the expert. Who are we to question his authority? Pastors, though, are not infallible, and they must be held accountable for what they are preaching. Even in the time of Moses, God warned the people, if you have a prophet who is preaching things contrary to God's commands, or is even leading you astray to follow after other gods, "you must purge the evil from among you." According to the law, that meant putting them to death (Deut. 13:6-9).

We can't do that in our culture, but it is important that we recognize the Lord's emphasis on the subject. If we don't purge our pulpits, we can't blame God for the putridness in our pews. If we can't purge the poison, at least we can refuse to drink it. We may not be able to spit it out, but we don't have to swallow it.

A Blessing or a Curse?

"The ark of God remained with the family of Obed-Edom in his house for three months, and the Lord blessed his household and everything he had."
I Chron. 13:14

The ark of God was a wonderful thing. It contained the ten-commandments that were written on stone tablets with the finger of God. It was usually in the Holy of Holies, for only the high priest normally had access to it. Yet, on certain occasions, such as warfare, the Israelites would take the ark of God and parade it in front of their army, to scare the enemy and to give courage to their own men. It symbolized that God was on their side, and that they were going to win. When God told them to use the ark in this manner, it provided the power and motivation that they needed.

However, when they were presumptuous and just took it anyway, even when God did not direct them, they lost badly, and the ark was stolen by the enemy (I Sam. 4:5-12). The Philistines knew that the ark held some kind of spiritual power, so they put it in the temple of their god, Dagon. The next morning, the idol was found knocked over. They set it back up, but the next morning they found it not only knocked over, but broken. Not only this, but everyone in that town was breaking out with tumors. So, they removed the ark to another town. The same thing happened to these people. All of the Philistines were now afraid of the ark, and they decided to return it to Israel just to get rid of this curse.

The Israelites, of course, were excited about getting the ark back, but seventy of them were killed by the Lord just for trying to look inside the ark out of curiosity. Even the Israelites became afraid of this holy object, so they left it in the home of this one Levite, just to get it out of the way. The Levite, I'm sure, was probably also afraid of this spiritual icon, but he treated it with honor and respect, and God blessed his whole household.

Depending on who had it, then, and their relationship with the God that it represented, the ark was either a curse or a blessing. When the Israelites took it into battle and lost it, they thought of it in the same terms as an idol, for they were idolaters at the time, and they just wanted some extra magical power to achieve their goals. The Philistines, also, put it next to their idol, thinking that it would give Dagon some extra strength.

God showed them all that he is not just another idol or magical power that they can just tap into whenever they want. He is the holy God, and he must be treated with respect, worship and humility. God is not a toy meant for our entertainment or our empowerment. If we treat God with respect and submission to his will, he will bless us. If we don't, our religious foolishness will be our curse.

September 5

Undivided Integrity

"I know, my God, that you test the heart and are pleased with integrity."
I Chron. 29:17

Success is something that everyone wants, but few achieve. Sometimes the problem is that one's goals are unrealistic, or expectations are too great. Sometimes one's ideals are unattainable because there are too many obstacles in the way, or one's personal weaknesses are constantly undermining their strengths. Sometimes people become so frustrated or impatient about not reaching their goals, that they try to bend the rules, cheat, lie, or put others down in order to lift themselves up. This happens in churches, families, and friendships, as well as the business world.

The Bible says, though, that God tests our hearts, and his standard for success is not outward prosperity or achievement, but integrity within. This is why Jesus says, "What good is it for a man to gain the whole world, yet lose his own soul?" (Luke 9:25). The key to success according to Christ is, "If anyone would come after me, he must deny himself and take up his cross daily and follow me" (Luke 9:23). The meaning of the word "success", in fact, means "to follow" someone who has reached his goals before you. From a Christian perspective, the only one who has done that completely is Jesus. Being successful as a Christian, then, means to be Christ -like.

What God wants, though, is not just for us to follow him when we feel like it, or when it coincides with our worldly goals. He wants us to be men and women of integrity. The word "integrity" means "whole, complete, pure, undefiled, undivided and indivisible." This is why the first and greatest commandment is to love the Lord your God with your whole heart, mind, and soul. Our love for him must be a love of integrity—holy and whole-hearted. It must be pure, genuine, and honest, and everything in our lives must be openly true and in the light, as he is in the light (I John 1:7), for to be successful, we must follow him.

Yet, having integrity is not just a matter of quantity, or the amount of ourselves that we need to give to him or to follow him. It is also a matter of what it does within us. When we walk with integrity, it makes us complete. The word "complete" within scripture means "mature". It means that there is a sense of stability that doesn't feel like it needs to waver with every wind of what is popular or accepted by others. The moral, mental, and emotional storms within us have been calmed by the Lord, and we feel that we are standing on a firm foundation, a rock that cannot be moved, the Lord himself. A person of integrity is solid as a rock in their beliefs, their standards, and principles that they live by, for their God is a God of absolutes, who does not waver.

If only there were more Christians today who had this kind of backbone. Then, maybe, there wouldn't be so many worms or snakes in our pews.

Revival of a Nation

"If my people, who are called by my name, will humble themselves and pray and seek my face and turn from their wicked ways, then will I hear from heaven and will forgive their sin and will heal their land." 2 Chron. 7:14

This verse is a tremendous affirmation of God's faithfulness and mercy to his people. Yet, it is usually taken out of context and misunderstood because people want it to say more than it does. Solomon and the Israelites had just completed the building of both the temple and Solomon's palaces. It was time for a formal dedication. Thousands of bulls and sheep were sacrificed in God's honor. Solomon prays a glorious dedication, promising the complete devotion of the people of Israel to their God.

Then God responds and accepts this new temple as the official place where sacrifices are to be given. Yet, God qualifies his acceptance. He makes it very clear that if they rebel against him, he will punish them severely, and that the only way for them to regain his blessing is if they humble themselves, turn from their sins, and seek him. Then, and only then, will he forgive them, and heal the Promised Land from any plagues that he has sent their way as punishment for their sins. He will heal their land because it is their inheritance, and it has been set apart as the center for his worship, as well as his reign when he returns to the earth as King of Kings.

God does not make this covenant or promise to the church, to America, or any other nation or group of people. That doesn't mean that these same principles of revival--humility, prayer, seeking God, and repentance—are not valid for everyone. They are. Individuals, churches, and communities can experience great revival from time to time. Yet, that doesn't mean that even if all of the Christians in America were to be revived at the same time that God would heal our entire country of all its wickedness or the consequences of sin. Like it or not, the majority of Americans are not Christians. They are lost in the delusions of a materialistic, hedonistic pagan world view, and the problems in our society are there with God's permission as payment for their spiritual rebellion. God is not going to heal this land of these problems for the sake of a minority of true, dedicated believers. It would not be the loving, merciful thing to do, because it would give the people the impression, then, that they don't really need God, and that everything is okay. God's goal is their repentance, not their comfort or happiness.

The only way that the national promise worked in Israel was if everyone turned back to God, not just a few devoted souls. They could turn back to God in unison because they all belonged to God, and they had all once followed him. That same circumstance does not exist in our nation or any nation apart from Israel. We can still be revived, but not by claiming verses that don't apply to us. People cannot be revived that were never alive to begin with.

A Special Honor

"He was buried with the kings in the City of David because of the good he had done in Israel for God and his temple." 2 Chron. 24:16

Israel had fallen into idolatry, and even the sacred objects in the temple were stolen and used in pagan rituals. The king of Judah, Jehoram, had killed all of his brothers so that he could become king. He was so wicked, in fact, that when he died, everyone was glad, and he was not buried with the other kings. Yet, evil continued to reign, and Baal worship was dominant.

Finally, a Levite priest named Jehoiada decided to take a stand. He made a covenant with the commanders of the armies, the heads of the Israelite families, and the other Levites, and he led a revolt against the pagan priestess and her followers. He killed the followers of Baal, and established the rightful heir to the throne as the new king. This new king was only seven, but he had been hidden in the temple, and raised by the priests. His heart was right with the Lord, and Jehoiada put aside any selfish ambition that he might have had to support this new king and the God of Israel. He then collected a temple tax which had been established by King David in order to restore the temple to its original glory. The people of Israel were glad to pay this tax because they caught Jehoiada's enthusiasm and zeal for the Lord, and they were excited again about the things of the Lord.

Revival had occurred, and it started with the faith and obedience of one man. In recognition of his contribution to Israel's God and the temple, this simple priest was honored by being buried with the kings in the City of David. What a privilege this must have been. It's interesting that one of the ways that we show honor to someone is by the way that we bury them. For the homeless, they only have pauper's graves. For those who die in battle, there are special tombs, parades, and twenty-one gun salutes. For kings, there is special honor and glory. For someone to be able to be buried with the kings, in spite of their not being a king, is even a greater honor, for it is not based on one's position, but the respect that one has earned through their bravery or integrity. It is earned, not just inherited.

In one sense, we as Christians, are in the same situation as Jehoiada. We, too, look around us and see the paganism that is prevailing, and we too must decide to follow the rightful king (Jesus). We, too, must have faith and be obedient, humbly laying aside our own ambitions or selfish interests, to follow the king. We must seek first the kingdom of God and his righteousness, and encourage others to do the same. We, too, are buried with the king, as we are crucified with Christ, buried in baptism of the Spirit, and risen with the King of Kings, in honor, to rule and reign with him for eternity. It is only those who have been buried with the king that can be risen with the king, not because we are kings also, but because we are his priests dedicated to serving Him.

To Hell and Back Again

"In his distress he sought the favor of the Lord his God and humbled himself greatly before the God of his fathers. And when he prayed to him, the Lord was moved by his entreaty and listened to his plea." 2 Chron. 33:12

How far can a person travel into hell before it's too late to turn around toward heaven? I know that this sounds like a strange question, for we think of hell as a location, and that once you are there, there is no turning back. Yet, in another sense, hell is experienced each day on this earth by people who are spiritually separated from God. In fact, the more that a person rebels against God, the deeper and darker is his hell. Maybe you have experienced this separation and lonely darkness, and you know the depth of despair and evil that imprisons the soul into this downward spiral. Maybe you have felt that you have gone too far into the dark side to return—that God wouldn't want you now. It's too late.

Let me tell you a story of a king in ancient Israel. His name was Manasseh. He did more evil during his reign than any of the other kings of Israel, and was actually more evil than even the pagan kings from all the other countries. He was the worst of the worst (2 Chron. 33:9). He worshipped idols, he built altars to the starry hosts in the temple of God, he sacrificed his sons to Molech, he practiced sorcery, divination, and witchcraft, and he consulted mediums and spiritists. He not only practiced these things himself, but he led all of Judah and Jerusalem astray as well. The Lord tried to speak to him many times, yet he refused to listen. He was determined to be God's enemy, and to be his own god. He was completely sold out to the Devil, and there was no turning back.

So, the Lord allowed the Assyrian army to conquer Judah, and to capture the king. They put a hook in his nose, and led him away bound in shackles to Babylon. On his way, while being dragged along like a beast of burden, he cried out to the Lord, begging for forgiveness, and humbly yielding his will to God. In spite of all that Manasseh had done in the past, with all of its blasphemy and Satanic worship, God felt compassion on the king, and God's mercy reached out to him. God forgave him and healed his spirit from its former bondage, and allowed the king to return to Israel. Manasseh immediately showed his gratitude by destroying all the idols and evil temples in the land, purifying the temple of God, and leading the people back into a way of holiness and worship according to the Law of Moses. There was a complete about-face, a transformation that only God could have performed.

It is so easy for us to write off the rebellious in our society, or ourselves, as if there is no hope for those who have gone too far. Yet, God has shown time and time again, through Manasseh, Paul, the thief on the cross, and us, that it is never too late to turn our lives over to God. He specializes in the impossible, including impossible people. Never give up hope.

When Friends are Foes

"I am angry with you and your two friends, because you have not spoken of me what is right." Job 42:7

Everyone is familiar with the suffering of Job, where Satan was given permission to take away his family, his possessions and his health in order to test his faith and character. Amazingly, Job was able to stand firm in his righteous reliance on God, saying in the midst of his pain, "Though he slay me, yet will I trust him" (Job 13:15). Yet, some of Job's greatest trials were not in the loss of physical blessings at all. When Satan asked permission to attack Job in the physical realm, he knew that this would create a chain reaction into the psychological, social, and spiritual realms, as well. God didn't give Satan permission to test Job in these other areas. They just got pulled into the turmoil on the coattails of the original onslaughts.

For example, Satan knows that we might be able to endure physical hardships, even to the point of facing death with courage and patience. Yet, he also knows that even when we are strong in one area, we may be weak and completely helpless in another. So he plays dominoes with our lives, stacking them all in a row, then watching how one knocked down can cause the entire row to tumble.

Satan knew that Job was a righteous man, and that he probably would be able to endure the loss of his prosperity with mature faith. The unknown factor, his ace up his sleeve, was Satan's plan to attack Job after the fact, using those friends and family who were still alive. First, he attacked Job through his wife, who told Job to give up and curse God (Job 2:9). Believe it or not, Satan can often use those closest to us to defeat us, even more than the wicked people on the outside. The people that we love can often hurt us, discourage us, distract us, tempt us, or destroy us just by the things that they say, and how they respond to the hardships that we are going through. The hardship is just the rock in the sling. Our loved ones are those who often cast the stone into our minds and souls to knock out any courage or faith that we still have left.

Job's friends were the same way. They used his trials to tear down his faith and self-esteem, as well as making him feel that he was all alone in his suffering. One of the hardest blows, though, was from those whom he had helped in the past. He had been kind to the poor and oppressed of his society, using his wealth and compassion to help them out of their own trials. Now they were turning their backs on him and mocking him.

Sometimes Satan's attacks are upfront and in your face, but many times these are only distractions meant to conceal the real attacks, which are the stabs in the back by those we trust. Fortunately, Job was not only righteous, but circumspect, being able to see the attack from all sides, and responding with strength. We not only need the patience of Job. We need his wisdom, as well.

Hidden Faults

"Forgive my hidden faults." Psa. 19:12

Have you ever gone through a "Fun House" at a carnival, where there is a maze of mirrors, and you have to find your way out? It can be lots of fun, or it can be pretty scary if you are claustrophobic and can't find the way to escape. It can also be very revealing if you are a little overweight, and you have never seen how you look from so many directions. In fact, you may be so embarrassed that you decide to never again enter this "house of horrors".

The same thing happens spiritually speaking. We all know what our main sins are—the more obvious ones, but we are not always aware of our hidden faults—the ones that others see in us, but that we are blind to. When it comes right down to it, even if someone tells us about these faults, we become defensive, and we either deny that we have such problems, or we "refuse to go there". In other words, we want our hidden faults to stay that way, and refuse to even talk about them. The hidden faults are the ones that are too difficult for our egos to admit that we have, so we keep them hidden in our sub-conscious level, and resent anyone trying to bring them up to the surface. That's why many people are never helped by going to see a psychologist, for they don't really want to know the truth. They just want someone to listen, to sympathize, and to say they are okay.

Yet, the Bible takes this self-delusion one step further. It says that we commit sins that we are not even aware of or "unintentional sins" (Lev. 4:27-28). Yes, it is possible to commit a sin by accident, without you or anyone else being aware of it. King David makes the distinction in the Psalms between these unintentional sins and sins of willful rebellion when he prays, "Who can discern his errors? Forgive my hidden faults. Keep your servant also from willful sins; may they not rule over me" (Psa. 19:12-13). The willful sins are apparent, for we have made conscious choices to sin against God. The hidden faults are not so conspicuous. They may be sins of the mind or heart, such as pride, lust, greed, envy, anger, or lack of faith, and we may not even know or understand the extent that they have blinded us or enslaved us.

What we need is a spiritual "Fun House" or "Mirror Maze" which will show us our souls from every perspective, so we can know the truth about ourselves, from God's perspective, not just our own. This is why we have the light of the Word and the internal probing of the Holy Spirit, to show us our unflattering true selves. Yet, even if we haven't matured to the point that we can handle the whole truth yet, we need to understand that we do have hidden faults that God wants to reveal to us. We need to ask God to expose our sins to us, so that we can confess them, and make ourselves right with him (Psa. 139:23-24). We also, though, need to ask forgiveness for the ones we don't know about yet, for our hidden faults are still sins even when hidden in the shadows.

Waiting on the Lord

"Wait for the Lord; be strong and take heart and wait for the Lord." Psa. 27:14

Waiting is one of the hardest things to do, especially when we are really excited about what we are waiting for, such as Christmas, a wedding, or a birth. It is also hard to wait when we are dreading something bad or difficult, such as an operation, an exam, or getting laid off. One of the best ways to cope with this waiting patiently is by using our time to do something constructive or to think good thoughts while we are waiting, so that our mind is not just focused on the negative, or how much longer we have to wait. We need to keep busy doing fun, interesting things, so that all our energy is spent on creating positive, empowering, edifying reinforcements to our faith and peace, instead of wasting our energy on self-destructive thoughts and actions.

So often we think of waiting as just a passive word, like just standing around until someone else takes the initiative to do something. In the Bible, though, waiting is an action verb. It means binding together, or tying together the loose ends. When we are waiting for the Lord, then, we are not just hoping that he comes soon because we are tired of just standing around doing nothing. We are helping him to come back soon by taking care of business here on earth. We are the welcoming party, waiting for the bridegroom to come get his bride, and we are doing everything we can to get ready for the wedding. We are binding together people into a closer unity in the Spirit, realizing that all Christians are part of the bride of Christ, and not just ourselves. We are tying together loose ends, doing everything we can to take care of all the details that might be necessary for his return. We are leading people to the Lord in every tribe and nation, seeking to reach every last soul that will come to know Him before He comes again. We are binding ourselves closer to Him, making sure that there is nothing between us, so that we are truly one, as husband and wife.

All of this binding and bonding helps us to take courage and to be strong, for we are not waiting alone. We give each other strength, faith, and hope, so that we can continue waiting until his perfect timing to call us home. We are waiters and waitresses, waiting on the King of Kings, serving him with everything that his heart desires, for that is our main goal.

Waiting on God is not tedious or boring, for He is life, power, love, truth, and hope. We can expectantly rise and shine every day, excited about serving the master, waiting on him right now, not just in the future somewhere. We can take heart that God will love us and meet our every need as well as we wait on him, for he is not only our Lord, but our betrothed. If he loved us so much to die for us, just imagine how that love will demonstrate itself when we live together with him for eternity. He will wait on us, just as we wait upon him, and all that binding together forever and ever will be well worth waiting for.

Taste the Lord

"Taste and see that the Lord is good." Psa. 34:8

This saying almost sounds cannibalistic. In fact, when Christ told his disciples later that they needed to eat his flesh and drink his blood, many of them refused to follow him anymore (John 6:51-66). In light of the pagan cannibalism and human sacrifice of many kingdoms in the past, it is no wonder that some were disgusted and offended by even the idea of tasting someone.

So, exactly what is David trying to get across here? The word "taste" does not mean to put into one's mouth. It means to thrust into or to throw into, to touch, to perceive, or to experience personally instead of second hand. To taste the Lord, then, is to thrust or throw ourselves into him completely, not just half-heartedly. It is like the trapeze artist who flings herself into the air, doing a double flip, and then expecting her partner to catch her before she falls. There has to be complete abandon and trust. It's also like the mother who fixes a sumptuous feast for her family for Thanksgiving, then calls out, "dive in". God wants us to" dive in" in the same way, totally focused on one thing, consuming, digesting, and internalizing Him. He is not asking us to just take a cautious sip of the Spirit once in a while. He wants us to be "filled with the Spirit" , and so drunk with his love that we never thirst again for anything else (John 4:13).

Once we have tasted the Lord in this way, we can perceive him in new ways because our "spiritual taste buds" have been sensitized to his touch. When he touches our souls in new ways, he heals the callousness that has built up through past abuse or sin. It is similar to a person whose tongue has been so exposed to harsh, spicy hot sauce for such a long period of time that they can't even taste the smooth, silky flavors of fine delicacies, or someone who is a drunk not being able to appreciate the difference between a cheap wine and one that has been aged to perfection. Sin does the same thing to our spirits. When God heals our hearts, we can taste his finest truths, even when they had tasted bland when we tried them before.

So often the truths that we learn come to us through other people. There is nothing wrong with this, for God has given the gift of teaching to certain individuals for this purpose. Yet, we should not rely upon this method of learning alone. God wants us to taste Him and his truth personally, straight from the chef himself. Imagine never eating any food yourself, but only having others describe what they are eating. We might appreciate the beauty of their descriptive language, but something would be lost in the translation if we can never taste it ourselves to verify what they say. God wants us to taste and digest the spiritual food that he offers us, which is not something that is separate from himself, like h'ors derves at a party. He wants to be the main course.

A Broken and Contrite Heart

"The sacrifices of God are a broken spirit; a broken and contrite heart."
Psa. 51:17

David lived during a time when animal sacrifices were required for a variety of reasons. Yet, he sensed at the same time that these acts of worship were only external rituals that some how missed the point, in and of themselves. They were not enough by themselves to accomplish anything. They couldn't cleanse from sin, make atonement, or gain greater access to the Heavenly Father. They were never intended to. They were merely external symbols of what was supposed to be happening internally in the hearts of the believers. Every time that a physical sacrifice was made, the person offering the sacrifice was supposed to be offering himself as a living sacrifice to the Father, completely yielding himself, in humble submission, seeking the will and mercy of Almighty God. If the believer just sacrificed the animal, but did not offer himself self-sacrificially at the same time, it was an abomination unto the Lord, for it was a disrespectful insult to the Father to offer this object of worship, when he knew that the person's heart was still worshipping self. David acknowledges this when he says to the Lord, "You do not delight in sacrifice, or I would bring it; you do not take pleasure in burnt offerings. The sacrifices of God are a broken spirit; a broken and contrite heart" (Psa. 51:16-17).

A broken spirit is one that has been humbled by one's own sin and inadequacy to live a holy life, the recognition that forgiveness can only come through the Lord's mercy and atonement, and the complete submission to the will of the Father. In other words, "I am nothing and can do nothing apart from Him".

Having a contrite heart takes this conviction one step further. The word "contrite" is the superlative of the word "broken". That means that it takes the meaning one notch higher. It is the ultimate or the extreme. Contrite not only means broken, it means crushed or pulverized. It is shattered to the point of being non-recognizable. This means that if I have offered myself as a living sacrifice to God, I am not only dead to self, the self has been transformed into something new.

It is like the caterpillar being transformed into the butterfly. We have yielded to the recreating power of the Master, and He has decided to take the lump of clay that we have offered to Him, and to make something else. What we gave him was badly flawed, so he decided to make a new creation, something special, which looks just like him. He has taken our pulverized dust and added the Living Water to make it more pliable. Then he places it in the fire of affliction and spiritual testing until it is purified and purged of any flaws, making it into a holy and acceptable sacrifice unto him (Gal. 2:20). What God wants is us, not what we have to offer. He will do the rest.

Rest in God Alone

"My soul finds rest in God alone." Psa. 62:1

There is so much turmoil and unrest in our world. There are wars and rumors of wars, terrorist attacks, rising crime rates, unemployment, inflation, political corruption, corporate greed, racial tensions, gender struggles, generational power games, moral debates and religious wrestling. What is the solution? Where does it all end? Unfortunately, in this life, tensions will never end between people, for we are all in our own individual spiritual warfare's, and our personal battles often conflict with those of others.

Yet, in spite of the ongoing struggles between people, we can still find rest in our own souls, even in the midst of turmoil. David tells us, "My soul finds rest in God alone". The word "rest" in our minds signifies sleep or non-activity, yet the Bible presents a very different picture. We never cease from activity in the spiritual dimension, for we are in constant battle with the principalities and powers in high places (Eph. 6:10-19), even when we are physically asleep.

The kind of rest that we have in God is not to stop functioning. The word "rest" here actually means to become silent. Silence before God is an interesting concept. As a husband, father, and grandfather, I know how rare and special silence can be. Don't get me wrong. The noise of loved ones cheerfully enjoying the Holidays together, or chattering happily over a cup of coffee, or playing a game with total abandon in the backyard brings joy to the heart. Noise is synonymous with life and love, and for these we are grateful. Yet, noise also brings bickering, and complaining, and whining, and tension, and with these we often pray for silence.

The word "rest" also implies "stillness", as a calm pool of water that is not agitated by any disturbance. As all the turmoil and noise continues around us, then, we can still find a place of calm rest in God, where our soul is at peace, not agitated by the problems that we face. We aren't busy complaining to God about all of the jerks that we work with or live with, the idiots in political office, the stupid neighbors or so-called friends, or even our inconsiderate family members. We aren't fretting about the bills, our bad health, or our vulnerability to the dangers around us. We aren't frustrated by the incompetence's or weaknesses of others, or caught up in the tension of judging others. All of these issues are very real, but they cease to bring us to the boiling point. We have already turned them over to God, and we trust in his wisdom and ability to handle each one in his own way and his own timing.

In other words, it's all settled. Nothing more needs to be said. It is being one-minded with the Lord, so that communication happens at the level of the heart, and there is no misunderstanding. He is in control, and that is all that matters. End of story. That kind of rest can only be found in God, and that kind of silence is golden.

Like an Olive Tree

"I am like an olive tree flourishing in the house of God." Psa. 52:8

King David was a mighty warrior, who killed Goliath with a sling, killed wild animals with his bare hands, and led armies to conquer enemies. He shed so much blood, in fact, that God would not allow him to build the temple. He was too violent to build a house of prayer. Yet, in spite of his faults, the Bible says that he was a "man after God's own heart" (I Sam. 13:14). He knew his failings, but he was truly repentant, and constantly sought to stay in tune with the Almighty. He was truly human in his sins, but divinely in touch with the glory and grace of God in his spiritual life. So, God was able to use him in a mighty way, not only to conquer the enemies of the Lord, but to write some of the most beautiful, powerful passages in scripture.

When David writes, then, that he is "like an olive tree flourishing in the house of God", he is using this simile to describe how God has transformed a very destructive force into a very fruitful, creative power in the lives of God's chosen people. The olive tree was never literally planted in the temple courtyard, but symbolically represents the spiritual growth that was taking place there. The olive tree symbolizes purity, peace and prosperity. David had found purity through God's forgiveness, peace internally with God, in spite of warfare on the outside, and prosperity in the blessings that God bestowed upon him.

We can always tell if a person has been touched by God by how much he is able to touch the lives of others. David's psalms filled the temple, praising God, and encouraging the hearts of the Israelites as they faced their own daily struggles with fears, anger, doubts, and sins. He was a living example of God's grace, from shepherd boy to mighty king.

The olive tree is a slow growing tree, but can live more than a thousand years. David had to go through a lot of struggles, and had to learn the hard way many times, but his slow growth did not hinder the strengthening of the trunk of his faith. The trunk of the olive tree may be gnarled, but the grain of its wood is rich.

The olive oil was used for the anointing of kings and priests, and David was God's anointed one, through whom the Messiah would come. He wrote in his psalms of this future king, but also of the suffering savior (Psa. 22). God was able to use David's own struggles with friends who betrayed him to help him to understand the suffering of the coming Christ.

Olive oil was also used as a healing ointment for the wounds of war. David knew first hand how God had healed him, and now he was turning around to heal others as well through the soothing ointment of God's love. His last years were spent in preparing for the building of the temple, for he knew that after he was gone, God's house would continue to help his people stay close to their eternal king, just as it had helped him.

Awake, My Soul

"Awake, my soul! Awake, harp and lyre! I will awaken the dawn.
I will praise you, O Lord." Psalm 57:8-9

I'm a morning person. My mind wakes up first, bouncing back and forth between what happened yesterday and what will happen today. I toss and turn for a while, wrestling with my thoughts, and then finally decide to get up. I have a cup of coffee and read the newspaper, for my mind is awake, but it takes my body a while to catch up. When my body and mind are finally both in sync, I sit down with my Bible in a quiet place and say, "Good morning, Lord".

I am now ready to have my soul awakened, to have God open the eyes of my heart, that my spirit might be molded by the loving hands of the Father. He gently lifts my soul, like a parent might lift a sleepy child from bed when it is time to get up. He embraces my spirit with a "big daddy hug", and then sets me on his lap to hear the story of His love and grace. It is a powerful time of rich, intimate bonding, where I feel that He is confiding in me the deepest secrets of His heart. I wouldn't trade this special time with my Heavenly Father for anything. It awakens my soul even before the sun is awakened, and I get the privilege of seeing the new day dawn with a heart that is already shining.

Although this might sound a little too idealistic to some of you, for it doesn't match your own experience, it is nevertheless very real. Yet, it hasn't always been that way. I have known the Lord for a long time, or at least, He has known me. Yet, something was greatly lacking. I was like Rip Van Winkle, in that, I was alive in the Lord, but in a deep sleep spiritually speaking for a long time. It wasn't until I was in a serious automobile accident and almost died that I began to awake. The problem was not in my faith, but in my focus. I had believed in the Lord for most of my life, but my focus had been on myself.

Self-centeredness and spiritual slumber go hand in hand. When I am asleep, I am in a comfort zone where I do not want to be disturbed. I want to remain in my fantasy world of dreams, where there are no boundaries or limits to my imagination. I don't want God, or anyone else to bother me, for I want to be the god of my own fantasies. Spiritual slumber is like a drunken stupor in some ways, in that my sensibilities are numbed to the real world. I become desensitized to the Holy Spirit's speaking to me. I don't want to hear his convicting voice. I don't want to change. So, I zone out and tune out the Lord and everyone else, becoming completely oblivious to the needs of others or what the Lord wants for my life.

Yet, now I hear my Father calling, "It is time to wake up!"? He is waiting to lift me up into his arms and to draw me closer to himself. I open the eyes of my heart and look into His face. He is the dawn of my new spiritual day. Awake, my soul, to see Him.

Pilgrimage to Paradise

"Blessed are those whose strength is in you, who have set their hearts on pilgrimage." Psa. 84:5

There are basically two different kinds of pilgrims—ones who wander aimlessly, and ones who are driven by a sacred longing to reach a place of holiness. When the Israelites were wandering through the wilderness for forty years, they fit the first classification of pilgrim, for they were going around in circles, just waiting for their turn to die. They wanted to get to the Promised Land, but they had forfeited their right to their inheritance through their rebellion against the Lord.

When this generation passed away, though, the next generation was taught how to walk with the Lord through trials, achieving victory after victory, and growing in their faith and love for the Lord. The psalmist, David, praises those whose desire is to follow after God and him alone. Their "hearts are set on pilgrimage", in that, they aren't satisfied with the status quo. They want to keep growing and becoming more like their holy King.

They know that going on such a pilgrimage will not be easy, for they must pass through the "Valley of Baca" on the way to their destination. The Valley of Baca means the Valley of Tears. In between the Jordan River and Jerusalem, there is a narrow valley that has steep cliffs on both sides, where graves or tombs are dug into the rocks. There are trickling springs coming out of the rocks, so the people who pass by on their pilgrimages to Jerusalem, are deeply moved by the spiritual symbolism of tears coming from the graves.

So, we, as we go on our spiritual journeys, must pass through valleys of tears or suffering, or the "valley of the shadow of death", but we don't have to be overwhelmed with grief or burdens of despair. If we keep our focus on our destination and why we are taking this journey, we can see goodness and create good out of even the worst nightmares.

The Israelites going through this valley have taken the time to dig basins at the bottoms of these cliffs in order to catch the water into pools for drinking. David tells us that as they pass through this mournful valley, "they make it a place of springs" (vs. 6). We, too, need to be willing to take whatever life gives us and to turn it into springs of life and growth, instead of drowning in self-pity and sorrow. When we face trials, we tend to get pulled down into depression, and often give up because we dwell on our problems and our weaknesses instead of the Lord.

The psalmist tells us that the pilgrims went "from strength to strength" till each appeared before God (vs. 7). They didn't dwell on their inabilities, or let anything or anyone deter them from reaching their goal, even the graves of those who failed around them. The power of their pilgrimage was their undying hope, just as it is with ours.

The Upside of Down

*"They bruised his feet with shackles, his neck was put in irons, till what he foretold came to pass,
till the word of the Lord proved him true." Psa. 105:18-19*

Joseph had been a favored child. His father, Jacob, had loved him more than any of his other sons. God also favored him, and gave him the gift of prophecy from the time of his youth. He had everything going for him. He was blessed by God and man. Then, his whole world was turned upside down. He was despised by his brothers because they were jealous of his favored status, and they sold him into slavery. One moment he was a "prince", and the next moment a prisoner.

Perhaps we too have had our world turned upside down, where our health, our job, our marriage, or our loved ones were all of a sudden taken from us, and we were left wondering, "What happened? Why has God forsaken me?" Well, God didn't leave Joseph behind. He used his adversity to move him forward. What happens when we are blessed is that we often get too comfortable, and we settle in to the "pat myself on the back" stage, and we become too content with the status quo. We're "in heaven", so why go any further? God wants us to keep moving and to keep growing. He doesn't want us stuck in front of a mirror admiring ourselves and our accomplishments. So, he often takes away what he has given us, so he can prepare us to get even more. He wants to develop our characters, so the next time we look in a mirror, we see Him, instead of ourselves.

God gave Joseph "giftedness", but he had to teach him humility. Even as a slave, everything came easy for him. He quickly became a leader, and was honored by his master. Yet, once again there were those who resented his personal power, and his master's wife got him thrown into jail. One thing that famous or important people quickly learn is that being put into the spotlight makes you an easier target for those who envy your glory. Yet, we need to remember that these are not just "attacks of the Devil". They are allowed by God to keep us humble, and to test our faithfulness to him.

When Joseph was in jail, his faith was tested. God continued to speak to him, and his gift of prophecy was as strong as ever. Yet, day after day, he was still in prison. Why didn't God just get him out of there? Certainly he could be used more effectively by the Lord in a palace than in a dungeon. God's purposes, however, are not always our own. God needed to prepare Joseph's heart for what he had planned for the future. Not only was Joseph to become a prominent leader in Egypt, he was to be a savior for much of the known world, as well as his own family, during a tremendous famine. The king even gave him the opportunity to teach his own children the godly principles that he had learned, as a favored child, as well as a prisoner (vs.22). God took his down-sides and turned them into up-sides, and he wants to do the same thing for us (Rom. 8:28).

The Rebirth of God

"Arrayed in holy majesty, from the womb of the dawn you will receive the dew of your youth."
Psa. 110:3

Have you ever really admired someone, and then they let you down? Maybe they were your parents, your teachers, your pastors, or your friends, but somehow they showed themselves to be a little too human. You wanted them to be the ideal "10", but they ended up being a zero. Sometimes the problem is that we are all sinners, and no one is perfect. Sometimes the problem is that we have false expectations because a person has presented a false front, and then they show their true selves later on.

In Christ's situation, however, the Israelites were disappointed with Jesus because they didn't understand his purpose or his timing. They were expecting someone to come from God to save them from their enemies. Jesus came to save the world from their sins. They expected immediate salvation from their physical oppression. Jesus offered immediate spiritual salvation, but postponed the physical restoration of the kingdom till later.

Somehow, from their perspective, Jesus was a little too human. He came from poor parents, from the wrong neighborhood, and he was critical of the establishment. He was a misfit rebel, and they were hoping for so much more. In modern terms, we might say, Jesus needs a "complete makeover". He needs someone, like a Hollywood press agent, to give him a better image. We want someone who is bigger than life, like a mega-star, not just a carpenter's son who hangs out with dirty, smelly fishermen, prostitutes and tax-collectors.

Well, God is going to give us what we want. He, in a sense, is going to be "reborn", with a new image. He is going to come again, but this time, instead of as a lowly human, he is going to come in all his power and glory as God. He is going to come as the triumphant king and Lord of Lords (Rev. 1:12-16). In one of David's messianic psalms, he describes Christ's second coming as if it is a rebirth. He says, "Arrayed in holy majesty, from the womb of the dawn you will receive the dew of your youth." Christ's first coming wasn't majestic. It was lowly. Yet, now he is going to come in all of his glory.

Notice, however, that it isn't the kind of glory that he has just received because of what he did as a human. It is the kind of majesty that he had as God from the beginning of time, from the "womb of the dawn". He will receive once again the "dew of [his] youth", the freshness and vitality of the Creator before creation, as if his glory had never been set aside in order to humble himself as a man. It will not be a matter of a man finally achieving the greatness of a god, like some cults teach, but of God reclaiming and reasserting the power and glory that he had from eternity past. The Messiah, Yahweh our savior, will be "born again".

The Cornerstone

"The stone the builders rejected has become the cornerstone." Psa. 118:22

It is obvious from the gospels that Jesus is the cornerstone that was rejected by his chosen people (Matt. 21:22). Yet, there is confusion on what exactly a cornerstone is. The problem is that there are actually three different kinds of cornerstones: the foundation stone, the capstone, and the keystone. Jesus, in a very important sense, is all three.

First, he is the foundation stone, which is used by builders to start the foundation, and to make sure that the building is square. Everything in the building is based upon this first stone. If it is not set properly, the whole building could fall apart or be terribly crooked and contrary to the architect's design. According to the apostle Paul, the apostles and the prophets are the foundation of the church, and Jesus is the "chief cornerstone" (Eph. 2:20). If the church is not built upon this foundation, with Christ as the standard, the church will not stand.

Another kind of cornerstone is the "capstone". The capstone was a large stone placed over the doorway. Jesus told his disciples that he was the gate or doorway that each man must enter in order to have eternal life (John 10:9).

The third kind of cornerstone is the keystone. It is placed at the peak of an arch or of the roof of the building. It is the highest point, the one that others must lean into in order to get the support that they need. Jesus is the one that we must all submit to and lean upon, for without him we are nothing. He is in the place of prominence in the church, in that, everything points up toward him. We, as Christians, then, must build our lives upon the foundation of Christ and what he did for us. We must follow him through the door of salvation and every door of opportunity that he opens for us in order to be blessed by him. We also need to seek first the kingdom and prominence of God in our lives, with Christ receiving all the glory.

If people reject Jesus as the cornerstone of their lives, Jesus warns that they will stumble and fall on this stone and be broken into pieces (Matt. 21:44). In order to stumble and fall on this stone, they have to be falling on the whole idea of Jesus being the necessary and only way of salvation, or the foundation stone that all must believe. If they continue to reject this foundation, and to rebel against God's provision for our sins, then not only will they stumble on the rock, they will be crushed by it (Matt. 21:44). In this case, it is Jesus as the capstone or the keystone that will fall down upon them, and their judgment will not be softened if they are good or religious people. There is only one foundation, one doorway, and one God to be glorified, and if any man or woman rejects this one way, there will be only one outcome.

Jesus is not a soft, cuddly, comfortable teddy bear savior that we can change, control or squeeze into any mold that we want him to be. He is a rock-redeemer with sharp, distinct corners, and we are the ones that need to bend.

Open My Eyes

"Open my eyes that I may see wonderful things in your law." Psa. 119:18

My dear Heavenly Father, I know that you are all-wise and all-knowing, but I'm having a hard time seeing what you see. I want to be wise too, and to have the mind of Christ, but I keep being blinded by my own self-focus, which blows things out of proportion and distorts the truth. I try reading your Word, diligently searching for your light, but I often read page after page without being enlightened. Sometimes I see with your vision, but many times I am just plain "blind". I want to see your shining face, yet it is like you are wearing a veil, hiding behind your mysteries, and I am left staring at your footprints in history instead of looking into your loving eyes.

Please help me, Father, for I know that I am one of your children, and you have promised that if we seek you, we will find you. Help me to have my vision clarified, Lord, for now I see you as only the shadow of your true self. Draw me nearer to you, Jesus, for now you seem like only a blur in the distance, and I long to feel your embrace. Take away the cataracts from my spiritual eyes that cloud all your wonders into a confusing haze. Help me to have the sense of wonder of a child, so every raindrop, butterfly, and rainbow reflects your glory.

Help me to see your grace, too, Father, in the ugly, slimy things of life that I often try to ignore. Help me not to miss a single gift of grace that you have freely displayed, yet I am often too busy or worried to see. Help me to take the time to drink in all your beauty that you have put into the lives of others. Help me to look for the good in people, and not just the bad. Help me to see the anguish in people's faces, and not just look past them. Help me to see past the makeup or disguises that people wear, so I can see the pain and pleasure in their hearts. Help me to look for potential in people, instead of just potential problems.

Help me to see past my own immediate desires. Help me to be circumspect, looking at the past, present and future, before making any important decisions. Help me to see my own pimples, warts, and deformities of the soul, so that I am not blind to my own failures to be like you. I want to look at you and to look like you, but I am like a child, who often is only pretending "dress-up" like daddy. How can I look like you when I only see you darkly, as if in an antique mirror, or the distorted mirrors at a carnival?

Please, Lord, open my eyes, for they are often stuck shut with sleepiness, as if I have been lured asleep by the world, and I can hardly get a blurred glimpse of your truth. I want to grow and to have deeper insights into you and your Word, but my growth is often stunted by my insensitivity to your Spirit and my foolish pride that thinks that it already knows everything. Please give me the vision of a wise prophet, Lord, but the heart of a humble saint, so that I never think that I know or see too much. Help me to see only you.

The Disciple's Decathlon

"I run in the path of your commands, for you have set my heart free."
Psa. 119:32

I used to be a runner. I loved to be out on the open road, out in the country, feeling the breeze blow through my hair, blowing the cobwebs out of my brain, as I enjoyed the beauty of God's creation. It set my spirit free from the stress of my life, and filled my body with a sense of strength and satisfaction that I could find in no other way. The psalmist, David, was also a runner, but he often had difficulty in getting up in the morning to run. He says, "I am laid low in the dust" (vs. 25).

Why on earth is David laying in the dust instead of out running the way that he is supposed to be? Well, he tells us that his "soul is weary with sorrow" (vs. 28). It isn't the kind of sorrow that comes from grieving the loss of a loved one. He is weary and depressed over the attacks from his enemies and friends. People are scorning him and slandering him, talking behind his back, not because he has done anything wrong, but because he keeps the laws of God (vs. 22). In other words, he is involved with spiritual warfare, where he is doing everything right, according to the leading of God, yet being afflicted from every side, for they resent his righteousness.

The Devil has an agenda, and he is playing his spiritual chess game, thinking that he is making all the right moves, and then along comes a white knight, who thwarts his plan by trying to play by the rules, instead of the deceitful way that he was playing. David is doing his best to play the game right, but Satan keeps trying to blow out the lights, so David has to play in the dark. He tries to keep knocking the chess board, so that David is knocked off balance, and always on the defensive, so he won't have the energy to be able to attack against the dark side. David wants to be focusing on the positive, serving and worshipping the Lord, and meditating on the Word, but his concentration is constantly being distracted by the enemy.

When I used to run cross country in college, we often ran away from the crowds. As long as we were around the judges and coaches, everyone behaved themselves. Yet, out in the woods or the back roads, runners would sometimes revert to purposely tripping and throwing off the other runners, even injuring them at times, just to get the upper hand. The Devil fights dirty too, and he tries to keep us from finishing the race by trying to get us lost by following the wrong leaders.

David says that he has "chosen the way of truth" (vs. 30) or the right path, and he is running according to the rules (vs. 32). The result is that the Lord has "set [his] heart free" (vs. 32), and he no longer feels burdened down by all of the spiritual distractions around him. He knows that it isn't going to be easy, that it isn't just a sprint to the finish. Life is a decathlon, with ups, downs, long jumps, and hurdles, but the Lord will run with us all the way to the finish line.

Worthless Things

"Turn my heart toward your statutes and not toward selfish gain. Turn my eyes away from worthless things." Psa. 119:36-37

Do we ever just waste time for the fun of it? We are tired of being useful and productive, and we just want to vegetate. Perhaps we have been stressed out at work, overloaded with responsibilities, and frustrated that the piles just keep getting higher and higher. We are worn out, and we feel that we deserve a break. It has often been said that a person's true character is seen when they are under stress. Yet, the opposite is also true. What we truly value is often seen in how we spend our time when there is no stress, when we are on vacation, or when we think that no one is watching. We may have trained ourselves to handle or even hide our true feelings when we are under stress, for we know that our job or our reputation is at stake. Yet, what are we like at home, or at the athletic field, or in the movie theater, or on the beach? The bedroom of our soul reveals a lot more about who we are than the living room that is just set aside for the guests to see. Who are we when we are alone? That is what really counts.

When we are at work or church, we may be the most respected individual around, full of customer service smiles and cookie-cutter clichés. How are we, though, when we can take off the make-up, throw on the grubbies, turn on the TV, and are free to be ourselves? Are we still our charming selves? Are we thoughtful of the needs of our spouse, or are we more concerned with watching our favorite show? Do we spend quality time with our children, or do we just zone out hiding behind the newspaper?

The problem is that we often justify our priorities based upon the pleasure principle rather than by what is right according to God's standard. David recognized this problem in himself, so he prayed, "Turn my heart toward your statutes and not toward selfish gain". That doesn't mean that we have to spend every waking minute reading the Bible or worshipping in church. It does mean that we need to live by God's principles, though, even in our spare time. There is no vacation time away from the Father. There is no day off from serving the Lord. The Bible doesn't say to seek ye first the kingdom of God whenever we are in public, but seek our own kingdom when we are alone.

Do we deserve and need the time to rest and relax from our hectic lives? Absolutely, as long as we acknowledge that God is still there with us, and that we want him there. We should not use our down time from work or church as a time of escape from being a devoted disciple of Christ. Resting from stress is good, but anything that increases stress between us and our Lord because of sin in our heart or life, is worthless, even if it gives us the temporary pleasure or happiness that we desire. There is no cure for dealing with stress in our lives that is better than peace with God. Find rest in Him.

A Wineskin in the Smoke

"Though I am a wineskin in the smoke, I do not forget your decrees." Psa. 119:83

I am beginning to accept the fact that I am gradually becoming a part of a unique group of people— Senior Citizens. Sometimes, through Senior Citizen's discounts, this is a welcome thing. However, not everyone appreciates the value of the older people in our society. They see them as nuisances or useless baggage that they would rather do without. Although this older group is often limited in what they can do physically, that doesn't mean that they are ready for the recycling bin. Many seniors, in fact, are able to remain very active in volunteer work, and choose to donate their time, instead of just sitting at home feeling sorry for themselves, or going on vacations to places that they don't really want to see. They feel useful and productive, and many keep going strong long after the younger crowd has grown bored and moved on. Many Christian organizations depend on the hard, unselfish work of these well-seasoned citizens, for without them, many ministries could not exist. The younger adults seem to be so focused on just getting ahead, getting more, or just getting a paycheck, that they often lose sight of the bigger goals of serving the Lord by serving others.

The world looks at the "old folks" and sees them as all used up, but God isn't finished with them yet. The psalmist, David, speaks of his own aging process. He says, "Though I am a wineskin in the smoke, I do not forget your decrees." When a wineskin was hung near a fire, the smoke would often cause the wineskin to shrivel up like a prune and be all dried up. David sees the same thing happening to his own skin, but there is something far more important to him than his appearance. He loves the Lord, and he constantly focuses on what God wants him to do with his life. What his body looks like is irrelevant. Man looks on the outward appearance, but God looks on the heart (I Sam. 16:7).

Unfortunately, the world doesn't usually take the time to look deeper than skin deep. Even the Christian world is guilty of this materialism. Yet, God knows our soul, and our spiritual journey of growth and service doesn't end when we retire from our jobs. Our responsibilities sometimes change with time, but our level of commitment to serve our Lord should never waver. Being on "Social Security" just means that we have more time to meet the needs of others, even if we have less money to give. It doesn't matter if our wineskins are all shriveled up, how much we sag or shuffle, or if we have more eyes than teeth. Even if we are on our death bed, we can still be a prayer warrior, and a faithful witness of the love and grace of God.

If our fruit is too ripe, so what? God can still make us into preserves or fruit roll-ups. If God can use Abraham and Sarah to produce and raise a child at the age of a hundred, he can sure use us when we turn 65. Look at how much God still does at his age?

How to Know God

"Then you will…find the knowledge of God." Prov. 2:5

Have you ever known someone for a long time, but then as you grow older, you find that you don't really know them at all? Unfortunately, this happens with spouses all of the time. You date, get married, have kids, buy a home and even go to church together, yet discover years later that they are completely different from what you thought they were. You thought that they were kind and generous, but they were only putting on a show. You thought they were faithful, but they were having an affair. You thought that they were a Christian, but then they walk away from God.

The same thing happens in our relationship with God, yet, in this case, it is our fault. We think that we know God, but through time, we find that we don't really know him at all. In fact, he even seems like a stranger that we aren't even sure that we want to know all of the time. Let's assume for now that we really want to know God. How do we go about getting to know the Almighty maker of the universe?

Solomon, the wisest man who ever lived, gives us some helpful guidelines. He says that first of all we must accept God's words and store them in our hearts (Prov. 2:1). The word "accept" in this verse means to "believe, to carry away with you, and to use". If we have read or heard the Word for a long time, and yet we do not believe it, make it a vital part of our life, or use its principles in daily choices, how can we expect to get to know the author of those words?

The second guideline for knowing God is "turning your ear to wisdom and applying your heart to understanding" (vs. 2). The problem with Bible study for many Christians is that they never get past the facts. They know the basic plot of the story, the main characters, and all of the exciting parts, but the Bible was never meant to be read like a novel. It is the very essence of God's spirit speaking to our inner being about the truths of the universe, his heart to ours. We need to be reading the scriptures from that perspective, truly listening to God's voice, and being focused on learning and growing, not just being experts in "Bible Trivia".

The third guideline is to pray for wisdom and insight (vs. 3). God promises to give wisdom to those who ask for it (James 1:5). God is wisdom personified. We cannot become wise, then, without coming to know Him.

The fourth guideline is to search for God and his wisdom as if it is hidden treasure that we value more than anything else (vs. 4). Our reading of scripture and search for the Lord is so haphazard and inconsistent, that it is a wonder of God's grace if we ever discover truth or get to know God, who is Truth. We need to be dedicated and driven to know God above all else, with total abandon and submission to whatever he teaches us.

Unfortunately, our desire to know God is often more out of curiosity than commitment, and God remains a stranger.

You and your Body

"A heart at peace gives life to the body, but envy rots the bones." Prov. 14:30

Our society is very "body conscious". We idolize the muscular and sexy. We try to imitate the latest fashions and fads because we want to look like the models that display them. We make fun of the fat or the skinny, laugh at the ugly or homely, and treat the handicapped with disdain. We go on extreme diets, join health clubs to push our bodies to the limits, and even jog in the snow if it means losing one more ugly pound.

What we are doing is trying to deal with the symptoms rather than the causes—the wrapping on the outside of the box rather than the contents. What we should be doing is trying to figure out why we eat too much, don't exercise enough, or feel so unhappy with the way that we look to begin with. What is the cause of so much discontent? Why do we have to try to be something that we are not, or to look like someone else?

Unfortunately, the deep-seated insecurities that drive these feelings and impulsive behaviors are often caused by being traumatized or neglected when we are young, or made to feel very inadequate by our family members, friends, teachers, or even preachers. Many people today, including Christians, in fact, probably need psychological counseling to get over their fears and inferiority complexes. That is why so many people today, including children, are on tranquilizers or other drugs to calm them down or get their anxieties under control.

Yet, beyond our difficult childhoods and the stress of our complex, manipulative, materialistic society, there is another reason we are so self-conscious about our bodies. It is that we lack peace with God. We are still struggling with who should be the Lord of our lives, God or us, and as long as there is this battle, there will be no peace. The Bible says that "a heart at peace gives life to the body, but envy rots the bones." Our relationship with the Lord, then, affects the health of our body. If we are riddled with guilt, fear, anger, or envy, it wears on us physically. The added stress that these things add to our body can take years off of our life, or make the years that we have left ones of misery. We can literally worry ourselves sick.

We can also make ourselves sick by longing to be something that we are not. It says that "envy rots the bones". If we envy the supermodels or superhunks, and yet no matter how hard we try, we still look like "Fat Albert", we could be putting a tremendous amount of strain on our heart and other organs by constantly going on crash diets, or gorging ourselves when we give up or when we are nervous.

We need to stop trying to deal with the symptoms and focus on the cause. We need to learn contentment with the body that God has given us, and to focus our energies on things that are more important than our appearance. We cannot be at peace with our "bod" until we are at peace with our "God".

Are You Listening?

"A fool finds no pleasure in understanding, but delights in airing his own opinions."
Prov. 18:2

Have you ever tried carrying on a conversation with someone who wasn't really listening to what you have to say, but was so wrapped up in their own opinions, that you were almost invisible? The Bible calls this kind of person a "fool", for they find "no pleasure in understanding". They are not interested in learning anything, for they think they know it all. They don't know how to listen, for they are too busy talking. They don't care about other people, for they are too focused on self. No one likes this kind of person, not even themselves.

Someone who is filled with pride doesn't necessarily have a good self-image. They talk a lot because they are nervous and insecure, and they are looking for attention—your undivided attention. So, they yank on your ear for hours as a way of holding on to you. You are a captive audience.

Unfortunately, we are often like that "fool" when it comes to our relationship with God. We do all of the talking, but aren't really interested in listening to what God has to say to us. We go on and on in our prayers talking about our problems, but don't listen to what God has to say about those problems in the Word. We think that we are spiritual because we spend time in prayer, but prayer is supposed to be a conversation, not just a speech. God is our friend, not just a "wailing wall" to come to so we can dump all our problems on him. He wants to have a sharing time with us, so we can share back and forth, we to him and he to us. God has a few opinions too you know. Why spend all of your time just sharing yours?

The Bible says that the Spirit of Christ dwells within us to communicate with our spirit, not just to listen to our whining. When we read the gospels, we never get the idea that one of the disciples tried to hog all of the attention by talking about themselves. They couldn't help but focus on Jesus and everything he did and said. Our problem is that we can't see or hear Jesus physically, so we sort of pretend that he isn't really there. We ramble on in our prayers as if God is more of a tape recorder or a secretary taking dictation, instead of our bridegroom that we want to have communion with, intimately sharing and listening to the heart of our loved one.

If we only go to God in prayer when we have a problem that we want solved, then we have limited God in our view to a spiritual policeman or paramedic instead of a soul-mate. Jesus wants to be our kindred spirit, our prayer partner, our trusted friend, our counselor, our healer, our comforter, and our encourager. He cannot be all of these things if we do all of the talking in our relationship. If God can't get a word in edge-wise when he is trying to talk to us, he probably will just stop trying to say anything to us. He wouldn't want to interrupt us. He is too much of a gentleman to do that.

The Patient Warrior

"Better a patient man than a warrior, a man who controls his temper
than one who takes a city." Prov. 16:32

One of the hardest things in life is knowing how to deal with the egotistical jerks who purposely try to annoy us—the ones who know that what they are doing irritates us beyond belief, but do it anyway. They are basically saying, "Here I am. Look at me. I don't care what anyone thinks. I am going to do whatever I want, and if you don't like it, that's your problem." They are self-centered, inconsiderate, spoiled brats, and they range in age from two to one-hundred and two. Police officers have to deal with this type all of the time. It doesn't matter if they have just pulled someone over for speeding, or stopped someone from selling drugs, they have to deal with people who lose their temper for no other reason than someone stopped them from doing what they wanted to do. The authority figure is the bad guy in their eyes, and so they throw a temper tantrum to protest anyone who dares to say, "No!".

The hard part for the police officer, or any of us, is to know how to respond to "the terrible two's" whenever we see them. Our most natural human response is to be angry back at them, and to lose our own tempers at their belligerence. They are challenging our authority or invading our space or disrespecting our rights, so we feel that we need to respond strongly and harshly so that they know that they need to stop, and not let it happen again. Although a strong response may be the correct one, losing one's temper in the process is never right. If we get angry at someone else's anger, then we share their guilt. If we become out of control when someone is being an egotistical pain in the butt, then we have allowed our own ego to be blown out of proportion.

An EMT or emergency medical technician cannot afford to allow their own emotions to get in the way of helping the people who are in need. Otherwise, they may refuse to help someone that they don't like, or cringe away from seeing blood. We, too, must be able to set aside our own feelings in order to help those who are suffering, even if their pain is psychological or spiritual, instead of physical. Our mature response needs to be calm and controlled, and responding in such a way as to bring the situation under control, as well. If we respond in anger, no matter how much they may deserve it, then things get even more out of control, and we become part of the problem instead of part of the solution.

What makes the situation even more critical is when we realize that the tension that has been created is part of spiritual warfare, and that we are warriors in battle. Our natural inclination is to react with even greater anger, for we know we are fighting against God's enemies, not just our own. Yet, God says, "Better a patient man than a warrior." That means that if we fight back, we have already lost the battle. Only the patient win this kind of war.

Peace Isn't for Everyone

"If it is possible, as far as it depends on you, be at peace with all men."
Rom. 12:18

Have you ever tried to be friends with someone, but no matter how hard you tried, they treated you like you had leprosy? If you are bold enough, you might have even had the courage to ask them, "What's wrong? Did I do something to offend you?", but get no reply, only a cold shoulder. In cases like this, it's easy to conclude that they have been told some bad rumor about you, and that they just don't want to be your friend. Or, perhaps it's a pride thing, and they think that you aren't good enough for them. In other words, they are social snobs.

Yet, besides being snubbed by the egotistical, who basically just try to ignore our existence, there are also others who bristle like a cat whenever we approach, like we are sand paper, and we rub them the wrong way. As far as we know, we haven't done or said anything wrong, but they act irritated and defensive when we are around, and we don't have a clue as to what caused the friction. They talk behind our backs about us, and do everything they can to disrupt our lives. These people aren't just snobs, they're enemies. We have done everything we can to be sweet, but they are determined to be sour.

Sometimes this happens just because some people are plain grouchy. They don't like people in general, and we are just another one of their targets. Their bitterness has nothing to do with us. They have had a hard life, and they hate life itself.

There are other times, though, when someone is very friendly to most people, but they just don't like us. It may be that we just have a personality conflict. They are aggressive, and we are passive. They are controlling, and we just like being left alone. They are conservative, and we are liberal.

There are many varied reasons why people just don't get along, from politics to the clothes we wear. The Bible, though, focuses on one particular area of conflict—spiritual warfare. Simply put, there are some people who hate God, and therefore they hate us. Solomon puts it this way: "The righteous detest the dishonest; the wicked detest the upright" (Prov. 29:27).

Although it is possible, then, to have non-Christian friends, a Christian who is dedicated to living a righteous life can not be friends with a person who is wicked. They detest us, and we detest them. It is hard enough to just be civil with a person that we detest, because we don't respect them. We know that they are an enemy of God, and so our defenses are up against them, for they will probably try to attack us in some way. They are determined to do whatever they can to defeat us and the cause of Christ.

We are supposed to be at peace with all men, as much as is under our control, but the situation is no longer under our control when someone else has already drawn their sword. God please help us to be wise, even when peace is not possible.

Rejoice in the Lord Always

"Rejoice in the Lord always. I will say it again—Rejoice!" Phil. 4:4

This seems like a simple request, but it is one of the hardest commandments in the Bible to live by. No matter how positive and cheerful we are in our natural disposition, it is still difficult to be joyful when we are trying to come to grips with a tragedy or failure, rejection or loneliness, or seeing someone that we love being self-destructive. It would have been much easier if God had just said, "Go ahead and be depressed. I know how tough it is being human, so go ahead and bawl your eyes out, get angry, or be sad. Nobody's perfect."

We think, "It isn't normal to be joyful all of the time. I will be a hypocrite if I just pretend to be happy when I'm really feeling down. Why can't God just leave me alone and let me be myself? Depression is just a part of life, isn't it?" Part of the problem here is in the confusion of terms. The Bible doesn't tell us that we have to feel joy all of the time. Even Jesus wept. What God asks us to do here is always act in such a way as to be an encouragement to others. The word "rejoice" is not a feeling, it is an action verb. It means to "leap up into the air, and to keep leaping." What this means is that we need to understand how our actions influence others, regardless of how we feel. We have a job to do, and that is to have a positive impact on other lives. We are supposed to forget about ourselves and our own problems, and focus on reaching out to others.

This is not a matter of just pretending that you don't have problems or sorrows. It means that we don't allow those problems or feelings to keep us from ministering to those around us. For example, I have a three year old granddaughter who is taking a gymnastics class. When she comes home, she likes to show us the new tricks that she has learned. One of the things that she does is to jump up in the air, to turn around, and land back down with the grace of a ballerina. Well, at least that's the way it looks from the perspective of a proud grandpa. When I go to her house at the end of a long day, and I am weary and sometimes grouchy, it lifts my spirits when I see her childlike joy. Then she gets me to jump up and down with her, and to try her "ballerina" tricks. I go along with the fun, trying to ignore everyone else in the family sitting there laughing at us, and I end up going home a different man. I have been edified by a three-year old, and I am loving every minute of it.

That is what God wants us to do. He doesn't command that we feel a certain way. He commands that we act a certain way—completely focused on uplifting the spirits of those in need. They need to be able to see us "leaping up and twisting in the air", not literally, but in how we cope with life. They need to see "rejoicing actions" even if the feelings aren't there, for their sakes, not ours. This isn't being a hypocrite. We are still true to ourselves, in that, we are true to our conviction that it isn't about us—point them to Jesus.

Look to the Rock

"Look to the rock from which you were cut and to the quarry from which you were hewn." Isa. 51:1

Stone masons can tell which quarry a certain kind of rock comes from. Some rocks are pretty generic and can be found all over, but others are more rare and localized. To a certain degree, people are the same. You can tell a lot about people based upon how they dress, their accent, their vocabulary, their food, their jokes, etc.. Yet, people today are a lot more mobile than they used to be, and they often have lived so many different places, that you can hardly recognize their roots or origins. They are a conglomerate of ideas and styles, and they have lost some of their original uniqueness.

The Bible, though, encourages us to examine our heritage. It tells us to "look to the rock from which you were cut and to the quarry from which you were hewn." Yet, in this context, it isn't referring to our physical roots as much as our spiritual origins. Where did your spiritual journey begin? Who was used in your life to help you to grow in your understanding of the Lord? Who took the time to mentor you along the way through the hard times and into deeper truth?

On one level, we need to look before our own life to eternity past, for that is really where our spiritual journey began. God, before the foundation of the world, designed a spiritual destiny for mankind (Eph. 1:3-10). He foresaw that man would sin, need a savior, and that he would be the only one who could meet our need. Our spiritual roots, then, begin deep within the heart of God and his purpose-driven provision for the salvation of the world. He is the rock that we are to look toward, that all spiritual life springs forth from since the beginning of time.

Yet, our roots also dig deeply into the soil of sin, for we are of the same quarry as Adam and Eve and the rest of fallen mankind. We need to remember our fallen heritage in order to appreciate how much we have gained through the grace of the Rock. We have been cut from the quarry of sinful humanity, but we are identified by the unique characteristics of our own individualized environment. If we have had a very difficult life, with spiritual erosion, mental mudslides, or tsunami storms of the soul, these all play a part in the kind of rock that we are today. If we have had it easy, on the other hand, we may appear like softened clay, for we are very pliable or moldable to whatever God wants.

God uses both kinds of rocks or clay, and he understands why we are the way that we are. It is good for us also to remember our spiritual origins, but not to get bogged down with the quicksand of regret. The quarry that our rock came from is not as important as the fact that we are now part of the temple of God, with Jesus as the chief cornerstone. He chose us, with all our sinful sediment, to be transformed and used for his glory. We are now a chip off the old block.

Boasting about God

"Let him who boasts boast about this: that he understands and knows me."
Jer. 9:24

Boasting is a common practice among politicians, athletes, the social elite, the intellectual elite, and the kids on the playground. People brag about their new house, new car, new job, new boyfriend or girlfriend, new sexual exploits and their newest extreme sports adventures. People boast about anything and everything, including religion. People boast about how big their church is, how many new members they have, new baptisms, new buildings, new pastors, and even how great the entertainment is in their churches. Non-Christians also brag about their religious experiences. They openly claim to have had spiritual experiences, such as channeling with other spirits from previous lives, being able to communicate with the dead, having magical powers, and being able to foretell the future, or see the past. People claim to have special connections with angels, spirit guides, or even gods and goddesses.

Yet, when a Christian claims that they know God personally, for some reason, this kind of bragging is considered wrong by secular society. We are seen as being arrogant and self-righteous, as if we are better than anyone else. From the world's perspective, it is alright to boast about all these other things, because it makes them feel better about themselves. It builds their egos. Yet, when we talk about knowing God, it is something that they cannot claim, so they see it as a put down. We have something that they don't have, and they don't like it.

Of course, they don't really want it either, but that is beside the point. They just don't like people saying that they have something which they don't have. It is a pride thing. It is a greed thing. It is a jealousy thing. It is a spiritual warfare thing. They don't understand that for us to admit that we know God is not really bragging at all. They don't realize that we only come to the Lord as spiritual paupers, fallen in sin, and that we are only saved by grace, not because we are better than anyone else.

To say that we have been saved, then, is not bragging rights. It is like a criminal who has been found guilty, but then pardoned by the judge. We admit that we are unworthy, yet rejoice that God has saved us in spite of our guilt. We aren't claiming to be better than anyone else. We are merely saying that we were once slaves to sin, but we were bought by a new master, who has given us our freedom. Is a cancer patient bragging if he has been cured from cancer? Is a drug addict or alcoholic boasting if they share that they have been clean or sober for a certain period of time? We applaud this kind of testimonial as an encouragement of hope for others who may be suffering. Why, then, is it wrong for us to share our testimonials about being set free from our own sicknesses or addictions? Would you expect someone who has been healed to keep silent? Why should we?

Does God have Cooties?

"Cursed is the one who trusts in man, who depends on flesh for his strength and whose heart turns away from the Lord." Jer. 17:5

I remember as a child playing at school with my friends, when all of a sudden, everything changed. A girl came up behind me and stole a kiss when I wasn't looking. She ran away giggling, for she had become the center of attention, and all her friends screamed with approval at her bravery. My friends, on the other hand, cried out, "He's got 'cooties'. Don't let him near you. He got kissed by a girl."

I felt just a little bit like a person in Bible times who had leprosy. I was abandoned by my friends, forced to go play by myself, and lived with the stigma of having "cooties" for the rest of that lunch time. Of course, soon as the bell rang, everything went back to normal, but those agonizing minutes of being ostracized and abandoned seemed like an eternity to a small boy.

Amazingly enough, God feels the same way. With great joy he readily accepts those who come to him in faith. He longs to abide with them and commune with them, for they are now his friends, and they have chosen to follow him. Then something happens in their life, some trial or temptation, and God doesn't meet their need or desire anymore. So they, like Judas, give Jesus a "stolen kiss" of betrayal and abandonment, and all of a sudden, Jesus has "cooties". They have decided that they don't want to have anything to do with Jesus, for God didn't live up to their expectations. They decide that they can make it better on their own, so they walk away from God.

The Bible says that "cursed is the one who trusts in man, who depends on flesh for his strength and whose heart turns away from the Lord". It is not talking about unbelievers here, who have always rejected the Lord. It is talking about those who once followed God, but then turned their backs on him. The phrase "turns away" here actually means "pulls away quickly in repulsion", as if someone has just touched someone with leprosy. It was bad enough for me as a child to be treated like that by my friends. Imagine how God must feel when a person who claimed to love him, then "pulls away quickly in repulsion". I'm sure that there is the same kind of grief that a husband or wife must feel when their spouse has just told them, "I don't love you any more. I'm leaving. I can make it better on my own."

On the other hand, what joy it brings the Lord when someone comes to him in total submission and love, wanting to be close to him more than anything else. The Bible says, "Blessed is the man who trusts in the Lord, whose confidence is in him" (Jer. 17:7). The choice is up to us. Do we want to be blessed or cursed by God? The answer is easy to determine—who do we put our trust in—God or man? Simply put, God will not bless us if we treat him as if he has "cooties". He's looking for friends who will stick with him, no matter what.

Spiritual Acid Reflux

*"His word is in my heart like a fire, a fire shut up in my bones.
I am weary of holding it in; indeed, I cannot."* Jer. 20:9

I love to hear a zealous preacher who speaks as if the Lord's message is a fire in their heart that they must share with others or be consumed themselves. There is an urgency of message, almost to the point of desperation, as if nothing else in the world at that moment was more important than hearing the heart of God speaking to me. I feel at that moment as if I am in the presence of a prophet, like Elijah, who has spoken to God face to face, and he is now confiding in me the special vision that God has given.

I am hungry to hear this kind of passionate sharing from God's Word. Unfortunately, there are very few preachers who hold this kind of passion in their bosoms. Most sermons today sound more like an entertaining speech at a Toastmasters Club, or a quiet conversation over a nice hot cup of Cappuccino. They are meant to make us feel better about ourselves, instead of moving our souls and empowering our spirits to closer walks with the Almighty. These preachers have a different kind of fire in their hearts. It is the fire of Jeremiah, the prophet. He didn't really enjoy his job. He tried sharing the truth with people, but they criticized his zeal, and ridiculed him for speaking out against their sins. So he decided to choose an easier path. When God gave him a vision, he held it inside, and refused to share it. He would rather deal with the wrath of God than the wrath of the people.

God, though, wouldn't let him get away with it. The Word of the Lord became like a fire in his heart and in his bones, and he couldn't hold it in any longer. He had to get it out before it destroyed him. This is something that is very difficult for us to understand. From our perspective, it seems that a person would feel honored by being chosen to be a prophet. After all, it is quite a privilege to have that kind of personal communication with the divine, and to know without a shadow of doubt that what we are saying to the people is God's truth. Yet, not everyone wants to hear God's truth, and not every prophet wants to deal with the rejection that comes with the job. Jonah, Jeremiah, and even Elijah, tried to avoid the conflicts that resulted from sharing God's Word at times. They would rather run away and hide.

God, however, doesn't like being told no. When Jonah ran away, he got swallowed by a whale. When Elijah ran away, his ministry was taken away from him and given to Elisha. When Jeremiah resisted his prophetic gift, God put a burning in his soul, a spiritual acid reflux, that caused such great spiritual torment that he had to share God's message or be destroyed.

Whether we are a preacher or prophet, or just a Christian who has been commanded to share the gospel with others, God is a fire. It is up to us what kind of fire God will be—one of zealous power to share, or a raging volcano ready to explode.

October 5

No Worries

"Blessed is the man who trusts in the Lord, whose confidence is in him. He will be like a tree planted by the water." Jer. 17:7

We have had a wild year of destructive storms. We have had terrible hurricanes, record breaking rain and snowfall, avalanches, floods, earthquakes, and even a tsunami that killed two-hundred thousand people. Many are saying that Mother Nature has gone crazy in her old age, or jokingly, that she is going through menopause or PMS. We believe, however, that God controls the weather, just as he controls everything else in the universe. Nothing happens without his permission, or outside of his plan. If he caused or allowed a devastating storm, then, that destroyed the lives of thousands, he must have had a purpose.

Sometimes these acts are driven by the wrath of God, who often uses "natural" events to judge those who have turned their backs on him, such as Noah and the flood. Yet, God is good at multitasking. He doesn't just do things for one reason, or for one person. Everything is connected. If God does something to judge one person, he also uses it to show mercy to someone else. By seeing God's wrath against sin, it should help us to avoid a similar downfall. It should help us to avoid our own suffering from self-destructive activities, as well as the loneliness and emptiness that comes from seeking happiness apart from God.

God is in control, and that in itself should be a comfort to us, even when tragedy occurs. We know that he loves us, so whatever happens, we know that it is for our own good, as well as everyone around us. God uses tragedy to teach us lessons, to help us to trust in him instead of the idols that we often lift up instead, and to make us more aware of his almighty power, so that we don't just live as if he doesn't exist.

The Bible says that if we trust in him, we "will be like a tree planted by the water". Our roots get plenty of nourishment, so our tree "has no worries in a year of drought and never fails to bear fruit" (Jer. 17:8). We don't have to become stressed out when the heat or storms of life come, because we know that God has a purpose, whether we understand it or not. Even if everything is taken away from us, through no fault of our own, such as in Job's case, it can still draw us closer to him if we trust in him.

We think of success and happiness in our world as being associated with possessions. So, when our "toys" are taken away from us, we are often devastated. We feel insignificant as if we have lost our self-worth and everything that is important to us. Maybe that is the problem—that these things are too important to us. God's priority is not our pleasure or our happiness in this life. It is our spiritual growth. That should be our priority as well. If it is, then our confidence is in him, not in the things that we might lose in the fire, wind, or rain. It is more important to bear a single fruit of the Spirit than to own a thousand trees.

Your Lying Heart

"The heart is deceitful above all things and beyond cure. Who can understand it?"
Jer. 17:9

When someone is struggling with what to do, or with how to solve a problem, the advice that they often get is, "Follow your gut feeling", or "Just follow your heart". Yet, would we believe someone who always lies to us? Would we trust someone who purposely tries to trick us and lead us astray? Would we even listen to someone who has a reputation for being deceptive or dishonest?

The Bible says that "the heart is deceitful above all things". That means that our heart is the biggest liar in the world. Not only that, but there is no cure for this spiritual disease. Once a liar, always a liar. This is something that Christians need to be more conscious of. Many Christians feel that once they are saved, this solves the problem. Sure, they think, that non-believers will have lying hearts because they are blinded by the Devil and their own self-centered natures. Yet, Christians are new creatures in Christ, therefore, for them, this won't be a problem anymore.

Ironically, if they think this, it actually is proof that the problem still exists, for their hearts have lied to them that they have been freed from this fault. The Bible says that this weakness in man is "beyond cure". For the unbeliever, this means that they lie to themselves that they don't need God, or that there is no God. For the Christian, their hearts still often tell them that they don't need God to help them, so they try to do a lot of things on their own, and only call on God when they have an emergency. Their hearts also lie to them about their sins, often justifying what they do by comparing themselves to others, or thinking that it doesn't really matter what they do, for God will forgive them anyway.

Even though there is no cure for the lying heart, there are still some pretty powerful treatments that help to control its influence. First, there is the light of the Word of God. It is pretty difficult for a thief to steal something if there are a lot of lights on. It's not impossible, but just more difficult. The same thing is true about our lying heart. The more light that we can shed on a situation, the harder it is for our heart to get away with deception. The Bible promises that the truth will set us free, but we have to know the truth first.

The Devil is the father of lies, and is constantly taking advantage of the fact that most Christians don't really know their "operating manual", the Word of God. So, they can be tricked easily. Our heart does the same thing. It lies to us all the time, and gets away with it, because we are ignorant of the truth.

Second, you need to stay close to the Lord. It's pretty hard to lie about someone if they are standing right there to refute it. If our heart embraces the light, it can't hug the darkness at the same time.

The Problem with Prophets

"Both prophet and priest are godless." Jer. 23:11

Would you waste your time going to a bank that didn't have any money? Would you go shopping at a grocery store that had no food? Would you drive a car that was out of gas? We expect certain places and things to have what we need. If they don't, they are useless. So we end up going someplace else, often very frustrated that the usual places or things are bankrupt, deficient, or on empty.

The same thing happens with churches. Sometimes the pastors are bankrupt spiritually speaking, deficient in being able to nourish others, or just on empty in their souls. In a very real way, they are like the prophets and priests in Jeremiah's time who were "godless". God rebukes them for being shepherds who have scattered the flock of God because they "have not bestowed care on them" (Jer. 23:2). They "follow an evil course and use their power unjustly" (Jer. 23:10). They are more into the pastorate as a power trip or status symbol rather than compassionately caring for the people. They "strengthen the hands of evildoers, so that no one turns from his wickedness" because they are doing evil themselves, or they avoid talking about sin because they don't want to offend anyone (vs. 14).

The Lord warns the people not to listen to such prophets because "they fill you with false hopes" (vs. 16). They try to cheer us up and make us feel good about ourselves, making us believe that we don't need to repent or change. These so-called prophets don't even preach out of the Word. They use inspirational books, tell jokes, read poetry, and tell entertaining stories. God rebukes them because "they speak visions from their own minds, not from the mouth of the Lord" (vs. 16).

Yet, in spite of how bad all of this sounds, the worst thing they do is to claim that they are speaking for God, while they are really speaking through the power of "Baal", Beelzebub or Satan himself (vs. 13). These so-called prophets are like the pied-piper leading God's children into death and destruction, while pretending to be their friend. Satan knows that he can lead more Christians astray from within the church, than by the temptations without. So, he uses the leaders to either put the church to sleep, or to alienate them so badly, that they stop coming to church, or seeking the face of God.

Some of these shepherds are purposely leading people astray because they have infiltrated the churches to serve the Devil. Others, though, are just spiritually immature themselves, and they cannot lead the people any further than they have journeyed themselves. It is the blind leading the blind. We need to be careful that we are not in either one of these groups—either the blind leaders or the blind followers. Don't get caught up in the feel-good fads of our generation, where there is more emphasis on "Jazzercise for Jesus" and "Self-help Seminars" than there is on hearing the voice of God.

Singleness of Heart

"They will be my people, and I will be their God. I will give them singleness of heart and action, so that they will always fear me for their own good."
Jer. 32:38

I would love to have a muscular body, bursting with energy. Unfortunately, I also love chocolate and relaxation. The problem is that I don't have singleness of heart. My desires are conflicting, and I often choose the easiest way. This is the reason that I have so much trouble following through on my New Year's resolutions, or practicing what I preach. I can be dedicated for a while, just out of human effort or stubborn willpower, but sooner or later, I give in to my lack of self-discipline or my double-mindedness.

Notice first in the scripture passage above that singleness of heart is a gift from God, not just the result of gutsy determination. God is not just looking for those who will work hard. A soft heart is more important to God than a calloused hand. God tenderizes and inspires single-heartedness through teaching us to fear him. He says, "I will inspire them to fear me, so that they will never turn away from me" (vs. 40). He wants to create a consistency between what is in our hearts and how we live our lives—"a singleness of heart and action". In other words, he wants to make us more like himself.

In this same passage, he promises to bless his people with his "whole heart and soul" (vs. 41). He is undivided in his purpose for us, just as we are to be undivided in our devotion to him. For him, singleness of heart and action is natural to his divine character. For us, it has to be given and inspired by God. He has to put his undivided nature into us. Singleness of heart, then, is a gift of God's grace, totally undeserved by us or attained by us through human effort. We can't squeeze ourselves into single-mindedness, like putting on a spiritual girdle. Our natural self is so out of control that it is bursting at the seams. We are double-minded, divided in our hearts and souls, speak with forked-tongue, and are two-faced so often that we hardly recognize ourselves in a mirror. "Which person am I today?" We have double-vision in a complicated world, and our heart keeps giving mixed signals to our brain.

The Bible says that "No man can serve two masters" (Matt. 6:24). Unfortunately, the two masters that we often try to serve are within us, not some outside forces. We waver back and forth between our old nature and our new nature in Christ, and we end up despising ourselves because we can never seem to get it right. We are always struggling, sometimes victorious, sometimes a failure, almost always frustrated by the never ending instability of our souls.

True stability only comes through singleness of heart and action, and they are only united as God's gift of grace. We can only be one-minded if we are one-minded with Him.

Hidden Manna

"To him who overcomes, I will give some of the hidden manna." Rev. 2:17

To a certain degree, we are all born spiritually blind or impaired, although we all have a God-consciousness that is inbred into our being created in the image of God. We can see, but it is like in a mirror darkly. God makes his spiritual truth and existence obvious to all through creation, yet in a very limited sense (Rom. 1). We can see that there is a God, and yet not really know him. In order to know God, we must not only be able to see him, but to hear him.

The Holy Spirit starts drawing us to God through speaking to our hearts, convicting us of sin, and teaching us about himself, even before we are Christians. Our spiritual eyes have to be partially opened first before we can understand enough truth to know that we need a savior. When a baby is first born, though, he cannot see very clearly. Someone who is born again also has blurred eyesight. The light of God is able to come into their souls, but as if through a filter, like sunglasses, to keep their sensitive eyes from being hurt or over-exposed to the truth.

The truth of God is sometimes harsh, sometimes comforting, sometimes at the surface, and sometimes deeper than the deepest sea. God adjusts what we can see with the filter of the Spirit based upon our level of spiritual maturity, or what he feels that we are ready for in preparation for his plan for us. Sometimes the youngest babe in the Lord can be shown wonderful things, for they are like a newly transformed butterfly hatching out of their cocoon, seeing the world through new eyes.

Yet, often spiritual growth takes place only through life's experiences, with the testing of our faith. Very gradually, we are able to see and understand things in the Word that we had missed before. It isn't something that is rushed, but happens over a long period of time as we grow closer to our Maker.

Occasionally, though, the Lord allows us to go through a traumatic experience which shatters our preconceived ideas, and almost instantaneously, we have blinders taken off of our eyes, which we never knew we had. It's like the growth spurt that happens at adolescence, where a child will grow six inches in one year. The same thing happens spiritually, where we go through a growth spurt, and our spiritual pants don't fit anymore. We have to make some major adjustments to our world view, for the old clichés just don't work as well as they used to.

When we overcome the trials or growth spurts that face us, God promises to open our eyes, so that we can find the "hidden manna" that others often miss. Manna is out in the open, for everyone to find. The hidden manna is like a secret treasure, stored in the heart of God, and revealed only to those whose eyes have been opened by their faithfulness, brokenness, and love for their Lord. It isn't something that can be found through human effort. It is a gift of God's grace, reserved for only a few.

The Fruit of Unfailing Love

"Sow for yourselves righteousness, reap the fruit of unfailing love, and break up your unplowed ground; for it is time to seek the Lord, until he comes and showers righteousness on you." Hosea 10:12

Righteousness is something that many people have trouble relating to. It seems too good, too divine, as if it can only be appreciated from a distance. We are glad that God is righteous, because we want him to be a just, holy God, but we just brush it off as something that is impossible for us, so why even try? Yet, we all long for greater love. We aren't satisfied with just the fleeting infatuation, or the puppy love that is playfully fun. We want the real thing—unconditional, unwavering, unselfish love.

Ironically, though, the only way that we can get what we really want is through what we don't really want. The only way to true love is through a righteous life. The Bible says, "Sow for yourselves righteousness, reap the fruit of unfailing love." The word "righteousness" means purity; unadulterated commitment and focus on being right with God in our heart and life; faithfulness to the priority of putting Christ first.

We cannot attain righteousness through our own human effort, and we will never be perfect in this life. Yet, we can continually sow the seed of righteousness in our hearts through the study and obedience of his Word and the following of his perfect example. We can submit to the convicting power of the Holy Spirit as He seeks to bring us more in line with his own divine nature, and we can encourage others to live in the light of his holiness as well. As we "sow righteousness" in our own lives and the lives of others, the Lord is the one who brings forth the harvest. He produces the "fruit of unfailing love".

In other words, he produces his own nature through us, which is both righteous and loving. The one part of God is never separate from the other, and it can never be separated within us. We cannot choose or accept the loving part of God, but reject his righteousness. If we refuse his holy standard for our lives, we will never experience his unfailing love. The two are married together in perfect harmony.

When we accept Christ into our hearts we have to accept who he is, not who we want him to be. In order to do this, we have to be willing to "break up your unplowed ground". Ground that has not been plowed is hardened and dried by the sun, filled with weeds, and unreceptive to growing anything. If we have responded to God's love, but rejected his holiness, we have only allowed the seeds of his word to stay on the surface of our souls. Unfailing love can only grow when nurtured in a softened, receptive, teachable heart. God's righteousness is the plow which digs deeply into our very being, turning over and breaking up the hardened clods of selfishness which keep us from being able to either love or to be receptive to it. When our souls are soft, God rains his righteousness upon us, and love grows.

The Lord's Repayment Plan

"I will repay you for the years the locusts have eaten." Joel 2:25

At times, Israel is judged because of great idolatry, rebellious disobedience, or extreme wickedness. When we read such judgment, our response is often, "How could they be so stupid? It would be foolish to stretch God's patience in that way. Why didn't God just wipe them out and start over?" Well, God almost did wipe them out, but it wasn't for any of the extreme sins that are listed above. It was for self-indulgence. The whole nation had become lulled to sleep spiritually speaking, where they took God's blessings for granted, and wandered away from God in a daze of drunkenness and lazy laxness (Joel 1:5). They had it too good, and they forgot that they needed God.

So God sent a terrible plague of locusts which wiped out their crops and vineyards, and then sent a drought which dried up their springs and streams. They are told to repent of their "relaxed religion" and to return to the Lord (Joel 1:13). If their repentance is genuine, God promises to "repay you for the years the locusts have eaten".

In other words, God will give back the blessings that he took away in punishment for their self-centered, pleasure seeking sins. Yet, God's repayment plan isn't just a matter of restoring what they lost. Just as in the story of Job, when God repays what has been lost, he multiplies the blessings with interest. He always gives back more than he takes away.

First, there is the temporal blessing: "You will have plenty to eat, until you are full" (Joel 2:26). Yet, it doesn't stop there. The greatest blessing is spiritual. The Lord promises, "I will pour out my Spirit on all people. Your sons and daughters will prophesy, your old men will dream dreams, your young men will see visions…I will show wonders in the heavens and on the earth…and everyone who calls on the name of the Lord will be saved" (Joel 2:28-32). That's right. The powerful enablement of the Spirit at Pentecost was a fulfillment of this prophecy, which was part of God's repayment plan for taking away all that was lost "for the years that the locusts have eaten".

We might be happy if God would just give us back what he took away in his anger. God, however, wants to give us so much more. Our focus is usually just on the physical realm, and we feel a great sense of loss when we lose something we dearly value. The Lord, though, sometimes takes away our physical possessions in order to get our eyes off of ourselves and refocused on him. When that happens, he not only will trust us with "things" again, he will fill us with himself to the point that our whole world is turned upside down, and everyone around us is impacted for him. He transforms a tragedy into a transcendent overflowing of his miraculous power and presence. All we want is a Xerox copy of what we used to have, and he gives us a multimedia, interactive, Power-point presentation of the Dynamic-Divine exploding in majestic splendor like fireworks of the soul.

A Brood of Vipers

"You brood of vipers! Who warned you to flee from the coming wrath? Produce fruit in keeping with repentance." Matt. 3:7-8

Sometimes we tend to make excuses for the Pharisees and Sadducees of Christ's day. Yes, we argue, they may have been hypocritical, but who isn't? Yes, they took a stand against Jesus and had him crucified, but considering how much he attacked them and their established religion, who can blame them? Was Jesus too hard on these priests, or did he know something that we don't?

First, we need to understand that the serpent in scripture is a symbol for the Devil. He tempted Adam and Eve in the garden of Eden, and he will be thrown into hell at the last judgment. Yet, now he is creating havoc by producing others just like himself. The word "brood" means offspring that have been bred and trained for a special purpose. These are "thoroughbreds" of Satan, who were prepared and placed in Jerusalem for this very purpose—to kill the Christ.

Vipers are a very poisonous snake, and they strike quickly at anyone who comes near them. They are very protective of what they have, and their first response is to attack instead of to run. The only other reason they use their venom is to conquer their prey so that they can eat them. The religious leaders of Christ's day were the same way. They were super protective of their positions of power because as Satan's special ambassadors, they would have had to fight their way to the top. The battalion of the Devil is very competitive, and they would stop at nothing to not only keep their power, but to attain more.

Human sacrifice is one of the main ways that Satan worshippers gain their power, so how much more would they gain if they killed God's only son? Jesus makes it very clear that these men were not just ignorant, disillusioned holy men. He says to the Pharisees and Sadducees, "You belong to your father, the Devil, and you want to carry out your father's desire" (John 8:44). They merely used the disguise of religion to carry out their evil schemes. They took advantage of people's religious training to control them, to teach them false doctrine, and to lead them astray by their hypocritical example.

Unfortunately, this same kind of viper can be found in many of our pulpits, seminaries, and Christian organizations, for they have infiltrated the church with the purpose of destroying it from within. They wear Christian masks, but bite with such ferocious venom that there is no confusing who their real father is. They are a wicked brood indeed, but too often, they have gained so much power before they show their fangs, that the ones who end up leaving are the ones they have wounded, instead of the vipers themselves. Beware the poison from the ones who try to control us through their sly "religious" tongues, at the same time they are wrapping their coils around our necks.

Believer's Baptism

"As soon as Jesus was baptized, he went up out of the water. At that moment heaven was opened."
Matt. 3:16

When Joshua and the Israelites stood at the threshold of entering the Promised Land, they had a daunting task. They had to cross the Jordan River. The children of Israel had learned through forty years of wandering in the wilderness that God could be relied upon, and that all they needed to do was to trust and obey. So, when Joshua told them that they needed to be consecrated before entering the land of Canaan, they followed the ark of the Covenant into the Jordan River, and they were baptized into a consecrated faith that was ready to follow God wherever he led, doing whatever he asked. Joshua had promised that "the Lord will do amazing things among you", and they were ready to be a part of the amazing (Josh. 3:5).

When Elijah was ready to be taken up into heaven on a fiery chariot, he also went to the Jordan River. He took his cloak and struck the river, and the waters parted, just as they had for Joshua and the Israelites. This time Elijah and Elisha walked through on dry ground, and Elisha was baptized into his commission of being a prophet by being given a double portion of the Spirit (2 Kings 2:8-14). He was now ready to also see the amazing things that God was going to do through him.

When Jesus came to the Jordan River to be baptized, then, it was not the baptism of repentance. It was the baptism of being consecrated and commissioned to do wondrous things in the name of the Father. It was the baptism of the prophet, priest, and king, ready to cross the river into the Promised Land, to claim the inheritance for the Lord. It was a consecration to do battle in a spiritual warfare, like Joshua and his army, fighting to conquer the strongholds of the Devil. It was the baptism of the Spirit, like Elisha, to be empowered to perform miracles and to proclaim the Word of God. It was a baptism of fire, a seal upon his soul, that he was God's chosen one to fulfill his purpose for mankind. And God shouted from heaven with his thunderous voice, "This is my beloved son, in whom I am well pleased" (Matt. 3:17).

I believe that believer's baptism today means the same thing to the Father. It is not just John's baptism, a baptism of repentance, although this is part of it. It is also something far more significant. It is not just a matter of saying I'm sorry for what I did in the past. It is a baptism of consecration and commission for service. It is enlisting into God's army, and reporting for duty. It is crossing the River Jordan spiritually speaking, with a readiness to trust God to knock down the walls of Jericho. It is being anointed and empowered by the Holy Spirit to be his prophet, his warrior, and his priest, and waiting with great expectation for the amazing things that the Lord wants to do through us. It is boldly saying, "I am on the Lord's side. Who will follow?"

Rest for your Souls

"Come to me, all you who are weary and burdened, and I will give you rest."
Matt. 11:28

We live in a very hectic, stressful world. It is so easy to get over-burdened with responsibilities and activities, that our heads are left spinning. We have our jobs, our families, our church programs, and our friends, and we are endlessly trying to juggle them all, without dropping any of the balls. We have the pressure of bills, kids driving us crazy, spouses that don't understand, bosses that are insensitive monsters expecting us to be machines, and the stress that we feel even from God to be better than what we think we can. We feel like running away to the Bahamas, hiding our head in the sand like an ostrich, and pretending like the real world isn't there any more. Then, we come across a verse in Matthew, which says, "Come to me, all you who are weary and burdened, and I will give you rest." "Wow! I want that," we think. "How do I get it? Can I buy it on EBay?"

First, in order to get this rest, we must understand that we can only get it by coming to Jesus, and this must be done with the faith of a little child (Mark 10:14-16). This is extremely hard for adults, especially those who lead the kind of complex life that is described above. Very busy, type-A, multi-taskers are usually not known for their childlikeness. They usually have too much ability and self-confidence to even want to slow down, for they thrive on the adrenaline rush that comes from being "in great demand". They love the sense of power that juggling life can bring, and their complaining is often nothing more than a prideful way of getting other people to notice how busy and competent they are. To come to Christ as a meek child, then, isn't really something that they want. They would rather come to the Lord as a proven warrior, with medals of honor, boasting to the Lord, "Where do you want me? I'm the one you were looking for".

God cannot give rest to this kind of person. They don't see the need. Yet, if they humble themselves, and come to Jesus as a child, they will find that the kind of rest that he offers is not from the trials of this life anyway. It is rest from the burden of sin. In fact, the stress of life may even get more hectic after coming to Jesus than before, for the Devil loves to make havoc of our servanthood to God.

On the other hand, Jesus does promise to take the load of sin from our hearts and minds, so that the weight of our sinful conscience will no longer crush our souls. God's rest is another way of saying peace with him, and peace with ourselves. Then, with this kind of peace, we can have greater clarity of thought to make wise decisions, and to know what God's will is for our lives. This, in turn, can help us to eliminate some of the over-busyness which is causing so much stress in our physical lives, so that our spiritual rest can actually help to bring physical and emotional rest, as well.

Fishing for Blowfish and Bottom-feeders

"Come, follow me," Jesus said, "and I will make you fishers of men." Mark 1:17

When Jesus first called his disciples, he didn't just ask for their adoration or worship. He gave them a mission-- "I will make you fishers of men". Christ's intention was never to create a monastery of pious priests in prayerful meditation. He wanted disciples who were willing to follow him out into the real world, reaching out to the disenfranchised misfits of society, as well as to the so-called normal people of their communities.

When a fisherman throws his nets out, there are no signs on the nets saying, for tasty fish only. He may try to specialize in the kind of fish that he catches by controlling where he fishes, the kind of bait that he uses, and how deep he is willing to probe, but he still ends up catching a wide variety of specimens. A preacher also may try to reach only a certain clientele, for he feels more comfortable around people who are like himself. Yet, he still gets the "angelfish", who are heavenly mild, the "blowfish", who are full of hot air, the "sharks", who go for the blood, and the "bottom-feeders", who always sink to the lowest plain, and feed on the leftovers and waste of others.

People are people, and it isn't up to us to choose which kind deserves to come to Jesus. None of us deserves the Lord. When fishermen fish, they go after the ones that they think are the most marketable. When we are fishers of men, however, we should be throwing our nets out to everyone, and not just the chosen few. We need to remember that we are not catching "fish" for ourselves. God's fish market includes everything from gold fish to whales, from sunfish to sushi, from eels to octopus. He is not a respecter of persons or "fish", and he doesn't want us to be either.

When Jesus called his disciples, he made it clear that to follow him meant to be fishers of men. There are no spectators watching from the wharf. If we want to follow Christ, we need to be willing to roll up our sleeves, get out into the boat, get seasick from the rough waves, and pull in whatever catch the Lord brings our way. When Jesus says "I will make you fishers of men", the word "make" means "band together with you as". He is not asking us to do something on our own. He wants fishing partners. He wants to unite together with us in the endeavor of bringing people to God. He will give us the strength that we need to pull the nets in. He will give us the wisdom of where to fish, how to fish, and what to do with the fish when we catch them.

He may ask us to do things at times which make no sense to us, like pull in your nets and throw them on the other side of the boat, but the harvest is always there if we obey him. We don't have to convince the fish to jump into our boats by using our own wisdom, elaborate worship services, or special programs. The Holy Spirit lures people in through their conscience, baits them with the Word, and we just pull them in. Jesus gets the job of cleaning them.

Teaching with Authority

"The people were amazed at his teaching, because he taught them as one who had authority."
Mark 1:22

Jesus was not the first one to teach with authority. Moses and the prophets also spoke with authority, but there had not been any prophets in Israel for more than three-hundred years. All the people had now were religious leaders who gave their own opinions about interpretations of the law, and who relied more on their traditions than the Word of God itself. They were dogmatic, but only about their legalistic religious practices, which they hypocritically didn't even keep themselves. When Jesus came along, then, and started preaching not only the Word of the Old Testament, but new teachings from God, as if he was God himself, people were amazed.

Imagine for a moment someone doing this today—claiming to be God, and speaking as if he knew all truth. Our response would probably be that he is either an anti-Christ, on drugs, or insane. We might laugh at him, mock him, or throw some change at him in sympathy. Yet, these people were not just amused. They were amazed. There was something about the teachings of Christ that went beyond the bizarre. There was power in his words. They spoke to people's hearts and transformed lives. They healed the broken-hearted and set the captives free. Jesus was not just healing people's bodies. He was healing their souls.

The Pharisees were suspicious of Christ because his words didn't get past their skeptical minds. They had barriers built up around their spirits that were bigger than the walls of Jericho. They weren't interested in changing or being transformed. They liked the status quo because they were in charge. Jesus' words were powerful, but they would not force their way through a stubborn heart.

People are the same today. When we try to share the gospel with others, some are receptive, and they hear the words as if they are from God himself. It's like we aren't really there. They are listening to God, and he heals their hearts. When someone is hardened, though, they accuse us of being arrogant and self-righteous, as if we are better than others. How dare we think that we can speak on God's behalf? How can we be sure what truth is, or that the Bible is true? How do we know that God is speaking to us?

We can't let ourselves be intimidated by such attacks. They are just like the Pharisees. They are suspicious of what they are hearing because it doesn't go past their minds to their hearts. If it doesn't make sense to them, it is not true. We shouldn't waste our time trying to "cast our pearls before swine" (Matt. 7:6). We need to teach and preach with the authority of God himself, for he has given us the message. It's his truth, not ours. We don't have to be embarrassed of the light because the light is not ours. We can speak with the authority of a prophet, as God speaks through us, and leave the results and reactions up to him.

Out of Alignment

"These people honor me with their lips, but their hearts are far from me."
Mark 7:6

When I drive my car, the steering wheel shakes, and the car rattles. I'm trying to drive one particular direction, but the wheels are not all in agreement with where they are supposed to go. Somehow, they have been knocked out of alignment. For whatever reason, they are out of whack, and unless I get them fixed soon, my tires will wear unevenly and quickly, and I will need to purchase four new ones all at once.

The same thing happens in our spiritual lives. Christ described the problem this way: "These people honor me with their lips, but their hearts are far from me." In other words, what they say they believe, and what they really believe in their hearts, are two separate things. They are spiritually out of alignment.

There are a number of reasons why this might happen. Perhaps they have just gone over too many bumps in the road of life, and they are just out of balance. They are so used to being in a rut, that they don't know how to drive on the smooth highway. Their spiritual tires still drive crooked, as if that is the normal way. The Bible calls this kind of spiritual alignment problem as hypocrisy. It isn't just a mechanical problem or one that can be fixed by just adjusting or tightening a few screws in our life. It isn't a matter of just making the highway smoother either, so that there won't be any more bumps to bring attention to our lack of alignment. Spiritual misalignment is an engine problem that gets right to the core. It's not as easy as fixing a car or replacing a few tires. The engine has been disconnected from the battery. The heart has been separated from its power source, the Holy Spirit. So, the lips are saying they love the Lord, but the heart is a stubborn rebel that doesn't want anything to do with the Lordship of Christ.

Sometimes, though, the battery cables are connected, but they are so loose that sometimes there is a connection, and sometimes there isn't. Sometimes we get energized by the Spirit, and sometimes we feel nothing at all. We fluctuate between being a high-powered race car to a junk heap abandoned by the roadside. Something is terribly out of sync, and the rattles and shakes of our misalignment are driving us crazy. We need the Master Mechanic, the Lord himself, to do an overhaul. We need a "revival tune-up" really bad, but we are afraid that it might cost too much. The Master Mechanic may ask us to give up some of the sinful gunk that is clogging up our spiritual carburetors, or to use more "Word-filters" to separate the truth from the polluted air of the world.

We need to try some fuel-injected prayer power, instead of just the usual band-aid on the gas tank. A Spirit-led prayer of humility will give us a lot better mileage and a much smoother ride than trying to drag-race while stuck in reverse.

The Personal Trainer

"Who, then, is the man that fears the Lord? He will instruct him in the way chosen for him." Psa. 25:12

Professional athletes, movie stars, and the rich and famous often have the luxury of having a personal trainer. This person's job is to tailor a training and nutrition program that is uniquely suited for the client's natural build, metabolism, conditioning, and special purpose for training. If the goal is to look sleek and toned, then there is one type of training. If the goal is to look strong and bulky, then there is another kind of emphasis. If the desire is to gain or lose weight, then diet plays more of a role. Whatever the purpose, the trainer's job is to help the client reach their potential, with the maximum benefit in the least amount of time possible.

According to the Bible, we have our own personal trainer as well. His name is the Lord. His emphasis, though, is not on our physical well-being, as much as our spiritual strength and growth, so that we can be better suited to serve his purposes. If we fear him, he has promised to give us the personal training that we need. The word "fear" in this context means respect, or in awe of. If we have this kind of respect and awe, we are teachable and submissive to whatever God asks us to do. He designs a training program for us which is uniquely suited for our maturity level and purpose, and we are taught by him personally.

The word "instruct" in this promise means to "train, direct, and fill". He trains us by having us exercise our faith, stretch our limits, so we have to trust him, and power-lift the burdens that he asks us to bear, with the power of the Holy Spirit. As we grow in our spiritual character, he directs us, one step at a time, into his perfect plan for our lives. As we face different trials along the way, he fills us with himself, empowering us to meet every challenge.

The word "instruct" actually implies "filling to overflowing". God is the living water, and he overflows his own life and character into us and through us, so that we, in turn, can instruct or train others. Whereas, the rich may hire a trainer to get the desired results in a hurry, the Lord takes his time. We may be in a hurry, but he has his own timetable. If a body-builder tries to rush his workouts, or tries to lift too much too fast, he will injure himself, and could set himself back in his training, instead of improving like he desires. The same thing is true spiritually speaking. We can't rush the Lord's schedule for our progress. He knows when we are ready for more stress to be applied, or more strength to be demanded. If we try to push our own agenda and timetable, we can not only hurt ourselves, but others around us with our bull-headedness.

We need to be patient and obedient, and to show our trainer the respect that he deserves. If we do, he has promised to train our minds, souls, and spirits into a trinity of unified purpose, totally prepared for whatever he asks us to do.

The Lord's Secrets

"The Lord confides in those who fear him; he makes his covenant known to them."
Psa. 25:14

One of the best things about having a best friend is that we can tell them anything and everything, and they will still be our friend. They won't spread rumors, or use our secrets to hurt us. They can be trusted with our deepest fears and failures, and they can trust us in return. It is unconditional love at its finest, for a best friend will love us no matter what. At least that's the way it's supposed to work. Unfortunately, there are limits to our trust and flexibility. We lose faith in people sometimes because they have gone too far, and even one bad action or cruel word can end a relationship.

God, on the other hand, is a different kind of friend. His love really is unconditional, and his commitment to us has no limits. So, when the Bible says that "the Lord confides in those who fear him", it is the Lord sharing his deepest secrets with us because he considers us as his friends, not just his servants (John 15:15). He wants us to know him intimately, not just as casual acquaintances. He's not interested in a one-night stand. He's looking for a committed relationship. He wants to be deep and personal with us, and to share things with us that he hasn't made known to others.

The Bible says that he "makes his covenant known" to those who fear him. The word "covenant" means "to cut", which comes from the biblical mandate to cut an animal in two, and then to have both parties making the contract pass between the two halves, signifying that even worse should happen to the one who breaks this compact. When God made a covenant with man, then, he was literally putting His life on the line for his promises. He was the lamb that was slain or cut in two as a seal of his promise that we will have eternal life if we just believe in him. He is the kind of friend who holds nothing back. His life is an open book—the Word of God.

The problem is that we often hold things back. We don't always want God to get too close. We hold him off at a distance when we want to slip into sin for a while. We like to keep secrets from him, even though we know we cannot hide from him. We also refuse to listen to what he has to tell us. We plug our spiritual ears with distractions that keep us from hearing his words to us. Here he is trying to tell his deepest secrets to us, and we are ignoring him, or talking back to him, not wanting to hear his words or thoughts.

Part of the problem is that we know if he tells us something, then we are accountable to live according to that truth. We would rather stay ignorant, so his truth doesn't bother our conscience. If we truly love the Lord, though, we should want to hear his every word. We should look forward to his intimate secrets being told to our souls, as much as if he were our dearest love whispering sweet words to our ears—because he is.

Keep your Eyes on Jesus

"My eyes are ever on the Lord, for only he will release my feet from the snare."
Psa. 25:15

It is easy to keep our eyes on the Lord if we stay close to him. Yet, if we wander away after our own sinful desires, thinking that we can keep sight of Jesus from a distance, we often find ourselves in deep trouble. There are a lot of snares out there that are left by the enemy to catch us unawares. The word "snare" means a net or trap that is hidden to catch animals or men in order to kill them or rob them. The Devil loves to set these traps because they keep us from following the Lord. We get separated from the Master, and before we know it, we can't even see him anymore. He has continued his mission, while we're stuck in a snare back in the jungle of life. We have yielded to the trap of lust, the snare of greed, or net of pride, and we are left far behind. We are stuck in the quicksand of self-centered desires, and the fog of confusion and frustration rolls in, making it almost impossible for us to see beyond our own nose. We can't even see the people around us, let alone see the Lord.

The Devil's wish is to end our lives, but the Lord is the only one who has the authority over life and death. Yet, Satan is allowed to rob us at will. He robs us of our joy, our peace, our love, and our self-respect. When we are caught in his traps, we have no way to defend ourselves. Our falling into his snares gives him permission to abuse us and take advantage of us. If we are tangled in his web of deceit and illusion, we can actually be eaten alive without even knowing that we have been trapped. The pleasure of sin acts like an anesthesia, and we are insensitive to the pain of his fangs piercing our souls. We can struggle and resist, if we sense that we have been taken prisoner by his tricks, but we do not have the strength or power to fight him off after we have fallen into his clasp. Humanly speaking, we are "dead meat". He has a noose around our necks, and the more that we struggle, the faster we suffocate.

Our only hope is in the mercy of our God. He knows our weakness and the frailty of our characters. He knows that we are no match for the wiles of the Devil, and that our fallen human natures have been cursed from the beginning of time. So, out of his grace, he reaches back to free us from the snare, and to heal us from any of the wounds that the Devil has inflicted while we were his prisoners.

Sometimes, though, healing takes time, because he doesn't want us to take him for granted. He wants us to understand the pain that our wandering causes him and others around us. As our Father, he continually has to remind us to keep our eyes on him and to follow in his steps. Otherwise, we may step on the land-mines of sin along the way, and be separated from him once again. He can always come to our rescue, but we need to think of all of the time and energy that has been wasted every time we have to catch up.

The Voice of Satan

"Get behind me, Satan!...You do not have in mind the things of God, but the things of men." Mark 8:33

A mother is at a playground with her children, and in spite of all the distracting noises, she hears her own child cry out in pain, "Mommy!" She knows their voices. When a birdwatcher hears a bird making a call or singing in the forest, she knows which bird it is because she knows their voices. In each one of these cases, a person is able to recognize the sounds or voices of another because they know them so well, and because they have decided that it is important to know them even better. Their goals of being a good parent or skillful birdwatcher are dependent upon being able to recognize the distinctiveness of each person or thing that they are in love with, and their inner heart's ear is in tune with the voices they hear.

When Jesus compares his disciples to sheep, then, he says that they will follow him because they will know his voice when he calls them (John 10:4). This also requires familiarity and love for the shepherd. The sheep have to learn to recognize his voice. It doesn't come naturally. There are so many other distracting sounds in this world, it is hard at first to distinguish his distinct voice. Yet, with time and maturity, the master's voice is clearly recognizable, and the sheep can tell even by the changes in how the shepherd speaks to them that he is either angry or pleased with what he sees.

The sheep can also recognize the sounds of the wolves in hiding around them. They know when they are in danger, and the shepherd does everything he can to comfort them. When Jesus was teaching his disciples, he was telling them about his coming death. Peter takes Jesus aside and rebukes him for saying such things. Jesus, in turn, rebukes Peter by saying, "Get behind me, Satan!" Jesus was not accusing Peter of being the anti-Christ or the Devil himself. Yet, he could recognize that Satan was speaking through Peter, because he knew his voice. That doesn't mean that Peter's physical voice changed, but his inner voice, attitude, or philosophy was obviously the Devil's.

As we mature in the Lord, we should also be able to recognize the Devil's voice. Jesus tells us what this means when he tells Peter, "You do not have in mind the things of God, but the things of men". The more that we understand the things of God, his voice and his truth, the more that we will be able to recognize Satan's counterfeit or lies. Satan will try to lead us astray by even trying to disguise his voice, so he sounds like an angel of light and goodness, but he always keeps his "down under" accent which gives him away. There is always something dark and devious about what the Devil says, even if it is just a slight twisting of the gospel truth. A wolf in sheep's clothing still sounds like a wolf. The more we recognize the voice of God, the more we'll know the Devil's too. We just need to make sure we are following the right one.

My God, My God, Why?

"My God, my God, why have you forsaken me?" Mark 15:34

I can't imagine God the Father ever forsaking Jesus. Jesus hadn't done anything wrong. He was completely innocent, and he had done everything that his Father had asked him to do. If anything, at the cross, Jesus was closer to the Father than ever before because he had been obedient unto death. What, then, is meant by this mysterious verse? One possible explanation is in the term that he uses for God. Jesus cries out, "Eloi, Eloi, lama sabachthani." The word "Eloi" or "Eli" means the strength and power of God. All of the names of God are more than just names. They are representations of his character. When Jesus cries out, then, he may not be calling out to God at all, or questioning why his Father left him. He may be just recognizing that his power and strength has left him.

This happened before, too, when he performed miracles. Remember when a woman who had been bleeding for years came up and touched Jesus when he wasn't looking? His response was, "Who touched me?", for he realized that power had gone out of him (Mark 5:30). Whenever Jesus performed a miracle, then, he was conscious of the fact the power had gone out from him—that the strength of God was released from his body. This can explain why he often left the disciples to go off by himself to pray. He was physically and spiritually drained.

Then, on the cross, the greatest miracle of all was taking place. He was taking upon himself the sin of the world and its curse, and he was having victory that would span for eternity. No wonder he was feeling the power and strength leaving him. It wasn't a matter of God abandoning him. It was evidence that this God-man, God-incarnate, was poured out wine, completely spent on redemptively saving the world and conquering Satan. He had fulfilled his purpose for coming to the world, and he was ready to give up his spirit. It was finished.

Sometimes it is possible for us to feel just a slight trace of what he must have felt. At times, when we have poured out ourselves for the sakes of others and the cause of Christ, we too can feel drained physically and spiritually. We know that God has not forsaken us, for we have done his will. Yet, we can feel empty, and the peace and joy of the Lord can seem far away. Not only are we on empty, we feel burdened by the weight of the sins of those we have been trying to help. We know that only God can truly bear the burden of their sins, but as their earthly shepherds, we may be asked to carry the lost or wounded sheep on our shoulders for a while. It is during these times that we too may cry out, "Eloi, Eloi, why have you forsaken me?", but we are not questioning God's faithfulness. God has promised to never leave us or forsake us. Yet, his strength and power may have been poured out through us to the point that we feel dry and ready for a "fill-up". Then we cry, "Revive us again."

Prove your Pain

"Produce fruit in keeping with repentance." Luke 3:8

When Jesus faced Peter after Peter's denial, he asked him, "Do you love me?" Peter's response was, "Of course I love you". Then Jesus said, "Feed my sheep". In other words, Jesus wanted proof of Peter's love. Words were not enough. He wanted action.

John the baptizer gave the same message. The Pharisees and Sadducees were coming out to the River Jordan to watch John baptize the people, pretending to be sincere themselves. The people were coming to confess their sins and to be forgiven. Baptism was the outward sign of their renewed commitment to obey God and the cleansing that they had received from him. John knew that the religious leaders were phonies. He knew that they were only there for the show, to impress people, and to check up on what was happening. They were imposters and intimidators, and John could see right through them. So, he boldly cries out, "You brood of vipers. Who warned you to flee from the coming wrath?" He knew that they were really evil, and that they had no intention of humbling themselves before God. So he challenges them—"Produce fruit in keeping with repentance".

So, once again we have the sentiment of Christ. If we really love God, then we shouldn't just say it. We need to prove it. If we are really sorry for sinning against God, then we can't just say "oops". We need to prove that we are truly sorry. The word repentance means "pain". In other words, we feel the pain that God feels when we sin against him, so we decide to stop the pain as quickly as possible. The problem is that we don't really feel God's pain. We are calloused by our sin and insensitive to how it affects others. We don't really care because we enjoy the pleasure of our sin too much. So what if it hurts others a little bit, or even hurts ourselves. The pleasure is worth the pain. The "high" is worth the hangover.

So, when we say we are sorry, we don't really mean it. We are just trying to ease the tensions that were caused by our sin, so we can get back to normal. Then when we are feeling safe and comfortable, we can do it again. This isn't true repentance. The only pain that we might be feeling is the pain of getting caught. True repentance not only causes us to turn from our sins, so that we don't do them again, but it produces "fruit in keeping with repentance". This means that there needs to be a definite movement in a positive direction, and not just a turning away from the negative.

For example, if we have had a problem with lying, then we need to get involved sharing the truth with others. If we have had a problem with stealing, then we need to be generously giving to others. If we have been self-centered, then we need to start forgetting about our own desires, and reach out to meet the needs of others. We need to prove our pain with the positive.

He Must Increase

"He must increase; but I must decrease." John 3:30

When John the baptizer saw Jesus, he proclaimed, "Look, the Lamb of God, who takes away the sin of the world!" (John 1:29). This is the one that he had been telling everyone about. The Messiah was finally here—the one that he came to prepare the way for. His mission in life, even from birth, was to prepare people for this moment. So, how does he respond to this moment of a lifetime? He baptizes Jesus, but only reluctantly, and then he goes on his way, as if nothing had happened.

In other words, he just kept on doing what he had been doing, baptizing people and calling them to repentance to get ready for the coming of the Lord. Wait a minute. Didn't he just tell people, "Here he is. This is the One. Here is the savior of the world." Why, then, is he acting this way? Wouldn't it make more sense if he stopped what he was doing, and became a disciple of Christ? Someone who builds the foundation of a house doesn't just keep working on the foundation after the house is already built. His job is done. He needs to shift gears. He needs to take on a new purpose, set new goals, and keep growing. He needs to be willing to be flexible with the changing needs, and not just be stuck in the rut of what worked in the past. He needs to seek new direction from God, and not just live in the glory of the past.

It took John a while to adjust to the fulfillment of his own prophecies. Even his disciples were confused by the dilemma. They wanted John to stop Jesus and his disciples from baptizing, as if they were somehow a threat to John's status as the resident holy man. Instead of being glad that the Messiah was finally here, John's disciples were trying to subdue Jesus so their own pop-hero could be glorified. Although John didn't quite get it right at first, and continued to go straight ahead without stopping, even though the sign clearly said, "Yield the Right of Way", he finally got the point—"He must increase, but I must decrease." This realization must have been similar to David's, when God told him he could do all of the preparations for the temple, but he had to let his son build it. That is a very humbling insight. "I did all of the dirty work, and someone else gets to reap the rewards. I was getting all of the attention, but now I'm a "has been". I had all these big dreams, but now that I have reached my goals, there is a huge letdown. Now what do I do?"

John humbly admitted that this is the way things were suppose to be, but seemed to lose his effectiveness in his ministry when his purpose had been fulfilled. He probably would have joined Jesus eventually, instead of continuing to do his own thing, but he lost his head before he had a chance to change course.

We, too, need to be open to God's changing our course, instead of continuing to plod along on the old king's highway. We don't want to miss seeing Jesus in the present because we are so busy looking for him in the past.

Everlasting Fruit

"I chose you and appointed you to go and bear fruit—fruit that will last."
John 15:16

There is a big push in a lot of evangelical churches today to lead people to Christ. Many of them even have "altar calls" at the end of their services to give people the opportunity to make a decision for the Lord. This trend, however, is not biblical. The purpose of the church was never to bring strangers into the assembly of believers so they could have a chance to hear the gospel. The purpose of church from the very beginning was to equip the believers so that they could go out into the world to lead others to Christ, not for them to sit idly by while the "professional believers" did the work for them.

There is absolutely no reason why it has to be the pastor of a church who leads people to the Lord, and yet in most churches, they are the only ones who even try. Yet, even the pastors are often amiss in their responsibility, for most of them rely completely upon their sermons to do the job for them, with very few ever leading an individual to the Lord outside of the church. The Bible says that the purpose of the church is "to prepare God's people for works of service, so that the body of Christ may be built up until we all reach unity in the faith and in the knowledge of the Son of God and become mature, attaining to the whole measure of the fullness of Christ" (Eph. 4:12-13). In other words, the church is supposed to be a nurturing place for Christians, where we can be taught, trained and mentored how to be more like Christ, so that when we go out into the world, people will see Christ through us, and they will want what we have. We are supposed to come to church to get our lights lit, so we can go out into the darkness to share the light of Christ.

Many churches have this turned around and try to bring the darkness into the church instead. They try to make their services appeal to the unsaved by using worldly standards, entertaining programs, and choreographed, multimedia sermons. If this same standard was used in the early church, they would have needed to get temple prostitutes in their services, because that was the popular thing in the pagan world, and they would have justified it by saying, "It might get people to come, and then we can share the gospel". It's the old secular maxim, "the end justifies the means".

Christ never bought into this popularity game, and neither should we. The purpose of our church services should never be, "How many people can we attract to our fantastic ministry?" It should also never be to just attract non-Christians so they can come to Christ. Eternal life should be our hope and goal for many in the world, but the purpose of the church should be in producing "eternal fruit", instead of just "eternal life". It should be focused on the kind of spiritual growth that will last, not just in planting the initial seeds. We are to grow mature disciples, not just newborns.

Separation from God

"They are darkened in their understanding and separated from the life of God because of the
ignorance that is in them due to the hardening of their hearts." Eph. 4:18

The Apostle Paul gives a clear description of the pagan, unsaved world here. They do not understand spiritual truth, they are separated from the life that only God can give, and they have hardened hearts that are insensitive to the voice of the Lord. Unfortunately, Paul is giving this description because many of the Christians in Ephesus were just like this. Paul forcefully says, I insist "that you must no longer live as the Gentiles do, in the futility of their thinking…Put off your old self, which is being corrupted by its deceitful desires" (4:17,22).

In other words, they had bought into Satan's lie that living for self was better than living for God. Whenever God tried to speak to their hearts to convict them of their sins, they hardened their hearts and refused to listen. This stubbornness created a huge barrier between them and God, so that they could not experience the abundant, fulfilling life that God intended for them. God tried to explain to them how foolish they were being, but they just couldn't understand how what they were doing was that bad. After all, they were Christians, weren't they? What else mattered?

Getting to heaven or salvation, unfortunately, is the only spiritual goal that many Christians have. They don't understand that that is only the beginning, and they don't really care. If they can get to heaven, and yet live a life a pleasure here on earth, they think they have the best of both worlds. This, however, is wrong, twisted thinking that has been created by the Devil. The purpose of our salvation is not just so we can be saved from hell, but so we can be transformed into the image of Christ. We are "to be made new in the attitude of [our] minds; and to put on the new self, created to be like God in true righteousness and holiness" (4:23-24). This isn't just some pipe-dream that is going to happen in heaven someday. This is supposed to be our vision and goal for right now.

In order to do this, though, we have to "put off falsehood" (4:25). We have to stop believing the lies of the Devil, and we need to stop lying to ourselves. There are eternal consequences to our sins, and we cannot afford to just take God's grace for granted. We cannot expect to live for the Devil, but be rewarded by God. We cannot "give the Devil a foothold" by allowing any sin to just come in and take over (4:27). We need to stop being so self-centered, and start focusing instead on "what is helpful for building others up according to their needs" (4:29). We are to "be kind and compassionate to one another, forgiving each other, just as in Christ God forgave [us]" (4:32). To put it more precisely, we are to "be imitators of God" (5:1), not of the Devil.

Restoring a Treasure

"Repent, then, and turn to God, so that your sins may be wiped out, that times of refreshing may come from the Lord." Acts 3:19

When I was young and foolish, I once owned a set of pure silver, antique candle holders. Then one day, when I was desperate for money, I had a garage sale. I sold everything that wasn't nailed down. I wanted money now, and that was all that mattered. So, I put low price tags on everything. I succeeded. I sold it all, including the silver candle holders. I only got one dollar a piece for these treasures, but money in my pocket was more valuable to me than treasures on a shelf. I realize now how foolish I was, but apart from a miracle, there is no way to undo my mistake.

At Pentecost, Peter gives a powerful sermon where he basically says the same thing. He tells the Jews that they have "disowned the Holy and Righteous One" and have "killed the author of life" (Acts 3:14-15). They once owned the greatest treasure on earth, a relationship with God himself, yet they disowned him because they failed to value his true worth. They were more concerned with meeting their own immediate needs and desires than they were with eternity. Money in the pocket was more valuable to them than a treasure on the shelf. Unfortunately, that is all that God had become to them. Judaism had become a lifeless excuse to pump up their pride, but their relationship with God had died long before they crucified Christ. The nails in the cross were just nails in the coffin of a religion that was already dead.

Peter graciously says that they "acted in ignorance", but that doesn't change the fact that they have just thrown away "the author of life", and that, apart from a miracle, there is no way to get him back. Then Peter tells them that the miracle that they need has already happened. All they have to do is to "repent" and "turn to God" and their sins will be "wiped out" (Acts 3:19). Christ has already paid the price for their sins, and has bought back the relationship with the Holy God on their behalf. They just need to accept this free gift and to value it for what it is really worth. Then, God promises "times of refreshing", or restoration of the treasure that they once owned, a right relationship with God.

It is easy for us, as Christians, to fall into the same problem as the Jews. We, too, can assume that because we are part of God's family, we can take God for granted. We can lose sight of his true value, and put him on a shelf, where we only dust him off when we need him. Our immediate physical pleasures are often valued more highly than being able to hear the voice of God or to spend times of fellowship with him. In our ignorance and foolishness, we would probably sell the Lord at a garage sale if we could, just to get some change. Repent, and have your treasure restored. God specializes in antique restorations, and he has been working at restoring his relationship with us since the beginning of time.

Speaking with Boldness

"Enable your servants to speak your word with great boldness." Acts 4:29

Boldness is an exciting concept. It means to rush forward with fearless courage and confidence. We admire people with the guts to take on the challenges of life with bravery, focusing on victory as their only goal. This is why we admire sports as much as we do. We may not even know the rules of the game, but we can still admire the spirit in which it is played. To watch anyone put their all into something is inspiring. We wish that we too could be out there succeeding at that same level of excellence, but we lack the ability or the courage to even try. So, we become enthusiastic spectators instead.

The same thing is true in sharing our faith with others. The word boldness means "confidence", which means "with faith". If we are to be bold in sharing the gospel, then, we have to have the faith that God will give us the words to say, and that the results are up to him, not upon our spiritual eloquence. Some of us, though, are naturally shy, and we hesitate talking about the Lord. We need to ask God to enable us, to not only give us the words to say, but the boldness to say them.

Some Christians, however, have just the opposite problem. They are naturally bold or aggressive, and they have a tendency to blurt out the truth like a weapon, thrashing the Word about, without thought to how it might affect others. They basically hit the people over the head with it, and feel justified by the truth that they proclaim, even though they may be doing damage to the cause of Christ. There is a big difference between boldness and rashness. Both of them rush forward without fear, but rashness does not take the time to consider the consequences.

Spiritual boldness is not only fearless—it is also wise. The difference is that spiritual boldness only comes to those who are filled with the Spirit, while rashness only comes to those who are filled with themselves. The Spirit-filled person only cares about the purposes of the Spirit, and only says those things which will contribute to his goals. The rash person has his own agenda, and says only things that lift himself up, or put others down. God does not need Christians to rashly and self-righteously proclaim the gospel in such a way as to actually push people away from God, instead of drawing them closer to him.

Spiritual boldness is not spiritual "bullyness". It is possible to talk about the love of God in a hateful way, and to turn the gospel completely upside down by making it a legalistic whipping post. Some Christians teach the Word like bulls in a china shop, raging through without concern for how many things or people they shatter in the process. The Bible says that the "love of Christ constrains us" (2 Cor. 5:14). That means that we shouldn't just say or do whatever we want in the name of Christ. Everything should be tempered, even boldness, with love.

The First Christian Martyr

"While they were stoning him, Stephen prayed, 'Lord Jesus, receive my spirit."
Acts 7:59

Peter, John and the other disciples were preaching openly and performing wonderful miracles. They were called before the Sanhedrin, imprisoned, and commanded not to preach about Jesus anymore. Yet, they continued, and God used them to bring many people unto him. They were so busy leading people to the Lord, in fact, that they didn't have time to take care of the needy in their community of believers. So, they appointed seven men to serve food to the hungry, so the disciples could concentrate on preaching the Word. They were asked to "wait on" the needy. The phrase "wait on" was the verb form of the same Greek word that we get the noun, "deacon". A deacon was a waiter, or someone whose main function was to serve food. Their ministry, though, became much more involved, for they were filled with the Holy Spirit, and God used them to perform many miracles.

When the Jewish leaders became frustrated with the powerful impact that the disciples were making through the name of Christ, then, instead of attacking them, they chose the deacons as easier targets. They couldn't out-argue the wisdom of the disciples, so they decided to pick on their lowly assistants instead. What they didn't count on was the fact that it was still the same Holy Spirit who inspired them all. When they arrested Stephen, for example, this lowly deacon was able to preach one of the most powerful sermons in scripture. This infuriated the Jewish leaders partly because of the truth of his message, and partly because this uneducated man was able to show them up.

So, they laid their clothes at the feet of Saul, and began to stone him. Stephen knelt and prayed that God would forgive those who were killing him. Yet, before he died, he saw a very remarkable vision. He saw "heaven open and the Son of Man standing at the right hand of God" (Acts 7:56). First of all, this was remarkable because God allowed him to see heaven, see himself, and see Jesus. Most of us have to die before we are allowed that privilege. Yet, even more astonishing is the fact that he sees Jesus "standing" at the right hand of the Father. This is the only place in scripture where Jesus is pictured as standing at his Father's side. Every place else, he is sitting.

It is almost as if Jesus, the Almighty Son of God, the Creator of the universe, stood up in Stephen's honor, for the great humility and honor that he was giving to his Lord and Master, even unto death. He may have been a lowly deacon to the world, but in heaven, the first shall be last, and the last shall be first. He may have been waiting at tables on earth, but he is going to be honored in heaven, and the Lord is standing to welcome him home. Stephen cries out, "Lord Jesus, receive my spirit", and the Lord must have answered, "It is my privilege. I've saved a place for you."

Change of Heart

"Do not be afraid; keep on speaking, do not be silent. For I am with you."
Acts 18:9

Have you ever been so fed up and frustrated with your job that you just wanted to say, "Take this job and shove it! I don't want to do this anymore. I've had enough. I don't need this garbage. I'm moving on."? Sometimes we may actually follow through with these feelings and quit our jobs. Sometimes, though, we have a change of heart, and we decide to stick it out. Something happens which changes our minds, or we weigh out the consequences, and decide it just isn't worth changing right now. Maybe later.

This same thing happens in Christian ministry. One of the most fulfilling things in the world is helping people to grow in their faith and spiritual wisdom. Yet, it is also the most frustrating. More than half of all pastors who said that they felt the call to the ministry when they left seminary, ended up leaving the ministry for good in the first five years of their pastorate. It's just plain too hard dealing with sinful people all the time.

The pastor begins with all of these dreams and visions of being used by God to change lives, and then he gets put into a church with a bunch of "morons" who don't want to change, who complain about everything he says or does, and who do more damage to each other than he can ever undo. Being a pastor is like being a Christian who has been fed to the lions. He gets eaten up before he has a chance to say, "Hello, My name is Pastor…".

Although this sounds bizarre, the same thing happened to the Apostle Paul. He was in Corinth, working as a tentmaker during the week, and preaching in the synagogues on the Sabbath. Then, God sent him Silas and Timothy to help, so he could devote "himself exclusively to preaching, testifying to the Jews that Jesus was the Christ" (Acts 18:5). It seemed like the ideal ministry for a while, but then he started having all kinds of trouble. They were a disorderly bunch, who "opposed Paul and became abusive"(18:6). He tried to correct them by teaching sound doctrine about the proper use of spiritual gifts, but everyone seemed more concerned with getting attention than in ministering to others. This is why he wrote I Cor. 13—the love chapter--Not because the people of Corinth were good examples, but because they were basically self-centered and needed straightening out. Finally, Paul gets so frustrated with them that he quits as their pastor. He "shook out his clothes in protest and said to them, "Your blood be on your own heads! I am clear of my responsibility. From now on I will go to the Gentiles" (18:6).

Then God changed his heart. He went to the house next door and preached a powerful sermon, and many people were saved and baptized. Then the Lord spoke to Paul and said, "Do not be afraid; keep on speaking, do not be silent. For I am with you" (18:9-10). In other words, "Don't give up. You're not in this alone."

The Power over Darkness

"Many of those who believed now came and openly confessed their evil deeds."
Acts 19:18

Tonight is Halloween, one of the most evil nights of the year. Although many just use it as a time to pretend to be someone else, there is much that will happen tonight that will glorify Satan, including human sacrifices in his honor. Yet, this is nothing new. Even the Apostle Paul had to deal with the followers of Satan. When he was in Ephesus, one of the main centers of paganism in the Roman empire, he confronted a number of people who were involved with witchcraft. Paul didn't take their powers lightly, nor did he run in fear. He just kept on preaching the gospel, doing what God asked him to do.

The result, especially in this witchcraft heaven, was astounding. The Bible tells us that "all the Jews and Greeks who lived in the province of Asia heard the word of the Lord. God did extraordinary miracles through Paul" ((19:10-11). Satan was not able to stop Paul or the gospel, even in his stronghold. In fact, God blessed Paul's ministry so much here that "even handkerchiefs and aprons that had touched him were taken to the sick, and their illnesses were cured and the evil spirits left them" (19:12). The power of the evil spirits was nothing compared to the power of God.

Not only this, but many of Satan's strongest supporters were becoming Christians. The Bible tells us that "the name of the Lord Jesus was held in high honor. Many of those who believed now came and openly confessed their evil deeds. A number who had practiced sorcery brought their (magic) scrolls together and burned them publicly...In this way the word of the Lord spread widely and grew in power" (19:17-20).

Many churches today think that they have to offer fun alternatives to the Halloween parties, so they dress in costumes of good people, instead of the wicked. Yet, aren't we still playing their game? Why should we celebrate the Devil's holiday at all? Why don't we provide the same alternative that Paul offered—the gospel? Why don't we have a revival service or a Christian concert on Halloween instead of yielding to pagan traditions? Paul didn't try to play the game of the sorcerers in order to win them to Christ. He reasoned with them from the scriptures, and the power of God and his Word were so much more powerful than what the Devil was offering, that people dropped to their knees in repentance, and turned their lives over to the Lord.

We don't have to be like the world in order to win the world for Christ. We just need to hold up his light so that others can see him clearly. God will do the rest. If nothing else, tonight needs to be a night of solemn prayer, not celebration. There are many people tonight who will be initiated into the dark side, and the stamp on their souls will be with permanent markers. Pray that they see the light before it is too late.

Keeping on Task

"I consider my life worth nothing to me, if only I may finish the race and complete the task the Lord Jesus has given me—the task of testifying to the gospel of God's grace." Acts 20:24

One of the hardest things to do is to drive a car without getting distracted. There are so many things going on along the road, and the people in the other cars are crazy at times. We can see women putting on their makeup while they drive, or holding a pet in their lap. It's tempting to talk on a cell phone while we drive, or to fiddle with the radio or CD player. Then there are the traffic jams, with bumper to bumper traffic, and the temptation to read a magazine or newspaper on the steering wheel. The passengers in the car can also grab our attention, and naughty kids in the back seat can keep our eyes focused on the rear view mirror instead of the road ahead. Many crashes occur for no other reason than having our attention drawn away from the task of just driving the car.

The same thing is true with our spiritual lives. The Lord has given us a map of directions, the Word, but we still keep getting lost because we allow ourselves to get distracted by things that seem more important to us at the time. The Lord wants us to go one way, but we decide that we know better, and choose a different route. We take detours filled with pot-holes and dead-ends. We end up making a lot of u-turns and backtracking because we didn't stay on course, and we waste a lot of time in the process. What we need to do is to come to the same place that Paul came to when he said, "I consider my life worth nothing to me, if only I may finish the race and complete the task the Lord Jesus has given me".

Nothing else should matter. Everything else and everyone else only takes on meaning in relationship to how they help to fulfill God's purpose for my life. If they don't help to move me closer to my goal, they are pulling me further away. What was Paul's goal that was more important than anything else? Being obedient to God's call. What was God's call? Testifying to the gospel of God's grace.

It wasn't to build the biggest church in the area. It wasn't to out-do all the other pastors on how many baptisms or conversions they have had this year. It wasn't anything that men use today to measure success, for Paul didn't have any personal ambitions, five-year plans, or retirement dreams. In fact, "in every city the Holy Spirit [warned Paul] that prison and hardships" were waiting for him. He knew that he would be martyred soon, but it just didn't matter to him. He lived day by day, moment by moment, testifying of God's grace in his every word and action, for he was an example of God's mercy and forgiveness in everything he did. Nothing could distract him from his task of proclaiming and demonstrating the love of God in his life, and this should be our goal as well. If we don't know how, stop and ask directions.

The Right Reputation

"Your faith is being reported all over the world." Rom. 1:8

The Roman Empire was the greatest empire that the world has ever known. The population of the empire was 85 million at the time of Caesar Augustus. Considering its time and lack of technology, it was amazing what they were able to accomplish. The Roman roads alone were a tremendous feat. The city of Rome itself was magnificent. Built upon seven hills, it had a population of more than one million people. One eighth of the city was set apart as parks or gardens, and one third of the year was designated as official holidays. They celebrated and did it royally. They had chariot races in a coliseum that held 200,000 people. That is twice the size of any football stadium that we have today.

Rome is also known for its pagan gods and goddesses. The name Rome, in fact, is named after Romulus, the son of Mars, the God of War. There were temples everywhere. This was not a friendly place for Christians to live. The spiritual warfare in this place was at its peak, with demons competing for power amongst each other, and working together against any one who dared to stand in their way. The moral corruption in Rome was so great that it ultimately led to its downfall. You can only have so much evil in a place before it begins to eat away at itself.

Within this den of wickedness, pompous pride, and pagan power, the Christian church took root. Although the believers were tormented with persecution, lured by temptations everywhere, and brainwashed by the many competing "popular religions", the Apostle Paul made an amazing statement about this unique body of believers. He said, "Your faith is being reported all over the world". Wow! What a powerful reputation. Considering the time and place that they lived, it was a miracle that they even survived at all. Satan, himself, probably had his throne at this time on one of the seven hills of Rome. It seems like with all of this opposition, the Roman church would have shriveled up and hidden in the catacombs.

Yet, opposition, though its intention is to subdue, usually produces just the opposite effect. Persecution at this time created even stronger Christians, for the testing of their faith forced them to depend more upon the Lord. Instead of defeating the Christians, then, the opposition was actually pushing them deeper into the arms of their savior. Of course, it helped to have Paul constantly remembering them in his "prayers at all times". I believe that he stood in the gap for these people, and took upon himself many of the spiritual blows that were intended for them. God, however, honored his prayers and self-sacrificial love, and even used Paul's perseverance in spite of his trials to help the Romans to grow in their faith even more.

Satan's flames are futile, for faith continues to flourish in spite of his fury.

Mutual Encouragement

"That you and I may be mutually encouraged by each other's faith." Rom. 1:12

You have been working hard all day, and you finally get home. Then, what does your spouse do but dump their own problems of the day upon you, and you just want to run away. Why are the Bahamas so far away? Why is it that everyone wants to be heard, but no one wants to take the time to listen? Or, if both people take the time to listen, it merely serves to build the flames of resentment and frustration at life, for one person's complaints merely build upon the other's.

Yet, isn't that what friends are for—being mutual dumpers and dumpees, so we can get it all off our chests. It's called therapy, and it's certainly a lot cheaper than going to a shrink. Yet, when we look at the life of Paul, we never find him just dumping on his friends. He only shares his trials as stepping stones to present his victories. "Yes, I had this problem, but you should have seen the way the Lord handled it." His sharing about his problems is never intended just to get sympathy from others. He uses it to encourage others.

That doesn't mean that he has no needs of his own. He writes the church in Rome saying that he hopes they will "be mutually encouraged by each other's faith." He needs their encouragement just as much as they need his. Yet, he doesn't get it by begging for pity. He is like Christ, in that, his main focus is to minister unto others, not to be ministered unto (Matt. 20:28). He reaches out in love first, and then his own needs are met as others respond to his love.

Paul says later on in his letter, "Let us make every effort to do what leads to peace and mutual edification" (Rom. 14:19). What we need to do is to make these two things the standard by which we gage the kinds of things we talk about with our friends. Do they lead to peace and do they edify? If we complain and cut people down all the time, that merely adds to our stress, and robs us of our peace and joy. If we dump our problems all the time, then that will leave us all in the dumps. We need to trash our "trash talking" and turn our landfills into gardens of praise.

Is it wrong to share a problem with a friend? It depends on the effect that it has on the one that you are sharing with. Are they being edified by what you share? Is it building up their faith, or making them discouraged too? Are you making them a scapegoat, where you rid yourself of your burden by making them bear it instead? If, on the other hand, the person that you are sharing with is not just a friend, but someone who is mature enough spiritually to turn your problems over to the Lord, instead of trying to bear them alone, then your problem can actually be used to strengthen the faith of both of you as you trust in the Lord together for a solution. Standing together with someone in the quicksand doesn't help anyone. Standing together on the Rock, will make you both stronger.

Hearing the Voice of God

"He who belongs to God hears what God says. The reason you do not hear is that you do not belong to God." John 8:47

Have you heard the Lord speaking to you lately? According to this verse, if you belong to God, you will hear his voice. If you haven't heard his voice, that means you don't belong to God. Yet, what exactly does this mean? Does God speak with an audible voice that we can actually hear with our ears? Although this is possible, most of the time God speaks to people through the Holy Spirit in their hearts. His Spirit communicates with our spirit at the core of our being (Rom. 8:16). If we sense this spiritual communication going on, it is evidence that we are the children of God—that we belong to him.

John 8:47, though, is not just talking about hearing God talking to us. The word "hears" in this context means "embraces". If we are genuinely in a love relationship with the Lord, we not only hear his voice, but we cheerfully embrace every word that comes from his mouth. We sincerely desire to know the mind and heart of the Lord, so we anxiously wait for even the slightest whisper from the Beloved. It is this longing to hear what the Lord says, not just the ability to hear, that sets the believer apart from the unbeliever. Even the non-Christian can hear the voice of God speaking to his conscience, trying to convict him of sin. Yet, only the true believer lovingly embraces what he hears.

Unfortunately, though, even the believer doesn't always cherish God's voice. When we are out of fellowship with him, or when we are immature, and not willing to grow, we may actually resent God speaking to us. Belonging to God, then, is not just a matter of becoming a Christian. It is a matter of Lordship. Have we really yielded our heart completely to him? Do we love the Lord our God with our whole heart, mind, and soul? If we don't, we don't really belong to the Lord. I'm not saying that we are unsaved, although this is a possibility that we need to examine. Yet, if we are still holding back part of our life from his control, we are not going to be anxious to hear his convicting voice. We may avoid listening to him at all so that we won't chance hearing what we don't want to hear.

In other words, we cut ourselves off even from the desserts of God because we are running away from the vegetables. We miss out on the chocolate because we don't like the lima beans. A wife may come to the conclusion that her husband doesn't really love her because he is constantly lusting after other women. He may be married to her, but in a very real sense, he doesn't belong to her. His heart is somewhere else. The same thing can be true of us spiritually speaking. We may be married to the Lord, in that, we have accepted Christ as our savior, but, we still have wandering eyes. Unfortunately, if our hearts don't really belong to God, he may stop trying to talk to us at all. Is he talking to us now?

The Desires of the Spirit

"Those who live in accordance with the Spirit have their minds set on what the Spirit desires."
Rom. 8:5

What do you want? What are your dreams? What are your desires?   These are all questions that we ask our friends, and that we ask ourselves. They are the focus of our attention, our energy, and our planning. Yet, how many of us really take the time to ask God, "What do you want? What is your purpose or goal for my life? What are your dreams for me?" According to the above scripture verse, "Those who live in accordance with the Spirit have their minds set on what the Spirit desires." In other words, for the Spirit-filled person, "what I want" is not important. What the Spirit wants is the key.

Yet, even knowing what I want is hard enough sometimes. How am I supposed to know what the Spirit wants? Well, the Bible helps us out. It says, "The mind controlled by the Spirit is life and peace" (vs. 6). These are his desires, and if our minds are controlled by him, then they are our desires as well.

"Wow! We think. That doesn't sound that hard. Almost everyone wants life and peace, don't they?" Yet, when we think of these terms, we are usually thinking of the physical world. Our goals and dreams are all filled with things that will bring us longer and more enjoyable lives, with plenty of stress-free, peaceful relationships besides. When the Bible uses these terms, though, it isn't talking about our bodies, our pleasures, or our friendships. God wants us to have spiritual life and peace, which only come through him.

Jesus said, "I am the way, the truth, and the life. No man comes to the Father but by me" (John 14:6). Jesus is life, and the only way to find peace with God is through him. That is not just talking about salvation. Even as Christians, Jesus is still the only way, the truth and the life, every day.

The Spirit wants us to be focused on him, not just the things we can do for him. So often we as Christians get confused between service and submission. We think that as long as we are doing a lot of good deeds for God and others, we are doing what he desires. We feel fulfilled and good about ourselves because we think our good deeds are scoring points in heaven, and making us happy too. The Bible, though, makes it very clear that good deeds by themselves mean nothing to God (Mark 12:33). What God wants, what the Spirit desires, is for us to love the Lord with our whole hearts, souls, and minds, and to love others as ourselves (Mark 12:31-32). In other words, His main desire for us is internal growth, not external achievement.

Our focus needs to be on our relationship with him, not what we can do for him. We might think, "But I don't feel happy unless I am doing something for the Lord." That's fine, as long as you realize that your happiness is not the main desire of God. He wants you to have life and peace and fulfillment, not just happiness. Don't settle for less.

Overcoming Evil

"Do not be overcome by evil, but overcome evil with good." Rom. 12:21

Do you have any enemies?   Do you know anyone who deserves hell-fire and damnation, and you wish that you had the power to send them there? Do you dream about ways to get back at someone for all of the harm that they have done, but you are too afraid that you might get caught? Believe it or not, there are many Christians who could answer "yes" to all of the above questions. So many people have been victimized by abuse today that the world is filled with rage. It is only through the grace of God that there aren't more hate-crimes, road-rage revenge, rape, murder and other violent crimes, because the world is filled with people who are so angry and hurt that all it would take is for someone to trigger their core pain, and someone is going to pay dearly for the abuse that was endured.

The question is, "What is the best way to deal with all of this anger and pain?" Satan, who is called the Serpent in scripture, wants us to react like a snake. When a snake feels threatened, it responds in one of two ways. It either strikes out against the enemy, or it runs and hides. Satan wants us to do the same thing. He wants us to either seek revenge, or to withdraw into a wounded isolation that broods in quiet depression and loneliness. Neither one of these responses, though, will help to heal any hurt. They will, in fact, only make things worse.

God is the only one who can heal our brokenness, and as our Great Physician, he prescribes one medicine to help—Do exactly the opposite of what you know that Satan wants you to do. That is a difficult pill to swallow, for Satan usually disguises his desires in the form of our own human desires, or even as justice or righteous indignation. We feel that we have the right to feel or respond certain ways because we have been hurt so much. God does not want us to just be in denial and pretend that the abuse never happened. He wants us to be healed. He knows that if we continue to harbor hateful thoughts against our abusers, then they in a very real sense, are continuing to abuse us through our memories. Our hate doesn't help to heal the hurt, it merely prolongs the pain.

So, if God's medicine is to do the opposite of what Satan wants us to do, that means to not be like the snake. Instead of striking back, seeking to inflict pain upon the abuser, we need to pay back evil with good. The Bible says, "If your enemy is hungry, feed him" (Rom. 12:20). You say that you can't do that, that it also would increase your pain. Alright. God understands. If the first pill is too difficult to swallow right now, at least try the second one—don't run away to hide. Instead, reach out to others in loving ways. Continue to be creative and productive, instead of dysfunctionally becoming a basket case. If you shrivel up in a cave of self-pity, you are admitting defeat. Overcome evil with good.

Where is the Wise Man?

"Where is the wise man? Where is the scholar?
Where is the philosopher of this age?" I Cor. 1:20

Have you noticed how our society tends to "dumb down"? In our schools, our media, and even in our Bible paraphrases, there seems to be an effort to bring the truth down to the people's level, rather than inspiring the public to reach to a higher plane. The only challenges we want are in extreme sports, video games and sexual conquests. Everything else we want to come easy. Although this lifestyle may be lots of fun, it is very shallow, and it discourages those who seek to look deeper. It rewards those who entertain us with fame, admiration, and large salaries. At the same time, it shoves the true scholars, philosophers, and wise men further and further into isolation and oblivion by starving them to death and ridiculing them beyond measure, for they are considered misfits and outcasts. They are either forced to compromise their principles, thwart their creativity and individuality, or dumb down their intellect just to make a living and be accepted by the world.

It is a real shame that the true geniuses of every generation tend to be subdued and persecuted by society, while those who are willing to play the game of seeking the praise of men are often rewarded. It is too bad that there are not more Christians like the Apostle Paul, who could reason from the scriptures, and stand toe-to-toe with the philosophers and scholars of his age. The world needs more Francis Schaefer's and fewer Jerry Springer's. We need more men and women who are willing and able to be critical thinkers, instead of those who are satisfied with just the popular or spiritual "baby food" that we are often fed.

That doesn't mean that the gospel of truth is only for the intelligent or independently-minded. We must all accept Christ with the faith of a little child. Yet, we shouldn't be willing to just stay child-like in our understanding. The Apostle Paul prays and asks God to fill all those in the churches with "the knowledge of his will through all spiritual wisdom and understanding" (Col. 1:9). Intelligence should never be the basis of our faith, because then it will also become the basis for our doubts. We should never, however, just dumb-down the gospel in order to make it easier for all of us to accept. The gospel is simple, but it was never intended to be easy. There is a big difference.

Jesus said that the gospel was meant to be a "stumbling block" that many people would trip-up on. Jesus didn't try to sugar-coat it, and neither did the Apostle Paul or the other writers of scripture. John, instead, promises in the book of Revelation, that he "who overcomes, [the Lord] will give some of the hidden manna" (Rev. 2:17). The thing that we need to overcome in order to receive the deeper truths of God is the attempt by the Devil to pull everything and everyone down to his level, including the Word, which is meant to lift us up.

The Power Source

"The kingdom of God is not a matter of talk but of power."   *I Cor. 4:20*

There are many different kinds of power. There is hydro-electric power, nuclear power, solar power, battery power, etc. Yet, the difference isn't so much in the electricity that is produced, as much as the source that produces it. The power source determines the quantity of power, the difficulty in capturing it for useful purposes, and its potential for harm to those who use it.

The same thing is true in the spiritual realm. There are a lot of spiritual power sources in this world, and they are very deceiving, for they often appear the same. They enable people to be able to do things which they could not do with just their human abilities. Sometimes these powers are used for obvious evil, but often they are disguised as good, so that people will be attracted to the power before they realize the negative side to it.

In Paul's time, there was a group of people in the church at Corinth who had certain powers. They had the power of persuasion, and they used it to convince the people that they should just tolerate their immorality and evil as if they didn't really matter. After all, we are all Christians, nobody's perfect, we should love one another, and we shouldn't judge one another, etc. Paul tells us that these people were so wicked that they were committing immoral acts that were even denounced by the pagans (I Cor. 5:1), yet they convinced the Christians to just look the other way.

Do we understand that this is not just the human ability to be persuasive? There is something demonic going on here. These people have the power to deceive others, making them blind to their evil. They can be full of smiles, full of laughs, and full of "the right talk", saying all the right Christian jargon, and yet be stabbing us in the back at the same time. They can be pouring poison into our water glass right before our eyes, and yet make us believe that everything is okay. Sometimes the Lord opens our eyes to see the deception before it is too late, but sometimes not. Sometimes it takes an objective person from outside to help us to realize how we are being pulled under.

Paul writes the church at Corinth that he will be coming soon to expose these liars, because he has heard of their immorality, and their ability to charm the people to silence. He tells them to have nothing to do with these people, for their Christianity is all talk, but their power comes from another source. They are supposed to excommunicate them from the church, and not associate with them at all (I Cor. 5:9-13). If they don't expel them from their fellowship, they will be destroyed by them, for they are like yeast in dough, and will affect the whole batch (I Cor. 5:5-8). We have to understand that we are not just dealing with people, but with spiritual powers that aim to destroy us. They may be dynamic people, but what is their source of power?

A Home in Heaven

"We...would prefer to be away from the body and at home with the Lord."
2 Cor. 5:8

What is our dream of heaven? Do we picture it as vacation house in the country, a mountain cabin by a lake, or a penthouse of wealthy luxury? We all have different images of our home in Paradise, from a fluffy cloud to a mansion on a street of gold. Yet, what does the Bible teach? Part of the problem is that the King James Version translated John 14:2 as, "In my Father's house are many mansions...I go there to prepare a place for you." Did Jesus really promise us a mansion in heaven? The Greek word used here doesn't mean mansion. It means a "dwelling place", and the word "place" in the verse actually means "a room" or a smaller part of the whole. So, it is possible that what Jesus was promising was really just a spare bedroom in his Father's mansion, and not a mansion of our own. We might be disappointed by this, for maybe we were really looking forward to having a place that we could call home, instead of sharing someone else's.

Let's take this questioning one step further. What is meant by "a dwelling place"? The Apostle Paul makes a very interesting statement in one of his letters to the church at Corinth which may help us to answer this question. He says, "Now we know that if the earthly tent we live in is destroyed, we have a building from God, an eternal house in heaven, not built by human hands. Meanwhile we groan, longing to be clothed with our heavenly dwelling...For while we are in this tent, we groan and are burdened, because we do not wish to be unclothed but to be clothed with our heavenly dwelling, so that what is mortal may be swallowed up by" that which is eternal (2 Cor. 5:1-4).

According to this passage, our mortal bodies are like tents that our souls live in while on earth, but someday, when we go to heaven, our souls will live in immortal dwelling places, or heavenly bodies, which will never see corruption. Is it possible, then, that Jesus, when he was promising "dwelling places" in heaven, was not talking about buildings at all, but spiritual bodies to house our souls?

Although we may like the concept of living in a nice condo in heaven's suburbia, is this really what we need? We are not going to need a place to rest, for we will never be tired. We are not going to need a place to keep our families, for there will be no marriage in heaven. We are not going to need shelter from the weather, for there will be eternal "Sonshine". In other words, we will not need houses to live in.

Private property will not exist in heaven, for everything will belong to the king. There will not be any trying to keep up with the Jones's, so we won't need a house that is bigger than the next guy. What we will need, however, is a spiritual body, so we can serve the Lord forever. What more could we ask for? Heaven is not a mansion. It is being in the presence of God.

The Lord's Work

"We continually remember before our God and Father your work produced by faith, your labor prompted by love, and your endurance inspired by hope in our Lord Jesus Christ." I Thess. 1:3

What are you doing for the Lord? Don't misunderstand me. I'm not asking what kind of ministry you are in. I'm asking, "What are you doing for him?", as opposed to "What are you doing for yourself?" You see, it is possible to be involved in a growing church, faithfully giving your tithe, going on short-term missions trips, singing in the choir, and feeding the homeless at the Rescue Mission, yet not be doing anything for the Lord. You might be doing all of these things just to impress people, to seek attention or praise, or to sooth your conscience for all of the bad things you have done. You might be acting out of a sense of duty, guilt, or pride, and the Lord has nothing to do with it, except in name only.

What, then, makes something the Lord's work, instead of just our own attempts at good works? The Apostle Paul tells us that it must have four ingredients. First, it must be bathed in prayer. Paul writes, "We continually remember before our God and Father your work." It is important that we have prayer partners who are praying with us about our work for the Lord. There is strength and wisdom in numbers. So often, when someone just tries serving the Lord on their own, isolated from others and their prayer support, the Devil is able to pull them down by making them self-focused and proud, or discouraged and defeated. Having others who are praying with us helps us to keep things in their proper perspective, and there is "group power", even when the individual is exhausted.

The second ingredient is that the Lord's work must be "produced by faith". Many times we depend completely upon our own natural abilities instead of relying completely upon the Lord. We don't really need the Lord unless there is some emergency. Otherwise, we would rather do it by ourselves. That way, we get all of the credit. The Lord's work, on the other hand, must be done by faith alone. Unless we feel that there is no way that we can do our ministry or service without the Lord's enabling and empowering us to do it, everything that we do is just for ourselves.

Third, our work must be "prompted by love." Even if we have the first two ingredients, but we don't have the third, everything that we do is worthless. Paul writes the church in Corinth, "If I speak (or pray) in the tongues of men and of angels, but have not love, I am only a resounding gong or a clanging cymbal...If I have a faith that can move mountains, but have not love, I am nothing" (I Cor. 13:1-2). All the good works in the world are worthless unless motivated by God's love, not just our own, for our own love is self-centered. It is only God's love that gives us the final ingredient, "endurance inspired by hope". Otherwise, we just want to quit.

Hearing the Word of God

"When you received the word of God, which you heard from us, you accepted it not as the word of men, but as it actually is, the word of God." I Thess. 2:13

When we hear the word of God being taught or preached, how do we know that it is really God's voice that we are hearing, and not just the opinions of the preacher? The Apostle Paul commends the people of Thessalonica for <u>knowing</u> that the words that were spoken by Paul were not his own, but actually the Word of God. How did they know for sure? How can we know?

Paul gives us some guidelines. First, he says, "We dared to tell you his gospel in spite of strong opposition" (vs.2). One sign that a person is speaking for God is that they are willing to tell us the whole truth and nothing but the truth, in spite of the opposition of those who want it all watered down. Second, they speak with authority. Paul writes, "We speak as men approved by God to be entrusted with the gospel" (vs.4). They know that they have God's approval for what they are saying, and that is all that matters. They "are not trying to please men but God" (vs. 4).

Many preachers today are so prone to produce sermons that are just meant to impress or entertain, that often the only thing that we remember from the sermon is the joke or good illustration. They want to be popular or praised, so they don't want to step on anyone's toes by preaching the truth. God's spokesman doesn't use "flattery" to butter people up or to make them feel better (vs.5).

Neither does he "put on a mask to cover up greed" (vs.5). If a pastor spends more time asking for money than he does speaking to our hearts, then we may want to look elsewhere for the Word of God. Building bigger buildings is never more important than building lives for God.

A pastor who speaks to the heart must speak from the heart. If we don't sense that the pastor really cares for his people, and speaks with a compassion that is both genuine and consistent, then his words are probably from his head rather than from the Lord. The Living Water can only flow through channels of love. Paul writes, "We loved you so much that we were delighted to share with you not only the gospel of God but our lives as well" (vs.8). Notice, too, how this love affected the way that Paul ministered to the people. He says, "We dealt with each of you as a father deals with his own children, encouraging, comforting, and urging you to live lives worthy of God" (vs.11).

It is no wonder that these people accepted the words of Paul as the Word of God. They could sense his authority, power, genuineness, humility, truthfulness, and love. Oh, that we too could find such men and women of God to teach us and to lead us by their examples. Oh, that we could be such leaders ourselves. What prevents us from being a spokesman for the Lord? The Lord will never share anything with us that he doesn't want us to share with someone else. We are meant to be a channel, not a dam.

Be Strong in Grace

"Be strong in the grace that is in Christ Jesus." 2 Tim. 2:1

Imagine living next door to a neighbor from hell. He hates you and everything about you. He has sworn to destroy you and your family, and he does everything he can to make your life miserable. He is your enemy, a terrorist intimidator of the worst kind. He is the Devil incarnate, and the flames from his soul are enough to melt the siding off your house. His nuclear negativity is so powerful that it could provide the electricity for your whole neighborhood, yet without any light. He is the Dark Side, and to say that he is evil would be considered a compliment.

Yet, to make things worse, God asks us to love him. "Oh, no! Not him! Anyone but him! I can't do it. It is too much to ask. It is impossible." Well, yes and no. It is impossible for us, humanly speaking, to love anyone this hateful and mean. Yet, with God, all things are possible (Matt. 19:26), even loving our enemy. After all, isn't that what Jesus did when he died for us, even while we were still his enemies (Rom. 5:10). "Yes, but Jesus was God," we argue. That is true, but when it tells us to "Be strong in the grace that is in Christ Jesus," the word "strong" means "enabled or empowered". We can't love our enemies with our own strength, but we can be enabled and empowered by the Holy Spirit to do that which is humanly impossible. We have been given God's grace, which is different than just mercy. Mercy is just being pardoned for something that we did wrong. Even a pagan can show mercy. Pilate showed mercy toward Barabbas, the murderer, by letting him go free, instead of Christ.

Yet, grace is only possible through the power of God. Grace is not only a gift of unmerited favor, but it must be given with a motive of unconditional love. To be "strong in the grace that is in Christ Jesus", then, is to not only accept his grace for yourself, but to be enabled to become a channel of his grace to others. This is why Jesus is able to tell us to "Love your enemies, and pray for those who persecute you" (Matt. 5:44). He would not tell us to do something that he wasn't willing to do himself, or that he wasn't willing to help us to do. He doesn't want us, though, to just show mercy, or to "love" them from a distance, but to avoid any possible contact. God's love is an action verb, not just a feeling. Jesus tells us, "Love your enemies, do good to them, and lend to them without expecting to get anything back" (Luke 6:35). We are expected to reach out to them without constraint, without limitations, and without expectations. In other words, "Get rid of all bitterness, rage, and anger...Be kind and compassionate to one another, forgiving each other, just as in Christ, God forgave you" (Eph. 4:30-31).

God is our example, and he will help us to be "strong in grace" if we are willing to be humble and submissive to his will. God's grace is impossible not because we can't, but because we say, "I won't".

Proof of your Ministry

"Keep your head in all situations, endure hardship, do the work of an evangelist, discharge all the duties of your ministry." 2 Tim. 4:5

What makes an effective, successful ministry? Is it how many people are led to the Lord, how many get baptized, how many members a church has, or how much money is in our annual budget? These are the standards that many pastors use to gauge success. Yet, the Apostle Paul gives a different set of criteria.

He says first of all, "Keep your head in all situations". This phrase actually means, "Keep calm, cool, and collected, no matter what happens." It's easy to be cool when everything is going smoothly, when all the people are praising you, and your ministry is growing by leaps and bounds. How do you respond, though, when things start falling apart, people start getting negative and grumpy, and the Devil seems to be attacking from every direction? Paul tells us to keep cool and to "endure hardship". The word "endure" means "to continue under pain or distress without sinking or yielding to the pressure". The word "hardship" is something which tries to shape you with pressure. In other words, when the hardships of life put pressure on you to quit, or get discouraged, or get diverted from what God has called you to do, keep calm, "This is only a test". When God allows us to be tested by hardships, it is to see if our priorities are the same as his, and to help our characters to be molded into the image of Christ. He wants to see if we will practice what we preach.

Paul tells us to "do the work of an evangelist". We have this image of an evangelist as one who leads great revival services, or who has his own television or radio program to reach the world. The word "evangelist" means "one who shares good news by demonstrating the validity of his message in his own life." Most "so-called evangelists" today are more like "hit and run drivers" than "divine demonstrators". They throw out their lines, reel in the fish, then leave them on the shore to wither and die. According to Paul, the minister is suppose to be an evangelist, in that, he is supposed to be "God's test model" on how faith is supposed to work under pressure. You are there to show them how faith works practically speaking, that "faith without works is dead". If it doesn't work for you when the going gets tough, how is it supposed to work for them?

You are to "discharge all the duties of your ministry". This includes leading by example, not just by a good sermon exposition. This last phrase actually means, "make full proof" of your ministry. What is the "full proof" that you are really called to the ministry? It isn't by being judged by the world's standards of success. It is proving to the world that the flame you hold up cannot just be blown out by the winds of adversity. Do you have this kind of enduring flame, or are you just blowing smoke?

The Divine Bodyguard

"The Lord stood at my side and gave me strength...and I was delivered from the Lion's mouth." 2 Tim. 4:17

The Apostle Paul went through hell on earth. He says that, "Three times I was beaten with rods, once I was stoned, three times I was shipwrecked, I spent a night and a day in the open sea. I have been constantly on the move. I have been in danger from rivers, in danger from bandits...and in danger from false brothers...I have known hunger and thirst and have often gone without food. I have been cold and naked" (II Cor. 11:25).

Yet, in spite of all this adversity, he still is able to say, "I have fought the good fight, I have finished the race, I have kept the faith" (2 Tim. 4:7). How on earth was he able to go through so much and yet still be victorious? Most of us would have given up after being hit with the first rod, feeling the first stone, or missing the first meal. Why was Paul able to endure?

Paul tells us that when "everyone deserted me...the Lord stood at my side and gave me strength". In other words, he could sense the Lord's presence with him no matter where he was or what he was going through. That isn't always true with us. We may feel his presence when things are going good, but he seems far away when trials come. Paul, on the other hand, felt the most connected to God when he had no one else to turn to. He knew that God's strength was made perfect in his weakness. The weaker he was, the more opportunity that it gave for the Lord to shine.

Yet, there was another reason why Paul was able to endure through hardships. It was his sense of destiny and mission. He knew that God wanted him to proclaim the gospel to the Gentiles, so he could count on God's protection and provision until his mission was complete. He says, "The Lord stood at my side and gave me strength so that through me the message might be fully proclaimed and all the Gentiles might hear" (2 Tim. 4:17). Paul knew that God had a purpose for his life, so it didn't really matter what happened to him. God would be there right beside him until the purpose was fulfilled, and then God would decide when his time would be up, not the enemy. He knew that the Devil would continue to try to defeat God's purposes in him, but God would bring the ultimate victory. He says, "I was delivered from the lion's mouth. The Lord will rescue me from every evil attack and will bring me safely to his heavenly kingdom" (2 Tim. 4:17-18).

The Devil may be able to nibble at our heels, and even have us clamped in his mighty jaws from time to time, but we can be assured that God will deliver us from the lion's mouth, and that he will deliver us also to his heavenly kingdom. He is our divine bodyguard with a mission, and he will not let anything or anyone stand in the way of our final destiny. The Devil may be breathing down our backs, but the Lord is at our side.

Direct Revelation from God

"In the past God spoke to our forefathers through the prophets at many times and in various ways, but in these last days he has spoken to us by his Son." Heb. 1:1-2

Don't you hate it when you get second-hand news, and somehow the message gets all screwed up because the messenger misunderstands or misinterprets what he has seen or heard. In one sense, this is what happened with the people of Israel. God revealed his truth to them through the prophets, but then, as the message got passed down from generation to generation, it got distorted and reinterpreted according to the limited understandings and perverted consciences of the religious leaders and rulers. The prophet who gave the original message was inspired by God, but all of the hearers were not inspired. They did not have the Holy Spirit to counsel or guide them into all truth. They had to rely upon their own learning and experience.

It is no wonder, then, that they were so far off base by the time that Christ began his ministry on earth. They had the words of God, but they didn't recognize the Word. They were spiritually blind, and they lacked the power to be able to look past their own egos into the mind of God. You know how difficult it is to understand scripture sometimes, and you have the help of God. Think how difficult it would be with no help at all.

Yet, we do have help. We can understand the prophets, through the power of the Holy Spirit, but we don't have to rely upon the prophets as our only source of truth, like the Israelites did. We have Jesus Christ living within us, and he has given us his spirit to teach us all things. We don't have to go through an intermediary to tell us what God wants us to know. God speaks to us directly.

That doesn't mean that we don't need anyone else to grow spiritually. Just because we have God within us, doesn't mean that we are to become hermits, and hide from the world outside of us. God put us within the body of Christ, the church, and gave us all different spiritual gifts, so that we could help one another to grow. We are not supposed to be unattached single-cell organisms. We are part of a whole, and we need each other.

It is true that God can speak to us directly, but what are we supposed to do with that revelation? We are not supposed to hoard it, hide it, or hinder it from reaching others. Receiving truth directly from the divine places a responsibility upon us to pass it on. God never gives us anything that he doesn't mean for us to share with someone else. Why do we need to pass it on, since they can get the truth directly from God too? It is because that God promises to reveal all truth to the church as a whole, but not to each individual in this life. He will reveal things to one person that he will not reveal to another, etc. So, we can hear certain sentences from the Lord directly, but we need the others to hear the rest of the story.

Crucifying Christ Again

"They are crucifying the Son of God all over again." Heb. 6:6

Imagine seeing Nicodemus and Joseph of Arimathea agonizingly taking the body of Jesus off the cross, and carrying it to the tomb. Then imagine seeing them wash his body thoroughly, bathing it with myrrh, and carefully covering it with cloth before slowly rolling the huge stone in front of the opening of the tomb. Think, then, of the tormenting days and nights following the crucifixion where the disciples met secretly, afraid that they too might be killed for their faith, and secretly ashamed and hurt that they had put all their hope in one who failed them, who didn't end up being the Messiah after all. Visualize, then, the disciples' joy when they saw the risen Lord, and had their spiritual eyes open to how everything made sense now, and how Jesus had fulfilled everything according to scripture. He was God incarnate, their Messiah-Shepherd-King, and he had conquered death and Satan. What a glorious day.

Yet, imagine then the disciples taking Jesus back up to Golgotha, and nailing him back up to the cross, even though they knew he was the King of Kings and Lord of Lords. That's impossible, you think, for they would never think of doing such a thing. It was bad enough to have the Roman soldiers pound the spikes into his hands and feet. How much more cruel and heartless to have his own disciples do the same thing to the risen Lord. Unthinkable!

Yet, that is exactly what we do, spiritually speaking, according to Paul, every time we as Christians turn our backs on our Lord and Savior. It is just as if we are taking turns nailing him back on to the cursed tree. He writes that "Those who have once been enlightened, who have tasted the heavenly gift, who have shared in the Holy Spirit, who have tasted the goodness of the word of God and the powers of the coming age…if they fall away…are crucifying the Son of God all over again" (Heb. 6:4-6). He isn't talking about the Roman soldiers here. He is talking about us. He is talking about those who have put their faith and hope in the risen Lord, but then walked away, and by our very lives are "subjecting him to public disgrace" all over again.

We have not only crucified him again, but we have spit in his face and poured salt in his wounds as the cross is being raised. We are worse than the Romans, for what they did, they did out of ignorance. When we nail Jesus back up to the cross by our rebellion and rejection of him as the Lord of our lives, we know exactly what we are doing. We are showing to the whole world that we, as his disciples, who knew him best, have turned our backs on him in shame, as if somehow he has failed us, and he is now nothing but a reject. Jesus, and everything he stood for, gets nailed to the cross when we do that to our Lord. If even his closest followers rebel against their savior, why should anyone else believe in such a "fraud"?

The Secrets of Service

"Each one should use whatever gift he has received to serve others." I Peter 4:10

Some gifts are being glorified today as being more important than others, as if we can't be part of the "in-crowd" unless we have them. The Bible clearly teaches, though, that spiritual gifts are not meant to glorify the individual, or to make him appear more spiritual than anyone else. The purpose of spiritual gifts, in fact, is to make us a better servant. Peter tells us, "Each one should use whatever gift he has received to serve others". So, the question should be, "How can I be a better servant, not how can I be more noticed?"

Peter gives us some guidelines. First, he says there needs to be an attitude of urgency: "The end of all things is near" (I Peter 4:7). I cannot afford, then, to have an attitude of laziness or procrastination. I need to do whatever I can to reach out to others now, for I may not have tomorrow. The attitude of urgency, in turn, pushes us to "be clear-minded and self-controlled" (vs. 7). When a paramedic comes to the scene of an accident, he cannot afford to lose it emotionally. He has to be cool, calm, and collected. We, also, need to have this same sensibility that self-control is crucial. What we are doing is too important to "lose it" in the midst of service for the Lord.

Ironically, this control of self is supposed to help us so we "can pray" more effectively. If we have the attitude that we can serve the Lord in our own power and ability, we have failed before we even begin. Complete dependence on God and being Spirit-controlled is the only way that we can be self-controlled and focused to the point of having all our energies directed toward our purpose of serving others.

Yet, the most effective service is never just about doing more for the Lord. The Bible says, "Above all, love each other deeply" (vs. 8). This isn't just a surface kind of acquaintance-love. Only genuine, unconditional love will work. Why? Like it or not, we are called to serve imperfect people, who are sometimes grumpy, ungrateful, self-centered, rude, and even plain mean. Only unconditional love will work because it "covers over a multitude of sins" (vs. 8), it helps us to "offer hospitality to one another without grumbling" (vs. 9), and to faithfully administer "God's grace in its various forms" (vs. 10).

We can serve others, then, not because they deserve it, but as an act of God's grace. We are serving God, not just men, and we are his channels of grace, love and truth. This should affect even the way that we talk to one another, for we should speak as if we are "speaking the very words of God" (vs. 11). We are God's ambassadors, representing his divine nature and purpose, not just our own personal agenda. We serve with the "strength God provides, so that in all things God may be praised", for that should be our ultimate goal in all that we do (vs. 11). If not, it is all just wasted energy.

Being a Good Shepherd

"Be shepherds of God's flock that is under your care, serving as overseers."
I Peter 5:2

Peter is speaking here primarily to elders in a church. Yet, the concept of an elder is not just a position of authority but one of maturity and influence. So often we look only to the "professional Christians", the pastors and evangelists, who get paid to serve others, as if they are the only ones who are supposed to shepherd the flocks of God. The term elder, though, merely means someone who is older and wiser, who can lead by their wisdom and example, even if they don't have an official title in the church directory. Everyone who has been down a certain road with the Lord, in fact, should then become a spiritual guide for those who follow. We don't have to be a pastor or teacher to be a leader.

Shepherds are not known for their intellect or scholarship. They are valued for their ability to lead the sheep to where the food and water is, to lead them away from the pitfalls that others have fallen into, and to rescue those who have gone astray. We don't have to be a theologian to share with others where we have found truth, or what has helped us along the way. We don't have to be a PhD to lend a helping hand, or to listen and respond to the cries of those who are wounded and afraid. God wants everyone who has learned from him to become mentors or shepherds of others.

He doesn't want us, though, to grumble about sharing what we have learned. One of the evidences that a child is growing more mature is their learning how to share, instead of being just self-centered. Yet, true maturity is not just learning to share because we have to, but caring enough about people that we want to give of ourselves to meet their needs. Peter tells us to be "overseers— not because you must but because you are willing, as God wants you to be" (I Peter 5:2). We should want to look beyond ourselves to the needs of others because that is what God wants us to do, and we have grown enough in our spiritual walk to be like-minded. We should be "eager to serve" instead of doing it out of compulsion, like someone is twisting our arm.

We also need to serve with humility, and not look down upon those that we are trying to shepherd, as if somehow they are less worthy than ourselves. Peter admonishes us to serve with the proper attitude, "not lording it over those entrusted to you, but being examples to the flock" (vs. 3). The idea of being a shepherd is never, "I know more than you, so you better listen and obey." It is merely continuing to walk where Jesus leads us, and then leading others by our example. They will want to follow us because they can see that we walk what we talk. The sheep respect and trust the shepherd because he is out in the wilds with them, and knows the dangers personally, not just as a spectator from the palace walls. This is why Jesus, our good shepherd, came down from heaven, to show us how.

Everything We Need

"His divine power has given us everything we need for life and godliness."
2 Peter 1:3

What do we need? When someone asks us that question, we might think big and say a new house, car, or a million dollars. Or, we might respond more in the immediate, like something to eat, drink, or enjoy. Or, perhaps we might take it to another level and say, we need a good friend who will stick with us no matter what. Yet, what is it that we really need, beyond the physical, temporal or even personal? The Bible says that God "has given us everything we need for life and godliness through knowing him".

In other words, knowing God is all that we really need. Yet, what does it mean to know the Lord? The word "know" means "to perceive, understand, or experience with clarity and certainty". Having God just as a casual acquaintance, then, will not meet our need. There has to be a oneness or intimate unity that is often compared in the Bible to the marriage of two people who are one in body and soul.

Are we really one with the Lord in that way, or are we still trying to study him from a distance? The verse above says that knowing God gives us everything we need to be godly, which means to be like him. It says, in fact, that he "gives us very great and precious promises, so that through them [we] may participate in the divine nature" (vs. 4). The word "promises" means "commitment". God, then, commits himself to giving us his divine nature. It isn't just an empty promise, but a solid dedication to an eternal cause. He is committed to helping us to know him.

If we come to know him by responding to his commitment, we will not only become godly or like him, but we will "escape the corruption in the world caused by evil desires" (vs. 4). Knowing him means moving ever closer to who he is, and ever farther away from who he is not. We can't really know God and love the world at the same time. God's nature is in direct opposition to the fallen nature of the world. The Bible says, "God opposes the proud" (I Peter 5:5). The word "opposes" comes from the same root as the word "opposite". Opposites may attract in human relationships sometimes, but in spiritual relationships they oppose one another.

If we know God, then, we will oppose anything that is opposite from God's nature, because it has become our nature also. We will not be corrupted or diverted, therefore, from becoming godly in Christ Jesus. We will, instead, receive grace and peace in abundance through knowing Christ, for we will be completely content with the understanding that knowing him is not only the most important thing in our life, but the only thing that we need. Everything else that is worthwhile merely points to him, for it shares some of his nature, for "every good gift and every perfect gift is from above" (James 1:17). Our job is to worship the giver instead of the gift, and to know the difference—to know him.

We are all Slaves

"A man is a slave to whatever has mastered him." 2 Peter 2:19

Someone at work really annoys us, and every time we see them, we writhe in anger. We fume with every thought of them, and we can't stop thinking about them until long after they are gone. We have nightmares about them, and even dream about seeking revenge. We are totally controlled by our rage. Like it or not, we are a slave to our anger, for "a man is a slave to whatever has mastered him".

We see someone that we know, and they have something that we want. We can't stop staring at them, and resenting that they have it, and we don't. We want it so badly, in fact, that we dream about ways of taking it away from them so we can have it for ourselves. We may even try to get God on our side, and pray that God would take it away from that person and give it to us—a divine conspiracy on our behalf. Believe it or not, we are a slave to our greed and covetousness, for the Bible says that "a man is a slave to whatever has mastered him." Trust me—If it controls our emotions, our thinking, and our motives for doing things, then we have been mastered by it.

We see a beautiful, sexy person walking down the street, and we can't take our eyes off of them. We are captivated by their sexual energy, and we feel ourselves being pulled toward their sensual magnetism. We start imagining them without their clothes on, and how it would feel if we had sex with them. Our physical fantasies take a hold of us, and we are a slave to our lusts. We can't help ourselves for we allow ourselves to be imprisoned by our desires. We are a sexual addict, and a slave to our appetites, for "a man is a slave to whatever has mastered him."

We are out of control, for we allow ourselves to be controlled. We can't pass by a store window without feeling a craving to go in, desiring to buy everything on sale, whether we need it or not. We go to every garage sale in the state, buy everything that is sold on the shopping network, order things without limit on the Internet, and max-out every credit card that we own, plus some. We are addicted to impulsive buying, and we are its slave, for "a man is a slave to whatever has mastered him."

It doesn't matter what the addiction is or how harmless it may seem, such as eating sweets or watching TV, if it controls us, we are its slave. If we are not willing to give something up, then it means too much to us. If we can't do without it, it is too important. The only thing that we, as Christians, should be controlled by is the Holy Spirit, and this is never by compulsion or addiction. We are bond-slaves of our master, the Lord, and we willingly yield ourselves to him because we love him. He never controls us like these other things do, for we are not meant to be mindless puppets. Being his slave never means being out of control. It is becoming one with the Master.

Perfected Love

"If anyone obeys his word, God's love is truly made complete in him." I John 2:5

Everybody needs love, almost everyone wants it, but very few actually find it. Even fewer ever experience love in its completeness or fullness. So, what's the secret? How can we experience love-to-the-max, and why do so few even have a clue what I am talking about? First of all, if we want to know how something works, we have to study the operating manual. In other words, we have to read the directions. Yet, just reading the directions doesn't always help. Sometimes they are so confusing that we end up throwing away the item that we just bought, returning it to the store, or just letting it sit on a shelf in a closet, never to be looked at again.

The same thing is true with Christianity. Many people have never taken the time to really study the "Instruction Manual", the Bible, and so they don't have a clue on how it is all supposed to work. Then again, for those who have studied, many find it too confusing or boring, so they just ignore what it teaches, thinking that their way sounds better.

Of course, they are wrong. God always knows best. So, when it comes to experiencing love, many people look in all the wrong places, or try to put the pieces together in the wrong order, as if sex is supposed to come first, then love. They have everything backwards and upside down. The only way of knowing the right order of things is by knowing and obeying the Word of God, for God is the one who designed love, and he is the only one who knows how to make it work properly.

So, what does the Bible say about love? First, we must understand that God himself is love (I John 4:8). We cannot, then, experience love to its fullest unless we know Him.

Second, we are commanded to love God with our whole hearts, minds, and souls. Then, we are to love others as much as we love ourselves (Matt. 22:36-39). Unless we have these priorities, we will never experience love to its fullest. Everyone falls under and knows the shadows of love, but very few ever experience the fullness of its light.

Third, there must be complete submission and reliance upon the giver of love and light. It is His way, or the highway. The love of God is not just a fuzzy feeling that comes through our own spontaneous gushes of emotions. It comes only through listening to what God has to say and obeying it without question. The word "obey" is actually a military term in this passage, which means "to stand guard or to watch with intensity, as if holding on to something that was worth risking our life for".

Are we that focused and determined to know and obey the Word of God? Unless we are, we will never know love in its completeness, for mature love in its abundant fullness can never be experienced apart from total abandonment to God's revelation of himself, whether through his word or the Word, Jesus Christ, our Lord.

Will we let God complete his love in us? Trust him, and obey.

November 22

No Fear in Love

"There is no fear in love, for perfect love drives out fear." I John 4:18

We are walking down the street, and we see a homeless beggar sitting on the curb. He is singing a sad song with his guitar, and his case is open to catch any tips. We walk as far away from him as possible, and maybe even cross the street to avoid him. We wouldn't think of talking to him or throwing some change his way. We don't want to be bothered, and it is annoying to us that someone would just sit in our path, as if he is pushing his poverty in our face, and expecting us to make it better. Who does he think he is? Why doesn't he just get a job like everyone else? He is a lazy, good-for-nothing bum, and he deserves what he has—nothing.

Although it is possible that the person is just lazy, have we taken the time to find out? What if he is really a hero, who fought in the war to protect our country, but now is home, and suffering from post-traumatic stress syndrome from having to face so much pain and death? He is so depressed that he can't work, and no one seems to care.

Or perhaps he lost his job because he is too old, and his boss wanted some fresh ideas. It doesn't matter that he worked faithfully for thirty years, without missing a day. Now he is a has-been, and he is too old to find a new career. He lost his house because he could no longer make the payments, and his wife and kids no longer respect him, for he is now considered a loser. So, he sits on the curb, hungry, tired, and defeated, hoping that someone will show a little kindness before he shrivels down to oblivion.

Or, maybe it's a young man, who got kicked out of the house because his friends tempted him with some drugs. He yielded because he thought it would help him to be more liked or accepted, but his parents found out, and now he is on his own. He is feeling rejected and alone, and is looking for anything that might take away the pain. Sure, he may buy cigarettes, booze, or even drugs with any money that we give him, but that is only because he is hurting so much inside. What he really wants is someone who will love him with unconditional love. He wants a friend who won't reject him because he isn't perfect.

Or it could be a young women, a girl barely into her teens. She's a runaway with tattoos, nose-rings, and dog-collar, offering her body to anyone who passes just to make a buck. She wouldn't think of going back home, for she was sexually abused by her dad, blamed for everything by her mom, and verbally abused by her siblings. She is dysfunctional and anti-social, and no one wants to be around her, except others like herself. She is driven by anger, fear, and loneliness, and she has become totally self-centered just out of survival. If she doesn't focus on her needs, she will die.

So, how do we respond to all these desperate people? Do we reach out in love, or look the other way? We say that we are too afraid that they might hurt us. "Perfect love casts out all fear".

Faith that Overcomes

"This is the victory that has overcome the world, even our faith." I John 5:4

Our bills are stacked up around us, the creditor is pounding at the door, and we are afraid to answer the phone because the bill collectors are harassing us morning, noon, and night. We are overwhelmed, and don't know what to do. "This is the victory that has overcome the world, even our faith." Even when we no longer believe in ourselves, and can't trust anyone else, we can trust in God. He will give us the strength to face this trial, and through our faith we can have the victory.

That doesn't mean that God will just dump a lot of money in our lap. He may be allowing this trial to teach us not to be so impulsive in our spending, or to wait on him when we have a need, instead of trying to solve our own problems through rash decisions. Yet, he will not abandon us. He has promised to never leave us or forsake us, so we can depend on his being there with us through it all. If we trust in him, he will keep us from drowning in the muck called life.

Maybe we feel lonely and dejected because no one seems to really respect us. They look down on us, make sarcastic comments to us all the time, and ridicule any little mistake that we make. We are like an odd piece of furniture, and people are annoyed at us because they keep stubbing their toes on our presence. We are always in their way, and if they can, they will look or walk right through us. They are callous, cruel, and downright mean.

"This is the victory that has overcome the world, even our faith." We don't have to worry or be hurt by these uncaring people. God will help us to have peace even in the midst of turmoil. We can feel loved by him, even if there is not another friend in the world who will give us the time of day. We can trust in the Lord to meet our needs, and as we reach out to others who are lonely and depressed, we will feel more fulfilled and happy than we would ever feel if everyone else liked us. If our personality or people skills need some work because of some abuse or neglect that we endured when we were young, then God can send someone our way to help us smooth out the rough edges. He specializes in the impossible, even if that means us.

It doesn't matter what the trial, temptation, or test, we can have victory through faith in the one who loved us enough to die for us. If he was willing to give up his life for us, and to have victory over death, he will be willing to help us to have victory in our daily life as well. There is no problem too big or too small that he will not help us with. We don't have to wait until we need a mountain moved before we start praying for help. We need to recognize that we need help even in our day by day drudgery., not just the emergencies. We can't make it on our own. If we think we can, we will fall flat on our faces. Yet, if we trust in Him, we can have the victory that overcomes the world—faith in Him.

The Poor in Spirit

"Blessed are the poor in spirit, for theirs is the kingdom of heaven."   Matt. 5:3

In growing up, I always thought that the Beatitudes were God's way of saying that he had compassion on "poor" people. Yet, interesting enough, not once in scripture does it tell us that Jesus went out of his way to help the poor to get out of their poverty. Yes, he fed the five-thousand, but that was regardless of how much money they had. He fed the wealthy along with the poor. Yes, he healed people that were poor, but it wasn't because they were poor. He was merely trying to demonstrate his power so people would listen to his message. He had compassion on the people in general, but never just because they were in poverty. Their spiritual poverty was more important to Jesus than their physical needs.

Today, it is just the opposite. We have it in our minds that to reach the world for Christ, we need to feed the hungry, build them houses, pull their teeth, or give them free condoms. It doesn't matter if we ever share the gospel with them, as long as we share the compassion of Christ, we are helping to relieve suffering. We are helping to make the world a better place, and that makes it all worthwhile.

What we are actually doing, however, is making the world a worse place, for we are giving the impression that all that matters is reaching the physical needs of people. It is no wonder that many countries around the world despise America, even though we have donated billions of dollars to world hunger and aid. We have fed their stomachs, but left their souls impoverished. We think that by giving someone a piece of bread that that translates that we love them. It does not. All it says to people is that we believe that the solution to any problem is throwing money at it. We don't understand that God has allowed poverty and suffering in the world so that people will turn to him. By alleviating their suffering, we get people to turn to the United States Government or the rich American churches instead.

What God wants is people who are "poor in spirit", who turn to him because they realize that there is no where else they can turn. There is no one else who can meet the hunger and emptiness of their souls. They need to feel the spiritual pain of repentance before they will turn to the living God to heal their aching hearts. They need to feel the full-weight of the consequences of their sins in order to draw them to a need for a savior.

When we try to reach out to the world by relieving them of those consequences, we think that we are doing the work of God, but we may actually be undoing it. We need to follow Christ's example and share the gospel along with the bread. Otherwise, we are just filling the empty tombs of their souls with crumbs that will decay. Ironically, sometimes Satan tempts us with doing good in order to keep the better from happening. If he can get us to fill the bellies of the poor, while starving their spirits, he will be our first volunteer to cook the meals.

Those Who Mourn

"Blessed are those who mourn, for they will be comforted." Matt. 5:4

As a parent, my natural inclination is to want to comfort my children whenever they are experiencing sorrow or pain of any kind. I know that I may not be able to stop their pain, but I can at least show them that I care. As a Christian, I know that I am also supposed to comfort those within the family of God who are suffering, and to show them that I care by "mourning with those who mourn" (Rom. 12:15). They need to know that I feel their pain, for we are all part of the same body.

When Jesus tells his disciples, though, that those who mourn "will be comforted", he is not just dealing with the kind of comfort that a parent might give to his child, or a friend to a friend. The word "mourn" in this context means "penitent" or "repentant". It is not, then, just talking about natural sorrow because of the trials of life. It is dealing with the pain of the soul that is caused when a person is truly sorry for the sin that they have committed. It is the pain of separation between their spirit and the Lord. The Lord promises to comfort those who are repentant, for they will be comforted with his forgiveness and the renewed relationship that they have with Christ.

Jesus makes this same promise when he tells them that he has come to heal the brokenhearted (Luke 4:18). He is not speaking of those who just got jilted by a boyfriend or girlfriend, or who are disappointed because they have failed to reach success. The word "brokenhearted" means "broken off at the root", like a plant being pulled up from its soil. The heart of a man is ego-centric and sinful. The Bible says, "The heart is deceitful above all things, and desperately wicked: who can know it?" (Jer. 17:9). To be brokenhearted, in this sense, then, is to be broken off from the root of sin in our hearts. It is to be humbled before the Lord as we bow down before him with a penitent heart, pleading for forgiveness and mercy, knowing that we don't deserve either one. It is with this brokenness that we mourn, and that we are blessed and comforted.

The word "blessed" means being given "a gift of happiness". This kind of gift is also a gift of grace, for we do not deserve to ever be happy or at peace with our Maker. The word "comforted" is the word "paracletus", which refers to our "Paraclete", the Holy Spirit. The word "Paraclete" means "walking along side of", as if walking hand in hand, or arm in arm. When we acknowledge that we have sinned against the Heavenly Father, and that it is only through Jesus, the Son, that we can have forgiveness for our sins, then the Holy Spirit is able to give us the comfort that we need as he "draws along side us", locks arms with us, and says, "Let's go. We are in this together from here on out. You can depend on me." With this kind of comfort, we can truly say with the psalmist, "Weeping may endure for a night, but joy cometh in the morning" (Psa. 30:5). Jesus is our Sonshine.

Arise and Shine

"Arise, shine, for your light has come, and the glory of the Lord rises upon you."
Isaiah 60:1

Israel has fallen into sin and idolatry, and Isaiah says in shame, "Truth is nowhere to be found, and whoever shuns evil becomes prey" (59:15). The Lord looks for someone who is willing and able to take a stand for righteousness, but he is "appalled that there was no one to intervene" (vs. 16). So, he decides to come himself, to be the Redeemer of Israel and everyone who repents of their sins (vs. 20). He promises that his Spirit will be upon them, and that His words will be with them forever (vs. 21). Then he tells them, "Arise, shine, for your light has come, and the glory of the Lord rises upon you" (60:1).

The Redeemer has come, and He is the Light of the World, and His light shines upon those who love him. Yet, the word "upon" does not just mean on or over. It means "through". That is why he tells them to "Arise, shine", but the light of God is meant to shine through them, not just on them. It is the "glory of the Lord" that rises upon them and through them, so it is not meant to give them honor. They are merely channels of his light.

In contrast, "darkness covers the earth and thick darkness is over the peoples" (60:2). God's people are not meant to blend in with the darkness. They are supposed to be lights upon a hill top where everyone can see the distinctiveness of their divine illumination. There will be, of course, evil ones who will always rebel against the light, but there will also be many who will be attracted to the light. Isaiah writes, "Nations will come to your light, and kings to the brightness of your dawn" (60:3). It is exciting when this happens, for they can sense that God is using them to bring people to himself. He tells them that when this happens, they "will look and be radiant", and their hearts "will throb and swell with joy" (vs. 5).

We, as Christians, can join in this joy, for we too know this same Redeemer, and his Spirit has filled our hearts with his light. We need to arise, shine and let God's glory glow through us to the world that is in darkness. If we allow God's light to shine through us, , then the Bible promises us, "The Lord will be your everlasting light, and God will be your glory. Your sun will never set again, and your moon will wane no more" (vs. 19-20).

In the physical world, the sun always sets, and we have to rely upon the lesser light of the moon. Yet, in the spiritual world, we can know a world where God's light never has to disappear or diminish. The darker the world gets around us, in fact, the stronger and more powerful the light of God can shine. The Dark Side of the spiritual dimension does not need to be a damper that puts out the flame. The Fire of God's glory and truth can blaze forth through us, and create prisms of power and love that reach deep into the darkest corners of the human heart. So, arise and shine and give God the glory.

Our Super Hero

"My God is my rock, in whom I take refuge." Psa. 18:2

It is easy for us to visualize God as the Rock of our Salvation, or our faithful fortress, for he is the same yesterday, today, and forever. He is a solid foundation, with all the stability and strength of Eternal Power and Truth. He is our safe harbor and our anchor. Yet, all of these images are stationary, unmoving and unmovable. They seem static or even stagnant at times, and we have a hard time relating to a rock. We want a God who is more vibrant, enthusiastic and energized.

Of course, God is all of these and more, and he came in human form to communicate that to us in ways that we can understand. Jesus was real flesh and bones, passion and compassion, and he reached out to man in unconditional love. God the Father, though, is still hard for us to relate to at times. We would like to think of him as being more interactive with us, but our minds just keep picturing him as a solid statue sitting on a throne somewhere in the distance, like the Lincoln Memorial, cold and lifeless.

King David gives us a little different picture of our Mighty God. David is crying out in anguish because of his enemies, and he calls out to the Lord to save him. Notice how this "sedate, antique, stone-cold God" responds: "The earth trembled and quaked, and the foundations of the mountains shook; they trembled because he was angry. Smoke rose from his nostrils; consuming fire came from his mouth, burning coals blazed out of it. He parted the heavens and came down; dark clouds were under his feet. He mounted the cherubim and flew; he soared on the wings of the wind…Out of the brightness of his presence clouds advanced, with hailstones and bolts of lightning. The Lord thundered from heaven; the voice of the Most High resounded. He shot his arrows and scattered the enemies, great bolts of lightning and routed them…He reached down from on high and took hold of me…He rescued me from my powerful enemy, from my foes, who were too strong for me" (Psa. 18:7-17).

Wow! So much for our putting God in a retirement home with other worn-out old has-beens. He is eager for action, afraid of no-one, and the greatest "Super-Hero" we will ever find. He is ready to mount his mighty cherubim on a moment's notice, and to rush to our rescue, using every weapon at his disposal. Then, when he has won the victory, he reaches down in love and draws us into his arms, and we feel the pounding of his adrenalin-filled heart, still pumped from the mighty battle.

Then David shares a very special, intimate moment with us. After God has rescued him, it says that the Lord brought him "out into a special, private place", just for the two of them, because the Lord "delighted" in him (vs. 19). To think that God is not just a lifeless observer up in the sky someplace is a marvelous thing in and of itself. To think that he is awesomely active because he delights in us: He Rocks!

The Divine Drill Sergeant

"He trains my hands for battle." Psa. 18:34

I've never been in the armed forces, but I have heard about the reputation that many drill sergeants have. They are lean, mean fighting machines, who eat nails for breakfast, can hit a bulls-eye with chewing tobacco at a hundred yards, and spew enough poisonous profanity from their mouths that they have to be quarantined to a toxic waste dump when they retire. Their justification for their acid temperaments—It's the best way to make men out of boys—to make real soldiers out of pampered couch-potatoes.

Well, God has a different plan of attack. Notice how he trains his soldiers. First, he doesn't just train us, like a drill sergeant, then hand us off to someone else to lead us into battle. He is right there beside us, helping us to "advance against a troop" (vs. 29). Second, he doesn't just try to build up our own strength. He gives us His strength (vs. 32). Third, whenever he asks us to fight a battle, he "enables" us to stand on the heights, so we won't be defeated in the valleys (vs. 33). He trains our hands for battle, showing us how to fight in our spiritual warfare, teaching us how to use the weapons that he has given us. Then, miracle of miracle, he doesn't just give us a shield to defend ourselves. He gives us <u>his own</u> "shield of victory" (vs. 35). He's been out there fighting the enemy, having one victory after another, and then we he returns, he gives us the shield that he used in battle. This shield has the dents and scrapes and wounds that were meant for him, so we try to hold it up to honor him. It is so big and heavy, though, that we start to stumble from its weight. So, his "right hand sustains" us (vs. 35), like a loving father trying to help a child learn how to ride a bike, letting go only when he knows that we are able. We end up falling, though, over and over, as we try to carry his shield and the sword of the Lord. So, he bends down to pick us up. Yet, it is more than that. David puts it this way: "You stoop down to make me great" (vs. 35). In other words, he lowers himself in order to lift us up higher, not just back to where we were before, but exalted to greatness. He picks us up and raises us to his shoulders, like someone might do to a hero or in recognition of special honor.

Wait a minute! What did we do to receive such honor? Didn't we just fall flat on our face because we couldn't carry the heavy load of his shield and sword? God knows that we are not perfect. We are little children trying to walk in our father's shoes. We are going to trip and fall. Yet, he knows that the best way to help us to grow into his shoes is by encouragement, not criticism. He, in fact, "broadens the path beneath me", so that I won't trip so easily (vs. 36). He does everything he can to help us to succeed, not by putting us down, but lifting us up; not by making things more difficult, but by making our ways straight. He wants us to be victorious. We are wearing his armor, and carrying his shield.

Deep Calls to Deep

"Deep calls to deep in the roar of your waterfalls; all your waves and breakers have swept over me." Psa. 42:7

As the Jordan River gushes from the natural springs in Mount Hermon in the Holy Land, it cascades down the cliffs and gorges, thundering and booming into the deep crevices, echoing into the dark canyons deep below the surface, and crashing like wave upon wave of majestic power and vibrant energy. The spring waters embrace the melting snows, and the power builds with this fluid marriage. The craggy, wrinkled face of the mountain side is splashed with bursts and billows of sparkling sensations, like an old mountain man recklessly splashing water into his face from a playful brook to wake up in the brisk morning. Everything is alive and fresh, and the rainbows play with the rising mist that floats upwards from the crashing depths of the waterfalls and rocks below.

It's no wonder that David was able to write many of his psalms about the mountains and rivers. I'm sure that he spent a lot of time basking in their beauty. Yet, some of these excursions were spent in hiding in the caves from King Saul, who was desperately seeking to kill him. Other times he sought refuge from his enemies in battle. Still others, he sought solace in his soul, for he was troubled by his own sin, and the tremendous weight of separation that is felt when one feels abandoned by someone they love. He went to the raging river to bathe in its washing waves of power to sense the cleansing presence of his Lord. It not only helped him to feel renewed and revived, but empowered and enabled to go on. It gave him a sense of God's strength and majesty, like a fountain of eternal youth purging his soul. He knew that he could go to the river in desperation, and cry out, "Why are you downcast, O my soul? Why so disturbed within me? Put your hope in God…Deep calls to deep in the roar of your waterfalls; all your waves and breakers have swept over me. By day the Lord directs his love, at night his song is with me" (vs. 5-8).

By the light of day, David can see God's directing power as the river flows and shapes its banks, like a master craftsman guiding and forging a work of art. By night, in the darker times of despair and desperation, he may not be able to see God's hand, but he can hear and sense the roar of the rumbling rapids, and know that God's power and strength is still there. He knows that the waterfalls must reach into the deepest caverns of his spirit, where no light appears, to cleanse the rocks of his rugged heart. He wants to be baptized by the booming billows, bouncing from boulder to boulder, crashing down the echoing chambers of his most inner being. He is God's anointed, and the river renews his vision of manifest destiny, that the Messiah will some day flow from his loins, like a wondrous waterfall of God's flowing love.

Fountains, Springs and Wells

"All my fountains are in you." Psa. 87:7

Have you ever noticed how reading the Bible is like going on a pilgrimage through a foreign land, seeking the Promised Land, or searching for the Holy Grail? Honestly speaking, there are a lot of dry deserts that we have to plow through as we desperately search for the next oasis. We hunger and thirst after righteousness, but our canteen is on empty, and even our camels refuse to take another step. Sometimes we are able to climb just one more sand dune, and there on the other side is a fountain that squirts up and dances like a mystical maiden in all of her sparkling splendor.

Sometimes God makes us wait till the last minute before he provides the refreshing renewal that we need. We search and search for truth and light in his Word, hoping to glean new nuggets of inspiration, or seeking to hear his gentle voice whispering to our spirits, yet sometimes it is like he is playing hide and seek, and we don't find the fountain of his shining face until we can't go anymore.

Other times, we aren't able to find the fountains at all. Instead, we are led to the more subtle springs of the Spirit, who bathes us with his refreshing joy and peace in the coolness of his comforting shade. It isn't splashy or vibrant like the fountain of God's glory, but it still soothes our souls as we drink from its deeply pure brook of new insights and perspectives into the very character of our Lord.

Still other times, we don't find any fountains or springs of truth at all. We read the Word, page after page, diligently searching and thirsting for more, but we find nothing already rising and bubbling from the surface. So, we have to do some digging. We get our commentaries, our concordances, our favorite devotionals, and every Bible study guide that we can find. We listen to J. Vernon McGee or John McArthur on the radio, hoping to get some inspiration, until finally we hit water. Sometimes we only have to dig a few feet to find the well, but other times we end up digging to China and back. Sometimes we have to dig through rocky ground, and sometimes we just sort of step through the sandy surface into a river right below our feet.

Even though it is hard for us to understand why God would ever want to withhold his truth from anyone, he does tend to filter through who gets what, how much, and when. Sometimes he speaks in parables, and sometimes in child-like truth. Sometimes he reveals himself through radiant light, and other times in the deepest darkness. Sometimes his truth is discovered like a fountain or spring, and sometimes we have to really dig for it. Yet, like any relationship, our bond grows as we experience our journey together. We are on a spiritual pilgrimage, and he has promised that anyone who truly seeks, shall find. Yet, don't always expect the Water of Life to be on the surface. We also must learn to dig.

The Soul Winner

"The fruit of the righteous is a tree of life, and he who wins souls is wise."
Prov. 11:30

Leading people to a saving knowledge of Jesus Christ is a wonderful experience. Yet, evangelism makes a lot of people very nervous, so they tend to leave it to the "professionals". It is such a glorious undertaking, in fact, that people refer to it as "winning souls", as if it is a competition or a prize to be won by the elite or most gifted. Where did people get this idea? Leading someone to Christ is a joyous experience, but also a humbling one. It doesn't give someone bragging rights because they have "won" more souls to Christ than someone else. This whole idea of winning anything in our walk with Christ, whether souls or crowns or rewards of any kind, then, is nothing more than self-glorification, rather than glorifying God. We don't deserve our salvation, and we certainly don't deserve '"winning" anyone else's salvation either.

So, what do we do with the verse that says, "he who wins souls is wise". Doesn't that encourage the idea of "winning souls"? Well, not really. The verse is talking about the eternal life that we personally have by being in a right relationship with God. The second part of this verse merely reinforces the first part. The word "wins" is mistranslated in this context, for in the Hebrew it means "receives, accepts, or grasps hold of". The word "souls" is also mistranslated, for the Hebrew means "anything that has life or vitality". In other words, this verse is really telling us that "The fruit of the righteous is a tree of life", and he who grasps hold of or seizes this life is wise. It is an admonition for us not to take our salvation or eternal life lightly, but to receive all of its vitality with gusto and eagerness to continue to grow. We should want to be bearing fruit, and not be satisfied with just being dormant. We should want the fruit of the Spirit to blossom within us, as evidence of the life that we now have in Christ. We should want to produce fruit that is righteous, or grown according to the guidelines of the divine gardener. We should also desire to share the vitality of our faith with others, so that they too can be fruitful in righteousness.

God wants us to lead others to him through our words and example, but it has nothing to do with "winning souls". There is no competition between ourselves and others, or between God and Satan. Jesus Christ has already been victorious over sin and death. We just need to share that good news with others, so that they would be willing to accept, receive or grasp hold of the same life that gave us eternity. If they believe, it is not because of any effort on our part, but the divine drawing of the Holy Spirit toward the Almighty. We may be used by the Lord as a tool in the process, but God only uses his rusty, old, beat-up tools to do his gardening, for he wants all the glory for the harvest, instead of the pride of the plowboys.

Circumspect or Disrespect

"A man is praised according to his wisdom, but men with warped minds are despised." Prov. 12:8

A circumspect person is not always wise, but a wise person is always circumspect. The word circumspect comes from the combined roots for the words "circle" and "respect". Someone who is circumspect, then, is one who has respect for the whole picture—past, present, and future---and not just the immediate impulsive desire. It is possible, though, to evaluate all of the possible consequences of an action, and yet still make an unwise choice—to choose the evil instead of the good. So, we can be circumspect without being wise.

When we are wise, however, we also must be circumspect. If we are wise we will always take into account the whole picture, both temporal and eternal, before making our decisions. The circle is a symbol for the eternal. This is why we exchange rings at weddings, to symbolize our lasting love for one another. To be circumspect, then, is to have respect for the circle, or the eternal. We are not only interested in our own perspective. We want to know what God's perspective is about everything.

According to the above verse, such a person will be praised. This is not always true. The world doesn't always honor or praise the truly wise. They are much more likely to praise the warped minds of our generation because they too are warped. Yet, those who value wisdom, will definitely praise the wise man. He will also be praised and rewarded by the Lord, for he has promised to honor those who honor him.

The person with a warped mind, however, is despised by those who value wisdom. The word "warped" here means "distorted, perverted, or twisted out of shape". They cannot see the whole picture clearly because of this distortion, so they usually stumble into their own foolishness. Their vision of truth is blurred so they keep bumping into the same mistakes over and over again. They never look back, so they are completely insensitive to the consequences of their actions or how much they have hurt others. They have no respect for their "circle" of friends, so they too are despised. They aren't circumspect. They're just going in circles.

God has a plan for our lives—a blue print or design—instructions on how things are supposed to work. We have a shape that we are supposed to conform to—Christ-likeness—but the non-believer, as well as the Christian who has been deceived by the world's delusions, has been twisted out of shape. The result is a perversion of God's purposes. God wants to produce a masterpiece, and we give him abstract-impressionism or childish finger-painting. We are not circumspect, so we earn his disrespect. We are not wise, so He will despise. We are not willing to look past our present desire, so we earn his disdain, and an eternity that's filled with fire. The wise will learn. The unwise will burn.

People Without Revelation

"Where there is no revelation, the people cast off restraint." Prov. 29:18

When the children of Israel were waiting at the bottom of Mount Sinai for Moses to return, they thought that maybe Moses had died on the mountain. So, their natural tendency was to revert back to the pagan practices of their past. It was what they were used to, what they were comfortable with. They had not been given the law yet, so as far as they knew, they were not doing anything wrong. Yes, God had proven his deity by helping them to escape the Egyptians, but that didn't mean that he was the only deity. They were raised to believe that there were many gods. Believing in Jehovah was just like adding another idol to the shelf. Without revelation from God, they had nothing to restrain their actions. Their consciences were calloused a long time before through their being used and abused, beaten and bruised. They had to become hardened just to survive.

God's people today have no such excuse. We have the inspired Word of God, and the Holy Spirit living within us to illuminate our understanding. Yet, how many times do we find Christians who never open their Bibles, let alone ask God to teach them from it. They even go to church without their Bibles, for they have learned to depend on the "Scripture on the Screen". This multimedia innovation is very convenient, but it is contributing to a whole generation of Christians who don't know the Word, and wouldn't know how to find something in it if their lives depended on it. They are more familiar with the TV Guide than they are with the Word of God.

It is no wonder that God has stopped revealing himself to us today, for we have almost completely ignored the revelation that he has already given to us. The God of the universe has done everything that he can do to reveal himself to us, including the humiliating entry into the world as a man, rejection, and crucifixion, all because he loves us, and we still just throw the Bible under the bed with our dirty clothes, as if it is just someone's dirty laundry that we would much rather just ignore. Is it any wonder that our young people today are casting off all restraints, and living pagan, hedonistic lives? Is it any surprise that even we as adults often play with sin, as if it didn't really matter, in spite of the fact that it grieves the Holy Spirit, and stirs up the wrath of the Almighty?

What does a wild animal do when it has no restraints? Whatever it wants. It doesn't give a second thought about killing or devouring others around it. It is self-centered, destructive, and focused only on the immediate needs and desires. Does this sound like anyone we know? Does it remind us of ourselves? Most of the time we ignore the revelation of God, not because we are lazy, but because we don't want to have God's restraints put upon us. We would rather be free to be our own gods. Reading the Bible might be bad for our self-image. It might just tell us the truth.

Stand Firm in your Faith

"If you do not stand firm in your faith, you will not stand at all." Isa. 7:9

I love to go to the ocean, to take off my shoes, and to wade into the water just far enough to get my rolled up pants a little wet. I love to just stand there and let the waves hit my legs, sinking slightly into the sand with each playful surge. This works fine until a large wall of water decides to crash into my daydreaming. I think I have my feet dug in deep enough to withstand the wave, but I am lifted up and thrown backward as easily as the wind might blow a leaf. I try to stand different ways, with my back to the ocean or maybe my side, but the same thing happens when the water rises. The tide is coming in, and the waves are getting bigger, and my once fun game has gotten me soaking wet. The ocean is no longer satisfied with knocking me over. It now wants to put me in its pocket and take me home. It is time to move to higher ground, or I will be washed out to sea. I need to find a rock to stand on that is high enough and sturdy enough to withstand the wild tempest, and I need to run, not walk, before the next big surge comes. I don't want to become like a fragile sea shell, and get shattered against the craggy cliffs. I leave, not because I want to, but because I want to survive, so I can come again to take my stand against the waves another day. I know that I can never win in this challenge against the mighty foe, but I love to dance with danger, and to hold out as long as I can.

Sometimes we get the idea that our spiritual stance is this same kind of dance. We think that all it takes is a change in strategy, or a slight movement to ward off the coming blows. Or perhaps if we just dig in a little deeper, we can withstand the mighty attacks from the Devil. Yet, over and over, sometimes when we least expect it, we get lifted completely off our spiritual feet, and thrown backward into the powerful, swirling sins of the world around us. We are startled by the ease with which we are thrown off guard, but we come back again, each time thinking that we just need to try a little harder, and eventually we will succeed. This, of course, is just as pointless as our trying to challenge the sea. The solution is not in more effort, taking a different stance, or even moving to the left or right. We need to find higher ground. We need to find a solid rock to stand on, and stop trusting in the sinking sands. We need to understand how fragile or weak we are, and stop trying to dare the Devil to a duel. We need to find our strength in Jesus, our Rock, and to take our stand upon the Word of God, instead of dancing with human philosophies, eastern religions, or even pagan rituals, as if we feel invincible to the surges of Satan. Just because we are Christians doesn't mean that we can't be knocked off our feet by the Devil's schemes. If we don't stand firm in our faith, we will not stand at all, and faith means trust, not just digging in our heels. Jesus is the only answer, and truth is the only way.

God's Guarantee

"The Lord was with Samuel as he grew up, and he let none of his words fall to the ground." I Sam. 3:19

When my brother got married, my wife made the wedding cake. It was a large cake, with several layers. On the day of the wedding, it was my job to carry the cake to the church safely. It was only two blocks away, so I thought that I could carry it that far without any problem. I had no idea how hard it would be. My arms felt so heavy that they felt like they were going to fall off. They didn't just hurt, they ached and throbbed. Then they got so weak, that I didn't think that I could take another step without dropping the whole thing onto the sidewalk. Yet, I knew that the wedding would be ruined if I dropped it, and I would have a lot of angry relatives that I would have to deal with for the rest of my life. So, I endured the pain, and used my stubborn will to compensate for my weak muscles. I made it, but barely, although I may have ruined some of the frosting with some of the sweat that poured from my brow. It's amazing what you can force yourself to do when you know that others are depending on you.

The Lord knows how weak we are, and how much we need him. He knows that our human natures are unreliable, and prone to break down under stress. So, as the manufacturer, he has offered a guarantee—his purposes will never fail. When God chose Samuel to be a prophet, Samuel was just a child. Yet, as he grew, God made sure that everyone knew that he was God's spokesman by fulfilling every prophecy that Samuel ever gave. That's 100% accuracy, because with God, there is no room for error. When God gave Samuel a message, God made sure that it happened just as he foretold. The Bible puts it, "He let none of his words fall to the ground". The "he" in this phrase is not talking about Samuel. There is no way that Samuel could have made sure that God's words were fulfilled. He was just a messenger. God is the one who guarantees his own words. He will never drop the ball, or the wedding cake, or whatever he chooses to carry. He never grows weak or tired, like we do. We can depend on him.

"Words" in this phrase are not just communications. This word in the Hebrew means "words, causes, promises, commands, and purposes". God guarantees them all. He doesn't just spew out meaningless or frivolous words like we do. Everything he says is profound, prophetic, and purposeful.

When it says that he will not let even one of his words fall, the word "fall" means "fail, be discarded for being useless, or allowed to die through neglect". We, as humans, might fail to obey his words, or discard them through rebellion, or allow them to die in the soil of our souls through neglect. Yet, that doesn't keep him from fulfilling his promises or purposes. We may drop the ball, but he is always there with his "catcher's mitt". God never fails.

Hind's Feet on High Places

"He makes my feet like the feet of a deer; he enables me to stand on the heights."
2 Sam. 22:34

The deer is one of the most graceful, gentle, and beautiful animals in the wild. While the male buck can be aggressive and violent in the protection of itself or its territory, the female doe is more prone to run away and flee any possible danger. It is the female that is talked about in this verse, for the word used for deer is the word usually translated "hind", which refers to the doe. That is significant, considering the context of this verse, for it is referring to a time of warfare. The verse before it says, "It is God who arms me with strength", and the verse after it says, "He trains my hands for battle; my arms can bend a bow of bronze".

So, how does this scene of idealistic beauty fit in the midst of this picture of conflict and combat? If it was the male stag, with its mighty antlers and muscular body attacking its foe, we could understand. Yet, it is the female hind, and she has run to the mountain tops to escape the bloodshed. What is going on here? Why the contradictory metaphors of beauty and the beast, of gentle bliss and gory battle?

This passage is actually one of the songs of David, and is repeated in Psalm 18. It is a song of praise to God for helping him to have victory over his enemies, and to be saved from the attacks of Saul. David was a picture of contrasts. On the one hand, he was able to conquer Goliath, and fight against the enemies of God without fear. On the other hand, he was a gentle man, who would rather flee from Saul than to take the life of God's anointed. He knew that he was chosen to be the next king of Israel, so he could have assumed that it was alright to take this position by force. Yet, he submissively waited for God's timing, and did everything within his power to seek peace with his enemy. He was a battling buck, but a humble hind at the same time. From the world's perspective, he should have just strutted his stag strength for all it was worth. From God's perspective, though, David needed to be submissive to the power and purposes of the Lord. He needed to recognize his own weakness, and his need to depend completely upon God, not his own strength.

So, the Lord helped him to have "hind's feet", ones that would flee to the mountains in submission to God, knowing that God would "enable" him there to take the stand that he needed to take. He would be able to experience the heights of God's love and blessing when he sought refuge in God's power and will, and he would receive the strength that he needed to go back down the mountain to fight the battles that he was destined to win.

The word "hind" is the same root as the word "hinder", for from the world's view, meekness is weakness, and it only hinders our drive to reach our ambitious goals. For Christians, to be a "hind" is never a "hindrance" to the will of God.

The Sovereign Lord

"The Sovereign Lord is my strength." Hab. 3:19

When do we trust in God? How do we know when he is blessing us? When do we have peace with God? When are we able to really rejoice in the Lord? Amazingly enough, all of these questions are usually answered the same way—when God provides all my needs and desires. We are so materialistic, that even our spiritual understanding is grounded in physical terms. "If you fill my stomach, I will feel full of the Spirit. If you make my business prosperous, I will feel that you love me. If you give me what I want, I'll give you a tip once in a while in gratitude." In contrast, if we don't do well, we tend to blame God. If our debts are huge, our credit cards are maxed out, and we never have enough left over to really feel like we've made it, we wonder why God doesn't bless us more. It is totally foreign to us to think of God in just spiritual terms. We have to anchor him down with the physical realm in order to visualize him. We, too, feel like we have to be anchored down by things. If we don't have them, we think we are worthless, life is worthless, and God is worthless.

Occasionally, though, there comes along someone who is completely unattached to things. They don't care about whether they have a nice house, or a car, or nice clothes, or any of the adult toys that we think of as necessities. Elijah, Paul, and Stephen are just a few of the Godly men mentioned in the Bible who are so unconnected to things that nothing in this world means anything to them except for sharing the message of the divine. It doesn't matter what happens to their bodies, their souls remain steadfast.

Habakkuk is another man of God who came to value God alone, and nothing else mattered. He humbly says, "Though the fig tree does not bud and there are no grapes on the vines, though the olive crop fails and the fields produce no food, though there are no sheep in the pen and no cattle in the stalls, yet I will rejoice in the Lord, I will be joyful in God my Savior. The Sovereign Lord is my strength" (Hab. 3:17-19). He doesn't just say, "Well, I don't like it, but I guess I can put up with it." He is able to find strength and joy in the Lord alone, <u>without things</u>.

His secret of contentment and rejoicing is found in the names that he calls his God. The first one is "Sovereign". This word means lord, master, ruler, or owner. If we believe that God is all of these things, then we have no ownership of our own. Things don't belong to us. <u>We</u> don't belong to us. We are God's. If we can't understand this one principle, then everything else in scripture is meaningless. If God is not lord of all, he isn't lord at all.

The second word for God is "Yahweh", which means "the self-existent one or the eternal "I AM". In these two names of God, then, we have the two principles involved in the sovereignty of the Lord--He is the only "I AM", and we are "I AM HIS". In these come real life and peace. Nothing else matters.

The Singing Savior

"The Lord your God is with you, he is mighty to save. He will take great delight in you, he will quiet you with his love, he will rejoice over you with singing." Zeph. 3:17

Wow! Can you imagine God actually singing? Maybe he is really George Beverly Shea incarnate, and his booming baritone blesses heaven with his daily concerts to packed houses of loyal fans. Maybe this is why the angels play their harps, to accompany the omniscient opera, with God as the lead virtuoso. Maybe this is how David was inspired to write his psalms—he heard the voice of the Lord singing to his soul. What on earth, or heaven, would cause the Almighty God to take the time to sing? It seems like he would be too busy with more important things to be involved with such a frivolous pastime. Even more amazing is the fact that he is singing about us. He isn't just praising his works of creation, or serenading the saints of long ago. It says, "The Lord your God is with you, he is mighty to save". He isn't just on some distant galaxy singing to the stars. He is here, right now, with us, and he is singing because he saved us. Even more astonishing is the fact that he didn't just save us because he felt sorry for us. We are not just a charity case, and heaven is not a celestial rescue mission. Believe it or not, God actually takes "great delight" in us. We bring joy to his heart when we come to him in repentance and faith. When we come with sorrow in our souls for the sins we have committed, and seek his forgiveness and grace, it says, "He will quiet you with his love, he will rejoice over you with singing". He will comfort us, and heal our broken hearts. He will tenderly wrap his arms of love around us, wipe away all of our tears, and sing to our hearts till they echo his joy. I can't imagine such love. It seems, from our human perspective, that he would be so discouraged with mankind, that he would just want to destroy it completely again, like he did with Noah and the flood. Why does he put up with our rebellious insolence, lack of faith, and total lack of love? Yet, time and time again in the scriptures, he gives accounts of how God responds to the wayward spirits of mankind. There is the parable of the prodigal son, where the father received his wild, ungrateful son back with great joy, as if he had found a lost treasure. There is the parable of the 100 sheep, where 99 stay close to the shepherd, but one strays away. The shepherd is willing to do anything just to get that one lost sheep back into his fold--such compassion, grace, and mercy. It's enough to make a poor sinner cry. It's enough to make the savior sing. At the end of creation, God celebrated by taking a day of rest. At the end of his re-creation, when he breathes life into a dead soul, and the Eternal comes to dwell in the mortal, the Mighty God doesn't just rest. He sings "Hallelujah", and he asks us to sing the harmony.

Time to Reconsider

"Give careful thought to your ways." Hag. 1:5-9

It is end of the year evaluation time. Your boss has asked you to fill in an employee review form, and you are asked to weigh your performance on how well you achieved your stated goals for the year. You are stressed out, afraid of criticism, very much aware of your own failures, and feeling very inferior to the task. You hate having to go through this process every year. Sometimes it even makes you want to quit, rather than go through the humiliation of admitting failure. It's all such a waste of time anyway. Nothing ever really changes. You have the same problems and weaknesses that you had ten or twenty years ago. Why can't they just accept you the way that you are? Your job is so meaningless anyway. What difference does it make how well you do? You are just going through the motions of busyness in order to get a paycheck. You feel like a machine, an insignificant cog in the wheel. You wiggle, squirm, and procrastinate as long as possible, and then you reluctantly scribble down a few things just to get it done, hoping that the boss doesn't look too closely, or dig too deep. Nothing ever changes.

Unfortunately, the above description is too often the case in many of our lives. There is never any growth, or change, or improvement. We just get older, and more set in our ways. The same thing is true spiritually speaking. So, our boss, the Heavenly Father, calls us in for a performance review. He says, "Give careful thought to your ways". It's time to reconsider your priorities, your purposes, and your principles. "You have planted much, but harvested little". You are wasting a lot of your time and effort. You are spinning your wheels. "You eat, but never have enough". You are never satisfied. Everything that you do leaves you feeling empty. "You expected much, but...it turned out to be little".

This is not a very good performance review. Yet, God doesn't stop with the problems. He digs deeper to the cause. He says, "What you brought home, I blew away. Why?...Because of my house, which remains a ruin, while each of you is busy with his own house" (vs. 9). In other words, your priorities are all wrong. You have been just living for yourself and your own temporal needs and desires, instead of focusing on the eternal things of God. It's no wonder that your life seems insignificant and wasted, because everything that you value is merely a puff of smoke. You are pouring all your effort, creativity and life into a bottomless pit of meaningless materialism.

When are we going to learn that only those things that are done for Christ will last? When are we going to start listening and growing, instead of falling into the same ruts of self-destruction year after year? We need to set our spiritual goals higher and our selfish goals lower. Only God can give an eternal raise.

The Peacemakers

"Blessed are the peacemakers, for they will be called sons of God." Matt. 5:9

I used to be a school teacher, and one of my hardest jobs was keeping people away from each other. I had to separate the boys from the girls at times, when the flirtations got a little too physical. I had to divide one rival from another, each trying to irritate the other to no end. I had to move some completely across the room from their best friends, because otherwise they would keep each other from learning. I felt like a referee in a boxing match at times, keeping enemies from destroying one another. At other times I felt like a lion tamer trying to tame and train a bunch of wild things from acting out their natural instincts. I was a peacemaker, at least from the world's perspective. Isn't that what peacemakers are supposed to do—go into a conflict or stressful situation and get the two sides to either shake hands, or agree to leave each other alone?

Although this is sometimes a necessary tactic, it should never be the primary goal. A peacemaker should never be just a control valve which regulates how much steam the pot gets before it blows its top. The peacemaker is not meant to be just a bully who uses their strength or power to make people behave. We can pressure people to conform, but we can never force peace. The spiritual peacemaker is first of all one who is at peace within. They are not struggling with their own ego or self-image, they are not fighting with others, and they are not wrestling with God. One of the meanings of the word "peacemaker", in fact, is actually "one who is committed to contentment". They are content, and they are committed to staying that way.

That doesn't mean that peace is just a matter of more effort. Another meaning to the word "peacemaker" is "one who abides in the giver of peace", who is God. If we abide in him, he gives us his peace, and then we share that peace with others. In other words, when we find someone who is struggling, we are able to help them find the same peace that we have already found. We are not a wall or policeman between enemies. We are a spiritual physician sharing the healing power of God that was given to us.

Another meaning of the word "peacemaker" is "one who is bonded together with another to share their burden". We help them to find peace through the comfort that they get from not having to carry their burden alone. We are a conduit of the Holy Spirit, our Paraclete or comforter, who "comes along side, sharing the assurance of his strength".

The last definition of the word "peacemaker" is "to have and to hold", which is a phrase that is used in the traditional marriage ceremony. We promise to "have and to hold from this day forward, till death do us part". The peace, then, that we are able to share with others is really a commitment of love, trust, and loyalty, without conditions and without end. Have we been this kind of peacemaker?

The Hotly Pursued

"Blessed are those who are persecuted because of righteousness,
for theirs is the kingdom of heaven." Matt. 5:10

No one wants to be persecuted. In fact, we will usually do everything we can to avoid it. Yet, when there is a cause that we really believe in, we are often willing to be persecuted if our own suffering means the success of the cause. We, in fact, may even be willing to lay our lives down for our beliefs. So, when the Bible tells us that those who are persecuted for righteousness sake will be rewarded with the kingdom of heaven, it makes it easier to put up with the abuse that we may receive.

This verse, however, may be saying exactly the opposite. The word "persecuted" here does not mean tormented or abused. It means "hotly pursued". This still may imply persecution, for we think of a police officer being in hot pursuit of a criminal, or an army being in hot pursuit of the enemy. Yet, it doesn't have to be something negative at all. It could also refer to the large crowds who were in hot pursuit of Jesus out of admiration when he was performing so many miracles. It could also refer to the total abandon with which the disciples gave up everything to follow after Christ. They weren't just pursuing the excitement of his powerful ministry. They were pursuing a more intimate, abiding relationship with Jesus himself. Their pursuit of God was all-encompassing. They not only wanted to be with him. They wanted to be like him. They wanted to be one with him.

This verse, then, can be both positive and negative as it relates to us, just as it was both positive and negative for Christ. There were those who hotly pursued Jesus to persecute him in every way that they could. There were also those who hotly pursued his lordship in their lives. Blessed are we, therefore, if we are like Christ, and are pursued for both our good example of righteousness, and because there are those who want to attack us because of that righteousness. If we can have such a strong testimony of God's power and truth in our lives that others will be drawn to our leadership and light, what greater honor could there be? That is the kingdom of heaven, not just some future retirement home in the sky. It is Christ's kingdom on earth, right now, in people's hearts and lives. If we are walking in the light, and others are led to the Lord by hotly pursuing the light that we are holding up, we are not only citizens of the kingdom, but torchbearers for the Lord.

If, on the other hand, we are hotly pursued by those who are enemies of Christ, who want to snuff out our lights, we should feel blessed and honored to be allowed to suffer for the sake of our Lord. To be pursued by both the good and the bad at the same time, some trying to lift us higher, and the rest trying to bury us, what an exciting mixture of pain and pleasure-- which is the only way that we can even taste a little of what Christ went through for us.

Signs of the Times

"This child is destined to cause the falling and rising of many in Israel, and to be a sign that will be spoken against, so that the thoughts of many hearts will be revealed."
Luke 2:34-35

Every parent has hopes and dreams about the futures of their children. They know that they will go through trials and hardships, but they hope for the best—that in the end, everything will be alright. Mary and Joseph had these same dreams, I'm sure, highlighted by the glowing prophecies of Jesus becoming the Messiah of the children of God. When they take him to the temple, then, to be circumcised and dedicated to the Lord, they are not prepared for the prophecy they hear. They knew that he would be great, but they had no idea what that would mean.

Now they are being told that he is "destined to cause the falling and rising of many in Israel". The word "falling" actually means "the crashing downfall" of many. He is going to be the sign of the times, and many on the road of life are going to crash into him. He is going to be a roadblock that many will not be able to get past. Some will be able to be directed by his sign, and will be able to rise toward heaven, but many will be casualties of the King's Highway. They will speak against this sign, as if it is the sign's fault that they crashed. It keeps them from going the way that they want to go, and they have road rage to the extreme. The sign has revealed "the thoughts of many hearts", and it isn't pretty.

Why is this sign so disturbing? Well, first of all, it keeps changing its message. No one likes to be told "No!", so it is no surprise that people do not like being told "Stop" what you are doing. It is sin. Then the sign changes to a different message, "U-turn okay". Jesus doesn't just want us to stop going one direction. He wants us to make an "about face", and go the opposite direction. Then, when we rebel and start yelling out the window at him for cutting us off, he changes to a "Yield" sign. We don't take "No" for an answer, and we demand to know "Why?". He tells us that it is because we are driving on a "One Way" street, and we are going the wrong way.

If we listen and turn around, we will be doing fine. We will end up in Paradise, which is where the signs are pointing to all along. If we refuse to "Yield", however, and keep going our own way, we will crash right into Jesus. There is no way to get around this "Dead End". Jesus tells us, "I am the way, the truth, and the life. No man comes to the Father but by me" (John 14:6). This "One Way" sign is probably the hardest for most people. They don't like having limits put on them. They think that they know better. They want to be in the driver's seat, and in their mind, God is just a back seat driver who is annoying them to death.

So, mankind crashes into Jesus' sign on the cross. Unfortunately for them, the sign is restored, and they are liable for the damages.

The Fig Farmer

"I was neither a prophet nor a prophet's son, but I was a shepherd,
and I also took care of fig trees." Amos 7:14

When it comes to election time, how do you decide who to vote for? Do you make your choice based upon their appearance and personality, or their voting record? Do you listen to their canned speeches, or are their debates more important to you? Do you weigh out the stances they have taken on all the major issues, or do you just want to know how they stand in one or two important ones? Are their morals and private life important to you, or do you just vote on how good they can do their job? Is their race or religion of value to you, or is it more important what political party they belong to?

It is amazing sometimes how little we really know about a politician before we put our trust in them. It's more like a gut instinct, than an educated choice. Yet, as much as possible, we don't willingly or knowingly elect someone who is incompetent for the job. With God, however, it's almost as if he purposely chooses the incompetent ones, just to show that they can't do their jobs without him.

First, he chose Adam to name all of the animals, even though Adam had no education, had never seen an animal before, and had no idea what species the animals were related to. He was a novice, yet he was put in charge of the zoo.

Then he asked Noah to build a huge boat out in the middle of the desert, even though he wasn't near any water, and may never have even seen a boat. He certainly had never seen one big enough to carry all the people and animals that he would need to take with him on his adventure. He was a tin-horn, yet was being asked to build the Titanic. What was God thinking?

Then, he chose Moses to lead his people out of Egypt into the Promised Land. First, he was raised and educated according to pagan religious principles, he was a fugitive for committing murder, he was a poor shepherd in a foreign land, and he had a speech impediment. Certainly God could have found someone with better credentials than that.

Then came David, who also was just a shepherd, except this one knew how to serenade his sheep. He was young and inexperienced, but God chose him to be king.

Then God chose Amos to be his prophet. When people complained about his prophecies, he honestly admitted, "I was neither a prophet nor a prophet's son, but I was a shepherd, and I also took care of fig trees. But the Lord took me from tending the flock and said to me, 'Go, prophesy to my people Israel.' Now then, hear the word of the Lord." He admitted that he was a nobody, and that he was unqualified for the job. Yet, God still chose him and commanded him to be his messenger. Amos didn't argue. He just obeyed. God is more interested in our availability than our ability. We just need to be willing to leave our figs, and start bearing fruit for him.

Putting Meat on the Bones

*"Think not that I have come to destroy the law or the prophets;
I am not come to destroy, but to fulfill."* Matt. 5:17

When I was in college, I was still pretty thin, and my grandmother would always tell me, "Come over to my house, and I'll put some meat on those bones". I had all the right structure, and I was plenty healthy. I just needed to fill out a little.

In one sense, strangely enough, the same thing is true of the scriptures. When God gave the books of the Law to Moses, it was like building a skeleton or framework for revealing the glory and character of God. Then came the prophets, who wrote down what God revealed about both the past and the future, which gave the skeleton its eyes to see things from God's perspective, as well as its muscles to demonstrate the strength of his power.

When Christ came along, he was accused of wanting to destroy these revelations of God, and starting something completely new. He said, "Think not that I have come to destroy the law or the prophets; I am not come to destroy, but to fulfill". The word "fulfill" means to "complete, fill in the gaps, and to embody". Instead of doing away with the previous revealed Word, then, he was going to complete it. He was going to fill in the gaps of understanding about God and his truth by embodying the nature of God himself. He, in a sense, was going to put some meat on the bones of the Old Testament, to flesh-out the skeleton of the Law.

It is hard to understand the nature of God just by looking at the skeleton of the Law and the prophets. We can see his holiness, wisdom and power, but it is harder to comprehend his love, mercy and grace. They are there, but it is as if they are often hidden in the marrow of the bones of the skeleton, rather than out on the surface for all of us to see.

So, Jesus came, God in the flesh, to demonstrate more fully the character and purpose of the divine. The letter of the Law had become old and brittle, and Jesus breathed new life into it. He gave it CPR, Christ's Powerful Redemption, and the pile of dry bones was revived.

In a very important sense, we too, must do the same. We are supposed to be Christ-like, demonstrating the character of God in our lives. The world isn't going to take the time to read the Bible to see how Jesus embodied the nature of God. So, Jesus breathes new life into us, so we can, in turn, show the world the eternal character of the Deity. The church is the body of Christ, and we, like him, must embody God's revelation of himself. Christ hasn't completely fulfilled all of his revelation of the divine plan and purpose yet, for there are still many prophecies that have yet to be fulfilled. Yet, we need to understand that we are part of this ongoing "fulfilling" or "fleshing-out" of God's spiritual skeleton, so we shouldn't skimp on the spiritual feasts that God prepares for us.

Doing Our Duty

"We are unworthy servants; we have only done our duty." Luke 17:10

Imagine working hard all day, dealing with all kinds of stress, and then, at the end of the day, when you are completely drained, your boss asks you to stay a couple extra hours to finish one of his projects, so he can go home. How would you respond? Would you lose your cool, or would you say, "Yes, Sir. I would be glad to," but then brood and steam in rage after he is gone?

Jesus actually tells a parable of this same thing happening. He tells of a servant who has worked hard all day plowing the field and taking care of the sheep. Then he comes home for supper, expecting to be able to get the rest that he needs. In fact, when he sees his master approaching him, he thinks, "Maybe he'll praise my work, show his appreciation, or even ask me to eat with him as a reward for my hard work." Instead, his master tells him to fix a meal for him, and then serve him till he has finished.

Does the master thank him for all that he has done? Not at all. At about this time, we would probably be fuming. Why can't he just say "Thank you" once in a while? Why does he treat me like a robot who is just here to do a job? Does he have any idea how hard I work? Does he even care?

One of the biggest struggles that we have to deal with, either at work, home or church, is not feeling appreciated. We feel that people take us for granted, and the only time they even notice us is if we make a mistake or don't get something done. We feel insignificant, unfulfilled, and empty, and all of our extreme effort ends up being meaningless.

Part of the problem in this story is the ungrateful attitude of the boss. People only think of themselves. Yet, Jesus doesn't use the parable to ridicule the master. His lesson is for the servant. He says that we should respond to the unfair demands that are placed upon us, and all the ingratitude, with an attitude of complete submission, which says, "We are unworthy servants; we have only done our duty."

Part of our frustration is that we feel that we deserve more, and all the self-help books out there try to convince us that we are special. If other people don't recognize that, it is their problem. Well, we are special, created in God's image. Yet, we are also spiritually fallen and deserving of hell. If we are saved, it is only by God's grace, and even the very best of our works is nothing but "filthy rags" in God's sight (Isa. 64:6).

It doesn't really matter, then, how we are treated by others. We are only servants, and never deserve anything more, no matter how hard we work. So, if we have to plow the fields, feed the sheep, or even feed the "pigs" of our society, we should do it expecting nothing in return, for that's probably what we will get. If we are truly serving Jesus only, we won't need the praise of men. If we do, maybe we are serving ourselves, and not Jesus at all.

Knowing God's Timing

"You did not recognize the time of God's coming to you." Luke 19:44

Jesus is on his way to Jerusalem to offer himself as King of the Jews, yet he knows that he will be rejected and crucified. So, he takes the time to perform two very different kinds of miracles. He stops first at Bethany, where he calls forth Lazarus, raising him from the dead four days after being put in the tomb. No one has ever seen such power. If this isn't the Messiah, no one is. You would have to be blind, deaf, and dumb not to recognize the mighty hand of God working through this man.

The crowds swarm him as if they are just waiting for the next big miracle to happen. So, he doesn't disappoint them. He calls Zacchaeus down from a Sycamore tree and tells him that he needs to stay at his house that day. Zacchaeus is a little man in stature but a big man in the community. He is the chief tax collector and a wealthy man. He is used to having power of his own and controlling people's lives. He is dishonest and heartless, for his job demands him to be such a person. Yet, when Jesus calls his name, he responds immediately. He not only takes Jesus home, he promises to give away much of his money, and to pay back all those whom he had robbed or cheated. Another resurrection has taken place, but this time it is a man who is dead spiritually, yet now he is alive. Jesus welcomes him freely into his family.

When Jesus gets closer to Jerusalem, then, the crowds grow bigger and bigger, and they call out, "Blessed is the king who comes in the name of the Lord" (vs. 38). It is the triumphal entry, in that, the crowds are willing to crown him king, for they have seen him raise Lazarus from the dead. He must be the one they are looking for. Yet, they miss the point of his second miracle, which is even more crucial. They are willing to accept him as their physical savior, but not as their spiritual savior. The first kind of miracle they can identify with, for they are concerned with the here and now and their own immediate desires and needs. They are completely blind to the second kind of miracle, though, for it seems like no big deal. Yes, they are glad to get their money back from this crook, but what does this have to do with anything? They are used to seeing rich people flash their generosity around just to get attention. They don't realize that a life has been changed.

Jesus tells them that they are going to be judged, and that Jerusalem is going to be destroyed. Why? He says, "You did not recognize the time of God's coming to you." Yet, aren't we guilty of the same thing? We look for God's presence in our lives, but we focus just on the physical miracles. We see people being healed in their bodies, and we feel that we have had an encounter with God. Yet, when God delivers someone from being egotistical, dishonest, or greedy, we praise the person for overcoming their problems instead of God. The Lord has been in our presence, and we haven't even recognized him.

Come to Me

"Come to me to have life." John 5:40

We attend church whenever the doors are open, we study the Bible every day, and we even go on short term missions trips from time to time. Yet, is it possible that we might be doing all of these things, but missing the point? Could we be doing all the right things, but for all the wrong reasons? Could we be learning about God and doing things for him, and yet not really know him?

We understand how these questions apply to the non-Christian, who may be confusing good works with knowing God. Do we understand, though, how these same problems are true for Christians as well? Jesus talks about the problem when he says, "You diligently study the scriptures because you think that by them you possess eternal life. These are the scriptures that testify about me, but you refuse to come to me to have life" (vs. 39-40).

The problem is that people want what God can give to them, but they aren't willing to come to Jesus to get it. They are willing to do things for God, but they aren't really interested in knowing him. They want to know about him, but keep him personally at a distance. Coming to God is never about good works, either as a non-Christian, or a believer. It is a matter of allowing God to draw us to himself, not us trying to build a huge scaffolding or another tower of Babel, trying to reach the heavens or some spiritual high, but not really caring whether God is there or not. We want eternal life and abundant life because they are good for us. We can understand how our self-centered natures can seek worldly goals just to uplift our egos, but we often miss the correlation when we become Christians, and our goals become spiritual ones.

Well, it doesn't matter whether our goals are our hormones or the heavenlies, they are all based on the ego unless our ultimate goal is getting closer to God himself, and not just our sense of achievement, or trying to sooth our own conscience. We need to seek a closer relationship to Jesus, and to pursue that more than any other goal. We need to recognize that God is pursuing a closer relationship with us, as well, and that we need to stop all of our busyness to wait for him.

Can we imagine a parent going from store to store at Christmas time, trying to buy the perfect gift for their child, and then at the end of the day remembering that they had left their child back at the first store? They were so busy trying to please their child through buying gifts that they forgot about the child himself. The problem is that we do the same thing in our spiritual walk. We spend all of our energy trying to find the perfect gift, or making the greatest sacrifice, or moving mountains for the Almighty, seeking to reach our goal, but losing site of God.

Jesus says, "Come to me to find life", but we aim for "life" itself, and never come to him. We are so busy for him, that we leave him behind.

God's Choices and Ours

"They cast lots, and the lot fell to Matthias; so he was added to the eleven apostles."
Acts 1:26

Jesus had ascended back to heaven, and now the apostles, with 120 other disciples, waited for the coming of the Holy Spirit. They knew that their lives were about to be energized, and their lives would never be the same. They were going to have an exciting adventure, and who knew where it would lead or what it would demand? So, they decided that they needed some help. They felt that they needed someone to take Judas's place as an apostle. Why? They had 120 disciples that were willing to help. Yet, somehow, they felt that it just seemed right to have twelve apostles, as if they had to compensate for Judas's betrayal. Jesus had chosen twelve, so that must be the ideal. Jesus had not told them to replace Judas, and Jesus, himself, did not take the opportunity after his resurrection to choose someone else.

Yet, the apostles went ahead with their plan, even without divine guidance. Yes, Peter did search the scriptures to see if there were any verses that might give them guidance, and he found a couple that he felt that he could use. The two verses that he uses, though, have nothing to do with Judas or their situation. He takes them out of context, as if he had already decided what he wanted to do, and merely used the Bible to support his conclusions, instead of the other way around. Both of the verses that he uses are from the Psalms, and they deal with the enemies of David. Although some of the Psalms are Messianic, and apply to both David and Christ, these two passages don't seem to apply to Christ at all. It is David, not Christ, talking when he says, "You know my folly, O God; my guilt is not hidden from you" (Psa. 69:5).

The psalm is about David's enemies, who mock him and abuse him for his follies, as well as his belief in God. David prays that God will punish his enemies, and that "their place be deserted; let there be no one to dwell in their tents" (vs. 25). Notice that his enemies are plural, not singular, yet Peter quotes from this verse as it is a prophecy about Judas.

The second verse that Peter uses is from Psalm 109, where David is complaining about the evil men who have accused him falsely. He prays that God would send an evil man who would, in turn, accuse his accusers in a court of law, and that they would be found guilty. His prayer, then, is that "another take his place of leadership" (vs. 8).

This verse cannot be speaking of Judas, for Judas never falsely accused Jesus, and he never was found guilty in a court of law for what he did. He just went out and hung himself. It seems that what we have here is another example of Peter's enthusiastic, impulsive personality rushing into something before he really had guidance from God. He wanted to do it, so he found justification to do it. God later corrected this decision by choosing Paul instead. If only Peter had waited.

To Silence the Critics

"So if God gave them the same gift as he gave us, who believed in the Lord Jesus Christ, who was I to think that I could oppose God?" Acts 11:17

In the early cowboy movies, it was very easy to determine who the heroes were and who the villains were. The good guys wore white hats, and the bad guys wore black. Sometimes, though, the writers and directors would add a different dimension by adding an air of mystery to the character, such as with Zorro. This hero wore all black and rode an all black horse, yet he was a man of integrity and honor. This confused many children because it went against the normal stereotype. They didn't know how to respond at first, but soon learned to admire him for his daring courage and determination to fight for the right. They had to learn to look past his clothes to see the true nature of his heart.

The Jews had the same problem during the early church. They were used to thinking in terms of the Law and Jewish tradition, so when the Gentiles started believing, they had a hard time accepting them. God showed them through the ministry of Paul and Peter that even the Gentiles were being accepted by God, so what right had they to reject them? By filling the Gentiles with the Holy Spirit and faith even without the Law, God proved that they belonged to him.

This was a totally foreign way of looking at things for the Jews. It was worse, though, than having the good guys wear black. It was like having the same guy who played the villain in the last scene, all of a sudden become the hero in the end. They had already decided to hate the villain, but now they are being asked to accept him as one of their own.

They went through the same dilemma when Paul became a Christian. They didn't want to accept him at first. After all, wasn't he the one who tried to kill all the Christians? There must be some mistake. Maybe he is just trying to trick us. Yet, God showed that it wasn't just some trick by transforming Paul's heart. He was filled with the Spirit and power, and used the scriptures to convince many people that Jesus was the Messiah. Peter's response to the Gentiles who became Christians was based on the fact that God gave them the ability to speak in tongues, as proof of the filling of the Holy Spirit. He was forced to conclude that they really were saved because God had put his seal of approval upon them. Who was he to argue with God?

We often fall into the same trap as the early church. We often have a hard time accepting people who are different than ourselves as being Christians. God says that it doesn't matter what color hat or denomination they might belong to. Have they been transformed and empowered by the Holy Spirit? That is the question. What kind of outer trappings they have, or how different they are to us, is irrelevant. If God has accepted them, who are we to argue? That doesn't mean that they are perfect. Neither are we. It just means that we have all been forgiven.

Two Extremes

"A group of Epicurean and Stoic philosophers began to dispute with him."
Acts 17:18

The Apostle Paul had to debate two of the main groups of philosophers of his day, the Epicureans and the Stoics. The Epicureans, on the one hand, believed that whatever brought you pleasure was good, and whatever brought you pain was bad. This was not just limited to the physical realm, but to the emotional, mental and spiritual realms as well.

On the other hand, the Stoics believed just the opposite, that pain was good, and pleasure was bad. So, they practiced extreme self-denial and physical abuse to the self in order to achieve the ultimate good. Ironically, this physical self-abasement led to spiritual and emotional pride and self-righteousness. They humbled their bodies so their souls could be the greatest.

Although Paul was dealing with two pagan belief systems, I believe that these two extremes are also found in the church. On the one hand, we have those Christians who believe that the purpose of church is to make people feel good about themselves. They pump them up emotionally, get them all excited, and hypnotically get them entranced into a spiritual high through power-praise songs that are based on repetition and a heavy beat. They don't think that they have been successful unless everyone is dancing in the aisles, raising or clapping their hands, or jumping up and down in joyful exhilaration. They believe that you can't be filled with the Spirit if you are just sitting still. If the Holy Spirit fills you with his joy, then you can't help but bubble all over with flamboyant praise. He fills you with his presence and his pleasure, and you respond with praise.

On the other hand, there are the Stoics in church, who feel that all this external display of jubilation is really a mask for pride, because it merely draws attention to self. They believe that we need to be self-denying, humble, and quiet in our praise, like spiritual wallflowers, who blend into the pews and life so no one notices them. Their emphasis is on repentance and their unworthiness before God, which fills them with sorrow for their failures and inadequacies. They feel that it is only right to sing somber hymns, instead of rowdy praise songs, for we must emphasize reverence and worship before our holy God. Ironically, even in the midst of this humiliation and "divine depression", there is still a lot of pride, for they feel that they are better and more spiritual than the spiritual Epicureans, who seem way too worldly for their taste.

Both of these extremes, unfortunately, spend a lot of wasted energy comparing themselves to each other, and fuming about how wrong the other side is. Paul tried to explain how real Christianity differs from both of these extremes, and we should do the same. God is looking for real seekers of Truth, not just those who already believe that they know it all, or those who believe that their way of worship is the only right way.

Open Confession

"Many of those who believed now came and openly confessed their evil deeds."
Acts 19:18

One of the hardest things to do is to confess our sins to other people. We can tell God in private, but to share them with others is considered too embarrassing. The non-Christian world doesn't seem to have this same problem. In fact, they may even brag about their sins to their friends. Of course, they won't call them sins. They'll call them exploits, adventures or conquests, and they are proud of them. As Christians, though, we are convicted of our sins by the Holy Spirit, and we are commanded in scripture to confess them not only to God, but to one another (James 5:16).

Since it can be embarrassing, the Catholic Church has instituted the confessional, where people can confess to a priest with a semblance, at least, of privacy and anonymity. The point, though, of confession is not to make it easy. It is supposed to be difficult to discourage us from doing the sin ever again. If it is easy to confess, it will be easy to sin again.

God wants us to first of all confess to him, because no matter what our sin is, we have sinned against God, and need to ask his forgiveness. Yet, he doesn't want us to just stop with admitting our sin to him. He also asks us to go to those that we have hurt, abused, or taken advantage of, and to ask for their forgiveness, as well (Matt. 5:23-24).

The purpose for this confession is not just to get something off our chest, as to clear our own conscience. It is to reconcile ourselves to the other person, as well as to clear the channels between ourselves and God, so he will hear our prayers. Reconciliation means restoration of fellowship. It implies more than just a sharing of words, "I'm sorry", but a total change of attitude or a personal transformation. Like a butterfly hatching out of a cocoon, reconciliation is supposed to set our souls free to fly because our hearts are no longer burdened by guilt or shame.

Since reconciliation is the main purpose of confession, whether to God or man, it is not necessary to confess to just anyone. In fact, we are only told to confess to those that we have sinned against. It isn't necessary, then, for us to get up in front of church and bare our soul, unless our sin is a public sin, and we need to confess to the congregation to renew our fellowship with them.

In the account in Acts that is recorded above, the situation is a group of sorcerers who come to know the Lord. They come and burn all of their secret scrolls of sorcery in public as a statement of their changed life, in a similar way that we might do when we are baptized. Their public confession is not just a matter of saying they are sorry, it is publicly acknowledging that they have put their sins behind them, and are now walking a new path. Again, this is only necessary if the sins are public sins.

Paralysis of the Parasites

"When Jesus saw their faith, he said to the paralytic, 'Take heart, son' your sins are forgiven'."
Matt. 9:2

When Jesus heals a paralyzed man, he also forgives his sins, implying in this passage that his paralysis is caused by his sin. That doesn't mean that all paralysis is caused by sin, but in some cases, God does choose to cause paralysis as a punishment for people's sin. I believe that this is not only a possible physical consequence, but an emotional, mental, and spiritual one, as well. When a person has been living in sin, they can become dysfunctional or paralyzed in their ability to do anything that is meaningful. They can become emotional or spiritual zombies, unable to move toward God.

Sometimes the paralyzed person can still feel things touching them, but they are just unable to respond to the sensations. Other times they have lost their ability to sense anything physically, for their nerves also have been damaged. Spiritually speaking, it is the same way. There are some people who can still feel things emotionally and spiritually, but they have lost their ability to do anything in response. Others have become so insensitized, that their consciences have been seared, and nothing affects them any more. The mind may still be telling them that they need to do different things, but they are paralyzed in their spiritual muscles.

Although we may immediately think of lust, anger, or fear as sins that might cripple someone spiritually, there is also another one that is often overlooked. It is that of being a spiritual parasite. It is interesting that the word "parasite" actually originated in reference to pagan priests who were going around to the farmers taking food from them to give as offerings to the gods. The priests were the parasites for they were taking food or nourishment from others without giving anything back in exchange.

Now-a-days, it can still be the priests or pastors who are the parasites, always taking from the people and begging for more, but never really giving the people anything in return. Yet, most of the time, I think that it is the people themselves who are the parasites, feeding off of the pastors, but giving nothing back. Oh, they may put some money in the offering, but that is not the same thing as giving a part of themselves. They have become like spiritual sponges that soak up what the pastor teaches, but never squeeze out any of the living water for others to share. They have become saturated and heavy, and almost immovable. They have become paralyzed by the sin of spiritual laziness, and have become co-dependent upon the pastor.

It is time to break free from the security of trusting too much on the teachings of others. We need to take up our beds and walk, not allowing any sin, even that of laziness, to paralyze our ability to respond to the commands of the head, Jesus Christ, our Lord. God wants more proselytes, not parasites.

God's Plan is Better

"Lazarus is dead, and for your sake I am glad I was not there,
so that you may believe." John 11:14

Sometimes when God doesn't answer our prayers, it is because of sin in our lives, and we need to get right with him before the channels are open. Other times, though, it just seems like there is a huge wall between ourselves and God, even though we have done nothing wrong. We are facing a crisis, and we pray for God's help or provision, and the help doesn't come. The tragedy happens, or the plan falls apart, and we are left feeling like we were in a relay race, and God dropped the baton.

I imagine that this is what probably happened when Lararus became ill. He was probably very brave, and told his friends and family, "Don't worry. Just let my friend Jesus know that I am sick, and he will come to heal me. We know that he is the Messiah, and that he has healed many before. He will not let us down." So, they sent word to Jesus, and there was plenty of time to get there to help him. Yet, Jesus chose to delay his trip, and purposely waited until after Lararus was dead. He dropped the baton; he failed his friend, or so it seemed.

He told his disciples, though, that he waited so that they "may believe". Believe what? Wouldn't they have believed if he had gone earlier and healed Lazarus? When Jesus finally gets there, he is challenged by Martha, the sister of Lazarus. She boldly says, "Lord, if you had been here, my brother would not have died". In other words, "Why weren't you here?! This tragedy wouldn't have happened if you had been doing your job!"

Jesus tries to comfort her by telling her that Lazarus was going to rise from the dead, but she shrugged it off. "Sure, I know he will rise again in the resurrection at the last day." But, that's a long way off. We wanted you to save him now! She didn't understand that that is exactly what was going to happen. Jesus had failed her, and she wasn't listening to reason. She still believed that Jesus was the Messiah, but somehow his halo got tarnished. At least until she saw her brother walk out of the tomb alive. Then her faith was strengthened beyond measure.

If Jesus had come earlier, when Lazarus was just sick, and he had healed him, the family would have been thankful, but that is probably about all. Now, not only their faith, but the faith of everyone who heard about this miracle was greatly increased. It is because of this one miracle that there was so much enthusiasm by the people at the triumphal entry, as Jesus made his final approach to Jerusalem. Since Jesus waited for his perfect timing, what would have been a simple healing was turned into a mega-miracle, like a sweeping wave of God's arms, embracing a multitude.

Life After Death

"Do not offer the parts of your body to sin, as instruments of wickedness, but rather offer yourselves to God, as those who have been brought from death to life." Rom 6:13

According to the Bible, the worst disease possible is leprosy. It attacks the vital fluids of the body, and starts decomposing parts of your flesh while you are still alive. You are a walking dead man. Your organs are still functioning, but parts of your body just start decaying so rapidly that they fall off. Since this disease is so bad, in fact, the Bible often uses leprosy as a symbol for what sin does to our souls. We may be still alive, but spiritually we are "decomposing" or walking dead men.

Occasionally, though, someone with leprosy has a reversal. They will be cured or healed, and the decaying process will end. When this happens in the Jewish community, they are to go through a purification process in order to rejoin their people (Lev. 14:1-9). The priest is to fill an earthenware vessel with pure spring or stream water. Then he is to kill a bird and pour its blood into the water. Since there is not a lot of blood in a bird, scarlet dye is also added to the water as a symbol for blood. Yet, it is not just a symbol, for scarlet comes from killing the larvae from an insect, and squeezing its vital fluids into the water.

Then comes the dipping of part of the Juniper tree into the water. This could be a symbol for new vitality, for the Juniper tree is a strong tree, which grows out of the rocks throughout the Sinai Peninsula, where the Israelites wandered when they left Egypt. Our new life, when we repent and turn back to God, also must come out of the Rock, Jesus Christ.

The Hyssop branch is also dipped into the water. Hyssop is a small bush-like herb which grows out of the rocks or the walls of a city. It is used like a paint brush to spread blood on the door posts at the original Passover in Egypt. Now it is used to sprinkle this symbolic blood mixture upon the person with leprosy, to represent his cleansing from sin, as well as the disease. The priest must sprinkle it upon the man seven times, which is a symbol for perfection or completeness. He is brought back into a right relationship with God, and he is revitalized spiritually, instead of decaying further into depravity.

Then the priest does a beautiful thing. He takes a second bird and dips it into the blend of pure water and blood, and then he lets it go. The bird flies away as a symbol for the new life and freedom that the man has in his new communion with God. The man has been cleansed and set free from his sin, as well as the disease. He has the freedom to have fellowship with his maker. He still needs to go through some additional ceremonies in order to be reunited with the community, but the barrier between him and God has been broken. Now his spirit can really soar.

The Birth of Christ in You

"Flesh gives birth to flesh, but the Spirit gives birth to spirit." John 3:6

The birth of Christ is a very special occasion to us. Even though it is not commanded that we observe this as a holiday, our hearts are drawn to the outpouring of God's love in sending his Son to the world as a little baby. Our hearts are overjoyed, and we want to celebrate. Yet, there is another birth of Jesus, and that is when he is born into the heart of each believer when we become Christians. We are born again because He, too, is born again, once in the flesh, and then in the Spirit.

Jesus in the flesh was conceived through the Holy Spirit implanting the divine seed within Mary. Jesus in the Spirit is also conceived through the Holy Spirit as He implants the seed of faith in our hearts. Jesus in human form was born in Bethlehem, which is the City of David, for He was to become the King of the Jews. The Spirit of Jesus is born in our hearts because He wants to be our King, as well.

The name Bethlehem means "The House of Bread". This is suitable for Christ, for He offered himself as the Bread of Life for all who would receive Him. He also broke the bread at the Passover feast as a symbol of his own body being broken on the cross for our sins.

We, too, must accept Him as the bread of life when he is born within us, for he not only gives us eternal life, but strength for each day. We must internalize Him into every area of our lives, feeding upon His truth, and digesting its meaning for us. When Jesus is born within us, it is like a seed being planted which grows into grain, which must be harvested and sifted, ground down and pulverized into a useful flour, and made into the Bread of Life within the brokenness of our own souls. This Bread of Life is then ready to share with others for it has been hand picked and prepared by the Master Gardener and Baker himself.

In spite of the wonderful idea of the birth of God as a human is, if he just stayed a baby in the manger, like an icon on the wall, his birth would have been useless. He needed to grow up to fulfill his purpose on earth, for he, ironically, was born to die. He also needs to grow up within us, and we, in a sense, then, need to die with him in our hearts (Gal. 2:20). We need to die to self, completely yielded to the will of the Father, just as Christ was. Then, and only then, is he able to rise again within us, with his resurrection power, and we are transformed into new creations in Christ.

We are born again when Christ is born within us. We die with Christ when we are able to fully identify with the sacrifice that he made for us, and we are able to sacrifice our own desires and goals to him. Then we are risen with him as he gives us new life each day as we walk in the light of his truth.

There is a lot more to being a Christian than Christmas. We need to leave Bethlehem, make a stop at Golgotha, and then move on toward glory.

Prophesying According to Faith

"We have different gifts, according to the grace given us. If a man's gift is prophesying, let him use it in proportion to his faith." Rom 12:6

"How much money do you have? It doesn't really matter. Just spend in proportion to how much you have. If you have a lot, spend a lot. If you have a little, just spend a little." Does this sound like good advice to you, or is it just meaningless drivel? Yet, this same advice is given by many commentaries, who choose to read the above verse as if it is talking about a "measure of faith" or a certain quantity. In other words, they think that the verse means, "If you have a lot of faith, then prophesy with this quantity of faith. If, on the other hand, you only have a little faith, then prophesy with this quantity. It doesn't really matter how much you have, just use it."

This, however, is not what this verse is saying. The word that is translated here as "proportion" is "analogia" or analogy. An analogy is a story or illustration, like a parable, where something in the physical world represents some truth in the spiritual realm. Something seen represents the unseen. The word "analogy" comes from "logos", which refers to a concrete communication of an abstract idea. This is why Jesus is called the Logos of God, for he is the physical representation of the Spiritual God. He communicates in the physical realm the exact nature and character of the divine.

That doesn't mean that Paul is implying that a prophet needs to be a good storyteller, although many pastors spend a great deal of time in their sermons just doing that. What he is saying is that there needs to be a direct correlation between what the prophet or teacher is saying and the principles of his faith. So often preachers today speak with forked-tongue. They speak with tongue in cheek theology, as if they don't really believe what they are teaching. They are just proposing some interesting ideas for us to think about, as if they are curiosities in a museum or circus, but optional for us to accept or reject. "Ripley's Believe it or Not".

The word used for "faith" here, though, means "the moral conviction in the truthfulness of something", the total reliance in the thing that you believe in, and fidelity or loyalty to your focus of faith." The prophet, pastor, or priest, then, is supposed to be a walking analogy. His life is supposed to be a physical representation of what he says that he believes. He is supposed to be the demonstration model that what he preaches really works. He needs to have such conviction and fidelity in what he believes, that there is no question as to where he stands. He is, after all, God's spokesman, not just some whimpy milk-toast trying to entertain or make people feel good. He needs to know what he believes, and believe what he knows. In other words, he needs to be a "logos" when he is teaching about the "Logos"—Christ-likeness incarnate.

Clothe Yourself with Christ

"Clothe yourselves with the Lord Jesus Christ." Rom. 13:14

All of us probably have a favorite outfit that we like to wear. Sometimes it is something fancy, that we like to wear when we go out someplace nice. Other times it is something comfy, which we love to slip into as soon as we get home from work. Men, particularly, have the tendency to latch onto a favorite hat, shirt, or shoes, and you can hardly pry them away from them even when they take a shower or go to bed. It almost becomes a part of their bodies, and identifies who they are when you see them even from a distance.

The idea of clothing yourself with Jesus is the same way. The word "clothe" means to actually "sink yourself deeply into a garment", as if you wanted to become one with it, or cuddle so close to it that someone else would not be able to tell where you and it were separate. Have you sunk yourself that deeply into Jesus that people can't tell where the "you" part stops, and the "Jesus" part starts?

When we are clothed with Jesus, we wear his spiritual eye glasses, which help us to see everything clearly from his perspective. We wear his favorite hat, the helmet of salvation, which guards and guides our thoughts, to keep them from being conformed to this world. We wear his favorite shirt, the breastplate of righteousness, for only his holiness can truly guard our hearts from the Devil's darts. We wear his favorite pair of jeans, having our loins girded with truth, for we cannot please him unless we walk in his steps. We wear his royal robe, for we are children of the King.

The whole idea of being clothed with Jesus is that we want to be identified with him. It's more than just a guy wanting to wear a football jersey of his favorite team, so others will know who he is rooting for. We are not just fans of Jesus. We are not just couch potato spectators of Christ or Christianity. We want to be recognized as a member of the team. We want to be "He-Men", or people obviously belonging to Him. We are not just children, playing dress-up, so we can look like the Father. When people see children playing like this, they do not take them seriously. They know that they are just pretending. We don't want people to think that we are just pretending to be like God, playing dress-up for the fun of it.

We want to clothe ourselves with Jesus, sinking deeply or immersing ourselves into his character, his love, his grace, and his truth. We want to be so much like him, in fact, that others see him when they look at us. We are not just impersonators or imitators, trying to win a "look-alike contest". Being clothed with Jesus is not a matter of trying harder to make a good appearance or give a good impression. Jesus first of all puts on his "underwear", by dressing our souls. Then our outward lives merely reflect what he has done on the inside, and our outward garments reflect his face.

The Mind of Christ

"We have the mind of Christ." I Cor. 2:16

I have often wished that I could get into someone's mind and to read their thoughts. I either don't understand what they are saying, or don't trust the words that are coming out of their mouth. If I could just get inside, I think, then I could know what they are really trying to say, or hidden feelings behind their words.

On the other hand, if I did know people's thoughts, it would probably drive me crazy, and I would probably lose a lot of friends. I would find out how self-centered, mean, and crude people can be at times, and some of the "nicest" people would probably end up being my enemies.

To have the mind of Christ, though, is not just a matter of knowing Christ's thoughts. It is having our minds transformed so that we have the same thoughts that he has. We don't have to worry about being offended with his thoughts, for we already know that he always wants what is best for us. He has no hidden motives that we have to be afraid of. He is never going to pretend to be one thing, and then do something else. In one sense, what we see is what we get.

There are times, though, where we just don't understand his words or actions, so we pray that God will reveal them to us. It's like reading a good book, and being able to ask the author for a more complete explanation than what is given on the surface. It's nice being able to know the author that well that we can ask him whatever we want.

Yet, imagine that we didn't have to ask him for an explanation, for we already knew the hidden meanings. Imagine still further to the point that we not only know God's deepest thoughts, but have the same thoughts ourselves. We think like he does.

How can this be true? We are still humans, aren't we? Yes, we are still humans, and very limited in our humanness. Yet, we also have the Spirit of God living within us, and Christ promised us that he would teach us all things (John 14:26). Then the Apostle Paul tells us that we not only can know God's thoughts, but have "the mind of Christ" too.

Imagine what that means for a moment. What exactly does the mind do? It not only processes information. It also is able to be creative. The mind is the source of our imagination. Having the mind of Christ, then, is what helps us to be like our Creator. We can create new ways to serve and glorify him.

The mind also controls our entire body. It tells our heart to pump, even without having to "think" about it. When we have the mind of Christ, we don't have to think about being Christ-like in every situation. It becomes second nature to us, and even our subconscious thoughts become his thoughts. We not only understand what he is thinking. We feel his feelings, and have his motives. Wow! Just think about that!

Watering the Seeds

"I planted the seed, Apollos watered it, but God made it grow". 1 Cor 3:6

Have you ever bought a beautiful plant, but then just taken it home and forgotten about it? Very gradually, the soil dries out, and the plant withers and dies. Some of us have a green thumb, and others have the touch of death. Some don't water enough, and others actually drown the plants that they are trying to save.

The same thing is true in the spiritual world. A lot of emphasis is placed in our churches on planting the seed of God's truth, but the responsibility of watering the seeds is either neglected or overdone. Our new converts are either dried up or drowned.

In order to correct this problem, we need to first of all understand what is meant by "watering the seed". Watering can mean anything that contributes to the nourishment and growth of the seed of faith. It can mean anything as simple as a friendly smile, or as complex as day by day mentoring. It means anything that will help the person not only to have faith, but to walk in that faith. It is encouragement, edification, friendship, giving direction, leading by example, feeding, and comforting. It is using one's spiritual gift to build up the body of Christ, mutually edifying one another. It is adding not only water of the Word, but mixing it with the fertilizer of the Spirit, through correction and rebuke, as well as patience and love.

Besides watering, a good gardener also makes sure that the seed or plant has the right environment. He cultivates the soil, and helps to remove any weeds that might try to choke it. He is also sensitive to what each plant needs. Some plants need a lot of water, so that their roots are swimming all of the time. Others can almost pull water out of the air, and do better in the desert than in green pastures. People are the same way. Some need a lot of encouragement in order to grow, and others are almost self-sustaining. If we give them too much attention, we can actually push them away from the church. Their faith is a very private thing, and they like the quiet spring of God's Word feeding their souls, instead of the wild class-five rapids of the Mega-Church's push toward greater involvement. The spiritual waterer sees the need, is sensitive to the boundaries, and provides either the gentle mist or the fire hose depending on the type of spiritual plant, and its stage of growth.

Some plants need a lot of water when they are just seeds, in order to get started and softened enough to grow, yet need very little water as they get older. The same thing is true with people. We must be sensitive to not only the need of the moment, but how the needs change through spiritual growth. We also cannot assume that when a person gets older that they need less watering. A Redwood tree needs a lot more water than its seed. Be a wise waterer, and God will do the rest. We control the flow, and God makes it grow.

Self-Centered Self-Sacrifice

"If I give all I possess to the poor, and surrender my body to the flames, but have not love, I gain nothing." I Cor. 13:3

We often think of self-sacrifice as being a Christian characteristic, for Christ was the epitome of selflessness and humility. Yet, there are many religions around the world which push self-denial or self-abasement as the ideal. There are the Buddhist monks who live in the caves of Tibet and sleep in the snow without blankets. There are the Native Americans who go on long vision quests, fasting for long periods of time to have their senses quickened, purified, and sensitized to the spiritual world. There are the Tahitian natives who pierce and tattoo their bodies with elaborate designs to open passage ways or windows to the world of their gods. Then there are the Muslims who encourage even martyrdom in the name of Allah, for no matter how evil a man may be in his life, he can be assured of a place in immortality if he dies for his god.

All of these actions are based on self-denial, with pain, suffering, and even death as being upheld as more valuable than pleasure or personal comfort. Yet, not one of these actions is based on love. They are all based on self-gain or fulfillment, and, therefore, according to the Bible, are worthless. Self-denial, in and of itself, is empty and meaningless, and our only reward is any building of self-esteem that it might give us for how self-denying we are. We are proud of our humility.

This, however, is not just true of pagan religions. It also rings true for many people and denominations which claim to be Christian. There are many Christians who give to the church, or give to the poor, for example, who only give because they have a guilty conscience, and they think that their self-sacrifice will earn Brownie points with God. Love is not in the equation. They are only giving for themselves. There are even those who would be willing to die for a special cause that they believe in, like the Muslims for theirs.

Yet, what good is martyrdom if we are only looking for the praise of others after we are gone? In one sense it isn't any different than just committing suicide, for we are willingly giving up our life, without any concern for how our death affects those whom we have left behind. We are more concerned with becoming a hero than we are with staying at home and lovingly supporting our family and friends.

If our cause is just an ego-trip, and we are not doing it out of love, then the Bible says that all your self-sacrifice, even death, is worthless in his sight. We might get praise from others for our efforts, but what good will that be for us when we face our maker in heaven? The Bible says that even if we surrender our body to the flames, but have not love, there is no gain spiritually speaking for us. We have burned out in the flesh, and we will burn out in eternity, for all our "good deeds" will be purged, and we will stand alone.

I Raise my Ebenezer

"Then Samuel took a stone and set it up between Mizpah and Shen. He called it Ebenezer, saying, 'Thus far has the Lord helped us'." I Sam. 7:12

Before I met my wife, she had been an avid mountain climber. She used to go backpacking and hiking up at Yosemite, as well as many other sites around California. Whenever she went someplace new, or had a special adventure, she would bring back a small "pocket rock" that she found on her journey to remind her of her unique experience. Sometimes she would even write on the rock where it was found and the date, to remind her of the history of each stone. It wasn't just a rock to her. It was a memento to a memory.

The prophet Samuel used to do the same thing. After a great victory over the Philistines, he set up a stone as a monument to the victory, and he called it "Ebenezer", which means, "stone of help", to remind all the people of the help that God gave to them on this special day. He knew how easy it is to forget how much God has given to us, and how we often take him for granted. He wanted this stone to be a memento to a memory, that would help one generation to pass the history down to the next, so they too could share in the joy.

God, also, has his Ebenezer. John tells us about it in Revelation 3. He says, "Him who overcomes I will make a pillar in the temple of my God. Never again will he leave it. I will write on him the name of my God and the name of the city of my God, the new Jerusalem, which is coming down out of heaven from my God; and I will also write on him my new name" (vs. 12).

In other words, he is going to make us into his Ebenezer. He will write on us his name as a statement of ownership and pride, as if he is saying, "This one is mine, and he is an overcomer". Yet, it isn't just a memorial to what we have done. It is also a memento of how he saved us and provided for us. We will have the name of Jehovah and his bride, Jerusalem, engraved on us, as well as the New Name of Jesus, as our bridegroom.

It is almost like a wedding certificate, with the name of the Father and his wife signing it as our two witnesses. He calls us a "pillar" in his eternal temple, for we will never have to leave him, and we will always uphold his truth and glory. We are his "support team", holding up everything he stands for and is. It will be a momentous occasion, and the beginning of our everlasting honeymoon with him.

Have you had any momentous occasions with the Lord, where he has spoken to you and changed your life? Have you written down your experience with God, or collected some memento to remind you of your encounter with the divine? This book is my Ebenezer, for it records each one of my encounters with the Lord over this past year. Whenever He spoke, I wrote. I offer this book as a memento to His grace.

Topic and Verse Index

Made in the USA
Columbia, SC
16 February 2019